THE BATTLE
OF THE
NARROW SEAS

THE BATTLE
OF THE
NARROW SEAS

A History of the Light Coastal Forces in the Channel
and North Sea, 1939-1945

by

LIEUTENANT-COMMANDER PETER SCOTT
M.B.E., D.S.C. & Bar, R.N.V.R.

INTRODUCTION BY ANTONY HICHENS

Seaforth
PUBLISHING

DEDICATED TO THE MEMORY OF THE OFFICERS AND MEN
SERVING IN COASTAL FORCES WHO WERE KILLED IN ACTION

Copyright © Peter Scott 1945
Introduction copyright © Antony Hichens 2009

This edition first published in Great Britain in 2009 by
Seaforth Publishing,
Pen & Sword Books Ltd,
47 Church Street,
Barnsley S70 2AS

www.seaforthpublishing.com

British Library Cataloguing in Publication Data
A catalogue record for this book is available from the British Library

ISBN 978 1 84832 035 2

Printed and bound in Great Britain by Cromwell Press Group, Trowbridge

Contents

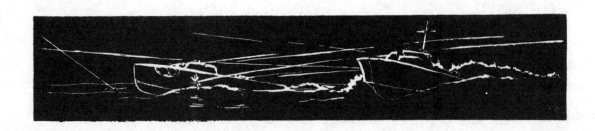

New Introduction

Peter Scott's *The Battle of the Narrow Seas* was published in 1945, in time for the first postwar Christmas market, as my own copy testifies it having been given to me as a Christmas present by my mother. My father, Lieutenant Commander Robert Hichens DSO* DSC** RNVR, features in it in many places and as a boy I thought of this book as a major contribution to Second World War naval history. Many years later it came as something as a shock to find that Captain Roskill's official history of the Navy in the Second World War made little reference to the stories of courage and adventure in Coastal Forces small warships which this book describes so freshly. It is indeed the feeling of immediacy which pervades the book, full of first-hand accounts of battles from which the smoke had hardly cleared, that distinguishes it from more analytical and objective naval history written later. Scott was himself a distinguished steam gun boat flotilla leader and he writes of his own experiences as well as those of other men he knew. He had clearly noted at first hand their descriptions of the actions they had fought and the book was compiled with official sanction while the war in the Channel of the North Sea still raged, possibly when Scott himself had come ashore to join the D-Day Directing Staff in 1944. Thus it has the strengths as well as the blemishes of an account drawn together at the time by one of the leading participants in that long naval campaign.

Scott describes the hesitant, amateur start of Coastal Forces in response to the sudden threat to the British convoy routes up and down the Channel and the East Coast after the Fall of France had, at one stroke, given the German Navy access to the Dutch, Belgian and French Channel ports. From these bases their well designed, fast and relatively heavily armed E-boats could sortie under cover of darkness to attack those vital highways with torpedoes and mines. Four years later, after the construction of hundreds of motor torpedo boats, motor gun boats and motor launches, manned predominantly by reserve officers and hostilities-only ratings, it was the British who snuffed out the capacity of the German Navy to escort its own coastal convoys on the far side of the water.

After 1918 the Navy had abandoned light fast fighting craft in order to concentrate available funds on heavier warships, a decision repeated ten years after the Second World War, so that this arm of the service had to be recreated in 1940. The early designs were inferior to the German E-boats and R-boats, but in war you learn quickly, or not at all, and by 1943 Coastal Forces had available to it an array of effective classes of miniature warships, many of them capable of exceptionally high speeds and suitable for taking the battle into the enemy's waters. Out of these fierce clashes, almost always at night due to the dominance of aircraft over the Channel by day, some remarkable reputations were formed, with men such as Pumfrey, Gould, Dickens, McDonald and, of course, Robert Hichens becoming as well known in naval circles, and indeed to the public, as naval leaders of far greater experience commanding infinitely greater destructive power in the destroyers, cruisers, capital ships and submarines of the greater fleet.

This is not strictly a history book. For Coastal Forces history read Peter Dickens' *Night Action*, Len Reynolds' *MTBs and MGBs at War in Home Waters* or Brian Cooper's *The Battle of the Torpedo Boats*. This is first hand recounting of wild adventures in which very young men led formations of small warships into yard arm to yard arm battles which were fought in darkness and at great speed, resulting in even greater confusion. The MGBs in particular fought at close quarters in an era when ships were generally sinking each other at distances measured in miles or under the surface by warships who seldom saw their quarry and only knew of his destruction through acoustic devices and the sighting of flotsam. Before radar directed guns, at night the enemy could only be seen at close quarters and the light automatic weapons were only then effective, so that action was routinely pressed home to point blank range. Although any naval war contains infinitely more hours of tedious patrol than it does of exhilarating contact with the enemy, when contact came it was exciting and stimulating. There is little doubt that the young men who fought in the North Sea and the Channel thought themselves fortunate compared with their comrades who put up with the hardships and tedium of Atlantic escort duty, which nevertheless would determine the outcome of the war to a far greater degree than these piratical clashes off Britain's shores. Another factor which made Coastal Forces so attractive to the young civilians who volunteered for the Navy was the ability to master the relatively simple technology of these small craft after only a few months of training and experience, so that in some cases men who had been at sea for less than a year were given command of their own ships and in time even flotillas. It was determination and raw courage, more than the mastery of complex technology and long naval experience, which defined successful MGB and MTB commanding officers and their crews.

It is inevitable that this book, compiled towards the end of the War, deals almost exclusively with the British point of view. German sources had not yet become available, beyond the transcripts of propaganda broadcasts which could easily be ridiculed. Neither side had a balanced picture of what damage it had inflicted on the other in those brief moments of contact, with night vision blinded by tracer and the flash of exploding shells and boats racing past each other at combined speeds of over eighty knots. What both reported in good faith when they returned to base sometimes showed irreconcilable differences of view about who had done what and to whom when compared years later. Yet the inexorable tide of growing British strength and competence in this form of warfare left its own unquestionable record in the attrition of German strength and finally a Royal Navy in confident control of the Narrow Seas. One of the few great E-boat successes of the latter part of the War, the sinking of American landing craft inadequately escorted by the Royal Navy across Lyme Bay on a pre D-Day night exercise, gets only the briefest of mentions. Perhaps it was still too sore a subject to record in more detail. Yet in spite of the inevitable bias of the time, and the lack of careful sifting of evidence, this is a magnificent story of how those young men fought and ultimately overcame their doughty and well armed opponents. It is beautifully illustrated, including many of the author's own vivid action paintings. To read this book is to relive the excitement, the determination and the optimism that were the defining features of the young men of Coastal Forces in the Second World War.

ANTONY HICHENS, July 2009

30 May, 1943

I have noted with admiration the work of the
light coastal forces in the North Sea, in the Channel and
more recently in the Mediterranean.

Both in offence and in defence the fighting
zeal and the professional skill of officers and men have
maintained the great tradition built up by many generations
of British seamen.

As our strategy becomes more strongly offensive,
the task allotted to the coastal forces will increase in
importance, and the area of their operations will widen.

I wish to express my heartfelt congratulations
to you all on what you have done in the past, and complete
confidence that you will maintain the same high standards
until complete victory has been gained over all our
enemies.

Winston, Churchill

x

Foreword

THIS is the history of the struggle for control of the Narrow Seas which stretch north-east and south-west from the Straits of Dover. It began in the summer of 1940 when the European ports from Bordeaux to the far north had fallen into enemy hands. For more than four years a battle went on to prevent the Germans from using coastwise shipping to relieve their roads and railways and, at the same time, to keep open our own convoy routes round the southern and eastern shores of England. A large part in this battle was played by our Motor Torpedo Boats, Motor Gunboats and Motor Launches, which are known collectively as Coastal Forces. They fought in these waters, mostly at night, against enemy convoys and their escorts over on the other side and against E boats which came across this side to attack our convoys.

Finally the time came for our armies to return to France, and our Coastal Forces had the job of leading them to their beaches and protecting their supply lines once they had landed. By the autumn of 1944 the enemy's ships had been drummed up the Channel as Drake drummed them long ago. But the battle went on in the North Sea until the end came on 8th May, 1945.

These were not the only areas in which Coastal Forces had been operating. They fought the enemy and the elements in the Mediterranean, in the Carribean, in the Far East, in West Africa, off Iceland and, nearer home, in the Irish Sea and round the coasts of Scotland. They figured in the war against the Luftwaffe and the war against the U boats; but it is with the battle in the North Sea and the Channel that this book is principally concerned, a battle in the new wide sense of the word, which, like the Battle of the Atlantic, lasted for years without pause, a battle of initiative and individuality and great dash, which can most effectively be described in personal narrative. For that reason much of the story is told in the words of the young men who fought their little ships in the Narrow Seas. They only achieved success at the cost of many promising lives, but by their daring and gallantry, their bold initiative and their contempt of danger, they lived up to the highest traditions of our Navy.

It would be easy, however, for some young man chancing upon this book in, say, ten years' time to feel that the life and work of these men must have been a glorious venture, an end in itself, and one which all men must achieve in order to satisfy an appetite for adventure, excitement and suspense. To him I would say this:

That when war comes to a country there is only one course for its people to take, and that is to fight as hard as they can until it is won . . . or lost.

That it is necessary for the sacrifice, the unselfish and continuing effort and the heroism of deliberate courage to be recorded so that it cannot ever be forgotten.

That the strain, discomfort and boredom which are the three predominant factors in modern warfare cannot be brought into their true perspective in a book of this kind, or it would be so long and dull that nobody would read it.

That there is no glory to be had out of war that cannot be had out of some greater and more creative enterprise.

That *nothing* will ever compensate us for the men we have lost, not even the way so many of them died. They were ready to die because they wanted to save their children and their children's children from future wars. The least and the most that any of us can do is to devote ourselves to finding a complete and lasting peace, and then to maintaining it with all our energy.

When you have finished this book, please turn back and read these few sentences again.

The book starts with an account of a typical torpedo attack which took place in 1942. It goes on to set the scene and describe the background of the battle, and then it begins at the beginning and tells the tale in chronological order. There has not been space to describe every engagement which was fought, nor to mention by name *all* those who played the principal parts. The necessity for secrecy, too, has placed certain limitations on the book.

My work in compiling it has been largely that of an editor, and as such my acknowledgements and grateful thanks are due to the following who have contributed in so many ways to complete the record:

For writing the stories of their adventures: Lt. M. Arnold Forster, D.S.O., D.S.C., R.N.V.R., Lt. Cdr. T. W. Boyd, D.S.O., R.N.V.R., Cdr. D. G. Bradford, D.S.O., D.S.C., R.N.R., Lt. Cdr. J. Cameron, R.N.V.R., Lt. Cdr. T. N. Cartwright, D.S.C., R.N.V.R., Lt. Cdr. P. G. C. Dickens, D.S.O., M.B.E., D.S.C., R.N., Lt. Cdr. D. G. Dowling, R.N.V.R., Lt. R. Q. Drayson, D.S.C., R.N.V.R., Lt. Cdr. C. W. S. Dreyer, D.S.O., D.S.C., R.N., Lt. J. Eardley Wilmot, D.S.C., R.N., Lt. R. A. Ellis, R.N., Lt. Cdr. G. C. Fanner, D.S.C., R.N.V.R., Lt. Cdr. K. Gemmel, D.S.O., D.S.C., R.N.V.R., Lt. Cdr. A. A. Gotelee, D.S.C., R.N.V.R., Lt. Cdr. I. R. Griffiths, D.S.C., R.N., Lt. P. G. Lee, D.S.C., R.N.V.R., Lt. N. G. Machin, D.S.C., R.N.V.R., Lt. G. D. Olivier, D.S.M., R.N.V.R., Cdr. E. N. Pumphrey, D.S.O., D.S.C., R.N., Lt. D. Rigg, D.S.C., R.N.V.R., Lt. Cdr. J. D. Ritchie, D.S.C., R.N., Cdr. R. E. D. Ryder, V.C., R.N., Lt. D. A. Shaw, D.S.C., R.N., Lt. Cdr. D. C. Sidebottom, D.S.C., R.N.V.R., Lt. W. S. Strang, R.N.V.R., Cdr. W. L. Stephens, D.S.C., R.N.V.R., Lt. J. O. Thomas, D.S.C., R.N.V.R., Lt. Cdr. I. C. Trelawny, D.S.C., R.N.V.R., Lt. Cdr. B. C. Ward, D.S.C., R.N.

For allowing passages already written to be published or reprinted: Cdr. D. M. C. Curtis, D.S.C., R.N.V.R., Mrs. Robert Hichens, Michael Joseph, Esq., Mrs. Derek Leaf, Michael Sadleir, Esq.

For much detailed information, technical assistance and helpful advice: R. F. Aickman, Esq., Lt. M. Arnold Forster, D.S.O., D.S.C., R.N.V.R., Miss J. M. Burge, H. Calkin, Esq., Lt. Cdr. P. G. C. Dickens, D.S.O., M.B.E., D.S.C., R.N., Lt. Cdr. C. W. S. Dreyer, D.S.O., D.S.C., R.N., Lt. Cdr. G. C. Fanner, D.S.C., R.N.V.R., Lt. Cdr. L. J. H. Gamble, D.S.C., R.N., Cdr. O. C. H. Giddy, D.S.C., R.N., Miss M. J. Gore, Lt. G. P. Griggs, R.N., 2nd Officer M. Hamilton, W.R.N.S., Miss Jane Howard, Capt. R. J. B. Kenderdine, R.N., The Rt. Hon. Lord Kennet of the Dene, G.B.E., D.S.O., D.S.C., Lady Kennet of the Dene, Lt. P. G. Lee, D.S.C., R.N.V.R., Lt. Cdr. R. K. Lloyd, R.N.V.R., Lt. Cdr. M. A. Pryor, R.N.V.R., Miss A. I. G. Reddington, Lt. Cdr. N. B. Stewart, R.N.V.R., Frank Whitaker, Esq., 2nd Officer M. K. Williams, W.R.N.S., J. J. Hedley Willis, Esq., Lt. D. Pipe Wolferstan, R.N.V.R., Sub-Lt. W. Hilton Young, R.N.V.R., Cdr. J. L. Younghusband, R.N., and various Admiralty Departments.

For permission to reproduce photographs and for other assistance in connection with the illustrations: Associated Press Ltd., Beken & Son, Central Press Photos Ltd., Fox Photos Ltd., Mrs. R. Holland, H. Jenkins Ltd., Keystone View Co., Mrs. Derek Leaf, *Life* Magazine, Ministry of Information, Planet News Ltd., Mrs. Nigel Pumphrey, Mrs. D. L. Rice, the Royal Netherlands Navy, *The Times*, The Topical Press Agency, Vosper Ltd., The Commanding Officer and photographic department of H.M.S. *Bee*.

PETER SCOTT.

1945.

CHAPTER I

"In the early hours of Tuesday morning, patrols of our light Coastal Forces, under the command of Lieutenant P. G. C. Dickens, M.B.E., R.N., and Lieutenant J. Weeden, D.S.C., R.N.V.R., intercepted a small enemy supply ship, escorted by two large trawlers close to the enemy-occupied coast of Holland.

"In the subsequent engagement, the supply ship and one of the two trawlers were torpedoed and seen to blow up.

"Our forces suffered one slight casualty and no damage, despite the fire of enemy shore batteries which joined in the action in support of the surface ships."

THAT kind of announcement was heard often in the News broadcast or seen in the daily papers, but such a picture is brief and necessarily incomplete. The whole story is, of course, much longer: it is full of expectation, suspense, exhilaration and fear. Here, then, in greater detail than can be told in a communiqué, is the same story—the story of a typical M.T.B. action in which, in spite of its success, there was also lost opportunity to be regretted. Few naval actions, if indeed any, are completely without such regrets.

THE M.T.Bs. SET OUT

During the afternoon of 18th January, 1943, five motor torpedo boats slipped out of an east-coast harbour, each with its crew, already dressed in their oilskin overalls, fallen-in on the fo'c'sle, and a string of brightly coloured pendants flying from the yardarm.

Once clear of the breakwater, they set course towards the east and increased speed. The noise of the engines rose from a deep hollow rumble to a fierce roar; the hulls lifted on to the surface of the sea and planed along with a burst of foam spreading like an arrowhead on either quarter and a milky road in their wake. Their formation was also an arrowhead, two boats keeping close station on each quarter of the leader. So they ran on, hour after hour, through the dusk and the darkness and the moonrise, until the coast of Holland was close ahead.

When the Senior Officer of a flotilla's own boat is out of action or undergoing its periodical overhaul, the Senior Officer himself often embarks in another boat to lead the force to sea. So it was on this night. The leading M.T.B. was commanded by Sub-Lt. P. Magnus, R.N.V.R., with Lt. Dickens on board as Senior Officer of the whole force. The Commanding Officers of the two boats on the starboard quarter, which completed the first division, were Lt. N. S. Gardner, R.N.V.R., and a New Zealander, Lt. G. J. MacDonald, D.S.C., R.N.Z.N.V.R. On the port quarter the two boats of the second division, which belonged to another flotilla, were led by Lt. Weeden. He was embarked in a boat commanded by Lt. J. H. Saunders, R.N.V.R. The second was commanded by Lt. R. Morgan, R.N.V.R.

When it was a few miles off the coast the force reduced speed and began to creep silently in towards the convoy lane where enemy shipping might be met. The moon was almost full, although it was hidden in cloud, and the night was bright, with a glass-calm sea.

It was 51 minutes past midnight when the enemy was first sighted directly ahead. That is the first great thrill in a night action—the moment of sighting. Suddenly there is a dark spot, half seen, half imagined. The binoculars sweep away from it and back again—yes, there it is—a ship—and another. Those are enemy ships. There are German seamen on board them, perhaps also looking out through glasses, perhaps also keyed up and expectant, although as yet unaware of the enemy who is looking at them. Soon they will know; soon the fight will be on.

The two enemy ships were large trawlers, and they were steaming southward at very slow speed. The force stopped, and Dickens told his Commanding Officers the plan of attack, shouting to them through a megaphone. Weeden was to work his division into one attacking position while Dickens worked his three boats into another, creeping round if possible unseen. As soon as the plan was clear to everyone, the two divisions parted and went off towards their positions. As Dickens crept in he suddenly sighted a third enemy ship farther inshore. The new target was a small ship of about 800 tons, but it was a target worth attacking. By 1.20 a.m. Dickens was satisfied with his position for a torpedo attack, and he turned in for the final approach. Six minutes later the boat was carefully aimed and the starboard torpedo was fired. The impulse charge which drives it out of the tube misfired and there was a moment's anxiety, but the seaman torpedoman hit the striker with a mallet, which is part of the misfire drill, and the torpedo leapt from its tube with a " whoosh " of discharge, a whir of propellers and a splash as it dived in and sped upon its way towards the enemy ship. For the Commanding Officer there is a tremendous feeling of relief once a torpedo has been fired. For better or worse, it is on its way. It is irrevocable. In a few seconds it will hit or it will miss. Nothing can alter its course.

This time its aim had been true. The enemy steamed on at no more than 3 knots, still unaware of the attack until the torpedo hit. The visible effect of a torpedo hit is very varied. Sometimes there is a flash, sometimes a dull glow, sometimes only a column of water. Dickens reports that on this occasion " the torpedo hit with a very large explosion for such a small ship." There was a vivid flash of bright red, evidently caused by the detonation of a magazine; burning ammunition was flung high into the air and exploded like a firework display. " When this had ceased," Dickens continues, " I saw only the bow of the ship sticking straight up in the air and nothing else."

Immediately after the explosion the firing boat turned away at high speed. A signal had been received on board from Weeden to say that his division was in position, and Dickens hoped that the attention of the trawlers might be diverted to himself as he disengaged. But for some time still there was no reaction from the enemy at all. For many long seconds, which seemed like minutes, the trawlers did not open fire.

The two boats of the second division were ready to attack when they saw the flash of the explosion, and they turned in to fire one torpedo each at a range of about 700 yards. But the moment that the trawlers saw the destruction of their companion they stopped immediately, so that the torpedoes missed ahead. Their tracks were evidently sighted from the trawlers, which opened fire at once with all their automatic weapons. Streams of white and green tracer bullets poured out in the direction of the two boats, which were making off at high speed.

After a few minutes the enemy fire had been outdistanced and the trawlers transferred their attention to Dickens and the first division. Weeden's boats stopped. Ten minutes later they began to creep back slowly, and soon they sighted the two trawlers again right ahead. This time the M.T.Bs. pressed in to 400 yards. At the last moment they were seen and a heavy fire was reopened by the enemy. But in spite of it both boats brought their sights on and fired their remaining torpedoes. As soon as they had fired they turned hard aport, increased speed and made a smoke-screen. " I followed the track of our torpedo," writes Weeden, " which struck one of the trawlers amidships. There was a large explosion and the trawler appeared to break in two." For some minutes the remaining trawler maintained a heavy fire, and splinters from near misses came on board both the boats. They did no damage, but Saunders—the Captain of the leading one—was slightly wounded in the face.

A New Target

The two divisions met again once they were clear of the action and discussed the situation, lying with their engines cut. The third trawler could have been finished off, but the boats of the second division had expended their torpedoes and those of the first division were equipped with a type of torpedo for which a trawler was not considered a sufficiently important target. So Dickens decided to send the second division home, and go himself in search of bigger game. His force still had five torpedoes left.

Soon after it had set off homeward, the second division sighted a ship on the starboard bow. Weeden stopped and made out that the new German force consisted of two more trawlers with a much larger vessel astern of them. Here was a fine target and he had no torpedoes left. The only thing he could do was to summon the first division by wireless message and try to slink away unseen so as not to put the enemy on the alert. High speed would have given him away by the noise of his engines and the plume of white water thrown up by his wake, which can be seen at night much farther away than the boat itself. As he went, the Morse key in the wireless office buzzed busily and more details of the enemy's movements were transmitted to Dickens and the first division. But after a few minutes the enemy spotted him and flashed a letter as challenge. Weeden still crept away slowly. Then came a bang, and a moment later a single star of light burst overhead followed by another and another. "We were silhouetted," he says, "by well-placed starshell and the enemy opened an intense fire with 4-inch, 2-pounder and Oerlikon. The boats again crash-started and disengaged first east, then north for about ten minutes and finally west at 38 knots, being constantly illuminated by starshells."

The two boats resumed their homeward journey, but half an hour later as they steered westward they were again in contact with enemy vessels. Three small craft were sighted on the port beam, steering on an opposite course towards Holland. At first they were taken for the three boats of the first division, though their course and high speed were unexplained. However, in a few moments it was clear that they were E boats returning from an offensive sortie off our coast. By the time they had been identified they were almost past. The M.T.Bs. began to give chase, but the E boats already had too much start, and, anxious to avoid upsetting the more important attack of the first division, Weeden decided to abandon the pursuit, and proceeded on his course for home without further incident.

Meanwhile the first division, which had seen the starshells of the second battle and had received Weeden's signal, was manœuvring at slow speed so as not to give away its presence, and trying to work into an intercepting position. After nearly an hour of fruitless search Dickens realised that the enemy must have got past him, and that the only thing to do was to start main engines and go in pursuit. He describes how as soon as he did this he was "immediately illuminated by starshell coming from the east north-east. I could tell this, as each shell showed a faint trace before it burst. It was therefore almost certainly not the convoy and I judged it to come from the shore."

However, the shore batteries contented themselves with starshell only; they evidently could not see the M.T.Bs. clearly enough to engage them with high explosive. Our boats continued on their course, and the starshell gradually dropped astern until eventually it stopped.

Dickens went on hunting until 6.20, by which time he decided that no enemy ships could now be near enough to give time for an attack before dawn. Reluctantly he abandoned the hunt and set course for home.

It was not until the middle of the forenoon that the boats reached harbour and berthed alongside. Their success was mixed with regret for the "might have been," but it made up for the fatigue and discomfort of their 18 hours at sea. They had sunk two enemy ships and suffered only one minor casualty.

CHAPTER II

THE OPPOSING FORCES

THE Coastal Forces which figure in this story are divided into three principal types of craft, each with a different function (although in some of them the functions have been combined).

The best known is the Motor Torpedo Boat, which is mainly concerned with attacking enemy shipping in enemy waters. Its hitting power is heavy for its size, and in that respect it is a parallel with the bomber.

The M.G.B.—Motor Gunboat—is the equivalent of a fighter aircraft. It is mainly concerned with fighting enemy light craft.

The M.L.—Motor Launch—which is slower than the other two, is used for a great many different purposes, sometimes offensive, such as laying mines or leading in the landing parties of a Combined Operations raid, but more often defensive, such as routine patrols and escorting convoys, minesweeping and the invaluable service of Air/Sea Rescue.

M.Ls. have been described a hundred times as the "maids-of-all-work" of Coastal Forces, but it is an apt description. They put in the longest hours of sea time, though little is heard of them, because when once we had taken the offensive in the Narrow Seas they were less and less often in contact with the enemy. The raid on St. Nazaire, however, was an operation in which they came into their own—a change from the spade work which they normally had to do, the dull convoy escort jobs. They have ploughed up and down the convoy routes round our coasts winter and summer, fair weather or foul, for months, sometimes for years, without so much as a smell of the enemy. An unkind story is told about one of these M.Ls., in which the navigational amenities are somewhat primitive. As one of the escort, it kept station throughout a very dark night on one of the smaller ships of a convoy. When the dawn came the M.L. was still close beside this ship, but the rest of the convoy was nowhere to be seen. Presently the ship ran aground on a sandbank, and a few moments later the M.L. ran aground too. The skipper of the small ship leant over his bridge with a megaphone. "I'm here for sand," he shouted. "What are you here for?"

But St. Nazaire made up for a lot of dull convoy work. Escorting the *Campbeltown* up the River Loire was a new sort of job for M.Ls., and very magnificently they discharged it.

These flotillas of M.T.Bs., M.G.Bs., and M.Ls. worked from about a dozen bases round our coast. Drawn up against them the Germans, working from such places as Ijmuiden,[1] Rotterdam, Ostend, Boulogne, Havre, Cherbourg and the Channel Isles, had a number of flotillas of E boats (corresponding to our M.T.Bs.) which they used for attacking our shipping with torpedoes and for laying mines on our convoy routes. The German name for these craft is *Schnellboot* (fast boat); the term " E boat " was officially adopted by us in 1940 as an abbreviation of " Enemy War Motorboat." (To speak of " enemy E boats," therefore, is a redundancy.)

Besides E boats there were flotillas of R boats (corresponding roughly to our M.Ls.), used for minesweeping and defensive patrolling along the occupied coasts. The name R boat is an abbreviation of the German name *Räumboot*, which means " sweeping boat."

The E boats' problem was very different from that of our M.T.Bs. Our coastwise shipping, which passed regularly in large numbers back and forth along our swept channels, was escorted as strongly as we were able, but with the U boat war to fight as well, our destroyers and corvettes and trawlers were fully stretched, and the escort forces for our south and east coast convoys could not be very large. The Germans, on the other hand, had few merchant ships and many escort ships. Often one of their convoys used to consist of one merchantman with a dozen or more escorting vessels. So as well as E boats and R boats there were destroyers, torpedo boats, " M " Class minesweepers and armed trawlers arrayed against our Coastal Forces; and besides these escorts there were patrols of armed trawlers and flakships specially stationed by the Germans to try to keep our M.T.Bs. away from their convoy routes.

There were three other factors affecting the battle in the Narrow Seas—aircraft, long-range shore batteries and mines.

Aircraft could attack the shipping on the convoy routes. In 1940 and 1941 the Luftwaffe took a heavy toll of our merchant ships, but their efforts by day and those of the E boats by night could not interrupt our traffic. Our counter-offensive was more successful. Blenheims and Hurribombers, and later Beaufighters, Whirlibombers, Mosquitoes and Typhoons made the Germans sail their shipping almost entirely at night along all that part of the occupied coast which lay within 100 miles of England. The patrols of both our own Coastal Forces and of E boats were limited by the threat of fighter aircraft, which might attack them at daylight if they had not regained the protection of their own fighter belt. And in the later stages the E boats and R boats were menaced even at night by aircraft such as Albacores of the Fleet Air Arm, Wellingtons, Avengers and others.

Secondly, there were the long-range guns on the occupied coasts, controlled by Radar, which often engaged our M.T.Bs., in attempting to drive them away from the convoy routes; and our own long-range guns, notably in the Dover Strait, which scored hits on enemy shipping passing through.

Finally there were mines: offensive mines, laid by our Coastal Force craft on the enemy shipping lanes and by E boats on our shipping lanes; and defensive mines, laid in large fields by both sides as a protective belt to seaward of their convoy routes.

These, then, were the forces which for four years were involved in the struggle for the control of the Narrow Seas.

[1] Pronounced, incidentally, " ay " to rhyme with " hay " and " maouden " to rhyme with " how now, brown cow."

THE EVOLUTION OF THE CRAFT

In our building policy for light craft we differed from the Germans just as we differed in the production of aircraft. They concentrated on one or two types produced in large numbers, while we developed a great many different types from which we were able to select the best points in a progressive system of evolution. At the beginning of the war we were ill equipped with M.T.Bs., just as we were with fighter aircraft. Our policy was slow, but it was a long-term policy, and at last it began to bear fruit.

The Coastal Force craft of this war were direct descendants of the Motor Launches and Coastal Motor Boats of the last war. It was in July, 1915, that the Admiralty ordered from America the first 50 Motor Launches, which proved so successful that an order for 500 more followed at once. These were 80-foot boats with two 250-h.p. engines and a speed of 20 knots and, like the M.Ls. of this war, they were used for a great variety of duties. They swept up minefields, they attacked U boats, they escorted convoys, and finally they earned undying fame in the blocking expeditions of Zeebrugge and Ostend.

At the end of the war some of them were sold as yachts or houseboats, but the majority were left lying on the mud in the Hamble River, a sad fate for such a gallant fleet. Recently, however, a number of them were put into service again as living quarters for the crews of some of the smaller landing craft, while they were waiting to invade France.

At the beginning of 1916, at the time the M.Ls. were first arriving in this country, the Admiralty approved the designs by Thornycrofts of a 40-foot motor torpedo boat, twelve of which were immediately built. They were known as Coastal Motor Boats or C.M.Bs.

The idea of a small torpedo boat was not a new one. The same firm had built a 60-foot steam torpedo boat in 1878 for the British Government, and a 50-foot M.T.B., carrying one 14-inch torpedo, was built for Russia during the Russo-Japanese war.

The 40-foot C.M.Bs. of 1916 were followed by a class of 55-foot boats, carrying two 18-inch torpedoes and driven by two engines of 375 h.p., with a speed of well over 35 knots. The C.M.Bs. had many and stirring adventures in the last war, along the Belgian coast and in the North Sea, and finally in Russia. Their greatest exploit was the raid on Kronstadt harbour on the night of 17th/18th August, 1919. Eight C.M.Bs. took part; under cover of a diversionary air-raid, they passed through two lines of island forts and entered the harbour. Here, for the loss of three of their number (two of them largely because they had the misfortune to collide in the entrance), they torpedoed two battleships and a submarine depot ship. This very decisive result entirely altered the balance of sea power in the Baltic at that time and demonstrated most forcibly the particular value of the small torpedo boat in delivering a surprise attack on an enemy well defended by batteries and minefields. But even this brilliant feat was insufficient to teach the lesson that these craft would, one day, once again become an integral part of our Navy.

Thus it was that, during the period between the two wars, high-speed motor boats were developed mainly by private individuals, until, in 1935, the Admiralty placed an order for twelve 60-foot M.T.Bs. with the British Power Boat Company, whose chief designer was Mr. Hubert Scott-Payne. They were to carry two 18-inch torpedoes and to be driven by three Napier Lion engines of 600 h.p. each. The first six of these boats, which formed the First M.T.B. Flotilla, under the command of Lt. Cdr. (now Captain) G. B. Sayer, R.N., were delivered in March, 1937, and in order to test them they made the passage to the Mediterranean under their own power, accompanied by a trawler—H.M.S. *Vulcan*—which had been converted into a depot ship. The second six boats were shipped to Hong Kong,[1] where they continued to serve until December, 1941, when Hong Kong fell.

In 1936 the firm of Vosper built, as a private venture, a 68-foot M.T.B., carrying two 21-inch torpedoes and engined with three 1,050-h.p. Isotta-Fraschini engines, which gave it a maximum speed of about 40 knots. This boat was the prototype of the 70-foot M.T.Bs. which have been used so successfully throughout this war.

The development of reliable high-powered marine engines is a very long job, however, and the entry of Italy into the war closed down the supply of Isotta-Fraschini engines. British petrol-engine production was still concentrating mainly on aero engines, and although some of these had been converted, there was, nevertheless, a difficult period before the 1,250-h.p. Packard engine could be supplied from America in sufficient numbers to maintain the required rate of expansion of Coastal Forces.

The M.T.B. of 1945 is far better equipped than the C.M.B. of 1917. It is much larger and heavier, and can operate in much rougher weather, but its speed is no greater. Power-weight ratios are complicated things, and it is partly the great increase in weight, but chiefly the lack of a suitable power unit, which is responsible for the apparent anomaly that the C.M.B., with two 375-h.p. engines, went over 35 knots, whereas some types of modern M.T.Bs. with four 1,250-h.p. engines do not go as fast. The E boat, powered by high-speed Diesel engines of great endurance and reliability, has always had an advantage over us in this respect, and we can only regret that more interest was not taken in Diesels in this country during the pre-war years.

The Birth of the M.G.B.

Meanwhile, at the beginning of the war, it had been anticipated that German U boats would operate in the Channel and North Sea and in British coastal waters, as they had done twenty-five years before. A small, fast Motor Anti-submarine Boat, known as a M.A./S.B. (usually pronounced Masby), was therefore developed from the British Power Boat Company's design, and fitted with Asdic, the U boat hunting device. These could only be used close to their bases and in fairly good weather, and it was soon apparent that the U boats had been driven from coastal waters by our air patrols. Their hunting-ground became the convoy routes far out in the Atlantic, and so the M.A./S.Bs. were without a quarry.

As long as the Continental coast remained in Allied or Neutral hands, German E boats were based too far from our coastal convoy routes to be a menace. But when France and the Low Countries fell the situation changed. The M.A./S.Bs. were, therefore, immediately converted into Motor Gunboats in order to tackle the E boats, now based so dangerously close to our shipping lanes. Thus the M.G.Bs. were born.

All these early M.G.Bs. were not ex-M.A./S.B.s, however; one of them, for example— a 70-footer—had been built by the British Power Boat Company in 1939 for the Netherlands Government. It was originally equipped with torpedo tubes, and it had an interesting history, for it was stolen and afterwards returned. At the outbreak of war it was undergoing trials at the British Power Boat Company's yard at Hythe in Southampton, Water; but as all available craft were needed, the British Government informed the Netherlands Government with regret that the boat could not be delivered to them. Lt. Cdr. O. de Booy, R.Neth.N., thought very little of this decision. He asked to be allowed, however, to complete the trials, now that they had begun, for the benefit of a number of similar boats still under construction in Holland. His request was granted, and in due course the M.T.B. sailed for these trials, which were to be carried out with a full complement of fuel. It seems

---

[1] To the Chinese they were known as " Wind Thunder Boats."

that the high-speed runs were all made in an easterly direction, and on completion the boat berthed, surprisingly enough, in a Dutch harbour, where she became at once part of the *Koninklijke Marine*.

When Holland was overrun by the Germans, H.Neth.M. M.T.B. 51 was under the command of Lt. J. van Staveren, R.Neth.N., and on 10th May, 1940, she was in Rotterdam, where hundreds of parachutists were dropped by the enemy to capture the bridges across the Maas. Under continuous attack by dive-bombers and fighters, the M.T.B. played a brilliant part in the defence of the bridges for hour after hour, raking them with fire until at last she was badly damaged by a near-miss. Her engines could still run, and when the position became hopeless, she escaped and came to England. By his courage and determination in the battle for the bridges van Staveren won the *Militaire Willemsorde*, which is the highest Dutch award for valour.

Back in England, M.T.B. 51 was converted into a motor gunboat and renamed M.G.B. 46. Soon afterwards she was manned again by Dutchmen and joined the 3rd M.G.B. Flotilla, in which there were British, Dutch and Polish crews: 46 was commanded first by Lt. W. A. de Looze, R.Neth.N., then by Lt. J. A. Schreuder, R.Neth.N., and later still by de Looze again; both of these were officers of great dash who fought in many battles in the Straits, in which Her Netherlands Majesty's ex-M.T.B. won honourable scars.

The prospect of U boat activity in coastal waters had led also to the development of a larger and slower type of motor craft, comparable with the M.L. of 1916, to be used mainly for the protection of coastwise shipping. Designs for these new M.Ls. were produced by the Fairmile Marine Company, who proposed building them on a mass-production basis, the parts being prefabricated and assembled at various yards throughout the country and overseas. The great advantage of this scheme was that the boats could be assembled by firms who had no previous experience of boat building. One such company, for example, which produced many M.Ls., was a well-known firm of piano makers before the war.

A number of M.Ls. were specially equipped and modified for Air/Sea Rescue work. They had a sick bay built as a deck-house aft, so that casualties could be looked after without being taken down through a vertical hatch to the living spaces below.

A smaller type of M.L. was designed for Harbour Defence. These H.D.M.Ls. have been used for patrolling booms at harbour entrances and suchlike routine duties. But they are excellent sea boats, none the less; two of them once made the passage of the Indian Ocean from Durban to Colombo under their own power. In the Mediterranean they proved themselves in battle many times. Their service at the fall of Tobruk was an example of the magnificent work they were able to do.

The small M.T.Bs. and M.G.Bs. were limited by reason of their size and their hull design to operating only in fairly good weather. Larger boats were therefore developed from the earlier Fairmile M.L. types. At the same time a steel steam-driven vessel was designed, to be known as a Steam Gunboat or S.G.B.

The design of Coastal Force craft is still going forward, though it will change with changing tactics and strategy; but the Coastal Forces are an integral part of the Navy now, and it is most important that this time they should remain so.

Much of the story of the struggle in the Narrow Seas, however, has to do with the days when our Coastal Forces were woefully few in numbers and those that were available to us were often underarmed and mechanically unreliable. Even when production of newer and better material was in full swing, the great offensive plans in the Mediterranean and the Far East swallowed up a large part of it. Veteran boats had many of them to remain in service year after year, and very fine work they did.

But fighting during the last five years so often, in the early days, with inferior boats and inferior weapons, our Coastal Forces kept the initiative. That is a condition which exists in men's minds rather than in material things. But the Germans are a materialistic race. In the strategy and tactics of this battle in the Narrow Seas, they were as materialistic and unimaginative as ever. An E boat carried torpedoes and mines against merchant ships. Should it meet anything else it must not become involved, but must retire behind a smoke-screen. So the E boat crews were instructed, and they patrolled in constant readiness to flee should any opposition be encountered. In spite of our frequent inferiority in numbers and armament, those were neither the instructions nor the traditions of our Coastal Forces, or indeed of any other part of our Navy.

One night in 1943, for example, a unit of our Coastal Forces was waiting at night off Cherbourg for a large enemy merchant ship passing up the Channel. The force met a German patrol which outnumbered them by three to one. The merchant ship was not amongst them, but our force was in contact with enemy ships and the Senior Officer decided to attack. In the resulting action several of our ships were damaged, and for a few days they were undergoing repairs. During that time the merchant ship slipped out and passed up the Channel.

From a material point of view the correct thing for the Senior Officer of our force to have done would have been to withdraw as soon as he had made certain that the merchant ship was not with the patrol. But from every point of view except the material one, such an opportunity of engaging the enemy on his own doorstep could not be lost.

In his Trafalgar memorandum of 9th October, 1805, Nelson wrote: " . . . no Captain can do very wrong if he places his ship alongside that of an enemy."

It is because that is our tradition and still our policy that British Coastal Forces were able to keep the initiative in the Narrow Seas.

Not only would it be unjust, however, but also extremely unwise, to belittle or underestimate the achievements of the E boat flotillas. Many of them have been most ably led and have wrought great destruction to our shipping, with a skill which cannot fail to be impressive to those in our own Coastal Forces who know so well the problems confronting them. The men who faced each other in the light craft, both British and German, were many of them yachtsmen before the war, who competed together in ocean races. The Germans are not a maritime nation in the way that we are, but their attention to detail makes them formidable opponents either in a night battle or a yacht race.

The Crews and the Maintenance Staff

In the larger types of Coastal Force craft the crews live on board their boats, but in the smaller types they live ashore in the base, in the same way as air crews live at an R.A.F. station. These bases are regarded as parent ships to the M.T.Bs. and G.Bs., and most of them are called after noxious insects—H.M.S. *Wasp*, *Midge*, *Hornet* and so on. Usually they consist of repair workshops and stores near the boats, with offices and accommodation housed in a converted hotel close to the harbour.

The crews of M.T.Bs. and M.G.Bs. vary from 8 or 9 in the smaller boats up to nearly 30 in the larger ones and, in a few, even more. They consist mainly of " Hostilities Only " ratings, men who have come straight from civilian life with a short training period when they entered the Navy and a further short period of special training for Coastal Force duties. Their officers nearly all wear the wavy stripes of the R.N.V.R., and have served their time as Ordinary Seamen before obtaining their commissions. They have a highly technical job to carry out, which is liable to grow daily more complex as more of the latest inventions are applied to their boats. They have suffered heavy casualties, but their morale has been unassailable and most of them would not have exchanged their job for any other in the Navy. Their spirit is typified in the story of the Leading Telegraphist[1] who came up on to the bridge as the M.T.Bs. were closing in towards the battle cruisers *Scharnhorst* and *Gneisenau*, and the heavy cruiser *Prinz Eugen*, which, with a protective screen of E boats and destroyers and an umbrella of fighter aircraft, were passing through the Straits of Dover at high noon. As he surveyed the fearful and majestic scene, the telegraphist rubbed his hands together and was heard to exclaim, " Roll, bowl or pitch, every time a coconut! "

Equally necessary to the operations of our Coastal Force craft are the maintenance staff of the Coastal Force Base. Internal-combustion engines, torpedoes, automatic guns, wireless and electrical equipment all require regular routine maintenance after so many hours' steaming, after so many days, after so many weeks, as well as the inevitable and continual minor repairs and adjustments. For this work a large staff of Motor Mechanics, Engine-room Artificers, Torpedomen, Ordnance Artificers, " Qualified in Ordnance " ratings, Radio Mechanics, Electrical Artificers, Wiremen and so on are held at each Base to keep the operational boats in working order. In some of these categories the work is done by Wrens, and very efficiently done too. Although these technicians do not normally go to sea, they take great pride, like the ground crews in the R.A.F., in the fighting machines which they maintain and which could not go out to fight without their care and attention.

Often their work goes on without pause for rest or even food in order that a boat may be ready for operations, and even occasionally the boat sails with the technician on board to complete the repair before the patrol area is reached. On one such occasion the Flotilla Engineer Officer had gone to sea and the enemy was encountered. It was the E.O's. first battle, and the story is told that in the middle of it he put his head up through the engine-room hatch; it remained there only for a moment, and as the multi-coloured tracer criss-crossed overhead, he was heard to remark, " Oh, I say—madly war, isn't it? "

Besides the personnel of the Royal Navy, many of the Allied Navies have been represented among the small ships. American, Dutch, Norwegian, Polish and Free French flotillas have been fighting side by side with our own in the Channel and the North Sea.

Most of the work of the Coastal Forces is done at night and most of it is uneventful. Normally, for every action there are many nights of fruitless patrol. So, even though this book is chiefly about the battles, it must be realised that these battles were only the exceptions which came occasionally to break the monotony of long nights patrolling, lying perhaps stopped and rolling helplessly in the trough of a short swell, or cruising at speed and drenched through with rain and spray.

The activity of Coastal Forces is largely governed by the weather. Although they can keep the seas in very bad weather, the boats cannot be fought under those conditions. It is useless for a force to struggle across the North Sea in half a gale if when it gets there the boats cannot be steadied for a torpedo attack and are rolling and jumping so wildly that the gunners cannot keep their sights on the target.

---

[1] This was Leading Telegraphist F. Langford, serving at the time with Lt. L. J. H. Gamble, R.N. He served later with Lt. C. W. S. Dreyer, D.S.C., R.N., in the Mediterranean, and became a well-known figure in Coastal Forces.

If, on the other hand, there is a spell of good weather, then Coastal Forces may be at sea night after night, sweeping the enemy convoy routes and patrolling against E boats. For the crews, life is a curious mixture of exhausting and gruelling operations and long days lying idle alongside the jetty waiting for a gale to blow itself out. In winter the weather is more often unsuitable, so that there is a great deal of irksome inactivity, but when the weather does moderate the night patrols are long and the strain is therefore heavy. In summer, when the seas are calmer, Coastal Force activity is limited by the short hours of darkness.

Darkness is the chief hunting-time for Coastal Forces for four reasons. First, because enemy convoys which have been much harassed by aircraft sail normally at night-time. Secondly, against an escorted convoy, some surprise is almost essential. Thirdly, although a few daylight torpedo actions have been fought by our Coastal Forces, the enemy escort would normally be too strong in fire power by day to allow the very close approach which is necessary for a successful torpedo attack. Lastly, both aircraft and shore batteries can be successfully employed against light craft operating near a hostile coast by day. The E boats found all this out, too, and were almost entirely nocturnal.

THE SENIOR OFFICER OF THE FLOTILLA

The spirit of a Coastal Force Base depends greatly upon the actions fought by the flotillas operating from it; and the spirit of those actions depends upon the leadership of the Senior Officers of the flotillas which fight them. So it comes about that the organisation both ashore and afloat revolves largely round the Senior Officers. There may be several flotillas based on the same port—perhaps one of M.T.Bs., one of M.G.Bs., and one of M.Ls.; perhaps two or more of the same kind. Let us follow, then, the day's work of a Senior Officer, who in the evening will be leading an offensive force of M.T.Bs. to sea on a night patrol against enemy shipping.

At nine o'clock in the morning the Flotilla Office in which he works will be crowded with Commanding Officers reporting that their boats are ready for operations or, alternatively, that some defect in the engines or the guns has been discovered which will take so many hours to put right. This information is transmitted to the Operations Staff of the Commander-in-Chief, who must know what strength is likely to be available that night. This staff may be many miles away from the Base, but the importance of close co-operation between the officers who plan an operation and the officers who are to carry it out has overcome much of the more ponderous mechanism of Naval procedure.

For the Senior Officer the forenoon is full of the administration of his flotilla. On his office table there are signals to be read, letters to be answered, reports to be rendered. They deal with a multitude of relevant and seemingly irrelevant subjects, and the Senior Officer's work on them will be constantly interrupted by the telephone. His mind will be called upon to jump from stores to weather reports, to discipline, to engine repairs, to tactics. Throughout the forenoon the mental acrobatics will go on: a hundred unrelated problems will arise about which he must know every detail and development.

Soon after noon there will be a meeting in the Wardroom of one of the boats, over a glass of gin. As he walks down to the boats the Senior Officer is watching the weather. He has been watching it all morning, looking at chimney smoke, at the ensigns of the ships, at the ripples in the harbour basin. Will it hold out till to-night? So far he knows only that four boats of his flotilla will be required. He may, when he spoke to the planning-room, have suggested one of his pet schemes for an operation—most Senior Officers of flotillas have pet schemes about how their boats can best be used—but he does not yet know whether the

Commander-in-Chief will approve of his scheme or require the flotilla for some perfectly different job.

In the Wardroom of the M.T.B. there will be discussion on tactics, on equipment, on past adventures. Not much talk about the night's operation, except perhaps some mention of the weather prospects.

After lunch some of the boats may be running an engine trial to make certain that a repair has been made good, or loading torpedoes or completing with fuel. The Senior Officer may be able to sleep for an hour or two, or he may browse over a chart in the briefing-room, waiting for the signals to arrive which will order the night's operation:

From : Commander-in-Chief—

SECRET IMMEDIATE

Striking Forces for to-night Friday, 3rd March:

Unit A   M.T.Bs. . . . .
Unit B   M.T.Bs. . . . .

Following patrols are to be assumed by 2100:

Unit A   position . . . .
Unit B   position . . . .

Object, destruction of enemy shipping. . . . .

Followed by the wireless frequencies and call-signs to be used. There will also be a "night movements signal" indicating the whereabouts of our own shipping during the night. The Senior Officer will work on the chart, plotting on the patrol positions from the signal and the course to reach them. The chart may be covered with a sheet of perspex or celluloid, in which case the route and the patrol line will be drawn on it with a chinagraph pencil, and the times and speeds written against it, to be used at the briefing later on. The possible movements of the enemy, the positions of his patrols so far as they are known or can be guessed, the bearing of the moon and the direction of the wind will all be drawn by the Senior Officer on the chart so that the strategical and tactical picture can be grasped both by himself and by the Commanding Officers of his boats. He will probably telephone on a secret line to the Staff Officer (Operations) to discuss in greater detail the way in which he plans to carry out the operation.

To Know Every Detail of the Plan

About half an hour before the striking force is due to sail, the Commanding Officers and First Lieutenants of the boats muster in the briefing-room. They will be dressed for sea with thick jerseys under their monkey jackets, and fleece-lined boots. The Commanding Officer of the Base may be there too. The Senior Officer[1] describes the general plan and object of the operation, reads out the orders and makes sure that each boat has a copy of the relevant signals. Then he goes through a list of details which everyone must know and understand. He tells them the latest information which he got from the Intelligence Officer, the results of photographic reconnaissance, the weather forecast. He draws in on the chart the scheduled "night movements" of our own shipping in the area, so that it may be avoided on the outward and homeward passage. He confirms that all boats have recorded on their charts the positions of the latest minefields and swept channels.

[1] In some of the bases a special Staff Officer (Operations) undertakes all the work of preparation and carries out the preliminary part of the briefing.

He tells them the time of slipping and proceeding to sea, the speed on passage and the speed while sweeping in enemy waters, the order of Fleet numbers and the cruising formation in which the boats will form up. He discusses the special tactics to be employed, how the force will deploy and where it will rendezvous after an action. Then he deals with such matters as the depth settings to be set on the torpedoes, the wireless frequency to be used, the collective call-signs for the force and a dozen other technicalities upon which the success of the operation depends.

Many questions will be asked during the briefing, for in no form of warfare is it more important for every Commanding Officer to know how his Senior Officer is likely to react in any particular circumstances, and for the Senior Officer to know just what his Commanding Officers will do when the time comes for them to use their own initiative.

The officers go back to their boats. The engines have been warmed through, and it is almost time to slip as the Senior Officer walks down the quay. The weather is holding; the forecast is good, a nice night for a battle; and there below him are the boats that he will take into action, waiting silently with their crews, dressed in oilskin suits, standing by the lines ready to let go. There are a few minutes before the force is due to slip. Empty nervous minutes, the climax of the tension that has been mounting through the afternoon.

" Start up." One by one the engines start into life and swell the rumbling roar which fills the harbour.

" Let go for'ard—let go stern rope—hold on to your after spring—slow astern starboard —stop starboard—slow ahead starboard—slow ahead port—take her down, Cox'n." The boat slips away down harbour, the others draw away from the jetty and follow. Once clear of the harbour mouth they form up in quarterline and increase speed. The coastline fades into the dusk astern. Another patrol has begun.

There follows a long period of uneventful steaming at cruising speed in waters where no contact with the enemy is likely. There may be moments of concern, a patch of fog, a rising wind, a breakdown in one of the boats. Should the patrol go on or turn back?—the Senior Officer's decision must perhaps be made quickly. Dimly up the voice-pipe or through the chart-house hatch he may hear the high-pitched note of a wireless signal being received by the telegraphist below. Various possibilities will be passing through his mind as he waits for the decoded version. It may be a routine signal, an alteration to the night movements, a warning that our heavy bombers will be passing over at such and such a time. With luck it will be an enemy report, perhaps from another unit or from air reconnaissance, giving the first indication that enemy ships are at sea in his area, that battle is imminent if the intercepting calculations are made correctly.

But probably the signal is a routine one. Addressed to Air/Sea Rescue craft " return to harbour," or referring to the night movements signal " My 031657 Cancel paragraph 4."

As the force approaches the enemy-occupied coast the crews go to action stations. The long tense hours of peering into the darkness have begun—glasses sweep the horizon ceaselessly, the eyepieces biting into the eye sockets until they ache. Will this be another of the fruitless nights? Will it drag slowly through until the faintest glow above the eastern horizon ends another dull patrol? Cocoa at midnight—and sandwiches perhaps. There may be nothing on the sea for miles around; or the enemy may even now be steaming the last half-mile before he comes in sight. The dark loom of the coastline is menacing. At any moment a flash may be the warning that precedes a salvo of heavy shells from the batteries.

As the night wears on it becomes harder and harder to believe in the dangers which seemed so imminent when the force first arrived in the patrol area. But for an effort the lookout would be less well kept. The effort must be made. A pitiless cold watch at action stations the whole night through. A constant awareness of the boats astern, to make sure they are following. One hour more and it will be time to start for home, but it is still very dark. Not much chance of meeting up with the enemy now, though. Another blank night like so many before it. As the glasses sweep a dark lump breaks the line of the horizon; it must be imagination, there are dozens of them now, whole convoys; imagination surely. No— there they are again—two . . . three. My God, they *are* there!

"Enemy in sight to starboard," is the signal. And to the Seaman Torpedoman: "Ready both," so that the two torpedoes are in instant readiness for firing. Now think—think hard. Think it out calmly; you haven't got long, but it should be long enough; move stealthily, creep. Start plotting, and plot their course and speed. And when the battle starts make a conscious effort at concentration. Forget about the blinding starshells and the lobbing, buzzing, zipping tracers; forget how dry your mouth is. Think which way he is going, take your glasses and see if you can see the escorting screen; think about the boats astern— do they know the situation, have they room for their attack and room to disengage? Think about your angle on the bow, about the risk of losing too much bearing, about the enemy report to be signalled to Base. What is the enemy's speed to set on the sight? What is the inclination? Make "Attack with torpedoes—Executive Signal" to the force. "Steer five degrees to port, Cox'n—Steady—Stand by—Five more degrees to port—Steady—BOTH." Torpedoes gone, seem to be running all right. "Hard a-starboard, Cox'n." "A arcs" are opening. "Open fire, Number One." Just listen to the Cox'n's language. No, don't— make "Attack completed." "My God! Did you see that explosion—see that, Number One? That must have been our fish. Keep those guns firing, Number One—make 'Attack completed, one hit.' God, that was a marvellous explosion!"

Smoke and tracer bullets, fire and noise; " . . . seconds to outlast eternity."

When the firing has ceased the Senior Officer must find out how his boats have fared. If they cannot answer the wireless signal at once, he will be anxious until they can or until he has found them in the darkness. If they are found and the casualties are not serious, he will experience a rare feeling of relief and the triumph of achievement. When they are all collected together, it may be possible to attack again. He has scored a hit and some of his boats are damaged; it is getting late and the wind is freshening. There are a dozen good reasons for going home now, but the object of the patrol was the destruction of enemy shipping, and "the object must be pursued with singleminded determination" says *The Principles of War*.

The Battle is Renewed

Our force may be battered, but the enemy is probably battered too. He is certainly more frightened. He is, for example, on the defensive against torpedoes. He has much more chance of having a swim before the night is out than the crews of the M.T.Bs., and he knows it. So the battle is renewed, to be fought until the approaching dawn, or the expenditure of ammunition, or the damage to our boats, makes it necessary to withdraw.

On the homeward journey there will be many regrets. "If only we had turned sooner, or if only we had closed faster; if only we had deployed earlier, if only . . . if only . . . !" Even apart from the casualties, few actions are fought without such regrets, but just occasionally a force returns so wholly triumphant that no single thing could have gone better. Then the Senior Officer will be walking on air. That feeling alone is full reward for the successful achievement of the object and for all the fruitless nights. But more often, far more often, the Senior Officer will be plunged in gloom, a gloom which deepens as the pure relief of survival wears off. This reaction after battle is part of the psychology of war, and many men have returned from a successful operation convinced of its failure.

The technicalities of the return journey will principally concern navigation, for, after the rapidly changing courses and speeds of an action, the Unit's position by dead reckoning cannot be very accurate. There will also be a signal to be made to Base, briefly reporting the results of the battle and the expected time of arrival.

When the sun rises a sudden change seems to take place. All that happened in the dark seems to be a dream. The boats following in station look the same as they did before dusk on the outward journey. Did all those things really happen in between? The world of everyday matter-of-fact things comes back with a cup of tea and a cigarette on the bridge. The Unit comes into harbour, a friendly place in the early morning sun. There are ambulances on the jetty, and the Commanding Officer of the Base, with the First Lieutenant and the Medical Officer. As soon as the boats are alongside, the crews collect in little clusters along the ship's side, retailing their experiences, and the Commanding Officers meet, probably on the bridge of the Senior Officer's boat, to discuss the action. The discussion goes on as they walk up to the Base, it goes on over the partitions of the cubicles in the bathroom, and on and on at breakfast.

After breakfast, the preliminary reports have to be made to the Commander-in-Chief by signal. Once that has been done, the Senior Officer is free to sleep. Later he will have to embark on the more detailed reports by letter of proceedings:

" Sir, I have the honour to submit the following report on the proceedings of the striking force under my command on the night of 3rd/4th March . . . "; and so on and so on.

Track charts and movements of all the boats, diagrams of the phases of the action, details of torpedo firing, setting on the sight, depth setting, the number of rounds of each type of ammunition fired, the lessons learnt, the recommendations for decoration, the proposals for improvement in training and equipment. All these things must be recorded as soon as possible so that the best use may be made of the experience that has been gained.

Meanwhile the boats are made ready again. If the weather holds, there may be another patrol laid on for to-night.

CHAPTER III

THE ENEMY WAS TOO FAR AWAY

THE first operational M.T.B. base in this war was formed at Felixstowe. By January, 1940, the 1st Flotilla was ready to operate from it. Under Lt. Cdr. Sayer's successor, Lt. Cdr. C. M. Donner, R.N., it had returned from the Mediterranean through the heart of France during the previous autumn. The boats had steamed up the Rhône past the Pont d'Avignon, and up the Saone; they had been towed through the canals into the Seine, and so down-stream again to Paris and the Channel, a journey fraught with many improbable adventures, and redolent of the " entente cordiale." These were the British Power Boat Company's 60-footers built in 1937. The trawler *Vulcan*, which had been their depot ship at Malta, was brought back and berthed in the Felixstowe basin, and one hangar of the Air Station was taken over for stores and for slipping the boats.

In March the 4th Flotilla, consisting of the new Vosper boats, and the 10th Flotilla, made up of an assortment of Thornycroft boats of various experimental types, some of them similar to the C.M.Bs. of the last war, also assembled at Felixstowe.

The enemy was still too far away for them; the nearest part of the German coast was beyond the range of the M.T.Bs., and their duties degenerated into a miscellaneous series of rescue operations, and finally even to routine trips, taking fresh provisions to ships lying off the harbour.

When the Germans invaded Holland on 10th May, 1940, however, new prospects were opened. The 4th Flotilla with a small base party was sent to Ijmuiden, where one of its functions was to prevent seaplanes from landing on the Zuider Zee, though the enemy never tried it. The flotilla continued to operate there until Holland had been overrun. At this period M.T.B. 24 (Sub-Lt. R. Parkinson, R.N.) scored the first Coastal Force success against aircraft, when she shot down a Heinkel 115 float-plane.

The work of the M.T.Bs. during the evacuations from Holland, Belgium and France was a small part of the vast operations undertaken by the Navy, but there were times when high-speed craft were of special and vital importance. The last boat to leave the Hook of Holland, for example, on two engines, with a miscellaneous cargo of refugees, as the Germans entered the town, was commanded by Lt. P. F. S. Gould, R.N., later to become one of the most daring and brilliant officers in Coastal Forces. He and Lt. L. J. H. Gamble, R.N., were amongst those who took part in the 1940 blocking of Zeebrugge and Ostend, taking off the crews of the blockships under fire.

There were terribly few high-speed craft in running order in those momentous days. A few M.T.Bs., a few M.A./S.Bs., that was all. During the withdrawal from Dunkirk, Lt. Gould worked along the beaches, and Lt. H. L. Lloyd, R.N., was busy ferrying important officers to and from France at the critical stages. Lord Gort returned in a M.A./S.B. commanded by Lt. W. G. Everitt, R.N. Lt. C. W. S. Dreyer, R.N., made eight trips to Dunkirk in his M.T.B., on the last but one of which he brought back General Alexander. He describes how on one of the previous days the destroyer *Keith* was bombed off La Panne, and as she was sinking he was called alongside to take off Admiral Wake-Walker and his staff, and ferry them into Dunkirk to carry on the organisation of the evacuation. The German dive-bombers must have realised what was going on, for thirty-five Ju. 87s made the M.T.B. the object of their undivided attention.

" The roads were very crowded and there were a good few wrecks," writes Dreyer, " so that twisting and turning were out of the question. I could only go flat out and hope for the best. Everything missed us and we sustained no damage, though one pair of bombs disappeared from view under the transom, and from our tiny bridge I was certain they had got us. During that hectic morning the two things I remember most vividly are my gunner, Able Seaman Stephens (later killed at St. Nazaire), and a mine-recovery drifter in the harbour. Every time we left Dover, Stephens clambered into his turret and sat there, behind his four little ·303 machine guns, until we got back; nothing would budge him. On this occasion he was looking up at the Stukas, his guns aimed and ready, waiting for them to come into range, the inevitable cigarette drooping from his mouth. I noticed his mouth moving and leant back to hear what he was saying. Over and over again he was droning, ' Come on, yer bastards,' just to himself, longing to have his crack at them. Then we got into the harbour and I landed the Admiral. There was a fairly hearty raid going on, and to my dismay he told me to wait for him. We had two wounded men from *Keith* and I had no morphia, so we went alongside the mine-recovery drifter, which was lying alongside the mole. On the fo'c'sle sat a sailor, peeling spuds; on a hatchway sat the drifter's captain. He had a loaf between his knees, a tin of marmalade in his left hand and a knife in his right. These two, quite unconcerned by bombs, falling aircraft, bursting shells and every other conceivable sort of noise, gave me morphia for the wounded, a morning paper and a tin hat, in place of mine which had gone overboard. ' My dear fellow,' said the captain, ' I don't want it. I hate the bloody things, anyway; they make my head ache.'

" On Monday night we made our last trip, carrying Admiral Wake-Walker again, to direct the bringing off of the Frenchmen. It was beginning to get a bit hot by then. A certain amount of shelling was going on, and the fires made it nearly daylight. We had a red and green light and a loud hailer, and our job was to tell the troopships when they could come in and when to go. It involved steaming up and down that little harbour amongst the wrecks, and I got fairly exhausted. I remember I had begun to reach that awful stage when one says ' if I hit something, I hit something, that's all,' but luckily we avoided everything, even the Brittany crabbers, who were superb, quite unmoved and entirely ignorant of the most elementary precautions for avoiding collisions.

" The French soldiers I shall remember always, fallen in along the pier and jetties, still and utterly silent—waiting. They were an unnerving sight, grim and resigned, symbolic of the coming years of their country, and one felt that even in those uncertain days, they knew that France was lost. They stood there, still, as we left, some thousands that we couldn't bring away."

The Last and the Smallest

The last boat to leave Dunkirk at the conclusion of the evacuation was a tiny 40-foot M.T.B. commanded by Lt. J. Cameron, R.N.V.R. Here is his account of the part played by his boat on the last night of operation " Dynamo," which was the code name for the evacuation.

" This was by way of an extra performance," he writes, " as the Vice-Admiral, Dover (Vice-Admiral Sir Bertram Ramsey), had called for one final effort to bring off as many of the remaining French troops as possible.

" In addition the blocking operation on which we had been engaged on the previous night had not been completely successful, as one blockship had been lost in collision on the way across, and tidal conditions had prevented the remaining two from being sunk in the predetermined positions. On this last night we set out from the Downs to do it again—three blockships, the destroyer *Shikari* (with us in tow, to save fuel), and a M.A./S.B. to take off the blockships' crews.

" My boat was 'experimental,' possessing one propeller, no reverse gear and a turning circle of phenomenal diameter which made manœuvuring in a confined space a matter of extreme delicacy. In addition, our single engine had to be induced to start by compressed air. It was frequently temperamental and the air bottles leaked; consequently once this thunderous piece of marine ironmongery had been set in motion we were loath to stop it.

" As night fell we slipped from *Shikari* and proceeded noisily under our own power, approaching Dunkirk by the usual and now familiar route. The night was very dark and full of rushing shapes, all of which appeared to be coming directly at us. These were the last of the rescue ships completing their final task. The flames over the city did not seem so fierce as the night before, but the pall of smoke, which none who saw will ever forget, still streamed westward from the dying town, and the ring of gun-flashes had closed in in an ever narrowing semicircle. It was plain that the end could not now be far off.

" From the nature of our operation it was essential to wait outside until the last of the rescue ships were clear of the harbour ; so the three ancient merchantmen with their attendant craft steamed very slowly up the narrow channel towards the harbour that was to be their grave and the scene of their last service to their country. As they went destroyers, sweepers and transports, their bow waves gleaming with faint phosphorescence, hurried past us and disappeared westward into the darkness; and as my little craft rocked in their troubled wakes I found myself meditating rather ruefully on the strange chance that had brought me, a settled barrister of forty, to be a witness of so stupendous a scene.

" We had still a short distance to cover before reaching the pierheads of Dunkirk and I had taken station about a cable on the port bow of one of the blockships when a violent explosion ahead, accompanied by a shower of very attractive-looking sparks, showed me where the *Shikari* had apparently been near-missed either by a bomb or a mine. Very soon afterwards there was another and much nearer explosion; this time our blockship had ' bought it ' and it was immediately plain that she was in a bad way. We made at once to close her, and with some difficulty secured alongside her fo'c'sle, while our companion ' Masby ' went alongside the waist. As the ship was obviously sinking, the survivors on board began to abandon ship into the ' Masby,' and before any from her fo'c'sle could reach my small and unhandy craft, her bows rapidly lifted—so rapidly in fact that our securing lines snapped before we could cast off—and she sank in a flurry of wreckage.

" The ' Masby ' shoved off with her survivors, and I remained to pick up those I could hear calling for help in the water. Owing to our lack of manœuvring power, the darkness and the amount of wreckage, it was obviously going to be a long and difficult job to find and recover anyone in the water, but in time it was done and not one was left behind. There were two moments of comedy. The first was when we recovered the Captain, an elderly retired Commander. He was most deeply disturbed by the loss of his ' brass hat,' which unfortunately we had been unable to salvage, so finally I gave him my scarf instead. The other was our abortive attempt to take one of the ship's boats in tow. This had apparently floated clear with one badly injured and one slightly injured man in her. I intended to transfer all my survivors to *Shikari*, as previously planned, and I thought it quickest to tow the lifeboat. We made little headway, however, which was not surprising considering that she was still attached by one of her falls to the submerged wreck.

A SCENE OF TRAGEDY AND DESOLATION

" During this time the remaining blockships had steamed slowly into the harbour, and later two heavy explosions told us that they had been sunk in accordance with the plan. The stream of ships had now ceased. The last ships we had seen leaving were the destroyers and

Dreyer's M.T.B. carrying the Admiral. In this M.T.B., probably the smallest war vessel to wear an Admiral's flag in action, a hasty 'lash up' had been made for a Rear-Admiral's flag. A dish-cloth with a red stripe formed the basis, red paint and ingenuity did the rest.

" By now we appeared to be alone; the rattle of musketry and machine guns from the shore indicated that the fighting was in the last stages, and some of the fire was being directed at us. In addition we were very near the spot where an unfriendly battery had taken a 'pot-shot' at us the night before, when transferring the crews of the previous blockships to the destroyer *Vivacious* after the first blocking attempt. By now also the day was beginning to dawn. So we proceeded into the harbour to see if *Shikari* was still there. She wasn't.

" The scene was one of tragedy and desolation. Silent and deserted wrecks, a few French fishing craft, a black and huddled line of Frenchmen waiting hopelessly on the eastern jetty— for them we could do nothing, but it felt rather like desertion to leave them there. Outside again more wrecks, the charred and blackened remains of many ships. The whole scene was filled with a sense of finality and death; the curtain was ringing down on a great tragedy.

" It was clear to me that there was nothing more that we could do, and it was already far too light for comfort, so, sadly, we set course for home. The route was familiar and luckily so, as the deviation of our compass was an entirely unknown but very substantial quantity; besides, there had been no time during the past week to bring the charts up to date. But in spite of these things and a fog which led us to become mixed up with the Goodwin Sands, we returned safely to Dover, the last and the smallest of the King's Ships to leave Dunkirk."

This was not the type of work for which the Coastal Force craft had been built, nor yet was it remotely like the work they were later to undertake so successfully in the Narrow Seas; but it was a part of the magnificent improvisation of the time when disaster was awakening the British people to a new unthought-of life of effort and determination.

Stewart Gould, Christopher Dreyer, Hillary Gamble, " Harpy " Lloyd, Bill Everitt— those were names which were to become famous in the battles of the North Sea and the Channel.

It was not for some months, however, that the typical Coastal Forces warfare was to emerge from those uncertain times. The unthinkable had happened: France had fallen; not only was the enemy separated from us on land by no more than the narrow moat of the Channel, but the skies above that moat were filled with his aircraft and there were few enough of ours to say them nay.

Having completed their work of evacuation, the M.T.Bs. were often used for rescuing the crews of ships which had been bombed. On the 25th July, for example, two M.T.Bs. under the command of Lt. J. B. King-Church, R.N., and Lt. R. Hennessey, R.N., were sent out at midday to run alongside a convoy which had become a target for the Stukas. As the ships were hit and began to sink, the M.T.Bs. took off the survivors and returned with them to Dover. Many trips were made to and fro, with the decks crowded with seriously wounded and dying seamen, whilst the walking cases filled all the available space below. At four o'clock in the afternoon there was a lull in the air attacks and E boats were reported to be heading across the Channel, evidently with the intention of finishing off the stricken convoy. Two destroyers—H.M. Ships *Boreas* and *Brilliant*—and the two M.T.Bs. were ordered to intercept them, and steamed off at once towards Cap Gris Nez.

It was a clear day, and after a while the German shore guns opened fire with enough accuracy to inconvenience but not to damage or discourage our ships. Eventually a long line of white smoke was sighted, and it was evident that somewhere behind it the E boats were hidden. The destroyers fired into it, and the M.T.Bs. were detached to try to break through and engage them. But they could not get much closer because of the batteries. If they had intended to venture forth, however, the E boats now abandoned the attempt; for the time being the threat to the convoy had been removed. All the while our ships had been receiving most unwelcome attention from a host of Messerschmitt 109 fighters. The water was constantly boiling around them where the bullets and cannon-shells struck. Just as it was becoming evident that the E boats could not be brought to action, fresh hordes of aircraft appeared in the sky, and one by one peeled off to attack the destroyers. They were Stukas, and at once they began their almost vertical dive-bombing. In a few minutes both destroyers had been hit, and one of them, with damaged steering, had turned back towards France, with her attendant M.T.B. beside her. The M.T.B's. steering had also been shot away and she was being controlled by the hand tiller which had been rigged up aft. From this black situation all our ships survived, nevertheless, and struggled back on a wobbly course, which no doubt helped them to avoid the bombs still raining down upon them as they went.

These same two M.T.Bs., with a third commanded by Lt. W. B. T. Bate, R.N.V.R., were patrolling one night between Cap Gris Nez and Boulogne. The three boats were spread along the coast, and the Senior Officer—Lt. King-Church—who was in the northernmost position, suddenly sighted some vessels rounding the cape. At first he took them to be merchant ships, but as the range closed very rapidly he realised that they must be E boats— E boats about which he had heard much but which neither he nor any of his flotilla had ever met before.

His boat, M.T.B. 70, was armed, besides his torpedoes, with six Lewis guns; moreover, although she had been designed for three engines, because of the supply situation only two had been fitted. In spite of these circumstances, King-Church "crash-started" and closed at maximum speed to engage the enemy with gunfire. There were six E boats, and M.T.B. 70 turned up the line, firing at each in turn. The E boats may have been surprised, but they recovered quickly and, realising the odds, at once gave chase. With only two engines M.T.B. 70 could not escape, and the E boats took station one on either side and four in line abreast across her stern. Cap Gris Nez searchlights now lit up the scene, and so for a while did the searchlights of two of the following E boats, though these were soon extinguished either by Lewis-gun bullets or by their owners' dislike of the fire they drew. Under a steady cross-fire from the E boats the M.T.B. struggled on for nearly twenty minutes, until the rising sun decided the enemy to turn back. Then she stopped to ascertain her damage. One bullet had slightly grazed the port depth-charge chute without causing any damage. Apart from that she was unscathed.

In the dawn M.T.B. 69 joined her and made fast alongside; for the sea was flat calm, and there was much to discuss about this their first action against E boats, as they waited for the third M.T.B. to appear. M.T.B. 72 was at last seen approaching at full speed. She passed at 25 yards range doing nearly 40 knots, and those on board the other two boats noticed that her two Lewis guns were trained upon them as she went by. Rather a stupid time to do a dummy attack they thought. After an interchange of signals on a lamp M.T.B. 72 returned at a more reasonable speed and drew up to apologise. The silhouette of the two M.T.Bs., secured alongside each other, had, it appeared, been mistaken for that of an E boat. As she made her attack, the order had been given to open fire, but by a merciful Providence both guns had jammed.

Those were early days in the Coastal Forces war, when there was indeed much to be learnt on both sides.

Air/Sea Rescue occupied a large proportion of the M.T.B's. time during the Battle of Britain. Always an important function of Coastal Forces, its particular urgency during

MOONLIGHT ATTACK

RETURNING AT DAWN

August and September, 1940, was well illustrated by the fact that whenever a pilot was picked up from the sea he had to be rushed into harbour, where a car would be waiting to drive him straight back to the aerodrome and another fighter in which he could take off at once. There was small margin of reserve in those critical days.

A BRUSH WITH TRAWLERS

On 13th August, 1940, three boats under the command of Lt. G. J. Mannooch, R.N., fought one of the earliest actions. Off the newly occupied coast, Mannooch came upon a party of what he took to be E boats, and decided to ram one of them. At the last moment he realised that the enemy vessel was something larger and turned off, but it was too late and he struck it a glancing blow. His boat was badly damaged and so, probably, was the German motor minesweeper. Meanwhile, Lt. Gould, commanding the second boat, carried on a running fight with the enemy. Lt. E. Hamilton-Hill, R.N.R., stood by the damaged M.T.B. and prepared to take her in tow. In those days some of the M.T.Bs. carried their torpedoes in the engine-room and released them by increasing speed and dropping them out astern. This required a portable outrigger protruding over the transom to guide the torpedo clear of the boat, and for the towing operation Hamilton-Hill had unrigged his outrigger. It was at this moment that six trawlers passed across the bows of the M.T.Bs. at ideal torpedo range. In one boat the outrigger could not be replaced in time, and in the other the damage had reduced the speed below the minimum for firing torpedoes. In a few moments the chance had gone. One of the trawlers turned out of line and pursued the M.T.Bs. in a half-hearted way, but they were able to make their escape and crawl safely home.

Soon afterwards, on the 8th September, 1940, came the first successful torpedo attack by M.T.Bs. to be made in this war. The three boats which took part were M.T.B. 17 (Lt. R. I. T. Faulkner, R.N.), M.T.B. 14 (Lt. Hamilton-Hill) and M.T.B. 15 (Lt. J. A. Eardley-Wilmot, R.N.).

"We were sitting on the lawn one afternoon," writes Eardley-Wilmot, "when a message was sent up for us to return immediately. At the Base we were told that a convoy of thirty merchant ships had been sighted by aerial reconnaissance and was now either in or approaching Ostend. When we got over the other side I nearly got lost, as I tried to attack what I thought was a floating dock, which turned out to be a wreck. I managed to catch up, and after stooging around for about three hours without seeing anything, 'Pip' Faulkner called us up and told us we would go into the anchorage of Ostend. Ham-Hill broke down and lost contact with us about fifteen minutes later, but the two of us went on in. The R.A.F. were having a lovely time when we got there and lots of muck was flying into the air. We found all the ships at anchor and 'Pip' flashed 'Disregard my movements' and went in to attack. I turned off to the largest thing I could see and fired one fish, with the speed of the current as deflection. Both he and I hit with one torpedo, then we came round and did another attack individually. Unfortunately there was so much explosive business going on, because of the R.A.F. and also because, we found out later, I had hit an ammunition ship, that it was impossible to see the results. However, on the way out the examination vessel started firing at us. Our organisation in those days was that all the stokers were armed with rifle grenades. As we passed about forty yards off (I hadn't seen the blasted thing till the last moment) these boys had a whale of a time, and what with rifle grenades and our Lewis guns we gave them quite a good innings. Next day an aircraft reported three new wrecks in the anchorage, but whether we got all three I do not know."

THE ANSWER WAS "NO"

One night in October, the monitor H.M.S. *Erebus* was due to bombard the occupied coast from the vicinity of the Kwinte Bank Buoy. Three M.T.Bs., led by Lt. Cdr. A. B. Cole, R.N., formed a covering force. Lt. D. Jermain, R.N., and Lt. N. Poland, R.N., commanded the other two boats.

During the outward passage they met two trawlers some distance north of Calais. They were behaving oddly, and they were in such an unexpected position that Cole thought there might be some mistake. So he shadowed them while he passed a signal to Base asking whether any of our trawlers could be in the vicinity. On receiving the answer "No," the M.T.Bs. turned in and attacked with torpedoes. Both trawlers were sunk and practically all of their crews were picked up by the M.T.Bs. and made prisoner.

During this action Lt. Dennis Jermain completed the destruction of one of the trawlers by dropping a depth charge under it. This was a method which he had studied and practised carefully. A few months later he was able to make even better use of it. On a night in December a patrol of three M.T.Bs. was investigating Flushing, with Lt. Cdr. Cole as Senior Officer, but his boat broke down and he had to return to harbour. Jermain and Lt. P. M. Corsar, R.N.V.R., carried on the patrol, but bad luck continued to dog them. They ran into an anchored convoy off the Scheldt rather farther out than they had expected, and while they were still running noisily on main engines.

Corsar's boat was hit by gunfire from the escorts, and had all her hydraulic equipment put out of action, including steering and torpedo-firing gear. She circled widely, out of control, lost contact with the other boat, and was unable to take any further part in the engagement; indeed she had some difficulty in limping back to harbour.

Jermain tried to torpedo one of the escorts, but he had trouble with his firing gear and the first torpedo was fired finally from so close a range that it ran under the target during the initial plunge before coming up to its set depth. A second attack was made, but again the firing apparatus failed, and this time Jermain had to swerve off just as the torpedo was fired by hand, with the result that it ran wide. He was now left with no torpedoes and a fat convoy at anchor in front of him; so he selected the biggest ship and made two depth-charge attacks on her, while his gunners fired upwards at anyone who put his head over the merchant-man's gunwale.

On the second run he went so close that the flare of his own bows touched the enemy ship. The depth charges exploded amidships each time and, although Jermain did not see the full result, the ship concerned made a wireless S.O.S. in plain language, which identified her and confirmed her estimated size of 6,000 tons.

Later in December came the opportunity for a raid on Flushing Roads which had been planned some time before. With the very slow, silent speed of these M.T.Bs., the tide had to be flowing with them as well as the weather calm.

"There were three of us," writes Lt. R. A. Ellis, R.N.—the Senior Officer of the force— "M.T.B. 32, my own boat, leading, then 29 (Kit James)[1] and 31 (Dennis Jermain). The conditions were excellent—flat calm sea, mist, and a fairly strong moon. We got a good fix[2] half a mile off Zeebrugge mole, and set course up the coast for Flushing at five knots, with the tide flooding under us. Never a sign of a sausage for hours, but very pleasant boating.

"I had some bad moments crossing numerous tide lines—there appeared to be only about 3 inches of water on the far side of these rippling lines, and it was a relief not to feel

[1] Lt. C. A. James, R.N.
[2] An accurate position from lighthouses, etc.

the boat drive on the sand. Porpoises were having fine sport with us, darting under the boat leaving phosphorescent trails behind, for all the world like miniature torpedoes.

"Eventually my No. 1, Jake Wright, said that if we held on much longer we should be in the Grand Hotel, Flushing. So I said, 'All right, we'll call it a night and go home.' This would be just one more of the fruitless patrols over the other side—all night on the bridge, feeling one's way through the sandbanks and wrecks, one's eyes glued to the binoculars searching every inch of water, keyed up for instant action, and never seeing a sign of a single object, whether landmark, buoy, wreck or ship.

"Whilst Jake was working out the course for home, suddenly, out of the mist about 100 yards right ahead, I sighted an enormous object and thought 'My God, it's the land—we're running ashore.' Then I made out the anchor chain and realised that we had come upon a dream target—a large merchant ship at anchor.

"As she was bows on to us, I had to pull out on to her beam to fire fish—this manœuvre probably didn't take very long, but it seemed like agonising ages, wondering whether she was going to spot us. However, thanks to the mist, our light-painted hulls and Peter DuCane's[1] excellently designed silent engines, Kit and I were able to get into a nice position on her beam about 300 yards distant, with our torpedo sights on her and our hands on the firing levers. We both, naturally, wanted to have a crack at her, so I shouted to Kit, who was very close, that I would only fire one fish and he could have the second shot. With a feeling of relief I pulled the port firing lever, the fish leapt out of the tube with a jerk and a flash, sending up a column of water as it entered its natural element for its brief but deadly journey.

"'There goes £2,000 of the tax-payers' money and my first torpedo fired in anger,' I thought. 'For God's sake, run true, little fish.' A dull thud and a column of water on the stern of the ship showed that it had indeed run true. Kit fired his fish immediately after mine had hit and this one put up a better show, striking right amidships with a large flash. As was to be expected, the Jerry gunners came to life (perhaps not for long), and started throwing red tracer at me as I did a crash start on the main engines and swung round to find a healthier spot. As usual, however, all the tracer went astern of us.

"While disengaging, I came upon a flak trawler, also caught with his trousers down, which received a good burst of fire from my gunner in his ·5 turret. Kit, whose attention was not disturbed by other things, was able to see the merchant vessel break up in two places and disappear a few moments after his fish had hit. I must hand it to the Jerry gunners, who kept their gun firing until the ship sank under them."

After that, the Germans began to be more careful of their big merchant ships. They did not leave them at anchor off their harbours any more.

So the night fighting began to develop in the Narrow Seas, in detail far simpler, but in pattern much the same as the battles which were still being fought in the same area more than four years later.

In the autumn of 1940 it had become clear that the Coastal Forces were about to increase greatly, and that there would continue to be a requirement for such craft both at home and abroad for some considerable time to come, if not indeed for good. It therefore became necessary to appoint a Flag Officer to co-ordinate all the maintenance, improvement and future construction of M.T.Bs., M.G.Bs. and M.Ls., and to act as a link between the Admiralty and the Commanders-in-Chief, who were to remain responsible, of course, for operating the boats in their particular commands.

In November, 1940, Rear-Admiral Piers K. Kekewich was appointed as Rear-Admiral,

[1] Cdr. (E.) P. DuCane, R.N. (retired), managing director of Vospers Ltd., the M.T.B. designers and builders.

Coastal Forces, with a staff of experts in every specialised branch relating to these craft. The Chief Staff Officer in this command at its inception was Captain A. W. S. Agar, V.C., D.S.O., R.N., whose Victoria Cross had been won in a C.M.B., near Kronstadt in 1919, when he torpedoed the cruiser *Oleg*.

For more than two years Rear-Admiral Kekewich directed the development, the personnel, the technicalities, indeed every detail pertaining to the Coastal Forces except their operation, first from his headquarters at Portland and then from Wendover Court, a converted block of flats in Golder's Green.

The way was now prepared for the vast expansion required to meet the demands for Coastal Forces, not only in the Channel and the North Sea, but in the Mediterranean and the Far East. Of necessity, however, it was some time before this effort of co-ordination could bear fruit; during 1941 Coastal Forces were still sadly short of boats, and what boats they had were slow and far from reliable. Those working in the Dover Strait, for example, could not at that time exceed 24 knots, but even with these few slow and unreliable boats the object was possible of achievement. This was demonstrated on the night of 8th/9th September, 1941, in the first successful torpedo attack to be fought on the pattern that was later to become typical of M.T.B. warfare in the Narrows.

INTERCEPTION OFF BLANC NEZ

On that night, the anniversary of the first successful M.T.B. attack of this war, a German convoy attempted the passage of the Straits of Dover. It consisted of two heavily laden merchant ships with an escort of trawlers and E or R boats.

Lt. Cdr. E. N. Pumphrey, R.N., was in command of the force of M.T.Bs. which intercepted them, and his own account follows :

"We were at long notice—one hour—that night, having been at sea for the five previous nights. The available boats were 35 (my own), 218 (Chuck Bonnell)[1] and a Norwegian boat 54, commanded by Danielsen.[2] We were all at the local leg show when the recall came through. 35 and 218 got away pretty quickly, but there was a hitch of some kind in 54 and we had to leave her to follow. The set-up was that the enemy vessels had left Boulogne northbound, and we would be in time to intercept them off Blanc Nez. We also knew that M.G.Bs. 43 (Stewart Gould)[3] and 52 (Barry Leith)[4] were at sea in the Varne area and would probably make contact with the enemy and shadow and report them.

"We set course for Blanc Nez, and when I reckoned to be two miles from the point of interception we cut wing engines. For me, that is the worst phase of any Coastal Force action. Apart from being considerably frightened, there is the real agony of anxiety that you may have messed up the navigation and will miss the interception. However, all went well, and at about 11.30 p.m. we saw them—two merchant ships around the 3,000-ton mark, loaded right down. Later, as we closed, we saw a lot of escorts all fairly close in. There seemed to be three trawlers and perhaps eight E or R boats.

"It was a flat calm night, moonless but not very dark. We saw them at 4,000 yards[5] and ran in unseen almost on their beam. It was desperately exciting, creeping in in the dark, still unseen and getting nearer and nearer. There had never been a serious M.T.B. attack from

[1] Lt. C. E. Bonnell, Royal Canadian Naval Volunteer Reserve.
[2] Lt. P. E. Danielsen, R.Nor.N.
[3] Lt. P. F. S. Gould, R.N.
[4] Lt. W. G. B. Leith, R.N.V.R.
[5] Two miles.

Dover before, and the escort was half asleep. We got right in, passing between two of the screening E boats, about 1,000 yards from the rear ship. As we passed the E boats we rung on wing engines in a crash-start, a noise to wake the dead, and the balloon was up!

"I didn't see any more of Chuck. The tracer came in green rivers, but it was badly aimed, mostly too high. The ships opened fire with heavy stuff, the flashes were blinding, but nothing fell anywhere near. 35 ran in to 800 yards and fired a promising salvo—as I thought. Then hard a-starboard and we disengaged astern. The German gunnery was getting a little less wild and 35 was hit three or four times. Our own point-fives were in action, and it was good to see the red tracer going away low and level. It looked good shooting. Then a great flash leapt up from our target and we felt an underwater explosion.

"The E boats made no attempt at pursuit, and after five minutes we were well clear and we cut engines. I confirmed that, as I had suspected, our starboard fish had misfired. It was still in the tube and available for further action."

M.T.B. 218 had meanwhile seen a medium-sized warship which may have been an "M" Class minesweeper coming up from astern. She turned and fired torpedoes at it, but either by chance or design it altered course at exactly the right moment to avoid being hit. 218 was pursued by two E/R boats[1] as she disengaged. She fired at one, and the two of them then fired at each other, whilst 218 escaped. Having expended her torpedoes she returned to harbour.

"We had just checked up on the cause of the misfire (a dud charge)," continues Pumphrey, "when A.B. Carruthers, my gunner, sighted a boat on the port side. We challenged and she replied correctly. It was M.T.B. 54.

"The time was now about ten minutes past midnight and M.T.B. 35 and 54 started on what was to prove a long, stern chase. My plan was to overtake the enemy on a parallel course to north of him and, when well ahead, to cut wings, creep into his path and lie in wait. Accordingly, I altered to starboard at about 1.20 a.m., convinced that I was far enough ahead. But the enemy had increased speed considerably, and I was, in fact, astern and would never have made contact had not Danielsen sighted them on our port quarter. I was unable to see them, so I told Danny to lead on.

"Soon the enemy were clearly visible to the northward. Suddenly a hail of tracer burst out, away over on our port quarter, perhaps two miles distant. We rightly took this to be the M.G.Bs. in action, though we didn't hear the story until later. Apparently Stewart Gould sighted four boats coming up astern of the convoy and naturally imagined them to be the M.T.Bs., whose arrival he was awaiting with ill-concealed impatience. The reply to his challenge, however, was a well-directed stream of green tracer which severely wounded both his Lewis gunners in the first few seconds. Undeterred, Stewart instantly closed the range to attack with depth charges. He led across the Germans' bows and placed one under the leading boat. Thereafter only three boats were seen, so the leader was certainly damaged and possibly destroyed. A hot gun action was meanwhile in progress, and the Hun liked it so little that he broke off and left the M.G.Bs. free to assault a trawler which was still on fire next morning when the R.A.F. went to have a look."

Gould set about the merchant ship as well as the trawler, and it is evident that the enemy was becoming rapidly demoralised by his determination, for he describes how during this engagement the enemy fire was wild and inaccurate. The escort were firing in all directions,

---

[1] The correct identification of ships at night is a matter of extreme difficulty. Even size is often impossible to judge, because the distance, and therefore the scale, is so deceptive. On a dark night almost the only distinction between an E boat and an R boat is the speed at which it is travelling. When there is doubt, the convention E/R boat is generally used.

and it appeared that at times the trawlers were engaging their own E/R boats. The two M.G.Bs. finally broke off the engagement at 2.55 a.m. and set off towards home. They had been fighting for well over an hour and 52 was in a bad way. One engine was out of action, and there was a serious leak in the engine-room which made continuous bailing necessary for six hours. But she got back to harbour, although she had to be towed by a trawler at daylight.

All this activity on the part of the M.G.Bs. had an excellent effect on the M.T.B's. prospects, as it diverted the attention of much of the German escort towards the convoy's port quarter, whereas the M.T.Bs. were on the starboard beam. M.T.B. 54, slightly the faster boat, had taken full advantage of her orders to lead the attack and was a cable ahead of 35, both boats going flat out. At two o'clock, 54 turned northward to an attacking course and fired her torpedoes at about 1,200 yards. She then made smoke and disengaged to port.

"We ran on through the smoke," Pumphrey continues, "and emerged to find four E boats converging on the starboard bow. However, our blood was now well up and we were going to make certain of it. At 600 yards the merchantman was sitting across the sights like a row of houses and the E boats were far too close and hitting us hard and often. The time had come to fire—and as I pulled the levers I saw the target obliterated by a great black column of water and wreckage. 54's torpedo had hit square amidships and mine was wasted.

"I turned sharp to port away from the E boats and found myself almost on top of a trawler. At 100 yards she was hitting us altogether too hard. Both wings coughed, spluttered and stopped. Then a 3-inch shell blew half the stern off and a big petrol fire started amidships. The steering was shot to pieces by the hit aft and only the centre engine remained running.[1] Out of control, we were circling slowly to starboard towards the trawler which was lying stopped. We tried steering with buckets but without success, so I had to stop. There didn't seem to be a lot of future.

"The fire was being dealt with—Sheldrick, my Number One,[2] had operated the fire extinguisher levers in the wheelhouse and Ordinary Seaman Gillings, with considerable gumption, had leaned far out over the side to squirt in Foamite through the shellhole. There were 700 gallons of petrol loose in the bilge and burning, and it speaks volumes for the methyl-bromide extinguishing apparatus that the fire was almost instantly put out. My Cox'n, P.O. Hadley, had gone aft to see what could be done about rigging hand steering. The situation there was pretty black, as only one of the rudders was fitted with a spare rudderhead to ship the emergency tiller on—and this was the rudder that had been shot away. To fit

[1] At this time Lt. Cdr. Pumphrey himself was wounded, and two of the crew—the telegraphist and the Seaman Torpedoman.
[2] Lt. H. W. Sheldrick, R.N.V.R.

the tiller on the other it would be necessary to file a square on the post of the remaining rudder, and this appalling job Hadley immediately and cheerfully undertook.

" The bright spot in our situation was that the trawler's fire had first slackened and finally ceased. For this there was a good reason. Able Seaman Carruthers at the point-fives was firing beautifully, with precision and economy. One by one he had silenced the trawler's guns. I walked aft to speak to him. He was as cool as a cucumber and utterly happy. He said: ' She's quiet now. I'm not wasting ammunition on her. Look.' I looked and saw an E boat, 400 yards away and slowly closing on our port side. She closed to 100 yards and then opened fire. The green tracer and the red crossed in mid air, but the green was too high, while the red tracer streamed into the E boat's hull and bridge, a lovely sustained burst of perhaps 80 rounds from each gun. The green tracer stopped suddenly and the E boat sheered off. Without a word Carruthers swung back on to the trawler.

" Meanwhile another complication had entered our life. In flooding the tank space with methyl bromide an error had been made and the engine-room had also been filled with the poisonous gas, and now the engine-room staff were tumbling up on deck gasping and retching, almost unconscious. Lt. D. G. Tate, R.N.V.R., spare Commanding Officer of the 6th Flotilla and ' out for the trip,' organised artificial respiration for them and had a good deal of success. After a very few minutes Gordon, the motor mechanic, was able to stagger back to his engines, and Mason and Scantlebury, the stokers, were not far behind him. Constantly vomiting and on the verge of unconsciousness, these men laboured away at the engines to such good effect that they were soon able to report that, in addition to the centre engine, I could have the port when I wanted it. This, however, was no use without steering-gear, and, as we anxiously awaited the results of Hadley's labours, our darkest moment came. The four E boats which had first engaged us had, for some obscure reason of their own, lain off at about 800 yards, stopped. They now started engines, formed up and steered slowly down our starboard side. I reckoned the time had come when all hope must be abandoned and the boat destroyed. The life-float was cleared away and floated alongside, and I gave orders to abandon ship as soon as the E boats opened fire. I was to remain to re-start the petrol fire. But to our amazement the E boats cruised past us at a range of 400 yards without firing a shot !

" Then everything went right. Hadley reported that we could steer after a fashion, the third engine was got going and, with Gillings and Jakes lying on their tummies and holding the tiller on to a flat one-eighth of an inch deep, we swerved off into the night on a most erratic course for home.

" That wasn't quite the end of it, as the damage aft had very nearly sunk the boat. The water was almost up to the engines, and though it rapidly drained while we were going at speed, she filled up again as soon as we eased down. So full speed it had to be, and as we had only a rough idea of where we were, highly erratic steering-gear, and a nice little fog to contend with as we approached our coasts, the situation was fraught with interest. Actually we missed the Goodwins on the wrong side and made the Thames Estuary just north of Margate! We entered Ramsgate at about 7.30 a.m.

" The great feature of this action was, in my opinion, the exemplary conduct of the ship's company under somewhat disagreeable conditions. The telegraphist continued to function although shot through the kidneys and barely conscious. Jakes, the torpedoman, worked like a black with Hadley and did not mention till we landed at Ramsgate that he was full of splinters in the legs. The engine-room staff, Cox'n and the trained man, Gillings, were all excellent, and I consider that Carruthers' performance as gunner was absolutely outstanding."

So ends Nigel Pumphrey's stirring account of the first great M.T.B. action in the Dover Strait, for which he received the D.S.C. Able Seaman Carruthers and Motor Mechanic

Gordon were awarded the D.S.M., and the First Lieutenant and the Cox'n were mentioned in despatches.

Able Seaman J. D. Lanfear, a gunner in M.G.B. 43, was also recommended for decoration for his calmness and skill throughout the engagement. Two nights later M.G.B. 43 was again in action in the Straits. In his report on that occasion Gould wrote:

" For the second time in three days Able Seaman Lanfear directed the fire of the after gun under heavy fire with outstanding coolness and skill. When seriously wounded he displayed gallantry and devotion to duty of the very highest order. Having suffered multiple injuries, being in great pain, and unable to stand, he seized a stripped Lewis gun and directed a rapid and accurate fire on the enemy until he finally collapsed from the effects of his wounds."

Able Seaman Lanfear was awarded the Conspicuous Gallantry Medal.

THE AUTUMN OF 1941 IN THE STRAITS

Before the successful M.T.B. attack of the 8th/9th September, there had been various unsuccessful skirmishes in the Dover Strait, two of them in daylight.

One of these was an attack on a trawler in low visibility, spoiled by the premature detonation of the torpedoes, which apparently hit the sea-bottom, and the other was an unsuccessful long-range attack on a single destroyer, escorted by two E boats. On another famous occasion torpedoes were fired at Boulogne breakwater which had been mistaken for a ship. On the following night our boats reported a red light on the breakwater, put there, no doubt (they said), to warn pedestrians of the hole.

But Lt. Cdr. Pumphrey had shown that success was possible even with the slow boats at our disposal, and a number of actions developed during the winter, a notable feature of which was the dash and courage of Lt. Gould and his M.G.Bs., acting in support. This team work between Pumphrey and Gould had a great influence on the development of Coastal Force tactics.

The most spirited action at this period was fought on 3rd November. That night Pumphrey and Lt. P. A. Berthon, R.N.V.R., between them sank a 5,000-ton ship and got away unscathed. They got away chiefly because of the very gallant and magnificent action which was being fought meanwhile by the tiny gunboats led by Gould. Whilst they were busy shooting up one of the trawler escorts, a " T " Class torpedo boat (the equivalent of a small destroyer) appeared on the scene, and the M.G.Bs. turned their attention to it. There followed one of the most astonishing actions ever fought by Coastal Forces. For five minutes the two sides steered parallel courses 400 yards apart at 25 knots—on the one hand the enemy warship of about 600 tons, firing 4-inch shells as well as heavy machine gun and cannon; on the other, the two tiny M.G.Bs. armed with their one Oerlikon and their Lewis guns. And this, in the words of Gould's report, is what happened:

" Both M.G.Bs. sustained damage and casualties. The enemy, after being frequently hit, broke off the action after about five minutes by turning away to the north-west under cover of smoke. The M.G.Bs. turned to the northward in pursuit." Such audacity was typical of the gunboats under Stewart Gould.

While pursuing the torpedo boat they came upon a stopped trawler, probably the one they had already shot up. They engaged it for a further ten minutes, after which they found themselves involved with the torpedo boat again and one of them was badly hit. One of her engines was put out of action and she was set on fire aft. Her Commanding Officer, Lt. M. G. Fowke, R.N., had to break off the fight and creep away on his remaining engine.

Gould was also in trouble. One of his engines stalled and the torpedo boat tried to ram him. The engine was started, however, and he drew clear just in time. The Oerlikon was out of action and the Lewis gun had run out of ammunition. The story is told that Gould called for the rifles and pistols to be brought up from below to carry on the fight. Meanwhile the Germans had them hemmed in against the shore, and it was only with the greatest difficulty that they managed to escape from the trap and get out to the southward. Once clear they stopped to find out how much they had been damaged and how many of the crew were casualties.

The boat had been badly holed, the wireless aerial had been shot away, one of the propeller shafts was vibrating badly; the First Lieutenant and two of the crew were wounded; they were three-quarters of a mile west of Boulogne breakwater and the wind and sea were rising.

They set off for home, but before they were half-way the boat became so waterlogged that she was in danger of breaking up. So they stopped and set to work to bail. They rigged a jury wireless aerial, but they found that the set had been damaged by the flooding and could not be repaired. At this stage motor-boat engines were heard, but Gould was not sure if they were friendly, and, since he could still see Cap Gris Nez quite clearly, he decided not to make any distress signals. At daybreak the English coast was also in sight and the M.G.B. was spotted by a fighter aircraft, which reported its position so that later it was taken in tow and brought safely to harbour.

Two weeks later Gould was in action on a very dark night. In the course of the battle he lost contact with the enemy, although he thought that they must be very close. As a last resort, to encourage the Germans to disclose their whereabouts by opening fire, he fired Very lights and tracer in all directions, but there was no response.

At the beginning of December, after Pumphrey's M.T.Bs. had delivered an unsuccessful attack on a small merchant ship, one of them, M.T.B. 218 (Lt. H. P. Granlund, R.N.V.R.), was holed below the waterline by a 4-inch shell, and damaged by cannon shells, one of which short-circuited the electrical system so that the compass light failed and the navigation lights and stern light were illuminated. The boat was rapidly becoming water-logged, although Leading Telegraphist P. Phillips had bunged the hole in the ship's bottom with blankets and pillows, which he kept in place by standing on them. Having extinguished the navigation lights, which were drawing unwelcome attention from the enemy gunners, and with 4 feet of water in the Wardroom and wireless office, 218 set course for home, passing a friendly M.T.B. to whom Granlund made no distress signal because he thought it possible that she had not completed her attack and felt that she should not, therefore, be distracted.

"An hour later," he records, "the situation was becoming serious, as the bow of the boat was below the level of the sea."

So the M.T.B. was turned about and proceeded stern first at 6 knots, although the reverse gears of the engines were not designed for such a heavy and continuous load. Leading Telegraphist Phillips remained in his position blocking the shell-hole for two and a half hours, by which time the water-level had reached his shoulders. Since it was midwinter, he was suffering from extreme cold and exhaustion, but still he had to be ordered to relinquish his post.

Granlund brought 218 into harbour five and a half hours after she had been hit. The water was then 1 foot above the wheelhouse deck amidships, but the trailer pumps were ready for her as she berthed alongside. "His skill and resolution on this occasion," comments the Vice-Admiral, Dover, "were of a high order, and his leadership was reflected in the admirable behaviour of his ship's company."

Scharnhorst AND Gneisenau

On the 12th February, 1942, the battle cruisers *Scharnhorst* and *Gneisenau*, with the heavy cruiser *Prinz Eugen*, passed through the Straits of Dover on their way from Brest towards Germany. The underlying reasons why the enemy succeeded in this bold movement do not concern this book, but one of the features of the passage was an attack by M.T.Bs. under the command of Lt. Cdr. Pumphrey. Here is his story of what happened:

"On the morning of the 12th February, I was sitting in my office doing a little placid paper work when the telephone rang. It was the ordinary exchange line, and I was rather expecting a call from the Naval Stores. The time was 1135.

"'Pumphrey?' said a voice which I recognised at once as Captain Day's,[1] the Chief of Staff. 'The battle cruisers are off Boulogne now. How soon can you get cracking?'

"It was a little startling. I told him we were at four hours' notice but would do all we could. I yelled into the Wardroom to man all boats at the rush and went up to the Operations Room. Hillary Gamble[2] was there—he thought I was pulling his leg. Eric Cornish[3] was there too, sick as mud, as his boat had gone into Wellington Dock that morning to exchange petrol tanks with 38. Both these two boats were out of it.

"There was a mad rush down to the boats. By an almost incredible stroke of luck, all the available M.T.Bs. were in running order; that is to say, not stripped down for maintenance, as one might expect at four hours' notice. The time was lucky too—all the crews were back from store parties and so on, and the boats were manned and started like lightning. The M.G.Bs. were unlucky. Stewart Gould and Roger King[4] were in the town, and there was no time to do more than tell the Duty M.G.B. officer to get hold of them. There wasn't a second to be wasted if we were going to make an interception of 27-knot ships with 24-knot M.T.Bs., which was all those particular boats would do.

"My own boat, 38, being in Wellington Dock, I had intended to lead the Flotilla in 219, Mark Arnold Forster's[5] boat. But when the boats were manned it was found that Paul Gibson[6] (221) was not present. Poor chap, he was up seeing about loan clothing and missed the fun. So I took 221 to sea myself.

"Manning the boats was a terrific scene. *Scharnhorst* and *Gneisenau* had become almost a myth at Dover—and here we were in broad daylight setting off after them. It didn't seem possible. Even apart from *Scharnhorst* and *Gneisenau*, to do an M.T.B. operation at noon seemed almost indecent. I shall never forget the chaps grinning all over their faces, pulling on their steel helmets and each boat making the V sign as they let go the ropes. 221 was the inner boat, and therefore last out of the ferry dock. The others waited for me in the harbour, and we formed up and screamed out at 24 knots.

[1] Captain A. Day, R.N.
[2] Lt. L. J. H. Gamble, R.N.
[3] Lt. E. A. E. Cornish, R.N.V.R.
[4] Lt. R. King, R.N., a Frenchman who had joined the Royal Navy when France fell.
[5] Sub-Lt. M. Arnold Forster, R.N.V.R.
[6] Lt. P. G. L. Gibson, R.N., another Frenchman who, like King, had lately joined the Royal Navy. King and Gibson were the names they had chosen for their service with the R.N.

" There were five boats—221, 219 (Mark Arnold Forster), 45 (Hillary Gamble), 44 (Dick Saunders)[1] and 48 (Tony Law).[2] We passed the breakwater in that order at 1155— just twenty minutes after the Chief of Staff had telephoned. It was good going: even allowing for the generous measure of luck in having everyone on the spot, it spoke well for the general preparedness of the M.T.Bs.

" We set course for number two buoy. It was pretty rough, with a strongish westerly wind, but with the weather behind us our speed wasn't affected much. At 1210 we saw fighters, masses of them, all Messerschmitts. A squadron flew over us very close—close enough to see the metal rim to the pilots' goggles. We all blazed away at them, but for some reason they didn't answer back. I imagine they were keeping their ammunition for the hordes of bombers they must have been expecting. Hillary Gamble shot bits off the wing of one. Simultaneously we sighted smoke in two distinct patches to the south-east, and almost immediately afterwards we saw the E boats who were laying it—ten of them in two divisions half a mile apart.

An Impossible Situation

" The M.T.Bs. were having a bit of engine trouble. 44 had lost one engine altogether and was miles astern. The others were struggling to keep up, but there must have been two cables between the leading and rear boat. The hell of it was that one couldn't afford to ease down. Course was altered 30 degrees to port to north 80 degrees east, a course that converged slightly on the E boats. When the range was down to 1,000 yards both sides started shooting, but at that range in a moderate sea it was almost a waste of ammunition. Then the main enemy force came clear of the E boats' smoke—three great ships with destroyers stationed astern of them. *Prinz Eugen* leading, then the two battle cruisers.[3] They were on the same course as the E boats, but 4,000 yards farther away. A swarm of escorting aircraft was all round them. I noticed that their guns were all trained fore and aft. I estimated their speed at 27 knots.

" The situation was an impossible one. The E boats barred the path of an M.T.B. attack, and though I ordered emergency full speed in an attempt to draw ahead of them, I felt pretty sure it would be useless. I was right. The E boats merely put on another knot or two, maintaining their excellent defensive position.

" The temptation to those ten E boats to turn towards us, close the range, and clean us up, must have been almost irresistible, but like the Messerschmitts, they resisted it. The initiative remained with me.

" There were two alternatives—either to try to battle through the E boats, or to accept firing at long range. The M.T.Bs. were on the ideal bearing—50 degrees on the bow of the leading battle cruiser, but the range was hopelessly long. I made the wrong decision and altered course to try to fight through the screen.

" It was a mad thing to do. The inevitable result would have been the loss of all boats before the range could have been reduced to a reasonable one—say 2,000 yards. But chance

[1] Sub-Lt. R. F. Saunders, Royal Australian Naval Volunteer Reserve.
[2] Sub-Lt. C. A. Law, Royal Canadian Naval Volunteer Reserve.
[3] Prisoners of war state that at this time the enemy ships were steaming in the order: *Scharnhorst, Gneisenau, Prinz Eugen*, which, if true, illustrates the difficulty of correct identification, especially of German heavy ships, even in broad daylight.

The story is told of a telegraphist in one of the boats at about this time who had just received Pumphrey's enemy report by W/T. " There's a chap down here who's just seen two battle cruisers, one cruiser, three destroyers and eighteen E boats—must be a ruddy exercise."

took a hand, and as I turned, my starboard engine conked and my speed fell back to 16 knots. In these circumstances there there was only one thing to do—to hold on until the E boat fire became a serious danger to my torpedo tubes and then to fire at a range of 4,000-odd yards.

" We steered in, in line abreast, until the E boats' range was 200 yards. Even then they scarcely touched us—it was too rough for shooting. We fired our fish carefully but without much hope and turned away. The whole operation had been most unsatisfactory. About three minutes after firing, *Scharnhorst* and *Gneisenau* turned 90 degrees away and our last hope of a lucky hit evaporated. *Prinz Eugen*,[1] on the other hand, turned about 50 degrees towards and presented Dick Saunders, who had recovered his dud engine, with a possible though very distant target. At the right interval after, I saw a curious plume of water under *Prinz Eugen's* bridge. It wasn't a characteristic torpedo hit, but, on the other hand, I don't know what else it can have been.

" The E boats resumed their smoke and the M.T.Bs. were rather gloomily collecting themselves together when suddenly, through the smoke, appeared a German Narvik Class destroyer,[2] closing the M.T.Bs. at speed. We made smoke, scattered and made off at our best speed. Without torpedoes we were pretty helpless—and she was overtaking us fast. Luckily her gunnery was weak. Still, the situation might well have become a very serious one had it not been for the sudden appearance of M.T.Bs. 43 and 41.

" Stewart Gould was hopping mad at having missed the fun. He had shot down two Messerschmitt's on his way across, which had slightly soothed him, but he was in no mood to be embarrassed by a mere Narvik. The two 63-foot boats went bald-headed for the destroyer, blazing away with their single Oerlikon guns. They intended to attack with depth charges. The German must have taken them for fresh M.T.Bs. still complete with torpedoes, for he turned away and rejoined his main force. The only other bright spot in this very sombre day was that on our way back M.T.B. 45 was able to pick up two of the very gallant airmen from the Swordfish, whose attack is one of the most splendid episodes in our Naval history."

Both Lt. Cdr. Pumphrey and Lt. Gould served in destroyers after leaving Coastal Forces in the spring of 1942. Pumphrey continued to fight in the Channel, first in command of H.M.S. *Brocklesby* and then H.M.S. *Goathland*. He played a prominent part in the Dieppe Raid, and later led a brilliantly successful attack on a convoy off the French coast, with H.M.S. *Albrighton* (Lt. Cdr. R. J. Hanson, D.S.O., D.S.C., R.N.) in company.

Gould returned, however, to command a flotilla of M.T.Bs. in the later stages of the African campaign in 1943. He was killed soon after fighting perhaps the most brilliant of all his actions, and one in which he displayed all the gallantry and daring which had made his name a legend in the Dover Command.

It was at the time of our final advances in Tunisia, and Gould had led his flotilla in daylight down the German-occupied coast of the Cape Bon peninsula, taking advantage of the enemy's disorder to engage targets ashore and even to enter their anchorages. His bag was two motor minesweepers and two aircraft on the beach destroyed and one R boat set on fire. In the early afternoon he was warned of the approach of an enemy merchant ship escorted by two destroyers and fighter aircraft. His own torpedoes had already been expended, but the other two boats of his force were available to attack. His plan of action was that he should hold the attention of the two destroyers single handed whilst the others attacked with torpedoes, and this plan

[1] According to prisoners of war this must have been *Scharnhorst*.
[2] This is now known to have been the *Friedrich Ihn*, which was of the " Maas," not the " Narvik," class.

he carried out, for fighting two destroyers with one M.T.B. were the sort of odds that Stewart Gould enjoyed. The merchant ship was successfully torpedoed, and the M.T.Bs. made their escape, but they were promptly attacked by the fighter aircraft and suffered heavy casualties. One boat was sunk and Gould was killed.

CHAPTER IV

THE MOTOR GUNBOATS ARRIVE

WHILE the Dover tradition was being founded in the winter of 1941–42, a new phase of Coastal Forces warfare was developing farther north on our coastal convoy route, which was becoming known as " E boat alley."

The first E boat attacks on the East Coast convoys had been delivered in early September, 1940, and by February, 1941, the menace had become serious, but the new motor gunboats, converted from M.A./S.Bs. were ready to enter the ring. The 6th M.G.B. Flotilla had been formed in December, 1940. It consisted of three boats previously converted, armed with four Lewis guns and one Oerlikon, and five boats built as M.A./S.Bs. for the French Navy, and armed with four Lewis guns and a Boulton & Paul aircraft turret operating four ·303 Browning machine guns. All these boats were the product of the British Power Boat Company.

The flotilla, under the leadership of Lt. Peter Howes, R.N., formed up at Fowey. Many of its officers were later to become famous in the annals of Coastal Forces: Lt. G. D. K. Richards, R.N.; Lt. R. P. Hichens, R.N.V.R.; Lt. I. R. Griffiths, R.N.; Lt. A. A. Gotelee, R.N.V.R.; Lt. L. G. R. Campbell, R.N.V.R.; Lt. G. E. Bailey, R.N.V.R.; Lt. G. F. Duncan, R.C.N.V.R.; Lt. R. M. Barge, R.N.V.R.

Early in March, 1941, the flotilla was sent to H.M.S. *Beehive*, the Coastal Force Base at Felixstowe. On the way it was bombed ineffectively off Anvil Point by a single aircraft which dipped suddenly out of the clouds. When it arrived little was known about the best method of using it, and various types of patrols were tried out. At first the M.G.Bs. operated with destroyers, but the noise of their engines gave away the presence of the patrol and the risk of being torpedoed made it impossible for the destroyers to lie stopped. By themselves, however, the M.G.Bs. were too difficult a torpedo target with their small size and shallow draught; it was unlikely that an E boat would waste a torpedo trying to hit one, so they could, and did, lie stopped, waiting and listening for the E boats' approach. They began to operate in scattered patrols in likely spots for E boats, and before long they were given the freedom of the North Sea from the Humber to the Hook and from the Texel to the Thames.

One of their first encounters with E boats came on the 29th April. Sub-Lt. E. D. W. Leaf, R.N.V.R., who was First Lieutenant of one of the two M.G.Bs., described the action in his diary: " Daybreak found us passing close to Brown Ridge Buoy. It was light enough to see two or three miles when we altered course for home and breakfast after a long night of waiting. Imagine our surprise at this late hour when we saw a German E boat approaching on a converging course on the starboard bow. He came nearer and opened fire with a long crackly burst as he crossed our bow about 75 yards ahead. We then shot him up from astern and turned to run alongside him. His tracers were fascinating. You could see them coming in little groups of eight or ten, mostly low overhead. One or two hit us and exploded. After a quarter of an hour a second E boat came up astern. We turned to port to depth charge her, but got caught with cross fire instead, and the first E boat escaped. As we were only about 20 miles from Holland and on fire in the after compartment, we broke off and made back home —none the more victorious. However, we did engage them for twenty-five minutes, and that was worth waiting for since last August when I first joined an M.G.B. We ought to have done so many things which we did not, but we are a lesson to the good and there's still plenty of time for more." How well Derek Leaf used that lesson, and the time, until he was killed in action off the Dutch coast, as Senior Officer of a flotilla, on 15th February, 1944, may be read later in this book.

This inconclusive battle gave food for furious thought. Heretofore gunboat tactics had been developed on purely theoretical lines. Here at last was some practical experience to bite on. The next encounter came on 25th May. This time it was a long-range brush, and again the result was inconclusive, but there was more new material with which to develop the tactical theory of fighting E boats with M.G.Bs.

"On midsummer night 1941," writes Lt. Gotelee, "we fought an action with five E boats again in the neighbourhood of Brown Ridge, which lasted fifty-five minutes and ended in us pursuing the E boats practically to within sight of Ijmuiden. To the lasting credit of Rolls-Royce engines, the action was fought at full throttle for the whole time, and in the middle of it my motor mechanic crawled up to me in the dustbin and said, 'For God's sake stop, sir.' I asked why, being extremely incensed at the time, and he said, 'You have been running your engines on full throttle for so long that all the dynamos are on fire. Give me two minutes and I will pull the leads out.' This he did without turning a hair and the party continued. By the time we had finished, one of my Browning guns was white hot."

But still the M.G.Bs. could not obtain a decision. They could not destroy an E boat, although the enemy realised that a new and potentially dangerous weapon was being forged against him.

The flotilla suffered a setback during this early period, when their Oerlikon guns were taken away for the Mediterranean campaign. Some of the officers " got into a car, went to an Air Force Station near Felixstowe and managed to beg, borrow or steal one last-war Cow Gun, one experimental Hispano and a very old ·5. We made our own mountings and carried on with these weapons for over a month before we were again properly armed."

In August Lt. Howes was appointed to a Signals Course and Lt. Hichens was promoted Acting Lt. Cdr. and took over as Senior Officer of the flotilla, the first R.N.V.R. officer to serve in such a capacity. During the next year and a half the name of Robert Peverell Hichens became a legend in Coastal Forces. He was killed in action in the early hours of 13th April, 1943. On the following night I myself was leading a force of gunboats down into the Baie de la Seine. Soon after nine o'clock one of the boats broke down and we all stopped while the repair was effected. In the silence as we lay there, someone shouted across, " Did you hear the nine o'clock news. Hitch has been killed."

Our patrol that night was uneventful, and I had long hours standing on the bridge peering into the darkness, long hours in which to think of the man I had known in peace-time and whom I had last seen only a few days before, when he had dined and stayed the night at my house in London. A fortnight later I had occasion to broadcast a B.B.C. Postscript for St. George's Day. After mention of the Coastal Force battles came the following passage about Hitch:

"In this sort of fighting, as I suppose in any kind of specialised fighting, there are men who combine those particular qualities of cool leadership and complete knowledge of the technical side of their job so perfectly that their battles are successful where others fail. Such a one was Lt. Cdr. Robert Hichens, R.N.V.R., whose loss two weeks ago was the most tragic blow to Coastal Forces and indeed to England. He was a man cut out for the job, because in peace-time his interests, apart from his work as a solicitor, were in motor racing and dinghy sailing. He won the Rudge-Whitworth cup in the 24-hour Grand Prix at Le Mans with his Aston Martin. I remember seeing that car completely in pieces in a shed at his home at Falmouth five years ago and driving in it again a few months ago at Felixstowe.

"In 14-foot dinghies he always went best in a strong breeze, and I used to reckon my boat went best in that kind of weather too. We had some good races in those piping days.

"He was known throughout Coastal Forces as 'Hitch,' and most of the tactical theory of motor gunboats was first developed and practised by him. But the chief thing about him was the way he could lead and the confidence he instilled into the officers and men of his flotilla. I remember one of them telling me that his only fear on going into action was that he wouldn't satisfy 'Hitch.' And it wasn't limited to his flotilla, this inspiration. It spread around and developed the spirit which put our Coastal Forces on top whenever they met the enemy, by virtue not of their guns but of their determination . . ."

To Lie in Wait for E Boats

It was in the early hours of the 20th November, 1941, that the 6th M.G.B. Flotilla under Hichens scored the first decisive victory over the E boats. On the evening of the 19th three M.G.Bs. were lying in harbour at short notice when E boat activity was reported from our convoy route, and they were ordered to sea with all despatch. Hichens was the leader and the other two Commanding Officers were Lt. L. G. R. Campbell, R.N.V.R. (known in the flotilla and subsequently throughout Coastal Forces as "Boffin") and Lt. G. E. Bailey, R.N.V.R.

The weather was perfect, sea flat calm, the moon still up, and the gunboats set course for the Hook of Holland with the object of lying in wait for the returning E boats more or less on their doorstep. But they had not gone far before Bailey's boat broke down and had to be left behind. A little later Hichens' own boat broke down. One engine was out of action without prospect of repair and his maximum speed was reduced to 18 knots. Many would have considered their boat in no fit state to meet the enemy, but Hichens decided to go on, and although he could not reach the prescribed position off the Hook, he steered to place himself some 20 miles to seaward of the area in which the E boats were operating and in the direct line of their retreat. Reports of their activities were still being received by the telegraphist in an almost continuous stream and passed to the bridge.

Soon after two o'clock in the morning the M.G.Bs. reached the stopping position and cut engines to wait and listen for the approach of the returning E boats. The moon had now set but the sea was still glass calm and there was a slight mist, so that the visibility distance for small craft was no more than a couple of hundred yards at most.

They had a long time to wait, but at a quarter to five the faint murmur of engines was heard to the westward. For eight minutes the murmur grew louder as the E boats approached and the bearing of the sound altered slowly to the southward. At last Hichens started up and set off to intercept, though with a maximum of 18 knots he knew it would be difficult enough, working only on the course and speed of the enemy estimated during the eight minutes they had been listening. After a little while, however, he stopped again, and quickly cut engines to listen. The E boats' rumble was much louder now and the bearing of the sound had altered slightly. The course was amended and the M.G.Bs. set off again at once. Hichens was wondering whether to stop a third time when a faint light flickered on his port bow. A moment later in the red glow of a flare he saw five E boats clustered together, either stopped or moving very slowly, having apparently reached their rendezvous position. In a few seconds the two gunboats were amongst them firing all their guns at a range of 50 or 60 yards. One E boat was engaged to starboard, another to port; a third received the full broadside of both M.G.Bs. at no more than 20 yards range and made no reply at all. A fourth was engaged for a short while on parallel courses; and then with their limited speed the M.G.Bs. lost touch with the enemy.

Hichens barely had time to discover that his main gun was jammed when a fifth E boat loomed up to starboard. The machine-gun turret on that side was also out of action. He describes the sense of frustration that he experienced at that moment as one of the liveliest and most vivid memories of his life. " After a year's search for the elusive E boat, to have one ranging nearer and nearer alongside at point-blank range and to be unable to fire anything at her except a rifle bullet was utterly exasperating."

Campbell, however, following astern, engaged her with all his guns; the E boat fired back wildly, turned sharply away and opened up to full speed. A minute later she was out of sight, for at 18 knots the M.G.Bs. had no chance to catch her. They followed for a little way and then Hichens decided to stop again and to listen. When the engines had been cut there was no sound of the enemy, the silence was complete. A quick survey revealed that the M.G.Bs. had been incredibly lucky. There were no serious casualties at all. The damage to Hichens' boat, though slight, was enough to reduce her fighting efficiency, but Campbell's boat was virtually unscathed.

" I was beginning to wonder what the next move was to be," writes Hichens, " when the Coxswain said:

" ' Do you think you hear something, sir, over there? ' pointing to the south-west.

" I told everyone to be quiet and listened. Very, very faintly one seemed to hear a low muttering, or was it imagination?

" ' Do you hear anything, Boffin? ' I shouted.

" ' Yes, I think so, to the south-west. Not very certain, though.'

" ' I think so too. Let's go and see.'

" The engines roared into life. We swung round to south-west and steadied."

The first dim light of dawn was beginning to show when they suddenly sighted through the mist the long low hull of an E boat lying stopped. There were minutes of suspense and suspicion before they discovered that the enemy vessel had been abandoned. Badly damaged in the action and involved in collision with one of her companions, presumably when the gunboats had burst in amongst them, the E boat had been left in a sinking condition, while the crew had been taken off by another E boat, the sound of whose engines had attracted the M.G.Bs. to the scene.

The derelict was boarded, but all efforts to keep her afloat were of no avail and soon afterwards she began to settle by the stern; not, however, before large quantities of equipment—charts, log-books, compasses, searchlights, revolvers and even pictures of Hitler, had been transferred to the M.G.Bs.

Hichens describes how, as she sank, her bows rose up until she hung vertically. Then she slipped quickly down and disappeared from view. " A cheer went up," he says, " but it was a feeble one. There is something awe inspiring and a little saddening about the sight of any ship, however small, however much hated, going down. It is so utterly irrevocable."

The M.G.Bs. returned triumphantly, flying the Nazi flag beneath the White Ensign, and received an enthusiastic welcome as they entered harbour.

THEY BELONGED TO BRUNO

Two more M.G.B. flotillas had been formed and were operating in the same part of the world. They, too, were learning by bitter experience on the rare occasions when contact could be made with the enemy. On the 29th November, which was a very dark night, the third boat of a unit led by Lt. H. O. T. Bradford, D.S.C., R.N.V.R., lost touch with the other two. Sub-Lt. Leaf—who was now in command of one of the M.G.Bs.—describes in his diary how they stopped and lay with engines cut hoping for the third boat commanded by Lt. C. Burke, R.C.N.V.R., to rejoin them.

"All of a sudden we heard engines approaching from the westward and guessed them to be Corney Burke's. Wrong! They weren't Corney's engines, they belonged to Bruno. However, we had come to the first degree of readiness and waited—only for about half a minute, during which we started up engines. Swish! There she comes—we still expected Corney—Howard Bradford challenges, she answers and keeps him guessing, then she's gone at 30 knots into the darkness. Quick! There's another. This time we knew what she was and we were after her; Howard first, then us a cable astern with wheel jammed hard a-port— fouled by a signal lamp which chose that moment to fall into its spokes. The wheel was cleared and we followed Howard. The E boat let fly with both guns and Howard was surrounded by tracers, but not a shot hit his boat. We tore after him and thought that Bruno had slipped us, but we knew it would soon get light.

"It was the E boat who next opened fire—again at Howard—but it gave us his position, and we opened up the throttles and went after him. Howard had hauled out to clear a jammed gun and there was the E boat ahead of us. All of a sudden it seemed that we were the only two boats in the whole of the North Sea. The E boat fired a long burst which snaked across our bows, through the rigging or down the side. We tore up his wake and then when within range steered off to let our guns fire, and what a relief it was to hear them blazing away. As we fired he stopped firing, but while we reloaded he fired again and hit us once or twice. Having altered course to bring the guns to bear on him, we had let him draw ahead again. So we turned back and entered his smoke. But soon we picked up his wake again, which was lucky, for he had turned hard a-port and we might have lost him. 'There 'e is, sir!' said the Cox'n, 'on the port bow.' 'Starboard a little, Cox'n.' This time the port point-fives and the Oerlikon opened up, and I think we hit him quite a lot for thirty glorious seconds. But the E boat fought back, and he shot off our Oerlikon gunner's arm with a shell which also damaged the gun.

"We began to overhaul him—the starboard point-five opened up, but the Oerlikon was out—I looked aft and saw it cocked up in the air and apparently half off its mounting. A stoker came and reported the Oerlikon out of action, and he was killed on the way back aft by a burst from the E boat. Another burst wounded the starboard point-five gunner and damaged both turrets. I decided to try as a last resort to get right ahead of the E boat and then cut across his bow to drop a depth charge, but a lucky burst of fire came across the water and holed us. The boat soon made water forward and amidships and lost speed. In my exasperation I picked up a tommy gun and fired the whole magazine at old Bruno, but he still carried on firing, and as all our guns had been put out of action I decided to break off; we had been going for twenty-five minutes, but it seemed like about seven only."

Then comes a paragraph in Leaf's story headed: "A MIRACLE?"

" We switched on lights and Howard came alongside while we surveyed the damage. We started off for home but noticed, after we had gone for about twenty minutes, that we were steering east instead of west. It may have been just because we were very excited at the time, but when we stopped it was quite light, and the first thing we saw on the horizon was a small boat. Howard took off one of my wounded men and then set off to investigate. In the boat were two Belgians, the sole survivors of seven who had left Dunkirk and been machine gunned by Messerschmitts a week before. Their motor and petrol had been shot up, and when we found them they were on their last legs—funny that we steered east instead of west!

" Old 89 brought us back to Yarmouth as fast as she could," he concludes, " and did we splice the mainbrace! We got a bottle[1] for entering harbour too fast and were told the action was a pretty poor show, but we were so tired we did not really mind. My First Lieutenant had a nasty wound in his hand which took months to heal. The motor mechanic was wounded in head and arm. I found out later that we had three shots through the engine-room and he had stopped up water leaks and put out fires and kept the engines going for twenty-five minutes during the action. (He was mentioned in despatches.) Carter, the Oerlikon gunner, had his arm amputated at the shoulder, but he appeared to be as cheerful as anyone in the ward the next morning, and he now works a lift in an office near Belfast.

" That evening I started back to Lowestoft through the Broads, but at dusk we fouled a seaplane obstruction and abandoned ship near Somerleyton. We left fire watchers on board and returned, via ' The Ship ' at Haddiscoe Bridge, in a lorry."

In spite of the fine spirit in which it was fought, this had been yet another indecisive battle, and it was nearly four months before the M.G.Bs. were able to follow up Hichens' success with another complete victory. This time it was the 7th M.G.B. Flotilla which fought the action—close to the Dutch coast in the grey light of early dawn.

THE ELECTRIC TRAIN BECAME AN ELECTRIC HARE

Amongst the anti-E boat dispositions in the North Sea on the night of 14th March, 1942, were three of the small fast M.G.Bs. of the 7th Flotilla. The Senior Officer of this flotilla was Lt. J. B. R. Horne, R.N., in M.G.B. 88, and in company with him that night were M.G.B. 87, commanded by Lt. S. B. Bennett, R.N.V.R., and M.G.B. 91, commanded by a Canadian, Sub-Lt. P. A. R. Thompson, R.C.N.V.R.

Late on that fine Saturday afternoon the three boats roared out of Lowestoft harbour and streaked across the North Sea to take up an all-night patrol 20 miles off the Dutch coast. What happened is described by the Commanding Officer of M.G.B. 87.

" At about ten o'clock our telegraphists began to receive a rush of E boat reports from the East Coast convoy. They came in so fast we could hardly keep pace with them. In the middle of all this, orders came for us to shift closer to Ijmuiden, to intercept the E boats on their doorstep.

---

[1] Naval slang for getting into trouble.

" We shifted, but nothing happened. We cruised up and down on a single engine throttled right down, in arrowhead formation. Half an hour before sunrise, when it was already daylight, we turned westward on a final sweep before streaking home again. The boredom of being closed up was beginning to tell. Slight mist made everyone imagine that they were seeing things, aerials of the other boats took on alarming shapes when seen against the horizon—battleships, smoke, mermaids—there it was again. . . . My God! it *was* something . . . a bow-wave formed by what looked like an electric train coming straight at us on our starboard bow—just a pale grey hull with enormous free-board, no mast, and a very small lump of a wheelhouse. She came on serenely enough, only ten miles from home and looking forward to a day's rest after her night's misdemeanours; but the Germans had another surprise coming to them as they saw three white ensigns fluttering in the breeze. The electric train became an electric hare as she swerved to port and our boats followed, giving tongue with their roaring exhausts. Every twist and turn was headed off as she tried to run for home, but she was finally kept on a course which was none of her own choosing. We had the legs of her and we slowly crept up, although she was doing 40 knots; and all the while we were giving her everything we'd got; bits were flying off her in all directions and a burst from one of her cannons stopped as abruptly as it had begun. Captains, First Lieutenants and Coxswains all found time to empty a few personal pans. The coxswain of 88 particularly distinguished himself by emptying his revolver at his opposite number in the wheelhouse of the E boat.

" Some of the crew jumped overboard," Lt. Bennett goes on, " and others scrambled on deck with their hands up. At last we could throttle down our engines which had been running for a good half-hour flat out. Mr. Packard might well rise from his grave and take a bow—not to mention the maintenance people ashore.

" We closed and prepared to board while 88 and 91 started picking up survivors. We all looked as menacing as we could while the boarding party of three (all that could be spared) got ready, led by the First Lieutenant (Sub-Lt. A. Phillips, R.N.V.R.), who had rather a raw deal when he was left hanging on to the E boat's guard-rails with his legs dangling in the water, as we came alongside a bit too fast. He scrambled up somehow, assisted by survivors of the German crew (a curious commentary on the contrariness of war); and unarmed, except by a ferocious expression, he herded eight prisoners on board, shouting " *vorwärts* "—all the German he could muster. The prisoners jumped on to our fo'c'sle, where they were received by the youngest stoker, who stood over them with a tommy gun, while the three who were unhurt dressed their comrades' wounds.

" No amount of gesticulations had been able to convey to the Germans that we wished them to strike their colours, so our telegraphist threw a White Ensign over, which the First Lieutenant nearly hoisted upside down, after furiously striking the other. This crisis was happily averted, and he soon reported that the E boat might float, though she had made water forward.

" Later four E boats were sighted to the eastward, spread out on the horizon and converging on us at speed. So reluctantly we took a last look at our prize with the White Ensign still flying, her bow well down and her three rudders and propellers shamelessly exposed for all the world to see. The E boats began to shell us at extreme range, and bursts were seen in the air as well as splashes all round us; but the situation was well in hand until, with a gesture of despair from Pete Thompson, her Captain, 91 began to lose speed. This was desperate and called for a quick decision. The grim thought struck us all that we were remarkably deficient in ammunition. A protective smoke-screen was the only thing and 88 and 87 supplied it."

The very unhealthy situation in which 91 now found herself can best be told by her First Lieutenant:

" I glanced ahead from the Oerlikon and immediately realised something had gone wrong in the engine-room. I stuck my head down the engine-room hatch and used some rather unsavoury language. This was greeted by the motor mechanic's beaming smile, as he said that the clutch would not engage. I jumped down and gave it a terrific pull, but realising I was beaten I got back to the gun cursing all engines and everyone who had had anything to do with them. The situation was now gradually getting unhealthy; shells were passing close, sounding like cracking whips. There were two E boats to port and two to starboard. The smoke-screen made by 88 and 87 enveloped us; I was relieved and grateful at the speed and efficiency of this operation. I recalled some instruction about ' smoke ': that it was pungent and one should wear a respirator. I took a sniff and thought it smelt fine.

" In the smoke the shells were going over, but not so close. As soon as we edged out they started hitting the boat. I noticed both turrets fully depressed and no one in them. There was just one gun still firing and only three pans left. As soon as we got out of the smoke, we fired short bursts; they were all very accurate, as the E boats on the starboard quarter tried to close; but on each burst they turned away. We had now lost the smoke and had E boats on either side, ready to make their kill; the situation was very ugly; the confidential books were all up and ready for destruction; someone was detailed to get through the heaps of cartridge cases and clips to axe the petrol tanks and set them alight. Two very accurate bursts from our Oerlikon caused an explosion on the inside E boat on the starboard quarter and she stopped. This was better, but not good enough—two E boats getting closer and only two pans left.

" Suddenly no E boats were visible. I thought it was the smoke again, but I soon realised it was thicker and better than any smoke; it was thick and glorious fog. One quick manœuvre in the fog to avoid an E boat dead across our bows, whose wash was plainly visible, and away we went to the northward. On emerging from the fog, although we had lost our consorts, we found we had shaken off our pursuers."

The other two boats had entered the fog a few moments earlier. It was patchy fog, and when they turned back to look for 91 they found the E boats still following. They led them away to the north-west and then cast back again to look for the missing boat. It was a fruitless search in the bad visibility, and shortage of petrol was beginning to catch up with shortage of ammunition, so that they had finally to shape a course for home with very mixed feelings. Had their operation been a total success or were they faced with one for one?

" We returned to harbour flying the Nazi ensign below our own and prisoners fallen-in on deck," continues Lt. Bennett, " but still no sign of 91. A great reception met our boats; as we came in the whole Base turned out. The Commander gave us three hearty, if embarrassing, cheers, while his First Lieutenant, in explosive German, took charge of the prisoners. We had just reported all our doubts and anxieties in the office when the news came through: ' 91 has come up with a signal '; and our day was made."

The First Lieutenant of 91 describes the condition of his boat as she limped homeward.

" The moment had come to take stock of our effectives. Out of the thirteen on board, including three officers, six had been wounded, and of the seven remaining, one was guarding the prisoners. Two of the gunners and the Sparker[1] were badly wounded; the latter, however, had tended the wounded until he became unconscious. The leading stoker who had manned a turret was also in a bad way. The aerial had been shot away. I bent down the engine-room hatch to see what efforts were being made to remedy the clutch trouble. All

[1] Telegraphist.

I saw was the stoker sitting on the starboard engine and supporting himself by gripping a pipe. I jumped down, seething with rage, to find that, though badly wounded in one arm, he was holding a rag over the fuel pipe which had been pierced by a shell. He remained in that position for many hours.

"One of the gunners, Smellie by name, had been wounded in the jaw, chest and legs, and was made as comfortable as possible in the wheelhouse. On the mess-deck there was an ugly mess—four of our wounded and two Germans—one of whom, with some poetic justice, had been wounded by one of the E boat's shells. The mess-deck was this gunner's cleaning quarters and he always got a special recommend for it at rounds. The Sparker called up from the mess-deck, 'Smellie, it's time you came down and cleared up your bloody mess-deck for Rounds.' We collected the bits of aerial, and the Sparker got up from the mess-deck into the wireless cabin, retuned the set and started sending out our 'Expected Time of Arrival' and details of the two prisoners and our six wounded.

"We crawled home by the usual channel, and on sighting land a terrific cheer from all on board momentarily drowned the engines. On entering harbour we went alongside the North Wall. Able Seaman Smellie, by sheer will-power, got himself on deck and, seizing an E boat fender, made himself useful. The Naval Officer-in-Charge came on board and, asking Smellie how he was, received this reply: 'All right, thank you, sir; we got out of Sunday Divisions, but we missed our tot.' "

E BOAT ALLEY

The M.G.Bs. were developing their campaign against an enemy who had virtually had his own way on our convoy routes for several months. The E boats by night and the Luftwaffe by day, and by twilight, had been taking a steady toll of our merchant ships supplying London, at a time when the U boats in the Atlantic were making one of their strongest bids to strangle the British Isles and finish the war.

E boat alley, which was, roughly speaking, that part of our convoy route lying off the coast of the counties of Norfolk and Suffolk, was an unhealthy place in the winter of 1941–42, for at that stage the attacking tactics were ahead of the defence, and our counter-weapon, the M.G.B., was still in its infancy.

Another branch of the Coastal Forces was also involved in the struggle. Each convoy was accompanied by a number of M.Ls. which acted as close escort. It was an unenviable task, as they had to be there whatever the weather, and, if an E boat action developed, they were more than likely to be mistaken for the enemy and shot up by the convoy itself. It was seldom enough that they had an opportunity of engaging the E boats themselves for more than the briefest brush, and their slow speed made it useless for them to give chase. But as rescue craft they were invaluable.

Writing of this period, Lt. Cdr. G. C. Fanner, D.S.C., R.N.V.R. (then lieutenant and without his D.S.C.) says:

"We worked in pairs, leaving Lowestoft in time to join the northbound convoy before dark; we got our orders from the Senior Officer of the Close Escort, took station, usually half-way down the seaward column or right astern, and endeavoured to stay there until daylight, when we would request permission to proceed into Immingham. After a rest of twenty-four hours, we carried out the same procedure coming south to Lowestoft again.

"Weather, during the early part of the winter of 1941," he goes on, "was shocking, and station-keeping was a nightmare. Those early M.Ls. had the wheel in the charthouse, the telegraphs there, too, and no revolution indicator. We worked on a system of buzzes on the engine-room horn, which was pretty clumsy, as you can imagine. . . .

" I remember spending one rather bad night, when it was blowing Force 5 or 6 from the east, in the lee of the biggest merchant ship in the convoy, trying to get some shelter, having a seagull's view of her decks one minute and a fish's view of her bottom the next."

Meanwhile, whenever the weather was possible, the E boats were almost certain to be active. They were, as Fanner says, " having the time of their lives. Their tactics were to lie on the far side of a lighted buoy, pick off the big ships in the lead and hare away for home."

Although the M.Ls. could do little to prevent these attacks in E boat alley, many hundreds of merchant seamen's lives were saved by them, often under most hazardous conditions. Picking up survivors from the water, or from rafts, or boats, or from the sinking, and perhaps burning, wreck of their ship, requires considerable seamanship, experience and ability in shiphandling.

Lt. Cdr. W. Whitfield, R.N.R., was Senior Officer of the 11th M.L. Flotilla, which played a leading part in this work, and Whitfield himself was involved in some of the most brilliant rescues. On one occasion he had to pick up the survivors from a ship which had been carrying bales of compressed paper. There was a heavy sea running at the time, and there was more than the usual requirement for haste, for the survivors were in more danger of being crushed between the floating bales than of drowning.

After an E boat attack one night, an M.L., approaching a sinking merchant ship, found her bows under water and a man dangling by a rope over the stern. Immediately beneath him, and now well out of the water, the ship's propellers were still turning at a good speed. It seemed at first a hopeless position, as the man would have been cut to pieces had he let go of the rope, but he had not the strength to climb back on board. The M.L. transferred some men to the sinking wreck and they were able to haul the man back on board, although by this time the stern was beginning to rise in a most dangerous way, which seemed to herald the final plunge. The survivor was so exhausted and so shaken by his experience that he could not stand, which complicated the problem of getting him across to the M.L. No sooner had it been accomplished, and when the M.L. had drawn no more than 50 yards clear, the stern of the ship lurched upwards and she sank.

On three successive trips—25th and 29th November, and 2nd December, 1941—M.L. 150, under the command of Fanner, picked up the crews of four ships. " The first two," he writes, " went up just after midnight near Hearty Knoll. One was a large tanker with a crew of over 50, of which only 17 got away alive. The second was carrying timber; there was no loss of life and she was eventually towed into Yarmouth.

" I learnt several things that night," he continues, " some unpleasant, like the awful timbre in human voices when they are in agony and danger, the terrific draught caused by a big fire, how slippery fuel oil, mixed with water, makes everything, including human bodies, how tired and exhausted one soon becomes doing that kind of work; and some pleasant, like the astonishing guts of the ordinary ' matelot.' I learnt, too, the extraordinary distance a cigarette end shows in the dark. The crew of the second ship had taken to the lifeboats and were found entirely by this means."

But from the routine work of defending convoys, two flotillas of M.Ls. were withdrawn early in 1942 for a special and dangerous task, more offensive and ambitious than anything that the Coastal Forces had ever undertaken before.

CHAPTER V

THE RAID ON ST. NAZAIRE

OF the ships that steamed up the Loire in the early hours of Thursday, 28th March, 1942, to carry out the St. Nazaire Raid, one was an old destroyer—H.M.S. *Campbeltown*—and all the rest were Coastal Force craft—15 Motor Launches, 1 Motor Gunboat and 1 Motor Torpedo boat. Such a prominent part in a combined operation had never before been played by the Coastal Forces.

"Looking back over a period of two years," writes Commander R. E. D. Ryder, R.N., who was awarded the Victoria Cross for his part as Naval Force Commander, "I regard the St. Nazaire raid from the Naval standpoint as primarily a Coastal Force achievement. More than this, it was at the time by far the largest single undertaking carried out by Coastal Force craft, and I believe that it still holds that position."[1]

The object of the raid was to destroy the entrance lock to the only dock on the Atlantic coast of France large enough for docking the battleship *Tirpitz*, an object which had a direct bearing upon the balance of sea-power. Secondary objects were to render tidal the basins containing the U boat pens and to damage as much as possible the harbour amenities of St. Nazaire, which was a vital German base in the Battle of the Atlantic.

The plan was for the ex-American destroyer *Campbeltown*, equipped as a blockship, to ram the lock-gate, for troops from No. 2 Commando to scramble ashore over her bow, and then, having started a delayed-action fuse, to scuttle her so that she would blow up with several tons of high explosive some hours later and demolish the gate.

Besides this, Commandos were to be landed from the M.Ls. at a small pier called the Old Mole and near a small lock-gate called the Old Entrance. All these troops had an extensive programme of demolitions to carry out on the other dock entrances and the pumping machinery. The Military Force, in this bold operation, was commanded by Lt. Col. A. C. Newman. (On return from captivity in 1945 he was also awarded the V.C.)

This, then, was a frontal attack by a small force carried in unarmoured ships against a heavily defended port, and its success depended more than ever upon the element of surprise. In many ways it resembled the Zeebrugge Raid of the last war, but this time the force was smaller. This time, too, it was much more liable to detection both by aircraft and radar, it had to go far up an estuary, and finally it had the disadvantage of the tremendous development in this war of close-range, rapid-firing weapons, a formidable threat to the wooden-hulled petrol-driven Coastal Force craft.

In the final plan the Force Commanders agreed that the destruction of the lock-gate by the *Campbeltown* should be the prime consideration. The light craft were to lead her in and give her all the supporting fire they could. An alternative scheme in which the M.Ls. would shelter behind the *Campbeltown's* steel hull was finally rejected. "In our minds and in our plans," wrote Cdr. Ryder, "we envisaged sacrificing, if necessary, everything in order to get the *Campbeltown* in. We all hoped to get well in undetected and then to bluff the enemy for just sufficient time to achieve our object. We had to realise, however, that, though we

---

[1] The passage was written two years after the raid, but before the invasion of the Continent, when, however, the Coastal Forces part was *relatively* less important.

might get in unseen and by bluff, there was no question of employing these means on the way out.   For this purpose we hoped that smoke would help."

The expedition sailed from Falmouth at two o'clock in the afternoon of Tuesday the 26th and formed up in its special cruising order.   " Guide of the Fleet " was H.M.S. *Atherstone*, one of the two "Hunt" Class destroyers provided as escort for the outward passage.   The Force Commanders were embarked in her, and she was towing M.G.B. 314, to which they had arranged to transfer for the final approach and assault.   Astern of *Atherstone* was *Campbeltown*, towing M.T.B. 74, which had been specially equipped for torpedoing, with delayed-action torpedoes, the smaller lock-gates in the Old Entrance, or if necessary the *Campbeltown* herself should the scuttling arrangements fail.   Astern of *Campbeltown* came *Tynedale*, the second destroyer of the escort, and, in two columns, one on either side of the destroyers, were the M.Ls.   Four of these were fitted with torpedoes for dealing with any shipping encountered either on passage or in the outer harbour of St. Nazaire.   The rest carried the Commando troops.   They had all been specially equipped with extra fuel tanks on deck to increase their range.

Because of the weather forecast the whole operation was staged a day earlier than was originally planned, and now that they were off there was a great contrast to the last feverish preparations which followed the weeks of training and organisation.   All that could be done had been done, and the crews, like passengers who have just caught a train, could only sit back and wonder what they had left behind.

The first afternoon was uneventful.   It was fine spring-like weather.   The swell coming in from the south-east caused sea-sickness amongst some of the soldiers embarked in the light craft, and it also made accurate steering difficult.   According to the captain of one M.L., the station-keeping " was pretty bloody."   To a less critical eye, however, the scene was impressive, as the escorting fighters circled the three columns of ships; and in the hearts of many who gazed back at the disappearing coastline of England there must have been deep thoughts as the night came down.

On the following morning the force was well out into the Atlantic.   Visibility was extreme when *Tynedale* sighted an object on the horizon which turned out to be the conning-tower of a U boat.

There was a grave danger that this U boat would report the force by wireless, but, as the *Tynedale* approached bows on, the enemy apparently supposed that she was friendly, for she fired a recognition rocket and proceeded on her way on the surface.   At 4,000 yards the *Tynedale* decided that she could approach no closer without being identified and that the U boat must not be given a chance to make a wireless report.   So she opened fire and the submarine at once crash-dived.   She may have been hit, for her periscope was sighted soon after, and as the *Tynedale* approached to attack with depth charges, she began to surface directly ahead.   Lt. Cdr. D. Tweedie, R.N., had to make an instantaneous decision whether or not to ram; if he did, the U boat would be destroyed but the *Tynedale* would be damaged and the expedition would be left with only the *Atherstone* as escort.   He therefore decided against ramming, but as the ship drew alongside the U boat a pattern of depth charges was released.   These exploded so close that the submarine's bow and conning tower emerged and she was at once engaged with 4-inch and automatic weapons.   The stern failed to rise and she gradually heeled over 40 degrees to port and disappeared stern first.

It is possible that the U boat was destroyed, but the result was not conclusive.   Meanwhile *Atherstone* had been to investigate two trawlers farther to the eastward.   Ryder was finally satisfied, however, that they were unarmed fishing trawlers, and since they were over the horizon from the main force and could not therefore have seen it, he did not think it

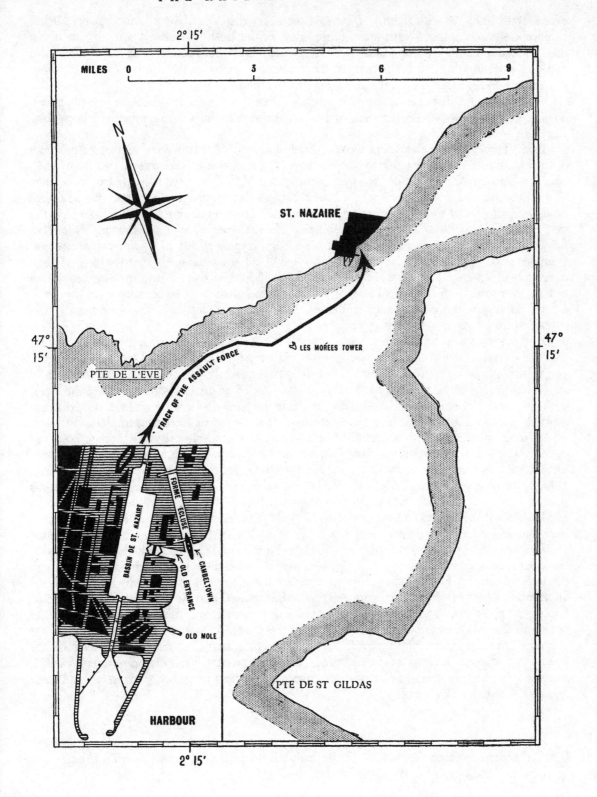

MILES 0   3   6   9

2° 15'

N

ST. NAZAIRE

47° 15'

LES MORÉES TOWER

PTE DE L'EVE

TRACK OF THE ASSAULT FORCE

47° 15'

BASSIN DE ST. NAZAIRE

FORME ECLUSE

CAMBELTOWN

OLD ENTRANCE

OLD MOLE

HARBOUR

PTE DE ST GILDAS

2° 15'

necessary to interfere with them. *Atherstone* then joined in the U boat hunt, but no further contact was made and, still with many misgivings, Ryder finally decided it was time to rejoin the *Campbeltown* and the Coastal Force craft. In case the U boat commander had eluded them and was watching through his periscope, the destroyers set off to the south-westward at first, in order to pretend that they were on passage to Gibraltar.

After these incidents reconnaissance aircraft, always a possibility, became a probability. The expedition now waited for their arrival to show that the vital surprise had been lost. But none appeared.

Later, however, more trawlers were sighted, and two of them, lying almost in the path of the expedition, had to be sunk by the destroyers' gun-fire after their crews had been taken off. Lt. Dunstan Curtis, R.N.V.R., who commanded M.G.B. 314, was detailed to go alongside the second one, board it and take off the crew and all the papers and charts. He describes how, when they saw the White Ensign, " the French crew on deck threw their hats into the air and shouted for joy. I said to the captain, ' Je regrette, monsieur la Patron, mais il va falloir vous embarquer et couler votre bateau.' He replied, ' Eh bien, si c'est necessaire. Pouvons nous apporter nos biens.' I said, ' Yes,' and they came on board with a strange collection of ' biens.' There were old blankets, half-cooked fish, a large fishing-net which got in everybody's way and a basin of potatoes which had been simmering over the fire." Curtis' apologies, more than once expressed, for having to sink his ship were met by the captain with the reply, " C'est la guerre."

In the evening a signal was received from the Commander-in-Chief, Plymouth, saying that five German torpedo boats had been sighted in the St. Nazaire area. This class is roughly equivalent in fire-power to our "Hunt" Class destroyers, so the five constituted a substantially superior force. But as the U boat had apparently failed to make any report and dusk fell with the force still undetected, Ryder decided that the torpedo boats must be accepted as no more than an additional hazard, and the expedition went forward according to plan.

At dusk the only serious mechanical breakdown of the whole outward passage occurred in M.L. 341 (Lt. D. L. Briault, R.N.V.R.), whose port engine failed. The Flotilla Engineer Officer was transferred from another boat, but for a time the trouble could not be located and Briault was in a dilemma. The *Campbeltown* had increased speed, and on one engine he was unable to keep up. Would the repair be completed before the force disappeared ahead? At last he decided that it was too big a risk to hold the Commandos on board his boat and that they should be transferred to one of the other M.Ls. When this had been done, the main force was out of sight. In the gathering darkness he followed the M.L. which had taken over his troops, as she made off to catch up, keeping her in sight with his binoculars until she disappeared ahead. For an hour more he crawled along, unsure of his position and with no apparent prospect of his engine being repaired. He realised that he had very little chance of finding the river mouth on his own, and he realised, too, that, even if he did find it, he would not be able, at his present speed, to reach it until the operation was all over.

When the Engineer Officer reported that he was no nearer to tracing the cause of the breakdown, Briault had to make his decision. With what bitter disappointment can be imagined, he turned his ship about and set course along the emergency track which had been arranged for such an eventuality.

THE APPROACH

It was at 8 p.m. that the Force Commanders transferred to the motor gunboat, and the force turned in towards the mouth of the Loire at 12 knots. " I was much stirred," says Curtis, " as I took my M.G.B. to the head of the line."

The cruising order was now altered for the final approach and the assault. Ahead of the *Campbeltown* were three of the Coastal Force craft—M.G.B. 314 leading and a torpedo-carrying M.L. on either bow—and following the old destroyer were two columns of M.Ls. and M.T.B. 74. The masterly navigation of Lt. A. R. Green, R.N., had brought the force directly into the mouth of the estuary in spite of the slight mist which had set in under the low clouds. The *Atherstone* and the *Tynedale* had parted company to carry out their patrol off the estuary until daylight.

Lt. T. W. Boyd, R.N.V.R., commanding M.L. 160 on the starboard bow of the *Campbeltown*, describes the kind of last-minute preparations being made by the crews on board all the craft, as they watched the R.A.F.'s diversionary air-raid ahead of them. " I had the deck petrol tanks emptied of the last dregs and filled with water, the hand tiller rigged and the medical gear all laid out in the wheelhouse. This kept all hands busy, which I thought to be a good thing.

" I shall never forget the sweet smell of the countryside as we steamed up the river. One could see both banks and make out hedges and trees on the port hand.

" Curtis went on ahead a little to find the buoys, which were conveniently lit for us.

" Before running in I was feeling frightened, but now that the show was about to start I felt absolutely calm, and I had great confidence. My crew were wonderful, bandying little jokes about as we ran in. ' This is a queer do,' I said to my coxswain. ' It will soon be a bloody sight queerer, sir,' was his answer."

When the force was opposite Les Morées Tower, still three miles from the town, a single suspicious searchlight swept the estuary. It swept twice through an arc that was just astern of our ships and then it went out. Almost at once, however, a challenge was flashed from the German shore signal station, and M.G.B. 314 replied with a bogus identification, followed by a signal in German that she was " proceeding up harbour in accordance with previous orders."

Another searchlight was turned on from the pierhead and shone on the M.G.B., but still the enemy was bewildered and again it went out, while our ships ran on at 15 knots. Still no shot had been fired and every extra minute was of vital importance.

There was little more than two miles still to go when the lights came on again; an automatic gun fired a spasmodic burst and the shells splashed in the water near the M.G.B. In answer, a recognition cartridge was fired in the hope of confusing the issue a little longer. The firing ceased. But by now the resources of bluff were running out. A few moments later ten or a dozen searchlights fell full upon the *Campbeltown*, and the fight began.

In the violent battle that occupied the next two hours there were many deeds of towering valour. Some were witnessed and recorded and others were not. Of the 18 ships which entered the river, 7 came out; of the 62 officers and 291 ratings who went, 28 officers and 140 ratings returned. At present the story can only be pieced together from the narratives of those who came back, but many who were left behind were taken prisoner, and in due time we shall know of all the bravery and all the horror that was seen by men who lived to tell of it. Still much will be untold, of the way men faced death and fought until they were killed, all of them, so that none survived to record their sacrifice.

THE STORM BREAKS

" It is difficult," writes Cdr. Ryder, " to describe the full fury of the attack that was now let loose on both sides; the air became one mass of red and green tracer travelling in all directions." Through it the *Campbeltown*, increasing to 18 knots, held her course straight for the lock-gate.

Success now largely depended on whether the German in his well-protected gun emplace-
ments on the buildings and jetties was a match for the British seaman standing more or less
unprotected behind the light quick-firing guns of our ships. "By all calculations the enemy
should have kept us out," says Ryder, "but there are many factors in war that cannot be
calculated.

"The gunlayers had been briefed to hold their fire for as long as they could, to spot
carefully where the enemy's tracer was coming from and to fire with good aim. When the
moment came the fire discipline was excellent. To begin with, the enemy had ceased fire
because there was no reply. Finally at the right moment our gunlayers fairly let them have it.
Soon it was evident that they were shooting to good effect, as there was a perceptible slackening in the enemy's fire.

"Although this was only temporary, it enabled us to get there, and it was a great feat of
arms for our guns' crews and those others who kept them in action when the proper crews
were wounded."

Abreast of the arms of the outer harbour the German guardship was anchored. The
force had to pass close by her and she was very roughly handled. "My pom-pom gunner,"
writes Curtis, "put about twenty rounds into her and knocked her forward gun overboard,
together with most of its crew. We left her to starboard, and as we passed her we pumped
a lot more into her bridge."

Out of the glare of the searchlights which had "turned night into day like a stage effect,"
Lt. Boyd's boat also came suddenly upon the anchored flak-ship. "I had to alter course
violently to avoid hitting it and gave it a very good burst as we went by. I looked astern and
saw the M.Ls. replying gamely to the fire from the shore, and felt very sad at heart as I saw
boat after boat hit and crash into flames or blow up.

"The *Campbeltown* looked glorious as she tore through the smoke and bursting shells
and dashed straight into the lock-gates with a crash which could just be heard above the
terrific gunfire."

In spite of the blinding glare of the searchlights, in spite of the hail of fire which was
concentrated on the bridge of his ship, Lt. Cdr. S. H. Beattie, R.N., kept her fairly and squarely
on her course at more than 15 knots until she struck her target at 1.34 a.m. After a journey
of 400 miles she was just four minutes late on the scheduled time.

"When she hit," says Ryder, "we saw a burst of flame on her fo'c'sle which seemed to
die away after a minute or two, and we could only see her Oerlikons firing hard."

With the *Campbeltown* firmly jammed in the lock-gate and sinking, Beattie had assured
the achievement of the main object of the raid and had most fully earned the Victoria Cross
which was awarded to him. When the time fuse exploded the gate would be destroyed, and
the Commandos were already clambering ashore down the ladders from the fo'c'sle head to
deal with the pumping-station and the lock machinery.

Meanwhile the M.Ls. were trying to get alongside the Old Mole some quarter of a mile
farther down the harbour, and they were meeting with ferocious resistance. The "perceptible slackening" in the enemy's fire, which was the result of their good shooting in the
earlier stages, did not last long. After the initial confusion, during which the Germans fired
on their own guardship as well as on our force, their gunnery again became accurate, and it
was particularly fierce in the neighbourhood of the Old Mole, which was the destination of
the port column of M.Ls. Already many of them had been set on fire and some had
blown up.

While they continued to try to land their troops there, the survivors in the starboard
column struggled on towards the Old Entrance near the *Campbeltown*. Here there was some

slight shelter from the enemy's fire, and M.L. 177, commanded by Sub-Lt. M. F. Rodier, managed to get alongside and land her troops. While she was doing so Curtis brought his M.G.B. alongside her so as to land Col. Newman and the headquarters party. "They went over the port side," he says, "full of beans."

Having put them ashore, the M.G.B. lay off for a while and then went alongside close to the lock, so that Ryder could go ashore and make certain that the *Campbeltown* had been properly scuttled. "After we had landed Cdr. Ryder, we lay touching the lock for three or four minutes until about twenty-five figures appeared from the nearby houses. I thought at first that they were Huns, and was about to give the order to open fire when one of them shouted that they belonged to the *Campbeltown*. They were all wounded, though mostly with superficial wounds, and many were suffering from the shock of the impact with the lock-gate."

Ryder returned on board the M.G.B. later. While ashore he had been shot at from one of the ships in the dockyard and had narrowly missed being blown up by the Commando's demolitions, but he had ascertained that the scuttling charges were exploding and that the *Campbeltown* was settling satisfactorily by the stern. M.T.B. 74 had been kept in reserve, as he had visualised the possibility of having to use her torpedoes on the *Campbeltown* had the scuttling charges failed. Now, however, when she appeared in the Old Entrance and her captain, Lt. R. C. M. V. Wynn, R.N.V.R., shouted, "What do you want me to do?" Ryder was able to shout back, "Go up the lock and torpedo the gates of the submarine basin." A few minutes later the delayed-action torpedoes were fired. Wynn returned alongside and went on board the M.G.B. to report, and Curtis tells how they had a quick drink together on the bridge: "Ryder said 'Well done,' and then told Wynn to push off. He went and I started to back away. The next thing I remember was seeing Wynn's ship go to a burning M.L. about 200 yards away. He tried to go alongside it, but his own ship caught fire."

It appears, however, that, in fact, M.T.B. 74 was not destroyed at this point. More light has been thrown on her fate by Lt. Cdr. W. L. Stephens, D.S.C., R.N.V.R., who was taken prisoner in the raid but escaped and finally returned to this country two years later.

"Mickey Wynn picked up some of the *Campbeltown's* crew," he writes, "and then set off for home. All went well for him because the Hun gunlayers did not realise that his boat was doing about two and a half times the speed of the M.Ls., and consequently all their fire fell astern of him. About half-way down the river he saw a Carley Float with some men on it, probably off one of the M.Ls. abandoned near the Old Mole, because with the strong current in the river they would have been carried down to just about where Mickey found them. He stopped his boat and started to pick them up, and the shore batteries got him right away. The boat went up in flames and they abandoned her. After being in the water some considerable time, during which many of them perished from exposure, the survivors were picked up by a trawler—Wynn amongst them.

"Mickey's action in stopping to pick up survivors, at a moment when he must have realised that he was at least well on the way to safety, was just what one would have expected from him, and it was indeed a tragedy that it should have cost so many lives and the loss of his boat. Incidentally, it also cost him the loss of an eye."

Meanwhile Curtis had been manœuvring his M.G.B. in the Old Entrance. "The scene," he writes, "was punctuated by the noise of the explosions on shore made by the soldiers. This noise was quite appalling. Among other things, they blew up the power-house, and a terrific shower of bricks landed on my bridge and decks."

Ryder had decided to go and see how the assault on the Old Mole was progressing. "On leaving the Old Entrance," he says, "we could see that matters had fared badly there.

The approaches were floodlit by searchlights from all directions and a deadly fire was being poured on the M.Ls. still gallantly attempting to go alongside."

Curtis observed that one of the gun-posts on the Mole itself " was keeping up a very heavy fire and there was a searchlight beam shining down, dead along the Mole. Two or three more guns—Bofors, I think—were firing straight down the beam and the Mole was getting pretty well blistered.

" I took station about 200 yards away and opened pom-pom fire on the German gun position. It stopped firing for some moments and I tried to shoot out the searchlight, but without success. Then we saw five or six Germans rush along the Mole to reman the gun which we had silenced. It opened fire once more, but we knocked it out again. We could not, however, silence the guns which were firing down the searchlight beam."

The gunlayer who sat so coolly on his exposed gun-mounting on the M.G.B.'s. fo'c'sle to carry out this bombardment was Able Seaman W. A. Savage, who, for his amazing disregard of danger and his unruffled precision of aim in the midst of this inferno of noise and flying tracers and bursting shells, won the Victoria Cross.

NEARING THE OLD MOLE

As we have seen, the M.Ls. had been " faring badly " at the Old Mole. The leader of the port column was Lt. T. D. L. Platt, R.N.R., in M.L. 447. His guns hit one searchlight on the Mole, but he was subjected to intense cross fire which killed the guns' crews and put the guns out of action.

An M.L. from the starboard column burst into flames and shot across his bows, apparently running aground on the seaward side of the Mole. This was probably Lt. Cdr. Stephens, in M.L. 192, who had been the leader of the starboard column and whose adventures we shall come to presently.

Platt took M.L. 447 in on the landward side of the Mole in accordance with the plan, but unfortunately she ran aground about 10 feet off the slipway.

" The officer in command of the Commandos on board came to me and reported that, as nearly all his men were killed and wounded, he did not think he would be able to make a very effective landing, but he would try.

" The M.L. was too far from the jetty to land anybody, so I decided to get off and go alongside the end of the Mole. During this time we were under fire from A.A. guns emplaced on the bank near the dry dock and on some buildings.

" Using ' full astern ' we managed to get off and, just as ' full ahead ' was rung, the engine-room received a direct hit with a shell of very heavy calibre. This put the ship out of action, and within a few moments the engine-room was an inferno."

The calmness which prevailed on board in this extremity is well illustrated by the comment of the Coxswain (Leading Seaman F. Overton): " It's no good getting excited about it," he said, " excitement won't help us."

" In view of the fact that it was impossible to control this fire," Platt continues, " and that both the guns and their crews were out of action, I decided to abandon ship, as, once the fire reached the tanks, she would blow up.

" I ordered the soldiers who were unhit to swim ashore and put two slightly wounded soldiers on a Carley Raft and told them to wait alongside. M.L. 160 (Lt. Boyd) came within hailing distance and was requested to come alongside. Under heavy fire from A.A. guns on the Mole and the South Bank, M.L. 160 took off the survivors and wounded of my crew and soldiers, also picking up some sailors from the water and the two wounded soldiers from the

Carley Raft. A careful inspection was made of the crew and soldiers lying on the deck to make sure that none was living."

When Platt ordered his crew to abandon ship Able Seaman Lambert, who had been wounded, remained behind to help to transfer the other casualties. In the words of Platt's recommendation, " This rating showed the greatest self-sacrifice and fortitude," and Commander Ryder adds, " When the order to abandon ship was given, the M.L. was hopelessly on fire and, with gallons of high-octane fuel in tanks on deck, it was liable to explode at any moment. I consider, therefore, that Lambert displayed valour of the highest order."

He was awarded the Conspicuous Gallantry Medal.

Platt himself won the Distinguished Service Order for his bravery in leading his column in to the Mole and striving against such fearful odds to get his boat alongside.

M.L. 160 had not drawn far away on one engine, with all the survivors on board, when the remains of M.L. 447 blew up.

A MURDEROUS CROSS FIRE

Little is known of the fate of M.L. 457, commanded by Lt. T. A. M. Collier, R.N.V.R., who was following Platt in towards the Mole. It is believed that she got into position, but that all the crew were killed in that murderous cross fire or by grenades lobbed on to her decks. She, too, ran aground and was finally burnt out. M.L. 307, commanded by an Australian—Lt. N. B. Wallis, R.A.N.V.R.—was following Collier's boat. She was doing 18 knots over the last half-mile and turned in at that speed, firing hard at the gun positions on the Mole.

" As we came in," says Lt. Wallis, " an M.L. on fire amidships came out stern first. This, I assume, was Lt. Platt's boat. Going full astern on both engines, I put the ship alongside."

She went alongside the landward or upstream side of the Mole, bows in, port side to, and she was protected by the 26 feet of the Mole from the gun positions on the top of it.

Just before she was berthed Wallis saw a German waiting on the Mole with bombs in his hands. Captain W. Bradley, an army officer, took a Bren gun " and gave him the works, firing from the shoulder." Three or four more grenade throwers were similarly dealt with.

" Ahead of me," continues Wallis, " standing off about 30 feet from the Mole, was another M.L. also afire and not moving.[1] On the other side of the Mole was an M.L burnt to the water-line.[2]

" As it was obvious that we were the first M.L. alongside instead of the fourth, according to plan, and as also we had on board only a medical party and doctor and a demolition party, it appeared a hopeless business to attempt to land."

The storming parties in the leading boats had not landed to clear the opposition, but in spite of this some of the demolition party got ashore and finally into the dockyard.

M.L. 307 was now under fire from a gun position on the top of a building, and Wallis decided that if he remained alongside his boat would suffer the fate of its predecessors and be destroyed. He picked up a soldier from the water, who was a survivor from Lt. Platt's boat, and then he drew clear.

Since his guns were still firing despite the casualties, he went across the estuary and engaged the batteries and searchlights which were causing trouble from that side. He also tackled a flak-ship in mid-channel and set its bridge on fire, before joining up with Lt. Boyd in M.L. 160.

[1] Perhaps Lt. Collier's.
[2] Probably Lt. Cdr. Stephens'.

Astern of Wallis in the port column was Lt. K. Horlock, R.N.V.R., in M.L. 443. As the force came in, he overshot his destination. He realised this when he had drawn abreast of some cranes, and he went about at once, turning to port. " The night was now as light as day," he says, " and I saw the Mole in silhouette about a mile away. I was angry with myself for missing it. Lt. Verity, the Naval Beach Master, was on the bridge with me, and when we saw it we both laughed; it seemed extraordinary that we had got through all that heavy fire and then missed the place. At that moment I had a feeling of absolute certainty that I was going to come out of this all right."

As he returned towards the Mole, his boat maintained a heavy fire on the gun positions and knocked out one on a house-top. " Blocking my way to the Mole," he continues, " was a burning M.L., probably Lt. Platt's. I opened fire on the two gun positions on the Mole. The Hun was going very strong. I saw no signs of life on the burning M.L. which had prevented me from getting alongside, and there were no M.Ls. alongside the Mole where they ought to have been. My gunfire seemed to be making no impression, and I thought that the German gun positions were probably protected by pillboxes. Lt. Shields was in charge of my forward gun and, try as we would, we could not quench the enemy's fire. It was then that I realised that this part of the operation was a flop."

The landing on the Old Mole had failed. The decks of the M.Ls. had been devastated by the enemy's automatic guns, of which there were far more than had been expected, and uncontrollable fires had been started on board too many of them. The balance was further tipped against them by a well-armed German ship whose position alongside in the submarine basin enabled her to fire on the approaches to the Old Mole, adding to the tornado of bullets which swept that area.

M.L. 446, under the command of Lt. H. G. R. Falconar, R.N.V.R., also overshot the Old Mole in the glare of the searchlights and went up past the *Campbeltown*.

Falconar returned as soon as he discovered his mistake, but as he closed in towards the Mole he found that most of the Commandos on board were wounded, including both the officers and the sergeant, and so were many of his own crew. Obviously under these conditions it was useless to try to land, and so finally he decided to withdraw. His after Oerlikon gunner was Ordinary Seaman A. W. Tew, who showed, according to Falconar's report, an inspiring example by continuing to lay his gun although seriously wounded and who only left his position when a direct hit had damaged the gun beyond repair. Tew was awarded the Conspicuous Gallantry Medal.

M.L. 306 (Lt. I. B. Henderson, R.N.V.R.) was last but two in the line. It appeared that she, too, overshot the Old Mole, and after suffering heavy casualties was forced to withdraw. The disaster which finally overtook her is described later in the story.

M.L. 298 (Sub-Lt. A. Spraggon, R.N.V.R.) was the last boat in the port column. Nothing is known of its fate, though it was almost certainly disabled and set on fire before reaching the objective.

THE STARBOARD COLUMN

While the port column had suffered heavily, the boats in the starboard column, whose destination was the Old Entrance, were even less lucky. Lt. Cdr. W. L. Stephens, D.S.C., R.N.V.R., in M.L. 192, was their leader.

" All went well," he writes, " until we were almost abeam of the Old Mole, and within 200 yards of our objective. We had been hit a number of times but were still quite seaworthy, and while we had some wounded, they were none of them serious. Then our luck turned and they got us twice at point-blank range with something very large, probably about 4-inch;

SEVENTY-FOOT M.T.B.

SEVENTY-ONE-FOOT-SIX M.G.B.

" B " CLASS M.L.

" D " CLASS M.T.B.

HARBOUR DEFENCE M.L.

" FIRE BOTH "

GERMAN "T" CLASS TORPEDO BOAT

GERMAN E BOAT "S.19"

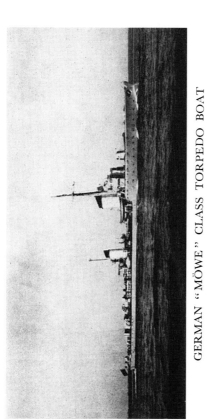

GERMAN "MÖWE" CLASS TORPEDO BOAT

GERMAN E BOATS—PRE-WAR TYPE

GUNNER IN A TWIN POINT-FIVE TURRET

LOADING POINT-FIVE AMMUNITION INTO THE TRAY

ADJUSTING THE SIGHT ON A POINT-FIVE TURRET—WITH ASSISTANCE FROM
THE BASE STAFF

LT. CDR. (NOW CDR.) E. N. PUMPHREY, D.S.O. AND
TWO BARS, D.S.C., R.N.

LT. P. F. S. GOULD, D.S.C. AND BAR, R.N.

SCHARNHORST AND *GNEISENAU* PHOTOGRAPHED FROM *PRINZ EUGEN*
DURING THE CHANNEL DASH

LT. M. ARNOLD FORSTER, D.S.O., D.S.C., R.N.V.R.

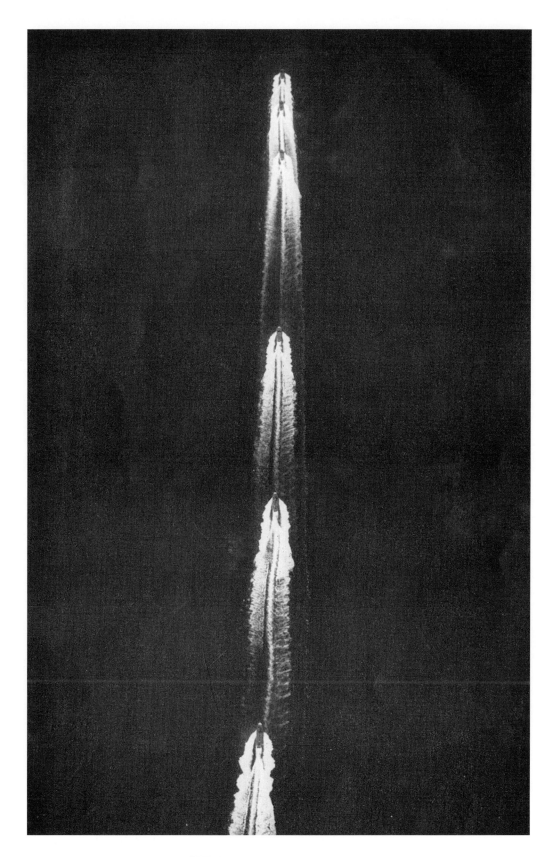

SIX M.T.Bs. FROM THE AIR

DUNKIRK—THE BEACHES

DUNKIRK—THE HARBOUR MOUTH

SEVENTY-FOOT MOTOR GUNBOATS

S.111 IN TOW OF M.G.B. 88, 15TH MARCH, 1942 (see page 38)

LT. CDR. R. P. HICHENS, D.S.O. AND BAR, D.S.C. AND
TWO BARS, R.N.V.R.

M.Ls.

M.T.B. 74 FITTED WITH SPECIAL TORPEDO TUBES FOR THE ST. NAZAIRE RAID

"B" CLASS M.L.

the results were sudden and disastrous; both engines and the steering went and the boat was swung hard a-port by the impact of the shells hitting her. By chance, however, we managed to come more or less alongside the Old Mole, allowing a few of the Commandos to climb up the wall and get ashore. My signalman also managed to get ashore, the idea being that we should put a line across to him and make fast. Unfortunately he was killed before he could do this, and the boat, having hit the wall of the Mole very hard, immediately rebounded some 15 feet and there we were with neither engines nor steering, and all the while being subjected to point-blank fire from a 20-mm. gun ashore. The damage was simply frightful, there was virtually no engine-room left, and some incendiaries must have hit our tanks, because we were blazing fiercely in the petrol compartment.

" I then decided that, as there was not the faintest possibility of saving the boat, the best course was to abandon ship and get ashore in order to join up with our own forces, who should by this time have landed a little farther up the river. We got everyone into the water all right, including our wounded, but owing to the number of soldiers that we still had on board there wasn't room for everybody on the Carley Floats and consequently a few had to swim ashore. I shall never forget my last moments on board. There was no firing at us by this time, it being only too obvious to the enemy that we had already ' had it '; they were concentrating on other targets. I stood right up in the bows and whilst getting out my flask to have a last ' quick one,' looked around me. The scene was indescribable. We were burning furiously, as were two other boats astern of us a little farther out in the river; that was a very sad sight. Tracer was still flying in all directions and the whole scene was brilliantly illuminated by searchlights. After a very long pull at my flask (little did I realise when I should next taste whisky), I slid over the bows on a line and into the water and, my God, it was cold! I started to swim, at first quite slowly and casually, because it was only 60 or 70 yards from the shore, then harder as I suddenly realised the current was carrying me fast downstream and away from the only possible landing-place. I kicked off my flying boots—something I was to regret bitterly later—and swam as I've never swum before. I had to fight to stop myself panicking. Slowly I began to make headway. Time seemed interminable, but I suppose I had only been in the water seven or eight minutes when I reached a small slipway and having arrived at it I just lay there half in and half out of the water and quite exhausted. At that moment I didn't really care much what happened to me; however, someone, I think it was my First Lieutenant, pulled me clear, and after a minute or two I was more or less normal. We found that only one of our party had not made the shore. Really remarkable considering how strong the current was just there.

" The next thing to do was to get along the docks and so join up with our own forces. If we had known a bit more about evasion in those days, we might have managed it, but as we tried it—almost marching in threes, and with not even a revolver amongst us—it was quite hopeless, and sure enough we were spotted by a platoon after we had gone about 20 yards. We all ran and tried to hide behind some huge rolls of wire-netting which were on the quay. After that it was just a question of minutes until we were rounded up and made to understand that we must hold our hands up; and so at 2.30 a.m. on the 28th March, 1942, I became a prisoner to the Huns."

How Stephens escaped twice and was recaptured, and then escaped a third time from a punishment camp to which he had been removed, how he reached Switzerland, and how, after more than a year there, he escaped again across France into Spain, and so to England, after the invasion of Normandy had begun, is no part of this story. We must return to the starboard column of M.Ls. which had been following the *Campbeltown* up the harbour of St. Nazaire.

Of the next three boats in the line nothing is known, though one at least of them may have reached the comparative shelter of the Old Entrance, which was their objective. These three boats were M.Ls. 262 (Lt. E. A. Burt, R.N.V.R.), 267 (Lt. E. H. Beart, R.N.V.R.), and 268 (Lt. A. B. K. Tillie, R.N.V.R.).[1] At what stage they were destroyed may never be known, or perhaps when the post-war reports are complete there will be news of them.[2]

M.L. 156 commanded by Lt. Leslie Fenton, R.N.V.R., was next astern of Tillie's boat. Early in the action a shell " transferred," as Fenton puts it, " part of the bridge and some shrapnel into my left leg and the leg of Captain Hooper, the Commando officer who was on the bridge with me."

So many of the M.Ls. ahead had been hit and disabled that there was some confusion towards the tail of the line. Two M.Ls. on the port hand burst into flames; two more crossed Fenton's bow from port to starboard and he had to turn hard a-starboard to avoid them. He made a complete circle, ending on a course towards the Old Entrance, and M.L. 177, which had been astern of him, came up on his port quarter. He could easily recognise Sub-Lt. Rodier, her Commanding Officer, standing on the bridge.

As he closed in he saw a signal being flashed from the *Campbeltown's* stern. Four M.Ls. were ablaze between the Old Mole and the lock-gate, two more on his starboard quarter and two on his port beam.

" I called the First Lieutenant and told him what the course was. Then I passed out."

The First Lieutenant was Sub-Lt. N. G. Machin, R.N.V.R., and soon after he reached the bridge the ship came under tremendous cross fire.

" Having given orders to make smoke, our steering went, and I reduced speed in order to try to torpedo a flak-ship which was doing us most damage. Instantly our engines went out of action.

" I gave orders for the hand steering to be manned and started to go aft to supervise, but as soon as I got aft of the funnel I was hit. I then made my way to the engine-room to see if we had any chance of starting the engines. The atmosphere down there reminded me of a Turkish bath. Steam was so thick one could barely see through it, because the watercooled exhaust pipes had been punctured by shrapnel. Leading Stoker Thompson, who was then in charge, was badly wounded in the leg, but he continued to hobble about and finally got the starboard engine going. Subsequently he remained at his post for more than five hours and was awarded a D.S.M., which he most richly deserved."

The Commanding Officer had been made as comfortable as possible between the torpedo tubes. When he regained consciousness, the engines were stopped and the ship was still lying in the cross fire. But the enemy seemed to think that the M.L. was finished and transferred their fire to the moving ships. Fenton was taken down below, where his wounds were dressed and he was given morphine. He sent for the First Lieutenant and Captain Hooper and told them that if the engines could be started he would try once more to get in.

" The smoke float was ditched," continues Machin, " and, as we crawled away, they opened fire on it, as it was throwing off a lot of flame. The port engine was completely out of commission, and we had to keep the starboard engine going full ahead to prevent it from stopping. As the ship was practically unmanœuvrable in these circumstances, it was impossible to try to get alongside or to let go our ' fish ' at the flak-ship, and so we proceeded on the course out. By this time I was weak from loss of blood, and although I looked at my watch I cannot be certain what the time was. I believe it was 2.40.

[1] Lt. Tillie was taken prisoner.
[2] It is reported by Lt. Cdr. Stephens, who was in the prison camp with her First Lieutenant, that M.L. 267 did get alongside and land her troops.

"After we had been on this course for a few minutes the Captain relieved me on the bridge while I had my wounds dressed. Then I returned and the Captain was persuaded to go below."

The last M.L. in the starboard column, 177 (Sub-Lt. Rodier) is known to have reached the Old Entrance. After landing her troops she was ordered to go alongside the after end of the *Campbeltown* to take off some of the destroyer's crew. She did this successfully, and at 2.20 she made a signal to say that she was leaving, but no more was heard of her.

Lt. Cdr. Stephens learnt the following details of her fate from fellow prisoners.

"Amongst the *Campbeltown* survivors Rodier embarked Beattie," he writes. "They were shot up on the way downstream. The boat caught fire and, due to leaking petrol, so did the water all round. I think this was one of the greatest tragedies of the raid. These men had done their job and done it magnificently by bringing the *Campbeltown* in, and then on the way out almost within reach of safety they were hit. Beattie and the others on the rafts had a hell of a time and were not picked up until next morning, by which time there were very few of them still alive."

Such, then, was the grim story of the two columns of M.Ls. carrying the Commando troops. There remain to be described the doings of the two MLs. with roving commissions which had been stationed on the bows of the *Campbeltown*.

That on the port bow was M.L. 270 under the command of Lt. C. S. B. Irwin, R.N.R., and his principal duty was to use the torpedoes with which his boat was equipped to sink any ship which might interfere on the way in or be met with in the harbour. He had, however, another and less enviable rôle. It was to steam up and down at high speed in order to draw the enemy's fire.

The fire of his own 3-pounder was particularly accurate, and amongst other targets it was able to dowse a searchlight which had been holding the *Campbeltown*. A little later, however, M.L. 270 was hit by a heavy shell aft, which put the main steering-gear out of action and damaged the auxiliary steering-gear.

After ten minutes of intense effort the hand steering was rigged and Irwin started to run downstream, attempting still to draw the enemy's fire and very successfully doing so.

During this run a German trawler was sighted silhouetted by the beam of a searchlight and was successfully engaged by the 3-pounder, most accurately laid by Able Seaman J. L. Elliott. The fire was being directed by the First Lieutenant, an Australian—Lt. C. W. Wallach, R.A.N.V.R.

The trawler's reply set the engine-room on fire, but, as one of the crew said, "We fired at his bridge and quietened him down."

Irwin had occasion to notice an M.L. which went alongside another boat that was blazing near the Old Mole. Many others saw and recorded with admiration this gallant rescue. It was Boyd, in command of M.L. 160, who was, as we have seen, taking off the survivors from Platt's boat, a proceeding which earned him the Distinguished Service Order.

Quite at Home in the River

M.L. 160 was the boat that had been stationed on the *Campbeltown*'s starboard bow on the way in. Here is Boyd's story of what happened to her after the destroyer had rammed the gate.

"I made the crew lie down behind the torpedo tubes and went in search of two 10,000-ton ships which were reported to be either in the river or in the dock. We were never out of the searchlights, and every time the tracer got too close I took violent avoiding action. Somehow we managed to keep clear of the heavier stuff.

" I felt relieved to know that the *Campbeltown* had done her job and even more relieved to find that I felt quite at home in the river. Everything appeared just as I expected it, and I blessed the model we had studied, lying on our tummies, for so many hours before we started. I think that model saved my life.

" I went on up the river past the huge skeleton of a half-completed French aircraft carrier which looked grotesque picked out in the glare of the searchlights. I could not find the two ships and disappointedly turned and came down river with the intention of going alongside the *Campbeltown* to offer any aid I could.

" Just before I got to the lock-gates I noticed a battery on top of a power-house, with two Bofors guns on it, shooting hell out of everybody, so I closed to about 200 yards, stopped the ship and gave them 30 rounds of high explosive and buckshot from the 3-pounder. I directed the fire through a megaphone, and McIver, the gunner, kept on saying, ' Och! that's hit the bashtards again.' As they could not depress sufficiently we got clean away with it and silenced the battery. But then things became too hot for us, and I yelled to No. 1 who was serving the gun to cease fire, and we got away from there as quickly as possible. The Coxswain kept crawling on to the bridge from the wheelhouse to make sure I was still alive; but I told him not to worry. My tin-hat became too heavy about now and I had to resort to my famous fighting hat, which gave me more confidence than the metal counterpart. I kept repeating to myself, ' By God, we're still alive.' It seemed to be terrific luck.

" Then I saw a ship anchored and manœuvred to torpedo it. I remember setting 10 knots enemy speed on the torpedo sight and then laughing and kicking myself because it was anchored. I fired at about 350 yards and only one ' fish ' ran. It seemed hours afterwards that the crash and column of water came up on the ship amidships.

" I was held in searchlights, and I could feel the ship shudder as she was constantly hit. Then came a blinding crash behind me and clouds of smoke issued from the engine-room; both engines cut and all lights went out. ' Well, this is it,' I thought. ' What a bloody end.' But my thoughts were broken off as both engines cut in again and I felt terribly happy and relieved. I called up control on the wireless several times, but could get no joy. Our deck petrol-tank was hit three times, and the water, which I had filled it with on the way up the river, all ran out. I turned and fired the other torpedo into the brown of St. Nazaire, as I was getting hit so often I thought it a bad plan to keep it on board.

" I closed the lock-gate and noticed the *Campbeltown* well down by the stern. I looked around for Curtis, but could not see him. I called again on the wireless and got no answer, so I decided to try to rescue anybody I could.

" A Silly Thing to Do "

" I saw a fellow in the water first of all, and heard a shout of ' M.L. ahoy.' Then I saw an M.L. fairly close to the Mole, smoking like hell with a red glow coming from the engine-room. I decided to go alongside, and did so in between him and the Mole, a silly thing to do. My stern crashed into his starboard side and we were locked together.

" The gunfire was intense, but we succeeded in getting off what soldiers and crew were still alive, including the Commanding Officer—Platt—whose ship had been crippled making a very gallant effort to get alongside under a withering fire." During this rescue the Cox'n of M.L. 160 went on board the blazing boat and carried off many wounded, tending them afterwards untiringly. His name was Petty Officer L. S. Lamb, and he won the Conspicuous Gallantry Medal.

" We pulled three chaps out of the water," Boyd continues, " and then I thought it was about time to be going. We were hit astern and caught fire in the tiller flat; we were hit in the engine-room and one engine was put out of action and the motor mechanic (C. D. Walker) was wounded in the face. Several soldiers were wounded by Oerlikon shells, and I remember calling up the wireless operator, Drew by name, and asking how he was getting along. He told me that a shell had passed in between him and his set, but he sounded wonderfully cheerful. I shut the one engine down to a fairly slow speed and crawled down the river, taking violent avoiding action. The big shore batteries nearly had us several times, but our luck was in and we managed to keep going amid the huge waterspouts thrown up by their shells.

"I decided I could not reach England on one engine and determined to steal a French fishing-boat to get back in. Whatever the odds, I was going to get my crew and myself back somehow.

"About 3.30 I went down to the engine-room and tried to start the port engine. The motor mechanic in spite of his wounds had repaired the ignition wires which had been cut, and finally we got it going."

Lt. Curtis' gunboat with Cdr. Ryder on board was probably the last to leave the harbour. They had been out to see how the M.Ls. were faring at the Old Mole, they had engaged the pillboxes and the gun positions on the house-tops, and they began to realise that the opposition was getting the upper hand.

"All this time," writes Ryder in his report, "we were lying stopped about 100 yards off the Old Entrance, and although fired on fairly continually and hit many times, we were, by the grace of God, not set on fire. On looking round the harbour, however, we could count seven or eight blazing M.Ls. and were forced to realise that we were the only craft left in sight that had not been destroyed.

"In consequence of this, a more concentrated fire was directed upon us, so we dropped a smoke-float while I called a council of war. No withdrawal signal had been sent and no contact had been made with the shore by wireless. There was still at least another half-hour before we could expect any of the landing party to reach the point of evacuation. We would have returned to the Old Entrance, but we could see a heavy cross fire across this inlet, and it appeared that enemy forces on both banks were shooting at each other. It was clearly impossible for us to return. With some thirty to forty men on board and our decks piled with seriously wounded, I decided at 2.50 that we were in no position to take off the soldiers we had landed. It was unlikely that we should survive another five minutes with the fire that was then being concentrated in our direction, and so we left at high speed."

During the withdrawal M.G.B. 314 was hit repeatedly on the starboard side. She overtook another surviving M.L. and laid smoke to cover her. She was floodlit by searchlights all the way down and, on passing Les Morées tower, the coastal artillery joined in and continued to straddle her with near misses until she was about 4 miles off the land. The withdrawal had lasted twenty-five minutes and, by the end of it, all the seamen on board had been wounded, and most of the wounded from the *Campbeltown* had been wounded a second time.

Just when she was beginning to get out of the searchlights she came upon an armed trawler, which opened an uncomfortably heavy, but fortunately not very accurate, fire which did no serious damage. Splinters from one of the last shells to be fired by the heavy batteries, however, caused further casualties on board and killed Able Seaman Savage, the layer of the pom-pom, and Able Seaman A. R. C. Stephens, the loading number, who had served their gun with such spirit throughout the whole action.

"By then," says Curtis, "Ryder and I were taking alternate tricks at the wheel, for I had sent my Cox'n to help with the wounded, of whom we now had some thirty. Fortunately the engine-room crew were unhurt though a large piece had been cut out of the tin-hat of the motor mechanic."

Curtis pays tribute to the way in which the official Press representative on board—Mr. Gordon Holman (author of *The Little Ships*)—attended to the wounded, for which he was subsequently mentioned in despatches.

" Below decks there was a mass of groaning men. We could show no light down there until the shell-holes in the hull had been blocked, otherwise we should have been spotted, so, to begin with, Holman and the Cox'n did their best, by the light of a dim torch, to help the wounded."

THE DESTROYERS IN ACTION

Of the seventeen boats which had entered, there were now some eight or possibly nine steaming down the estuary to meet the destroyer escort which was waiting for them. *Tynedale* and *Atherstone* had been patrolling off the river mouth all night. When the presence of the five enemy torpedo boats had become known to the Commander-in-Chief, Plymouth, on the previous evening he had at once ordered two more " Hunt " Class destroyers—*Cleveland* and *Brocklesby*—to proceed with all despatch to reinforce the escort, but at dawn they were still more than 80 miles from the mouth of the Loire.

As day broke the five enemy torpedo boats, which had apparently been recalled from escort duties farther to seaward, were sighted by *Tynedale* and *Atherstone* steering east.

A short battle followed, in which the two " Hunt " Class tried first to draw the enemy to the southward, so that he would not meet the last of the M.Ls. that were now limping down the estuary, and then out to the westward, from which direction the *Cleveland* and *Brocklesby* would be expected to appear.

The two " Hunts " were heavily outnumbered, and unfortunately it was a case of leading rather than driving. But the enemy did not follow. Instead, he broke off the action and went up river, hoping to bottle-up the remains of the British raiding force and destroy them. He was too late, although German prisoners have since stated that two M.Ls. were, in fact, caught and sunk by the torpedo boats. One of these M.Ls. was probably 306 under the command of Lt. Henderson who, when met by a torpedo boat, engaged at such short range that the enemy captain called on him to surrender over a loud hailer. He refused, although he was being raked from end to end by the German guns. His own guns went on firing until they were all put out of action and all his officers and most of his crew had been killed. The Germans then boarded, took off the few who were still alive and took their battered prize in tow. It is recorded that the captain of the torpedo boat commented on the amazing bravery of the M.L.'s crew in the face of overwhelming odds. The prisoners he took were unusually well treated, receiving immediate medical attention, dry clothing and hot drinks, a circumstance attributable only to the impression created by the gallantry of their fight.

Tynedale and *Atherstone* returned to collect together the remnant of their brood—the seven boats which had escaped. Three, apparently more seaworthy than the rest, had already pushed on ahead to the westward. These M.Ls. were commanded by Boyd, Wallis and Horlock.

It was now daylight, and *Atherstone* came first upon M.L. 156 (Lt. Fenton). She was badly damaged, and there was still every chance that the enemy torpedo boats were following and would appear on the scene at any moment.

With her telegraphs shot away the M.L. had the greatest difficulty in coming alongside the destroyer. Lt. Cdr. R. Jenks, R.N., the *Atherstone's* captain, hailed her and shouted,

" Ram me and I'll catch you," which, according to Machin, her First Lieutenant (who was then conning her), is just what the M.L. did.

She had been so badly damaged in the fighting that she had to be abandoned and was left sinking after the crew had been safely taken on board the *Atherstone*.

Meanwhile M.Ls. 270 (Lt. Irwin) and 446 (Lt. Falconar) had joined company with M.G.B. 314, and soon afterwards they sighted *Atherstone* and *Tynedale*. Jenks describes how he learned with great thankfulness, as soon as 314 was alongside, that Ryder and his navigating officer were safe and unwounded.

The M.G.B. was towed alongside *Atherstone* at 8 knots in the glass-calm sea, while the seriously wounded were transferred, and volunteers from the destroyer's crew went on board to replace casualties.

Ryder re-embarked in the *Atherstone* and, at eight o'clock, the party set off to the westward—two destroyers, two M.Ls. and the M.G.B. Already the German reconnaissance aircraft had found them and were circling round out of gun range. One of them, a Heinkel 115 float-plane, bombed the abandoned and sinking hulk of M.L. 156 far astern.

At 9.0 the *Cleveland* and the *Brocklesby* hove in sight from the westward and approached at high speed. From the signals they had received they knew that *Atherstone* and *Tynedale* had been engaged with the enemy torpedo boats, and their arrival considerably improved the balance, should the Germans follow up in pursuit.

The captain of the *Cleveland*—Cdr. G. B. Sayer, R.N. (who had, before the war, commanded the 1st M.T.B. Flotilla in the Mediterranean)—was then the Senior Naval Officer present, and Cdr. Ryder immediately placed the force under his command.

A British Beaufighter had been escorting them since just before 9 a.m., but a little later it attacked a Ju. 88 and destroyed it at very close range. Whether the two aircraft collided or not will never be known, but the Beaufighter also crashed into the sea and there were no survivors.

Enemy aircraft were now constantly in attendance, but after *Brocklesby* had shot down another Ju. 88 into the sea astern, they kept their distance, circling and observing, and, no doubt, reporting the movements of our ships.

" An appreciation of the general situation at this time," wrote Cdr. Sayer in his report, " seemed to indicate that a heavy air attack was imminent; in addition to which an attack by the surface forces known to be in the vicinity was considered a strong possibility. . . . In view of all these circumstances and the additional necessity of getting the critically wounded men to port as soon as possible, the abandoning of the M.Ls. now had to be considered."

Already the increasing head wind had reduced their speed from 16 knots to 10, and eventually it was clear that they could not maintain even that speed. In M.G.B. 314 the water was gaining slowly, in spite of the efforts of her crew, and finally one of her engines broke down.

At last the sad decision had to be made. The crews of the three Coastal Force craft were taken off, and the boats, which had served them so bravely through the fury of the fight, were sunk by the gunfire of the destroyers.

That was the bitter end of M.Ls. 270 and 446, and of M.G.B. 314 which had led the force up the river, fought so fiercely in the battle and come last away from the smoking fiery scene with her load of wounded.

M.G.B. 314 had a crew of three officers and fourteen men: Cdr. Ryder had taken two more officers and a signalman with him, so that there had been on board altogether twenty-one naval personnel. Among them were awarded two Victoria Crosses, three D.S.C.'s and four D.S.M.'s—a fine tribute to so small, but so gallant, a ship.

Without the Coastal Force craft the destroyers were now able to set off for home at high speed with the survivors.

"We Picked up the Lizard"

The three M.Ls. which had pushed on to the westward during the *Tynedale* and *Atherstone's* battle met the *Cleveland* and *Brocklesby* hastening eastward as reinforcements. At first they took them for enemy ships in the early morning light, and Lt. Boyd describes how he threw his charts and confidential documents overboard to prevent their capture before the two destroyers could be identified.

Later in the forenoon the German aircraft did not neglect these three boats. A Heinkel came to look at them. " As it came down to have a closer look everything opened up. The first rounds hit him in the glasshouse and he crashed at once. It was a fine sight to see the iron crosses smash into the sea and the plane break up. We all cheered and I gave the boys two rations of rum. The shooting of the other two boats was very very good. We turned north at five in the evening and were attacked again at dusk by a seaplane which dropped a 1,000-lb. bomb just astern of me.

" We were not troubled further, though I feared surface craft would get us before we got round Ushant. But our luck held, and next morning about 10 a.m. we picked up the Lizard— a place I know well [1]—and pushed on into Falmouth with a little over an hour's petrol left."

So the three triumphant M.Ls. returned safely to England under their own power three days and three nights after they had started.

The Aftermath

It was not until noon on the morning after the raid that the *Campbeltown's* demolition charges blew up and the main object of the raid was achieved. The lock-gate was blown off its sill and seriously damaged, and the dock itself was put out of commission for the rest of the war. Despite great effort, repairs to it were never completed.

Full details of the damage to the machinery and other installations will not be known until the German records become available, but there is no doubt that the activities of Colonel Newman's troops ashore were effectively destructive.

One merchant ship was sunk and several other German ships were damaged and possibly sunk, including one which was fired on by its own batteries ashore.

The secondary objective of the U boat pens was not reached because of the failure at the Old Mole, but to set against this there were unexpected developments which ended disastrously for the Germans during the few days that followed the raid.

To begin with, some thirty or forty senior German officers were on board the *Campbeltown* when she blew up. They are believed to have been lulled into a sense of security by two of the ship's officers, who led them on board well knowing that, although two sets of fuses had failed, there was a third which would shortly become operative. All on board were killed by the explosion and so were many of a large crowd which had collected round the dock.

On the afternoon of Saturday, 30th March, nearly three days after the raid, the first of the two delayed-action torpedoes fired by Wynn's M.T.B. exploded in the lock-gate of the Old Entrance. About an hour later the second one went off. Apart from the damage to the lock

---

[1] As First Lieutenant and Navigator of an M.L., Boyd had once been aground near the Lizard in a fog, which had earned for him in some quarters the nickname of T. Lizard Boyd.

itself, these explosions caused an astonishing panic amongst the dockyard workers and the Germans.

Indiscriminate shooting began when the crowd forced a barrier at one of the bridges. In the fighting which followed German fought German and the French workers in the crowd were mown down by machine-gun fire. More than 250 people are reported to have been killed.

A number of workmen of the German Todt organisation, dressed in khaki overalls, were mistaken for British Commandos by the German soldiers whose officers had been wiped out in the *Campbeltown* explosion and who were now leaderless and thoroughly unnerved. The fighting went on during the night, and it is reported that between three and four hundred Germans were killed.

Such, then, were the unplanned and unexpected results of the raid.

The reactions of the German naval forces are also worth remark. The five torpedo boats presented, as we have seen, a much stronger force than our own. "They put to sea," writes Cdr. Ryder, "shortly before our arrival in order to escort a merchant ship. When our presence was reported in the river they were out at sea, and when they re-entered the river to drive us out we were gone. Although we expected them to follow us under the cover of their own aircraft, they did not apparently care to do so and we were allowed to escape."[1]

That is part of the story of the greatest single undertaking ever carried out by Coastal Forces. Another part will be told when the German reports and those of the prisoners of war have been correlated, but perhaps the biggest part of the grim and glorious happenings of that night will never be known at all. That is why the citations of many of the high decorations which were awarded expressly state that they are in recognition of the valour of those others, unnamed, who did not return.

[1] Some explanation for this reluctance has since been given by German prisoners of war, who state that three of the torpedo boats were limited, by engine defects, to a maximum of 18 knots.

CHAPTER VI

An Introduction to the Coastal Forces

MEANWHILE the M.T.Bs. at Dover were developing their tactics along new lines, first suggested and exploited in Pumphrey's successful action of the previous September.

Early in March, 1942, I was sent down to Dover for M.T.B. experience, having newly joined the Coastal Forces, and I arrived on the evening of the 3rd. It was, I found, a busy time. Two nights previously Lt. Hillary Gamble, Lt. Paul Gibson, and Sub-Lt. Mark Arnold Forster, had torpedoed a tanker, supported by Lt. Stewart Gould and Lt. Roger King, in their M.G.Bs. The tanker did not sink, but was stopped and drifting with the tide, and Lt. Cdr. Pumphrey had been sent out later in the night to finish it off; but in the fog which had now set in he was unable to find it. He did, however, meet some of its escort, who were also apparently looking for the tanker, and he was himself wounded in the action which followed.

It was into this active atmosphere that I was introduced " for M.T.B. experience," and the following account was written soon after.

" It was already dark when a taxi from the station deposited me on the steps of the Lord Warden Hotel, now H.M.S. *Wasp*, the Coastal Force Base. I had been told to ask for Hillary Gamble, who was acting as Senior Officer M.T.Bs., since Pumphrey was in hospital, and so I asked the first person I met inside the Hall—an R.N. Lieutenant—who replied that his name was Gamble and how could he help me.

" I told him that I wanted to go to sea with the boats if they were going, and he said that they had already gone. Harpy Lloyd had taken John Weeden and Robert Varvil after a small convoy, and it appeared that one of the boats was in trouble. John Hodder and ' Flatters ' Sidebottom were just off this very minute to the rescue, and if I would like to go with them I would have to run.

" Ten minutes later, and not twenty minutes since my train had pulled into Dover station, I was steaming out of the harbour entrance on the bridge of a " C " Class M.G.B. (322), under the command of Lt. J. H. Hodder, R.N.V.R., while close astern followed M.G.B. 330 (Lt. D. C. Sidebottom, R.N.V.R.).

" M.T.B. 31, commanded by John Weeden, had made a signal to say that she was near the North-east Varne buoy and required immediate assistance. In bright moonlight we set course for the North-east Varne, and soon after we sighted a dim flicker of light and turned towards it. In a haze of smoke we came upon the burning wreck of the M.T.B. Some of the crew were still on board and shouted to us as we drew alongside. ' There's a raft with the wounded on it about a quarter of a mile away to the eastward,' they said, and Sidebottom went off to find it, while we made fast alongside the burning boat.

" The First Lieutenant was on board organising a fire party, and they were ready to take the hoses which had been laid out in readiness on our decks.

" Apparently they had successfully torpedoed a ship, but had been pursued by E/R boats and badly shot up. John Weeden had been seriously wounded and so had the coxswain and one or two others, and the Seaman Torpedoman had been killed. The boat had run clear before the engines packed up and the fire took hold.

" Macdonald, the First Lieutenant, an imperturbable New Zealander,[1] had placed the

[1] This was my first meeting with Sub-Lt. G. J. Macdonald, R.N.Z.N.V.R., afterwards to become one of the great M.T.B. leaders of the war.

wounded, including the Commanding Officer, in the Carley Raft, while he and the able-bodied members of the crew had abandoned ship by holding on to the splinter mattresses, which had been cut adrift to act as additional rafts. For some time they had lain off, but then the boat did not blow up and the fire seemed if anything to be abating. So Macdonald, who was a great swimmer, swam back and climbed aboard, and finally got some more of the crew back, and began to tackle the fire. It was at this stage that we had put in our most welcome appearance.

" It seemed that M.T.B. 31 was not past salvage. The fire, though not yet extinguished, was no longer spreading. The engine-room and tiller-flat were slowly flooding, but it was only a short distance to Dover. We began to tow her alongside, while we continued in our efforts to put out the fire. These efforts finally led us down through the charred chart-house into the smoke-filled forward mess-deck. The leader of the fire party was ' Teek' (Sub-Lt. H. Teekman, R.C.N.V.R.), one of the Maintenance Officers from the Base, who plunged down into the smoke below without a thought and finally finished off the fire.

" Behind the bridge was the body of the Seaman Torpedoman lying face downwards in a huddle of shiny black oilskins. He had been killed instantly, and there was nothing that could usefully be done but leave him for the present in the corner where he had fallen.

" Towing became awkward off Dover, where, in the mist which had set in, we found we had been swept to the north of the harbour, and the popple on the sea made the two boats crack together with ominous splintering noises. By the time we had passed the breakwater the stern of the M.T.B. was 2 feet under water, and only our forward speed, we thought, prevented her from sinking altogether. We finally beached her in the entrance to the Wellington Dock. She took the ground about five yards from the shore, and John Hodder's M.G.B. had to leave her there, as the tide was falling and he almost became stranded himself. There were three of us left on board 31 which, with her stern on the bottom, was almost vertical in the water. We looked like remaining perched precariously on her bows till morning, but some very senior officers who had come down to meet us passed a ladder across to us, over which we were able to scramble ashore."

That was my first introduction to the Coastal Forces. For their work that night both Weeden and Macdonald were awarded the Distinguished Service Cross. Their success in sinking a merchant ship was one of an increasingly large number which the M.T.Bs. had recently been scoring in the Straits.

AGAINST FEARFUL ODDS

The new technique had put us ahead, and it was clear that it could not be long before the enemy's reaction would develop. When it came it was in the form of a greatly strengthened escort for all important shipping passing through the Narrows. From now on the number of escorts was doubled, and the main target was, as it were, embedded in their midst.

On 12th May, for example, an Armed Merchant Raider made the passage with an escort, which included four " Möwe " Class torpedo boats, eight " M " Class minesweepers and about ten E/R boats.

The full details of the battle which took place are not known, for the Senior Officer of our M.T.Bs., Lt. E. A. E. Cornish, R.N.V.R., did not return; he and many of his crew were killed, and his boat, M.T.B. 220, battered almost beyond recognition, was salvaged by the enemy. But we do know that during the hour and a quarter of fighting two enemy torpedo boats—the *Iltis* and the *See Adler*—were sunk, although the raider got through. Cornish hit one torpedo boat, and it is believed that she may have rammed him before she sank. The other was hit by Sub-Lt. Barry Easton, R.N.V.R., who made a patch of smoke and then fired his torpedoes as the pursuing enemy came round the corner of it.

Sub-Lt. Mark Arnold Forster was so closely pursued by torpedo boats that he had no chance of turning on his pursuers, and his situation was not improved by the breakdown of one engine, which greatly reduced his speed. At one time the E/R boats joined in the chase and Arnold Forster decided to summon to his assistance the M.G.Bs. under the command of Lt. Tom Fuller, R.C.N.V.R., and Lt. " Ronnie " Barge, R.N.V.R. So he made a signal, " My position, course and speed so and so, six E boats in company." Some time later the E boats seemed to have been shaken off, and Arnold Forster went down to the wireless office and gave instructions for a further signal to be sent, " My so and so (referring to the time of origin of the last message), E boats no longer in company." While the signal was being coded the E boats reappeared on the port quarter. This was reported to him by the First Lieutenant down the voice-pipe, and as he made for the bridge he turned to the telegraphist: " Change that to ' My so and so, E boats still in company,' " he said.

But the M.G.Bs. could not make contact before the E/R boats abandoned the pursuit. The enemy had successfully completed his main task in that the raider had safely entered Boulogne, but two important ships of Hitler's hard-pressed fleet had been sent to the bottom. Against the odds which prevailed that night it was a notable achievement.

" PUT AWAY THE COFFEE "

While the technique of the Coastal Forces in the Straits continued to develop in its rather specialised way, an entirely different technique was emerging in the North Sea against the E boats.

Both Lt. Cdr. Hichens' and Lt. Horne's successes had been against the E boats on their homeward journey. The next stage was to try to intercept them outward bound before they could reach our convoy route with their torpedoes and mines.

Early in April, 1942, a flotilla of E boats began to operate from Ostend. The nights were growing shorter, and it was becoming impossible for them to make the long passage to and from their hunting-ground during the dark hours if they started from Ijmuiden or the Hook. From Ostend it was little more than half the distance. The plan was for the M.G.Bs. to be as close to the enemy's harbour as they dared to be by dusk, and to wait for the E boats to emerge.

On the first suitable night after a period of strong winds and rough seas, our boats were unable to patrol because of a special operation on which they had been engaged. The E boats came out and laid a minefield, and on the following day two merchant ships and two " Hunt " Class destroyers were mined. Hichens was sent to bring in the casualties from one of the destroyers—H.M.S. *Cotswold*, whose First Lieutenant was Lt. P. G. C. Dickens, R.N. This was the first meeting between these two men; later they were to work extensively together at H.M.S. *Beehive* as Senior Officers of M.G.Bs. and M.T.Bs. respectively.

" We were off Ostend the same night," wrote Hichens, " in a very vengeful mood. But the E boats were celebrating their success and we waited in vain." On the following day— Tuesday the 21st April—the weather was still calm and again our motor gunboats set out early in the evening to lie in wait. Four boats made up the force, which was split into two divisions lying five miles apart in order to increase the chance of interception. At the same time this plan meant that whichever force did make contact would fight against heavy odds. The E boats usually worked in groups of six at least: it would be six against two. Hichens accepted the odds.

"We had stopped at ten o'clock," he writes. "At 10.35 I suggested having some sandwiches and coffee as we waited in the 'dustbin.'

"'We may not have much time later on,' I added. And I was right. George Bailey,[1] who was with me as a passenger, held the cups and I unscrewed the thermos top. As I did so the faintest steady whispering beat fell upon our ears like the rhythmic rustle of a flowing ball-dress; the sound came from the southward. We stayed motionless, intent, the coffee and cups held poised, forgotten. Thus we must have remained for a minute or more. No longer was needed; the sound and its portent had become unmistakable.

"'Put away the coffee,' I said quietly, 'we shan't want it yet awhile.'"

Curiously, that little remark, indicating that the fight was on, was to spring to mind whenever we recalled this action.

There was not long to wait. The E boats were coming towards them, but the bearing of the noise was gradually changing. Hichens was waiting until it drew almost level. When he was sure that the enemy would pass close to the eastward of him, he warned his second boat under the command of Sub-Lt. R. A. ("Bussy") Carr, R.N.V.R., to stand by to start up. Lt. G. F. Duncan, R.C.N.V.R., leader of the second unit, lying five miles to the westward, was called on the R/T to join them, Course North 60° East. By this time an enemy report had been made—"Am engaging E boats in position . . ."—the "sibilant murmur and the muffled throb" were very close.

"Start up."

Six engines roared back their answer.

As the boats raced in to join battle Hichens describes how he had "a queer feeling in the pit of the stomach; but what man," he says, "determined upon performing an unpleasant duty, has not?"

The enemy were visible now, in line ahead, four—certainly four, probably more than four. Hichens increased speed: he would get in close before opening fire. But already he had been seen. The enemy did not wish him to come any closer. First a single stream of brilliant light and then heavy remorseless fire sought him out. He was making 38 knots now, and knew himself to be a difficult target as he continued to close the range. He closed to within a cable of the rear E boat, the gunners doing good work all the time; their shells could be seen bursting on the enemy's hull. Suddenly the next E boat ahead loomed up and the gunners switched their attentions to her, leaving their earlier prey to Carr. As they closed she broke away and the next E boat loomed in her stead. And so they passed up the line shooting at each in turn.

Carr, meanwhile, having engaged the rear E boat, which also succeeded in breaking away, had lost touch with the enemy, owing to the intense tracer fire which was at times completely blinding. Hichens' boat had suffered severe damage. One turret had been put out of action, but not before it had fired 1,000 rounds; there were two ratings wounded and Bailey had a splinter gash below his right eye. The battle went on.

Not until all six enemy vessels in turn had been engaged and driven off to the eastward in confusion did they have time to consider the situation. Was the enemy likely to carry on with his intention? Would he turn again towards our convoy route or had he had enough? They listened—the enemy could be detected almost due east. All four M.G.Bs. were now together, and it was decided to turn north-east, run for six miles or so at full speed and then cut and listen again. This would intercept the E boats if they were still sufficiently determined to carry on with their original intention and were heading again towards England. The M.G.Bs. sped away, making 36 knots. Hichens dealt out morphia for his five casualties from the supply

[1] Lt. G. E. Bailey, R.N.V.R.

which he kept in his pocket during action.   Three of them were very serious: one was obviously dying.   He reflected that he had good cause to be thankful that none of the thirteen shell-holes was below the water-line; luckily, too, his was the only boat with casualties or real damage.

Having reached their chosen position they stopped, " slumping into silence instantly before the way was off the boats, as the flotilla had been trained to do when hunting E boats where seconds might count."   There it was, the far-off murmur, to the south this time. So the enemy was making for home: Hichens decided to go after him.

There was by now a southerly breeze with increasing mist: 36 knots was no longer a possibility.   When they reached an estimated position 3 miles off Ostend, they stopped once more to listen.   It seemed certain that the E boats had made Ostend and entered the harbour.

Hichens with his telegraphist (Leading Telegraphist Roberts) then transferred to Lt. Duncan's boat, while Bailey took over M.G.B. 64 and raced her homeward with the wounded.

The other three boats remained in the vicinity till dawn, but the E boats did not come out again that night, nor for many nights afterwards.   With a single Oerlikon gun and two twin ·5 machine-guns, Hichens had achieved a major victory over a vastly superior enemy force; for this he was awarded the Distinguished Service Order.

THE ACTIVE SEASON

The tracer bullets and the flying spray, the torpedo attacks and the high-speed gun battles —these are the spectacular aspects of Coastal Forces, the " Spitfires of the sea "; but in the Channel and North Sea they made up much less than one-tenth of the work of our light craft.   They were interspersed at rare intervals amongst long fruitless sweeps off the enemy coast, long nights on anti-E boat patrol, on tedious convoy protection and escort work.

But it was to take advantage of these rare opportunities of meeting and fighting the enemy that the preparations had to be made.   It was to that end that the boats and their crews had continually to be exercised.

The number of times these opportunities arose depended on many things, not least the season of the year.   Generally speaking, the chance of making contact with the enemy was proportional to the number of hours spent in search of him.   In winter these hours were curtailed by bad weather, which often interrupted operations for days, sometimes weeks at a time.   In summer the short nights greatly reduced the time that could be spent on the hunting-ground.   It was therefore the spring and the autumn which were the peak seasons for Coastal Force activity.

In midsummer, when the weather was good and the nights were short, the activity was greatest in the Dover Strait, where the opposing forces were based nearest to each other.

Apart from the fierce fighting which followed the Allied invasion of France in 1944, the summer and autumn of 1942 made up perhaps the busiest period for the Coastal Forces in the Narrow Seas.   A long spell of good weather, combined with extensive E and R boat minelaying operations and an increase in the numbers of our own boats, produced a continuous series of battles, often several on the same night.

This run of battles started in June when the nights were at their shortest, and continued with a steady crescendo into the autumn.

Lt. H. L. (" Harpy ") Lloyd, one of the most outstanding leaders at that time, with a unit of two M.T.Bs. began the month with a spirited and successful attack on two " T " Class torpedo boats proceeding eastward from Dunkirk.   He was illuminated by the enemy and engaged before firing his torpedoes, but in spite of that the attack was well pressed home, and the second of the two M.T.Bs. (commanded by Sub-Lt. T. Neill, R.N.V.R.) scored a hit on one of the torpedo boats.

A week later came a night when there was great activity in the Dover Strait. Two groups of E boats were laying mines, one off Folkestone, the other off Rye; there was a friendly convoy eastbound and another westbound through the Narrows, and a friendly destroyer bound for Portsmouth, which was ordered to turn about because of further enemy mine-laying off Selsey Bill.

Under cover of these things the Germans cunningly chose to pass a convoy from Boulogne eastwards through the Straits, containing a large and important tanker.

This tanker was the one that had been hit and damaged by Gamble's M.T.Bs. on 1st March, 1942, and again by an explosion in Boulogne harbour in April. This time they were determined to get it through, and it was guarded with the usual heavy escort of ten or twelve ships.

Amongst the Coastal Force craft despatched in pursuit of this target the Allied nations were well represented. The forces comprised three M.T.Bs., of which one was Dutch, and five M.G.Bs., of which one was Polish, another Dutch and a third commanded by a Frenchman.

The M.G.Bs. under the command of Lt. G. D. K. Richards, R.N., had bad luck.

Their job was to lay mines ahead of the convoy, and as the leading sweepers turned in towards Calais the mines were laid between them and the harbour mouth.

The M.G.Bs. were detected, however, illuminated by starshell and searchlights, and engaged, with the result that the lay was spoiled.

Only the leading sweepers turned in to Calais and the tanker and its escort stood on towards Dunkirk. Richards subsequently made contact with it, and had the mortification of shadowing it for over half an hour unobserved, but with no means of destroying it now that his mines had been expended.

Meanwhile, at about 2 a.m. the M.T.Bs. under Lt. G. L. Cotton, R.N.V.R., were making their interception, though unfortunately it was detected before the attack could be completed. At once the air was full of starshell and tracer, but Cotton, with magnificent determination, went straight on in, closely followed by Lt. E. H. Larive, Royal Netherlands Navy. Which of the two boats fired the torpedo which is believed to have hit will probably never be known, but both M.T.Bs. passed through the screen of some seven or eight E boats and a number of flak trawlers. In the action which followed the result was inconclusive. It was less successful than many M.T.B. battles, but, as an example of human fortitude and determination in adversity, the story must take a high place.

Cotton describes in his report how, because of the blinding glare, he was not at first certain whether a ship ahead of him was a merchant vessel or a trawler, so he fired one torpedo at a range of 300–400 yards. Too late, as the torpedo left the tube, he realised that it was only a trawler.

"At this juncture," he writes, "we were hit on the bridge by an E boat firing from astern of us. I was wounded and the coxswain was temporarily knocked out; the wheel was taken by the Canadian spare officer, Sub-Lt. I. D. Moore, R.C.N.V.R.

"A large vessel was sighted immediately ahead which appeared to be the tanker, extremely light, as she was high in the water. She engaged us with very heavy gunfire. The remaining torpedo was fired at a range of 300 yards or less, and we turned to starboard, passing approximately 50 yards from the target's port quarter.

"Shortly after the second torpedo was fired, the spare officer and the gunner clearly saw and heard an explosion, while others felt the concussion; the gunner maintains that he saw smoke rising from the fore hold of the ship. I personally did not see any explosion, as my attention was occupied elsewhere.

" By this time one engine had been put out of action by a hit on the salt-water pump. In turning away from the tanker we passed an E boat at fairly close quarters, but it did not open fire. Two trawlers, however, engaged us as we were still turning, with extremely heavy and accurate fire, hitting us so often that the remaining engines and the guns were put out of action, a small fire was started, and many of the crew became casualties. So bad was the damage that the boat stopped, disabled, about three-quarters of a mile from the nearest trawler. Both trawlers continued shelling intermittently, so that finally the order had to be given to jettison the confidential books, and destroy all secret equipment.

" The state of the personnel at this time was as follows:

Commanding Officer	..	Wounded.	Signalman ..	Killed.
First Lieutenant..	..	Wounded.	Motor Mechanic ..	Very seriously wounded
Spare Officer	..	Badly wounded.		(died before reaching
Coxswain	..	Wounded.		Base).
Telegraphist	..	Slightly wounded.	Leading Stoker ..	Killed.
Gunner ..	..	Wounded.	Stoker	Badly wounded.

Only the Seaman Torpedoman and the ' Trained Man ' were unwounded.

" At 0220 I gave the order to abandon ship, intending to lie off in the raft while the trawlers continued shelling, and this was carried out during a lull in the firing. One trawler then trained a searchlight on the boat and the firing continued intermittently for about half an hour, after which both trawlers disappeared.

" I then ordered the boat to be reboarded and an endeavour to be made to get her under way. This was successful, and at 0340, proceeding on one auxiliary engine and hand-steering, course was set for Dover. The boat was making water rapidly, though the few still capable were endeavouring to their utmost to keep the level down by bailing and operating the hand bilge pump. At 0745 two High-speed Launches of the R.A.F. closed us and took off the badly wounded. An attempt was made to tow, but by this time the bilge pump was out of action and at 0848 she turned over and sank."

Forwarding Cotton's report to Admiralty, the Commodore Commanding, Dover— Rear-Admiral R. L. B. Cunliffe—after remarking on the " valiant efforts to save their vessel " made by " her gallant and much tried crew," goes on to say that there is no conclusive evidence of the damage inflicted on the enemy, but although three weeks had elapsed since the attack " the tanker, it is observed, still remains in the docks at Dunkirk."

THE NELSON TOUCH

Exactly a week after Cotton's attack on the tanker came a most spirited action, fought by a lone M.G.B.

The E boats were still busy minelaying in the Straits, and on the night of 21st June two small M.G.Bs. were amongst the patrol dispositions. These were the Polish M.G.Bs. *S.2* and *S.3*. The Senior Officer was Lt. E. Wcislicki, Polish Navy (known throughout Coastal Forces as " Whisky "), who describes how just before 11 p.m. *S.3* developed an engine defect so that he ordered her to return to harbour, and went on alone.

Paragraph 4 of his report of proceedings reads: " At 2310 (11.10 p.m.) a signal ordering M.G.B. *S.2* to return to harbour was received, but owing to the telegraphist's error was not then understood." So *S.2* remained on patrol.

An hour and a half later she was manœuvring to get the advantage of the moon as she sped off at 30 knots to intercept E boats which had been reported by wireless signal.

"At 0105," the report continues, "six E boats were sighted on a course of south-west, speed 15 knots. M.G.B. S.2 opened fire immediately without challenging at a range of 200–300 yards. At 0106 I turned hard a-starboard, and when on the same course as the E boats they replied with intensive, but inaccurate fire.

"The E boats increased speed to about 30 knots and altered course to south. M.G.B. S.2 increased speed to 35 knots and closed to 100 yards. Fire from M.G.B. S.2 was accurate and several direct hits were observed; at least one E boat is considered to be damaged. M.G.B. S.2 was hit by cannon shell above the petrol tanks in the ammunition space.

"At 0110 the E boats had formed a half-circle around M.G.B. S.2, the leader proceeding south-east. As M.G.B. S.2 had expended nearly all the ammunition in the Oerlikon magazines and all the point-five ammunition, I withdrew to reload. The enemy continued to fire until 0117, apparently at each other."

S.2 withdrew to the North-east Varne buoy, where later she was joined by four larger gunboats, and with them carried out a sweep to the southward; but they did not regain touch with the retiring enemy.

The Commodore Commanding, Dover, in his covering letter to the Admiralty which accompanied Wcislicki's report, mentions the signal ordering S.2 to return at 2310. "I am not without suspicion," he writes, "that the misunderstanding in paragraph 4 of the enclosure was not a case of turning the blind eye, and if so, results fully justified this following of precedent.

"There can be no doubt," the Commodore concludes, "that by this spirited action M.G.B. S.2 successfully diverted the enemy from his purpose, which was probably to lay mines, but may alternatively have been an attack with torpedoes on the Channel convoy."

THE PACE INCREASES

Besides this masterly single-handed engagement there were several other brushes with minelaying E boats in the latter half of June, and a number of attacks on convoys and patrols. Two new types of Coastal Force craft had just come into the arena, and it was during this month that they both had their first experience of action. The Steam Gunboats had a quick and indecisive exchange of fire with a "T" Class torpedo boat which ran away, and a few days later, on 18th June, operating in company with a "Hunt" Class destroyer, H.M.S. Albrighton, they sank a merchant ship in the Baie de la Seine. Lt. R. Barnet, R.N., who fired the successful torpedo, lost his boat and was himself taken prisoner, with nearly all his crew.

The newest design of the British Power Boat Company—their 71-foot 6-inch M.G.B. with which Hichens' flotilla had lately been reboated—also made its debut at this time. On 20th June Lt. "Boffin" Campbell took the first of these boats into action and shot up a trawler very successfully, and on the following night he was in action again. The value of these actions was enormous, for it is only in battle that the success of a new fighting machine can be proved.

By the ever-increasing numbers of engagements, too, the German was learning that he could expect our Coastal Forces prowling in his waters, not occasionally, not even frequently, but on every single night that the weather would allow. This was a reflection of our steadily increasing numerical strength, though only a proportion of our boat production could be devoted to the war in the North Sea and the Channel. The demands in the Mediterranean were great and the Far Eastern theatre could not be neglected. Still, new construction was opening a new phase of activity during this summer of 1942.

But the old boats were in it too.   The month of July began with a lively attack on an enemy convoy.   This time Lt. P. A. R. Thompson, D.S.C., R.C.N.V.R., who had taken part in the destruction of the E boat in March, led three of the old 70-foot M.G.Bs. in to engage three escorted merchantmen—one of them a tanker—off the Dutch coast.

The Commanding Officers of the other two boats were Lt. M. T. C. Sadler, R.N.V.R., and Lt. E. D. W. Leaf, D.S.C., R.N.V.R.   It was the first time that this flotilla, which was primarily concerned with hunting E boats, had become involved with an enemy convoy, and it is clear that Pete Thompson (later a prisoner of war after his capture in the Straits of Messina) was not going to let the chance of an offensive action pass him by.

Leaf wrote a spirited account of the battle, admirably illustrated, in his diary:

" It was a thundery summer night.   Pouring rain and pitch darkness one moment and five minutes later a clear sky with bright moonlight illuminating the clouds around us.   We were creeping down the coast during one of the bright intervals when a bright, hostile-looking white light challenged us.   We turned to investigate it.   Dark shapes appeared up moon— E boats?   No!   E boats don't carry balloons!   This is probably one of those convoys we read about which the aircraft of Coastal Command often attack.[1]

No time to speculate — what is Pete, the leader, going to do? Crikey! He's going in to attack! O lord! What with? We have no torpedoes only two depth charges. This should be interesting. This is what it looked like to me though of course it was really very much darker — thank goodness:—

We approached up-moon and made for the gap. Suddenly, as if we had all finally made up our minds we increased speed and waited for what was bound to come. Nearer and nearer ..... Fizz! A starshell right over our bows then it came. We were "travelling" by then and we had spread out.

" It was marvellous how we got through—the shooting was plentiful but not quite good enough; perhaps we were not expected.   A lot of the stuff was going over our heads.   I was fascinated by one ship on my port beam which looked just like a giant catherine wheel on Guy Fawkes night.   Something made me look ahead again, and it was just as well, for we were steering straight for one of the merchant ships (' A ' in the picture).

" My point-five gunners were concentrating on its bridge and a few sparks were flying off it.   We had to go hard a-port to avoid ramming her, and I just remembered to pull the string which drops the depth charges.   The first did not go, but the second went all right. I could see the name on her bow, but it somehow did not stay in my memory—at the time it seemed rather like some French word like *Aiglon*; perhaps it will come back to me one day. For ages, it seemed, the charge did not go off, then I felt a bump, and simultaneously the

[1] The passage which follows is a facsimile extract from Lt. Leaf's diary.

escort vessel 'B' opened fire, to which we replied. I could see Pete and Tom ahead, but I did not look round to see the effect of our attack. The Oerlikon gunner saw it go off abreast her foremast, so it probably strained her a bit. Later we looked back and saw a good deal of shooting going on at random in the convoy. They did chase us for a bit, using starshells, but we got away. One man was wounded, and so was Pete in 83; apart from that the boats were unscathed except for a few odd bullet- and small shell-holes. We returned just before breakfast, and were we dehydrated!"

Later in the month depth charges were used again against German shipping off the coast of Holland, this time by Lt. Cdr. G. E.. Bailey, R.N.V.R.

Since Jermain first worked it out in the winter of 1940, the depth-charge technique had rarely been used against surface ships. Because of the very short distance ahead of the enemy at which the depth charges must be laid, this type of attack is the most hazardous of all. Each opportunity that arose called for outstanding determination in crossing the enemy's track only a few yards from his bows.

For a dashing attack under the bows of a trawler, in which his boat was riddled with gunfire and only one of his crew remained unwounded, Lt. Cdr. Bailey won the Distinguished Service Order.[1]

THE MENACE FROM THE AIR

By the end of 1941 our aircraft had begun to challenge the Germans in the air supremacy which they had held over the Straits and the Channel since the fall of France. Even then, however, it was many months before we could claim to have established an equal supremacy ourselves.

During those months our Coastal Forces returning at dawn from operations off the enemy coast were liable to air attack unless fighter escort could be provided and maintained, and often, of course, this depended on weather conditions over the aerodromes.

The job, for example, of escorting landing craft on one of the many minor combined operations which were becoming more and more numerous during the summer of 1942, a job often carried out by M.G.Bs. or M.Ls., was, for this reason, extremely hazardous.

On the south coast Lt. Cdr. W. G. Everitt, R.N., was the Senior Officer of a flotilla of motor gunboats which attended almost every one of these early raids, including the assault on the radar station at Bruneval; and Lt. Cdr. T. Cartwright, R.N.V.R., who subsequently commanded the flotilla, carried on the work at Dieppe and on many other raids.

The danger from air attack by cannon-fighters was clearly demonstrated on the morning of 5th June, 1942.

Three M.Ls. were disposed in support of the landing craft returning from the commando raid on Boulogne, when, soon after sunrise, six Messerschmitt 109 fighters took advantage of the temporary absence of the Spitfire escort. For twelve minutes they were able to press home their attack on the M.Ls., passing no more than 100 feet overhead at the end of each run. M.L. 137 was singled out and bore the brunt of the attack. Her Commanding Officer, Lt. W. Tomlinson, R.N.V.R., was very severely wounded at an early stage, but he continued to con the ship and to fire a Lewis gun until the end of the action. The coxswain was hit by a cannon shell which severed his leg, and in the subsequent attacks two officers and ten of the crew were seriously wounded. Fourteen of the total ship's company of nineteen were now casualties.

In these dreadful straits there were many examples of magnificent courage and fortitude.

---

[1] He was killed two years later in July, 1944, when the ship in which he was serving was torpedoed by E boats north of Le Havre, during the early stages of the invasion of Normandy.

Able Seaman L. Bowden, with a broken arm and a wound in the leg, crawled into the tiller flat to attend to the airlocks in the piping system of a part of the anti-aircraft armament. Able Seaman A. Cross was severely injured in the hand, but remained at the wheel, and later, when the steering-gear had been put out of action, manned the emergency tiller.

The coxswain, Petty Officer B. W. Matthews (in the words of the official report), " although suffering considerable agony, remained cheerful and showed great spirit until his death."

Meanwhile the First Lieutenant, Sub-Lt. L. J. Hutchins, R.N.V.R., " seemed to be in every part of the ship all the time, firing guns where a man had been wounded, coping with the many pans of ammunition which had been jammed by enemy bullets, and even finding time during the action to give tablets of morphia to the more seriously injured. The action over, he worked indefatigably at the task of administering first aid to the casualties." This description of Hutchins' resource was written by a fellow officer who was wounded and who concludes, " I find it impossible to pay him too high a tribute."

Besides the steering-gear, the starboard engine had been put out of action and the port engine damaged; but the M.L. still kept going.

A steam gunboat commanded by Lt. I. R. Griffiths, R.N., which had been part of the covering force for the commando raid, now came to the rescue and began to tow the damaged M.L., while another S.G.B., commanded by Lt. J. D. Ritchie, R.N., came alongside, took off the casualties and proceeded back to harbour at high speed.

These two gunboats were engaged in a short, sharp action a few weeks later which inspired the German propaganda machine to more than usually ambitious flights of fancy.

From the *Völkischer Beobachter*

" British M.T.B. sunk by ramming

" Berlin, 12th July.

" In the campaign in the Channel the comparatively rare occurrence in modern naval warfare of the sinking of an enemy warship by ramming took place.

" During the night of 9th/10th July, a few German motor minesweepers were carrying out their task in the Channel, when they were suddenly engaged by superior British naval forces, consisting of two destroyers and at least four M.G.Bs. One of our small motor minesweepers had to defend herself at close range against an attack by several enemy vessels. In these circumstances the Commanding Officer of the motor minesweeper decided to ram. He turned towards the nearest British M.G.B. at utmost speed and throwing the helm hard over, rammed her in the way of the bridge. The enemy vessel was cut half through. When the wreck became disengaged it was set on fire and sunk. By this daring action the Commanding Officer shook off the remaining enemy vessels. In spite of severe damage to his own boat and casualties among the crew, the daring young Commanding Officer, Leutnant zur See (Sub-Lieutenant) Mohn, and his brave crew, managed to bring their boat back safely to base."

The story was amplified by the Calais Radio in a broadcast in English in which a full report by Leutnant zur See Mohn was quoted:

" Shortly after midnight yellow strips of tracer bullets suddenly appeared, but soon quietened down. The only thing seen in the pitch darkness was the foamy wake made by the floating part of the minesweeping gear. Later on, the dark shadow of a vessel emerged from the night. It was an enemy motor gunboat. There were sure to be a lot of Tommies hanging around somewhere under cover of night. The enemy were absolutely superior in size, artillery and speed. The British boat was clearly silhouetted against the horizon, so we could approach without being discovered too soon. The minesweeping gear was cut away and the minesweeper dashed on at full speed, getting the gunboat right under the bridge. There was a thundering crash. The stem of our boat ripped open the side of the Britisher. The collision was so tremendous that the bows of the minesweeper were forced up on to the enemy vessel, crushing it down into the water. Then our boat glided back to its normal position. Water was pouring in through a gaping hole in the enemy vessel, which listed and began to sink. One of our gunners had fired one round of incendiary ammunition at the enemy. We had no time to look for survivors, as enemy naval forces might emerge from the darkness at any moment.

" Our patrol boat, which proceeded to the place at dawn, found nothing but a couple of half-burned life-jackets and wreckage. There was no doubt that the Tommy had sunk, because with a leak like that there could have been no chance of its being towed home. On our side, the shock was terrific. One of the gunners was sent sliding from stern to bows. Many a man complained of an awful headache for some time after having been hurled against some hard part of the ship. The guns were temporarily put out of action, but the engines and hull of the ship were not seriously damaged and there was no need for us to be towed back to port. In a few days, the boat will have recovered from the night's task.

" This is the first time that such a thing has happened in the Channel and is just another eloquent proof that nothing is impossible for our light naval forces."

What Really Happened

Our force consisted of two Steam Gunboats (not " two destroyers and at least four M.G.Bs."), under the command of Lt. Ritchie and Lt. Griffiths, and as they steamed north-ward up the enemy convoy route off Etaples, on this very dark and rainy night, they met six or seven German R boats sweeping for mines.

" Some time after 2 a.m.," writes Ritchie, " I spotted a shape on the port bow, on opposite course, going quite slowly and passing about 200 yards away. It was against a lightish bit of the horizon at the time, though there were thick clouds ahead, and I decided to engage on opposite courses, turn round his stern, and then fight it out on the same course from the other side.

" Before the enemy was abeam I could see three ships, so we engaged the leader, Griff joining in about five seconds later. We both got a number of hits on this leading boat, and when I saw Griff had taken it on, I shifted target two to the right, hoping he would shift one right when he had finished with the front one. My Rolls two-pounder gunner was doing a grand job, scoring a hit every time, at a range of about 100 yards. We could now see two more Huns, and each was closer to us than the last, so they must have been in port quarter line. We shifted target again to No. four, who'd started to challenge us, and we hit him for about fifteen or twenty seconds. Then I put the telegraphs to full ahead to get round astern of No. five, who was, I thought, last in the line and we fairly plastered him at about 50 yards, but for a very short while, for I suddenly saw No. six only about 30 or 35 yards ahead. I think I was just putting the wheel over to go round to port when I saw him through the pom-pom flashes, and I don't think I managed to say anything before he hit us.

" We were doing about 20 knots at the time, so we hit fairly hard, and he came into the mess-deck, 16 feet of him, poked his stem head through the upper deck and dented the pom-pom mounting. The hole he made was 22 feet high and 18 feet long at the upper deck level, roughly triangular in shape with the apex 10 inches short of the keel.[1]

[1] " I'm afraid it's a bit too big for the collision mat, sir," the First Lieutenant reported later to the Captain, with a large grin on his face (so the story is told).

" We were all thrown on to our faces and our only casualty was suffered at this period—Ron Ashby,[1] my relief, who was to take over command of the boat at noon next day, broke a tooth on the rudder indicator. As all the water rushed in we heeled over to about 30 degrees and came upright only very very slowly. When we did get there John [2] broke the verbal silence with: ' Has anyone got a nasty taste in his mouth? ' which wrecked my vivid mental picture of a cold wait in the sea and a not-far-distant acquaintance with an Oflag.

" The Hun broke round alongside and Able Seaman Ross, the pom-pom gunner (aged 19), seized the opportunity to empty all his Ready Use ammunition into the fo'c'sle and bridge of the R boat. As she came clear John put the telegraphs to slow, and I remember very vividly seeing her, rather like a drawing in the *Illustrated London News*, by our special artist, with most of her starboard side removed to show the interior and with no bows at all. There was no one in sight on her bridge or upper deck and she didn't fire at all—not even the ' one incendiary ' claimed by the Calais Radio. The Rolls gun took up the battle as soon as he could bear, and there were some lovely hits on what remained of the starboard side of the unfortunate R boat.

" We were by then quite out of control, and the waves were breaking over the bows a little. The lights in the mess-deck were all on, so there was a blaze of light out into the darkness around, which may account for the German story that they set us on fire. John put some of them out by breaking the bulbs, but finally we had to remove the fuses, and, until he could find the right ones, the L.T.O. switched off all the lights, so that for the next ten minutes the ship was in darkness. As soon as we had lost contact with the enemy, we stopped and proceeded to ditch ammunition, move it aft, get the crew (or as many as could be spared) aft and to try to get some water into the after mess-decks. When we stopped I saw we had about a foot of freeboard forward, and went ahead again, slow, so as to keep moving."

Meanwhile Lt. Griffiths records his part from the beginning of the action:

" When I took over R boat No. one from Jock Ritchie, my West Country Dead-eyed Dick—Leading Seaman Jordan—did the most marvellous job with the Rolls two-pounder. His first shot hit it and set it on fire, and then, with A.B. Doran shoving the ammo in at colossal speed, he continued to hit the target which he had so nicely illuminated. All other guns were right on the target too—I had slowed right down, and at 90 to 100 yards they couldn't miss it. She went up finally with a big wallop and I passed directly over the spot where she had been, but saw nothing but some bits of wood. I believe that that R boat was destroyed.

" I had seen two others go past, and knowing Jock had gone off to the northward and not wanting to get mixed up with him in the dark, I went to play my own game with the two I'd seen. I engaged at about 100 yards and had closed in to about 50 yards, firing all the time and seeing lumps fly off their superstructure, when the starboard point-five gunner yelled ' Torpedoes starboard quarter, sir! ' I looked over the side and saw two minesweeping floats whooshing along. Immediately came the thought, ' This is no place to get propellers and wire rope mixed up,' so I turned hard a-port, and while I did so the Germans altered course away, made smoke and cut their sweeps, so that I lost touch with them.

" By this time I wondered what had happened to Jock, so I signalled ' Am disengaging.' A horrid flat voice from Drew, my telegraphist, said ' No acknowledgement, sir,' up my voice-pipe. I remember feeling my face go white with anxiety. I turned to old Woj Bate [3]

[1] Lt. R. R. W. Ashby, R.N.V.R., who had escaped from Hong Kong, where he had been serving in the Power Boat Flotilla there—the " Wind Thunder Boats."
[2] Sub-Lt. J. C. Erskine-Hill, R.N.V.R., the First Lieutenant.
[3] Lt. W. O. J. Bate, R.N.V.R., the First Lieutenant.

and said, ' We'll bloody well stay here until we find Jock—all day if necessary.' I poked off to the northward to hunt for him, and a great weight came off my mind when he piped up to Dover W/T."

Ritchie was under way again, although, as he says, " the most maddening business began. All I wanted to do was to get the brightly lit French coast behind me, but I couldn't get it to stay there. It went slowly round for about 170 degrees and then after a spell of ' half ahead port, slow astern starboard, wheel hard a-starboard,' it started to move off in the other direction for 170 degrees. However, things got better as we moved the weights aft, and I soon went on to 8 knots, half ahead together, steering by rudder only.

" About this time I sent a signal to Griff : ' My course 321 degrees, speed eight knots.' I said 321 degrees because it was the course from the scene of the action to the Bullock Bank buoy, which was lit in those days, and which I wanted to find; also I wanted Griff to know that I was going there. When Griff found us, a few minutes later, he was much amused that a ship yawing 90 degrees either way should make a signal with a course so nicely stated.

" Now that Griff had joined up I went on gradually (for I was rather nervous of the bulkhead, in spite of the excellent job of shoring it up, begun by the telegraphist and completed by John Erskine-Hill) to the revolutions for 14 knots, which meant that we were making good about 12. Griff kept some way ahead to navigate and lead us. We went under our own power to within a quarter of a mile of Newhaven, and then Griff took us in tow alongside, bows to stern, and berthed us."

So much, then, for Leutnant zur See Mohn's claim that " there was no doubt that the Tommy had sunk." Whether the collision was a manœuvre of the Leutnant's own choosing can be known for certain only to the Leutnant himself and perhaps to his helmsman and those who heard him give the orders on his bridge. Amongst others who hear the story, there will be many sceptics.

There remains one further comment, by Griffiths, on the German account. " I don't believe any of it," he says, " except about the headaches. Those headaches were of a permanent nature and the complaints were made to the Devil in Hell. It seems that the Nazis can communicate directly with their fatal casualties."

CHAPTER VII

AIR/SEA RESCUE

AIR/Sea Rescue is a duty shared between the Royal Air Force and the Royal Navy. The R.A.F. uses H.S.Ls. (High-speed Launches) and the Navy uses specially constructed R.M.Ls. (Rescue Motor Launches), which are larger and slower. Besides these vessels specially designed for the work many other ships have been required to go to the assistance of airmen in distress, amongst them all kinds of Coastal Force craft.

Air/Sea Rescue is an all-weather job, for the airmen are just as likely to crash into the sea when it is rough as when it is smooth; the boats must put forth in foul weather as well as fair, for broken hull frames are of no consequence when there are lives to be saved. The R.M.Ls. based on the east coast, for example, have done their unspectacular work magnificently, far out in the North Sea, searching in all weathers for the crews of our own and American aircraft damaged in the air battles over the Continent.

With the steady increase in air activity, A.S.R. work increased proportionately. One day some time ago a number of Flying Fortresses of the U.S.A.A.F. ran out of fuel when returning from a raid. Their fuel consumption had been worked out to a nicety, providing a certain margin for attack by enemy fighters. This attack had lasted much longer than expected and they had consequently run out of petrol over the Channel. Ten of them had to make forced landings in the sea, but every one of the hundred men who took to their rubber boats was rescued.

With our ever-increasing control of the skies, the danger of being attacked by enemy aircraft while engaged on A.S.R. work grew steadily less. But in the summer of 1942 it was still a serious menace. For example, on the 15th July in the course of a fighter sweep, Wing Commander " Paddy " Finucane, D.S.O., D.F.C., was shot down into the sea 7 miles southwest of Boulogne. Two H.S.Ls. and two M.Ls. were directed to attempt the rescue, although it was later discovered that he had not survived the crash. The boats had reached the Bullock Bank in mid-Channel at about 1.20 in the afternoon when the first of a series of devastating attacks was carried out on them by ten Focke Wulf 190 fighters. First H.S.L. 140 was hit, suffering casualties of one killed and one wounded. One of the aircraft, however, was seen to be damaged. The remainder made H.S.L. 138 (commanded by F/O. W. E. Walters, R.A.F.) the object of their concentrated attention.

Walters was wounded in the first attack on his boat and fell forward into the fo'c'sle; the forward gunner was also wounded, but in spite of that the H.S.L. kept firing until all its ammunition was expended. By that time it was burning from stem to stern. The nursing orderly, Aircraftman W. Morgan, who had been badly wounded in the arm, continued to carry out his duties and attended to the casualties below. Every member of the ship's company had by now been wounded and the fo'c'sle was full of smoke. The attacks continued and a moment later Morgan was killed.

Flying Officer Walters and Aircraftman M. Pring, themselves both wounded in the legs but realising the imminent necessity for abandoning ship, struggled to carry the gunner to the upper deck.

When finally they succeeded they collapsed on the deck. Aircraftman Pring was the first to come to, and he pushed the other two over the side and joined them in the water.

Having set the H.S.L. on fire the German fighters switched their attack to M.L. 139. Her Commanding Officer—Lt. A. R. S. Hodgson, R.N.V.R., records that they made five runs, in the first of which the fuel tanks were set on fire. The second caused another fire aft and a number of casualties, but in each of these runs one aircraft was damaged and the second time pieces were seen to fall off the target. Each successive attack increased the damage and the casualties.

The fires were the most serious menace, however. The methyl-bromide extinguishers had been released in the petrol compartment, but the fire was only partially extinguished and the compartment was filled with the deadly gas. In spite of this, Acting Chief Motor Mechanic L. Adams and Able Seaman G. Sandford, armed with hoses and Pyrenes, entered this most inaccessible compartment without breathing apparatus and put out the fire. They both worked in this confined space well knowing that the tank, with over a thousand gallons of high-octane spirit, had been pierced and that petrol vapour was present which might explode at any time; and in addition the ship was still under fire. In the opinion of the Commanding Officer the ship was saved by the bravery and resource of these two men, who were later awarded the C.G.M.

When the Germans flew off and the fires had been brought under control M.L. 139, with two officers and two ratings wounded, went at once to the assistance of the burning H.S.L., where three survivors were taken from the water.

M.L. 141 which had so far escaped attack, although she had been engaging the Germans as they attacked the others, rescued seven more survivors of the H.S.L. from their raft and proceeded to destroy the blazing wreck by depth charges. Twenty minutes later six more F.W. 190s appeared, and although our Spitfires were protecting the other M.L., the enemy managed to carry out one run on 141 from ahead, in the course of which one officer was killed and three ratings were wounded. The Commanding Officer, Lt. P. M. C. Williams, R.N.R., records that several aircraft were seen to be hit, two of which emitted clouds of black smoke which was clearly distinguished from their exhaust smoke at full throttle. One of these was seen to crash some distance away.

That was the last attack, and the three damaged boats came safely to harbour with their load of wounded. The courage of their crews under this fierce onslaught showed most eloquently how the human spirit can rise above such grim horror and misfortune and the ugliness of war.

THE BATTLE SPREADS WESTWARD

During this active summer of 1942 a new scene of action for the Coastal Forces made its appearance when the E boats began to explore the possibilities of the Western Channel as a hunting-ground; and at first they met with considerable success there.

Clearly they must be dealt with, and who better to deal with them than Lt. Cdr. Hichens and his flotilla, who had had wide experience of E boat fighting in the North Sea? His flotilla was now fully reboated with the new and more heavily armed " seventy-one-foot-six " M.G.B. and renumbered the 8th Flotilla. The night of the 14th July, the next night after his arrival in the West Country, found him with a force of three boats lying in wait 12 miles North of Alderney for the E boats which were known to be operating from Cherbourg.

Should no E boats appear before two o'clock in the morning, the force was allowed to close in towards the French coast or the Channel Islands to seek out enemy patrols or convoys. The time approached, and Hichens, watching the Alderney light flashing 4 every 20 seconds at full brilliancy according to its charted characteristic, decided that failing all else and despite the freshening wind he would go through the Alderney Race and have a look at the coastline so familiar to him in peace-time. They started up, and he led them south until the outlines of the island itself were clearly visible. Suddenly—

" Light bearing green 65, sir."

Hichens looked and saw a small white light on the horizon. He continued his quiet 12 knots on two engines close under the north shore of Alderney. Soon through binoculars he could make out two dim hulls and in a few minutes he realised he was gradually overtaking them.

" The little lamp, carefully shaded from ahead, flicked out the thrilling signal: ' Enemy in sight,' " writes Hichens. " Silently, signlessly, the unit fell into line ahead—the fighting formation."

With a strong head wind they could not be heard, and it was so dark that they were unlikely to be seen. The enemy ships were large trawlers, clearly visible now, proceeding on a westerly course and making about 8 knots. The leading gunboat was soon level with the rearmost enemy vessel. She challenged, and Lt. Cdr. Hichens gave the order to fire.

" The next few minutes," he writes, " provided a welter of impressions for me, beginning with a crescendo of noise and light, passing through tense anxiety and ending with stark fear such as I had never known before. All our guns burst into life. With the gun muzzles a few feet from one's ear the noise was terrific, the light from the muzzle flashes, the tracer, and the bursting shells dazzling and bewildering, the effect most gratifying. That trawler, hard hit and surprised, scarcely returned the fire at all."

The gunboats were increasing speed again, and as Hichens was overhauling the first trawler, with intent to make across her bows towards the second, he saw also a small tanker ahead. So that was it—an escorted tanker, with the rest of her escorts ahead of her no doubt. The time to attack the tanker was now—the way was open and already one of the rear escorts was subdued. Hichens flashed to the gunboat immediately astern of him to disregard his movements. He was planning a depth-charge attack.

" I lifted the throttles high as we headed in across her bows. The little boat leaped forward quivering with unleashed power, her guns projecting streams of brilliant light into the rapidly nearing hull.

" Head[1] was by me now. ' Stand by to let go port depth charge,' I yelled. The stream of shells hitting the enemy vessel, some penetrating, some bursting on the outside, lit up the outline of the ship, as though she was one of Brock's famous firework images on the last night of Henley. In the vivid scintillating glare her bow waves, pressed outward and upward at what must have been her maximum speed, caught my eye and held me transfixed.

" I had been conning the coxswain on, at least so I thought; but in the uproar and confusion I doubt if he had heard or understood. Would we clear that upthrown white bow wave, that sharp straight bow? I thought not, but I could do no more. It was out of my control, Curtis had the wheel and I must leave it to him. I remembered anxiously how we had practised this very attack on a trawler off the entrance to Harwich; how control on that occasion, too, had slipped from me in the end; how Curtis had flipped the stern of old 64 right in under the overhanging bows; how the trawler's crew had run in astonishment to watch, and had received our wash right over them and high up on the wheelhouse; how we had missed them by a bare two feet; how I went back to apologise and how stuffy they had been. Well, there would be no going back to apologise this time! "

They cleared the enemy's bows by less than 10 feet, receiving, as they did so, a tornado of fire, not only from the escort vessel they had maltreated, now astern and to port of the tanker, but also from the outraged tanker herself. Blow after blow fell upon them and the boat trembled; but they had got there. The depth charge went down and a few seconds later

---

[1] Lt. F. J. Head, R.N.V.R., his First Lieutenant (since killed in a motor-cycle accident).

came a shattering underwater explosion. "Just one of those rare occasions when everything goes right," remarks Hichens at this point, and goes on :

"It was at that moment that I knew real fear. The wheelhouse was a blaze of brilliant light. It seemed that we must be irretrievably afire. It was obvious that the entire upper deck crew had been knocked out by that infernal blast. Something had to be done about it at once. My sensations at that moment are still vivid. I was stricken with fear, real fear. I remember thinking desperately, 'I shall never get back, I shall never see Catherine or the children again.' I fancy I was near to panic; but fortunately the fear of panic had a stimulating effect. I was literally galvanised into activity, the activity that was required."

The wheelhouse was ablaze as Hichens stepped into it. Head followed him. Together they battled with flames distorted and magnified by flares which had been lit by the exploding ammunition. When darkness was restored there, they turned to the blazing oil which, escaping from the power pipes serving the pom-pom, had reached the after magazine. The flames were licking round the loaded Oerlikon pans. They rushed down the narrow passage-way to jump on the pool of fire and worked desperately until, in a few minutes, this situation, too, was in hand.

When Hichens returned to the "dustbin" he found the throttle hard up and the boat, light of fuel, making 45 knots (over 50 miles an hour) and leaving a clear straight wake behind her. Petty Officer Curtis, whose superb steering in the action drew unstinted admiration from Hichens, had swept her away to seaward in a wide curve ahead of the amazed forward convoy escorts, and they were now tearing north.

The attack had taken place less than 2 miles north of Alderney, and with glasses the tanker could still be made out—stopped and burning in a cloud of smoke. An occasional starshell burst there to the southward, and in the light some small fast craft could be seen circling about her.

Hichens stopped his boat and called up the others: all was well with them. His boat was damaged. One of his crew had been killed and another mortally wounded, but the enemy had been surprised and badly shaken. He had further surprises to come. In the six weeks that the 8th M.G.B. Flotilla remained in the West Country, this was not the only time they made their presence felt.

INTRUDERS AT CHERBOURG

During the last fortnight of July, Hichens waited in vain for the E boats. They knew well enough that he was after them and they became wary. They established a secondary base at St. Peter Port in the island of Guernsey, so that it was never certain whether they would return there or to Cherbourg after an operation.

On the 1st August, 1942, four boats of the 8th Flotilla—"the estimable eighth," as it had been named by Cdr. R. F. B. Swinley, R.N., the Training Commander at the "working-up" base—set out from Dartmouth on a typical anti-E boat patrol. Hichens was embarked with Lt. "Bussy" Carr, and the boats following astern were commanded by Lt. "Boffin" Campbell, Lt. G. F. Duncan, R.C.N.V.R.,[1] and Lt. T. Ladner, R.C.N.V.R.

Darkness found them reducing speed in a thick belt of fog. It did not look like being a happy patrol. At midnight, however, their spirits rose, for they received a report of E boats to the north of Cherbourg making for our coast. Hichens thought quickly. Cherbourg was 65 miles away; they would make for it and, lying off, await the enemy's return. From later reports it seemed that there were two groups of E boats operating, both on a northerly

---

[1] Known in the flotilla as "Fearless and resolute George."

course. Whether they intended mining or patrolling on our convoy route, they would be out some time; there was no hurry.

Then a different report came. The E boats had turned back—probably disliking the fog. "There was only one thing to do," writes Hichens. "Go like hell."

The E boats had only about 26 miles to go before they made safety—but they would see no reason for hurrying in such weather conditions. The gunboats had 65 miles to go before they could give battle—but they were going all out. It was fair enough.

The gunboats sped on. The impression of speed seemed to be enhanced, rather than lessened, by the poor visibility. Then the fog began to lift and soon they found themselves roaring through a clear still night, without pause, until they sighted the lights which the enemy had ordered against his own boats' return—the Casquets, Alderney, Cap de la Hague. Once past Cap de la Hague it was a case of action stations, tin-hats, and an ever-growing excitement.

At last the chosen position, 3 miles due north of Cherbourg, was reached: a row of lights along the breakwater reassured them of the accuracy of their navigation. They cut engines, and in the sudden silence they caught a sound, "a subdued rumble like the residue of a long drawn-out and slowly dying thunderclap." It came from the harbour and meant, they realised angrily, that the E boats must be just entering. But surely not all of them? The reports had clearly indicated two groups of E boats; possibly one only had arrived and the other was yet to come, having taken the more westerly route indicated by the reports, and sweeping south to pick up the Alderney light. Dismissing the unwelcome thought that these E boats might have put into St. Peter Port, they waited, reckoning that the enemy, if he came, would be on a south-easterly course close in to the shore.

Their luck was in—first the faintest murmur, then the muffled throbbing: they were coming.

"Start up."

It was a great chance for the gunboats. The enemy could not be more than 2 miles from the breakwater, and they would be going slowly now.

"Course south 15 east."

When they were within a mile of the breakwater they saw the dark hull of a motionless ship lying half a mile to the south-east. Soon it was possible to make her out: she was apparently a German torpedo boat, like a small destroyer. What a chance, had they only carried torpedoes! But they were gunboats and could only spare her a wistful thought. The E boats were the things—and there they were, four in line ahead and scarcely moving, probably awaiting permission to enter harbour. "I felt a great surge of triumph," writes Hichens. Altering course slightly to starboard, the gunboats came in astern of the enemy, and, beginning with the rear boat, moved slowly up the line raking each in turn with devastating fire. The Germans were completely and utterly taken by surprise. The German torpedo boats, of which they now saw two, and watchers on the shore must have found the scene astonishing: its significance was not in fact grasped for eight minutes, during which the gunboats slowly circled the unfortunate enemy craft, who made practically no reply. Then the enemy began to wake up. Here is Hichens' own description of what followed.

"Shore batteries put up innumerable starshell, and 4-inch shells from the torpedo boats and other batteries began to sing by, bursting with brilliant effect. The sight was unforgettable. Pale yellow-green luminosity from the slowly dropping shower of starshells, fierce red, green and yellow streaks of tracer interlacing in fantastic patterns, vivid splodges of light where the big shells were bursting; roar of engines, crash and stutter of guns; the almost silent, motionless line of E boats, glittering white in the artificial radiance and seemingly strangely helpless in their immobility; the dark line of the breakwater spitting bright flashes of flame irregularly, viciously, up and down the line, like a crazed xylophonist striking his keys wantonly and at random; the cautiously approaching towering hulls of the two torpedo boats lit brightly by the occasional bursts of our 2-pounder shells on their sides, still obviously puzzled, but the flashes from their guns gaining in momentum as they closed; the line of gunboats weaving and storming round their quarry, still magnificently together in tight line-ahead formation, the spray thrown back at 24 knots reflecting the green effulgence of the starshells in a luminous halo round the hulls.

"It was," he comments, "no time for losing oneself in the wild beauty of the scene."

However inaccurate the enemy fire from their big guns, it was inevitable that the gunboats would be hit and, if they stayed too long, stopped. For twelve minutes Hichens had dominated the situation, but many of the guns were falling silent with stoppages, as the pace of the action began to tell. The moment had come to make a get-away, and he took it. The M.G.Bs. gave the still surprised torpedo boats the benefit of a final burst at point-blank range as they passed to seaward as swiftly and unexpectedly as they had come.

"It was a full ten minutes," says Hichens, "before the enemy appreciated our absence. To our unbounded delight the battle still raged behind us." Shore batteries were belabouring their own ships, and they, spurred to tardy and misplaced retaliation, were firing towards the shore.

Four miles away, the M.G.Bs. paused in the friendly dark to "count the cost and enjoy the fun." They had two casualties—neither serious, a few holes in the boats, two of which were leaking forward: that was all. They had got off as lightly as they deserved. Looking back, they could see a distant glow in the sky which resolved itself into two bright pillars of fire and a cheer went up from the gunboats. Two of the enemy craft were well and truly on fire.

Hichens guessed that the enemy would be angered by this assault upon his very doorstep. The measure of his anger was clearly demonstrated by the broadcast from Breslau, given out in English at 11.30 p.m. on the 2nd August:

"This evening in its nine o'clock News Service the B.B.C. gave a totally false account of the naval engagement which took place in the Channel last night. It stated that two German motor torpedo boats had been sunk and added the absurd allegation that the Germans had opened fire on their own ships. The facts were clearly stated in to-day's German war communiqué, in which it was reported that off the French coast German patrol boats were engaged with British E boats and gunboats. It is probable that two of the British E boats were sunk, and it was observed that several further British craft suffered hits. None of the German vessels was either sunk or damaged. From the prominent place given to this item in the B.B.C.'s News Service it is evident that the British Government is experiencing the greatest difficulty in discovering material upon which even false reports of success can be based."

The First of the "D" Boats

Meanwhile the crescendo of activity in the Straits of Dover was rising to its climax. The night of the 20th July brought an example of what a small, but really determined, force of motor gunboats can do to an escorted convoy using, as their principal weapon, the threat of torpedoes which, in fact, they were not carrying.

The force of three M.G.Bs. was led by Lt. H. P. Cobb, R.N.V.R., and it was to search for enemy patrols south of Boulogne. The other two boats were commanded by Lt. G. D. A. Price, R.N.V.R., and Lt. A. Gotelee, R.N.V.R.

There was an additional interest in this battle in that Gotelee's boat—M.G.B. 601—was the first of a new class. This class was the result of a requirement for a larger boat, with greater range of action, that could stand up to heavier seas. Designed by the Fairmile Company, it was the lineal descendant of the " C " Class M.G.B. and was known as the " D " Class. The " D " boats were mass produced on the Fairmile prefabrication system, and, in the years that followed, they were destined to achieve great things in the Coastal Forces war.

This night of the 20th July, then, was the first on which a " D " boat had been in action. It was following astern of two " C " boats. At about midnight the force was diverted from its original patrol and ordered to intercept a group of enemy ships near Boulogne. Three-quarters of an hour later, a few miles north of Cap Gris Nez, they came up with the convoy, which consisted of a merchant vessel escorted by several armed trawlers and a large number of smaller craft, probably R boats.

The Senior Officer of the M.G.Bs. reported to the Vice-Admiral, Dover, that a torpedo target was present in the hope that it might be possible to despatch M.T.Bs. to deal with the convoyed merchant ship; but the weather was too rough for the small M.T.Bs. to reach the scene in time. A signal was made informing the Senior Officer of this and telling him to withdraw if the enemy were in superior force.

It seems that Cobb did not receive this signal. The enemy was certainly in superior force, but so far from withdrawing, he led the force straight in to the attack with the greatest resolution, engaging the enemy merchant vessel at close range to starboard and several of the escorts to port. His intention was probably to deliver a depth-charge attack, passing close ahead of the merchant ship. He turned towards the enemy and went straight in, in face of a terrible concentration of fire from the escorts. The boat was hit time after time, and before the attack could be completed she was ablaze. Possibly she was rammed by one of the trawlers after her engines had been put out of action, and in any case it is believed that she subsequently blew up, because a large explosion was seen soon after her last signal had been received reporting that she was on fire. Some survivors were taken prisoner by the enemy, but Cobb was not amongst them.

Several of the enemy ships had been hit and were also burning. Gotelee, who was badly wounded, writing of his part in the action says: " I was almost at once completely out of touch with the others owing to my wireless set having been blown to pieces, and thereafter I had to play by myself. We succeeded in doing this for fifty-five minutes, and I like to think that by crossing the T of the convoy and keeping moving with varying speeds, mostly rather high, we did persuade the convoy to turn back."

The amount of destruction actually wrought amongst the escort vessels by these three gallant M.G.Bs. cannot yet be known, but the convoy remained stopped for some twenty minutes before turning back at about half-past one, and later re-entering Boulogne.

On the debit side Pat Cobb—a brilliant and courageous officer—had been lost, with his crew and their boat; but on the credit side the first action experience of the " D " boat had been gained, and some of the modifications which were found to be necessary could at once be incorporated in the " D " boats that were still building.

THE PASSAGE OF THE SCHWABENLAND

By August, 1942, the passage of a single German merchant ship through the Dover Strait had become for the enemy a major operation.

In most forms of warfare there is a continual race between measure and counter-measure. The German convoy defence at this time was running neck-and-neck with the new forms of attack which were developing, and on the night of the 6th August, three days after Lt. Cobb's gallant action, it might be said that the counter-measures were leading by a short head.

The steamship *Schwabenland* arrived in Boulogne from the west in the early morning of the 6th. She was a merchantman of about 4,000 tons, and she had an escort of at least fifteen warships—" M " Class minesweepers, flak trawlers and E/R boats. The Germans were determined that she should get through. Soon after eleven o'clock that night her escort formed up round her for the next stage of the journey, and she set off again through the narrows towards Germany. At the same time, a force of M.T.Bs. under the command of Lt. C. W. S. Dreyer, D.S.C., R.N., was creeping in towards the French coast to intercept her as she passed. In company with the three M.T.Bs. were three " C " Class motor gunboats under the command of Lt. D. C. Sidebottom, R.N.V.R.

Suddenly the sky was lit with starshells, while streams of red and green tracer skimmed out over the calm sea. But this fire was not directed at our boats. Some miles away to the south-west the convoy was rounding Cap Gris Nez. Apparently, the outer screen of E/R boats had been mistaken by the inner screen for the British boats which were expected to appear at this juncture. The misunderstanding was watched by our forces " with interest and appreciation " as they crept close in under the French cliffs; for the Senior Officer had conceived the bold plan of crossing ahead of the enemy so as to lie in wait on the shoreward side.

" As we crossed the enemy's bows we could clearly see one of his unfortunate outer screen of E boats brightly lit by a well-placed starshell and being unmercifully shot up by his larger comrades inshore—a pleasant enough sight in itself, but a warning of what we should get the moment we ourselves were discovered."

That moment very soon came, and during the twenty minutes that followed it a violent battle was fought with the powerful forces which surrounded the main target. When our force was discovered, the E/R-boat screen increased speed to attack, and the last of the three M.G.Bs. turned back to engage and draw them off, whilst the remainder went in towards the " M " Class minesweepers of the inner screen. For a brief moment the merchant ship was sighted from the M.T.Bs. before everything was blotted out by the maelstrom of flying tracers and the glare of starshells overhead.

In the first few seconds the Commanding Officer of the second M.T.B. was mortally wounded, and the boat was out of control, while the steering-gear of the third boat had been shot away. Dreyer, in the leader, says, " As we drew closer it really got very hot—I never wish to see anything as hot again. Almost immediately I realised that there was no future at all in my present tactics. So I altered away to port and began to ease down. As we altered round a 40-mm. shell went through the engine-room, putting all three engines out of action, and wounding all the engine-room crew. I had intended to haul off and then go in again, but all question of further attack for us was now finished. We had no engines, steering, guns or wireless, and we were pointing directly away from the convoy and towards Cap Gris Nez.

" The motor mechanic came up to the bridge. He had lost a finger and got some splinters in his arm, but he was very cheerful. ' We've had it, sir,' he said. ' All the electrics are gone and I can't start the engines.' I told Clarkson[1] to prepare to destroy his ship and abandon it, and looked round carefully to see if I could find any of our side. I saw nothing but the

---

[1] Sub-Lt. V. F. Clarkson, R.N.V.R., was the Commanding Officer of the boat in which Dreyer was embarked as Senior Officer of the force.

convoy, which continued to pass us about 500 yards away, keeping up a heavy and moderately accurate fire at us. I had a nasty feeling of complete helplessness, which was greatly enhanced by a lovely sight of the main target lit by a lone starshell. She was passing across our stern at ideal range, bumbling serenely on her way, and we, with two beautiful torpedoes at the ready, couldn't turn round."

Meanwhile, Sidebottom describes how the gunboats steamed down the enemy's line engaging first a minesweeper and then the big ship herself.

" Being so large, she was easy to hit, and the bursts from our shells on her hull and super-structure looked good. It did not occur to us, in the heat of the moment, that it was rather like throwing stones at a house. Perhaps we broke some glass.

" We were so deeply engrossed in our duel with the big ship which was keeping up a heavy and accurate fire and causing us considerable damage, that for a short while we did not appreciate the significance of a stream of tracer coming at us from dead ahead. In a moment, however, it was seen to be coming from another " M " Class minesweeper. We altered course only just in time to avoid being rammed and passed down her starboard side, both boats giving her all they had left. She replied with interest and at first accurately, but the volume of her fire quickly decreased and it was soon evident that both sides had been fairly badly damaged by those close-range broadsides. Almost all our guns were out of action, either through casualties to their crews or having jammed.

" As we passed this last enemy ship one of the M.T.Bs. which had been hit on the bridge and was out of control, though of course we did not know it, was seen approaching us at high speed. She passed close to the leading gunboat and crashed almost head on into the second one."

The Commanding Officer of this second gunboat, Lt. T. J. Mathias, R.N.V.R., rang down full astern, in order to try to avert the collision, but it had no effect, and he subsequently discovered that his telegraphs had been shot away. In spite of this difficulty, however, he managed to manœuvre his boat alongside the more seriously damaged torpedo boat in order to get her in tow. This evolution was interrupted once by two E/R boats, and the gunboat had to draw clear in order to bring her guns to bear and drive off the enemy. At last, at about 2.15 a.m., they were able to get under way and creep slowly towards home, the gunboat with six of her own crew wounded, one of them fatally, towing alongside her the torpedo boat, whose Commanding Officer, Sub-Lt. W. Hay, R.N.R., had been killed and three of her crew wounded.

After passing the last minesweeper, the leading M.G.B. also stopped to take stock of the situation. There was a fire in the mess-deck, where an incendiary bullet had set alight some of the men's bedding, but this was quickly dealt with. The steering controls were cut and an emergency tiller had to be shipped. There were casualties—two of them serious—and these had to be made as comfortable as possible. The jammed guns had to be cleared and men told off to replace the casualties in their crews; and finally one engine was out of action without much prospect of repair.

But in spite of all these things, Sidebottom was chiefly concerned with the fate of the other boats:

" From our own experience it seemed more than probable that they were in need of help, and I decided to follow up in the wake of the disappearing convoy and search for them. There was nothing to be seen at first and the darkness and emptiness of the sea was in marked contrast to the activity in the same area a few minutes earlier, when starshells and gun flashes and tracer had lighted it like the Crystal Palace, and there had been more ships than we really cared to see. After a few minutes we caught a glimpse of the two boats which had collided.

M.G.B. AGAINST E BOATS

E-BOAT ACTION

On 21st April, 1942, Lt. Cdr. R. P. Hichens turned a group of six E boats from their purpose soon after they had left Ostend. In the picture the leading E boat has fired a burst from its forward gun of which four rounds have hit the water and the fifth is striking the M.G.B. above the water-line

It was only for a moment, in the faint light of a distant starshell, but they appeared to be under way. We continued on this same course, until we estimated that we had covered the whole length of the scene of action, without seeing anything more; then we turned to search back again, but closer in shore."

"Gay Laughter from Below"

The boats which had collided were also sighted from the disabled M.T.B. Dreyer was not at all sure whether they were enemy or friend. He signalled with a dim lamp, but they did not answer—indeed, they were very fully occupied with their own problems at the time. With the faint possibility of a tow, the work of destroying the boat was temporarily suspended, and holes which had been made in the hull were plugged. But when the two boats moved off the work had to go on. Dreyer describes how with Cap Blanc Nez no more than a mile away and a breeze that was blowing them slowly ashore, they completed their preparations. "We got the Carley raft overboard and joined the mess-deck cushions to it by a painter so that we shouldn't drift apart. The motor mechanic broke the fuel leads so that the engine-room began to flood with petrol. I remember hearing crashes and gay laughter from below— Minns, the leading telegraphist, was smashing the wireless equipment. All the crew were got overboard and paddled about 50 yards away, and I fired a Very's pistol into the engine-room hatch.

"I had intended to dive overboard as I fired and thought I had done so. I can remember thinking in rather a worried way that I was taking a very long time to reach the water; the next thing I remember was being towed to the raft by the cox'n—O'Garr. The boat had blown up.

"We set out to paddle to England; the sea was quite warm and calm, but we had the slight wind dead against us. What remained of the boat was burning furiously, and we could see right through the skeleton of her afterpart. Slowly she reared up till she was vertical and then slowly slipped down. There was a slight hiss as the fire was quenched by the sea.

"Her going made us feel very lonely, although the cliffs of Blanc Nez were still so close. We paddled fairly ineffectually for nearly an hour, and I was beginning to think of saying that, after all, we might have to go ashore in France, which was getting closer despite our efforts, when we sighted a boat. We shouted and blew a whistle, and it came closer. Almost simultaneously Clarkson, O'Garr and I said, 'Good God! it's an E boat,' and we kept very quiet. Then out of the night came a lovely and very English voice. It said loudly and with some annoyance: 'I can't see these bloody people anywhere.' It was Sidebottom."

The blaze of the exploding M.T.B. had been seen from the gunboat, and she had closed towards it cautiously because of the risk of grounding.

"After some time a float was seen and we stopped engines," Sidebottom goes on. "Owing to one engine being out of action we had difficulty in manœuvring alongside and eventually we decided to chance the Germans on shore having lost interest and gone back to bed; so we turned a signal lamp on the float, which lit it up brilliantly and showed it to be empty. But we hardly had time to feel disappointed, because immediately the light showed a chorus of catcalls and whistles arose from some distance inshore. They were clearly of British origin, so we steered slowly towards them, wishing they would restrain their enthusiasm lest the enemy on the shore should hear them.

"At last we found the float filled with men and with more in the water holding on for support. Heaving lines were thrown to them and they were hauled alongside and quickly hoisted on board. We wasted no time in making away from the all-too-close French cliffs.

"Half-way across we passed the gunboat with the torpedo boat in tow, but because of our casualties we went on at our best speed. Off Dover a large convoy of our own was slowly passing up-Channel. We dodged through the ships like a dog crossing a street and made for the harbour entrance. This was normally lighted with red and green lights on either side of the entrance, when ships were expected to enter or leave, and on seeing these I told the coxswain to steer for them while signals were flashed to the shore. When these were acknowledged, I looked again for the entrance lights and was horrified to see them very close and with a mast standing high between them. We had been steering to pass between the port and starboard navigation lights of a large steamer coming out of the harbour to join the convoy. We made a violent alteration of course and she passed close by, when the real harbour lights appeared behind her and we entered harbour without further incident."

Another attack was launched against the *Schwabenland* that night just east of Calais by a force under the command of Lt. H. P. Granlund, D.S.C., R.N.V.R. His men watched the progress of the earlier battle as they roared across the Straits to take up position for their own attack, and they were well able to see the very fierce resistance they would eventually meet from this powerful escort.

This force had no more success, however, than its predecessor off Cap Gris Nez, and all the torpedo boats were damaged and driven off before they could fire their torpedoes. That commanded by Lt. B. Easton, R.N.V.R., made three determined attempts. At an early stage one engine, his gun turret and his steering were all put out of action, but in spite of that he closed in to attack. Another engine was put out of action, but he made yet a further attempt. He was, however, intercepted by five R boats and so blinded by the tracer that he was forced to disengage without firing torpedoes.

So the *Schwabenland* got through and the Coastal Forces set themselves to work out a new answer to the latest German methods of defence.

DECISION BY RAMMING

The Germans found the attentions of our Coastal Forces, during this active summer of 1942, so embarrassing that in August they decided to lay a defensive minefield in mid-Channel with a dual purpose, partly in order to keep our boats away from their convoy route and partly in order to protect their coast against landings. These mines were laid by E boats and R boats.

The laying was, in itself, a hazardous operation, and led to several brushes with our

M.G.Bs., so the enemy tried various methods to catch us off our guard. On the evening of 16th August, for example, they came out some time before dusk, hoping to complete their lay before our night patrols would be likely to be in position. They chose an evening of poor visibility, so that they would not be spotted by aircraft, and they came out in great force—between twenty and thirty of them.

Two of our small gunboats, led by Lt. G. D. K. Richards, R.N., were just setting out when the alarm was raised, and three other M.G.Bs., under the command of Lt. Sidebottom, were still in Dover harbour, but preparing for a normal anti-E boat patrol. The message came through just as the crews were getting into their seagoing clothes, and four minutes later the three M.G.Bs. were passing out of harbour on their way to intercept the enemy. Thus, two separate forces were closing in on the German minelaying R boats in mid-Channel. Their combined numerical strength was less than a quarter of the enemy's.

During the preceding week the German minelayers had managed to elude our forces and complete their lay on several occasions. Once, when our boats were about to intercept them, engine trouble combined with a signal error spoiled the chance, and the E boats escaped again. On this account, our boats were all the more determined that this new opportunity should not be lost. They did not know, however, that they were about to fight one of the classic Coastal Force actions of the war.

In the dark automatic guns are very difficult to sight, so that quite a long action can be fought at close range without any decisive result. But on this summer evening the sun had only just set and it was far from dark. It was 9.25 p.m. when Sidebottom's gunboats sighted a line of six ships, about the same size as themselves, steaming across their bows on a south-westerly course. The main enemy force had evidently split, but this part of it still out-numbered, by two to one, the M.G.Bs. that were now sweeping in to attack them.

" We closed them fast," writes Sidebottom, " challenging them with a signal lamp to identify themselves. They did not reply. They were clearly the enemy. When we were within 400 yards of their line they had neither opened fire on us nor increased speed to escape, and as we closed still further we could see that they were R boats, and we knew that their maximum speed was no more than 20 knots. We therefore decided to attack the rear of their line, as they were double our strength, and we thought that by throwing their rear into confusion we should make it difficult for their leader to distinguish friend from foe, and so prevent him from coming to their assistance.

" When separated by no more than one cable, we turned to starboard to steam on a parallel course. Our three boats were now in close order in line ahead, with the enemy also in line ahead, but with greater intervals between his boats, 200 yards to port.

" Just as we manœuvred into this position to attack, the other force of two gunboats was sighted away to starboard approaching at high speed, and we flashed them an identification signal so that they would know who was who.

" We were now in a perfect position to make our chosen form of attack, and still without any interference from the enemy. It seemed almost uncanny to be allowed to come nearly alongside them without being fired on, but they either mistook us for another of their own units or they hoped we should mistake them for one of ours and let them pass. They soon had their doubts resolved. At 9.27 p.m., two minutes after first sighting, I pressed the button. The open-fire signal blared at each gun position and a simultaneous broadside of all weapons swept from our three boats into the last two in the enemy line.

" Their reply was instantaneous, not only from the boats we had engaged, but from every gun which could be brought to bear from up their line. In that light and at that range, neither side could easily miss. The air was filled with bright tracer as though all the neon signs in Piccadilly Circus were flying to and fro. Our 2-pounder shells were bursting all over the enemy's hulls, showering sparks like a hammer on an anvil. In a matter of a minute all the guns on our engaged side were out of action after direct hits, and the guns' crews were casualties.

"If the leading boat turned away to disengage, those astern would probably follow her, for the action was too intense for a signal to be passed to them, and the opportunity for them, as yet comparatively undamaged, to finish off the two badly hit enemy vessels would be lost. If she continued as she was, she would be a sitting target and would almost surely be sunk. The other alternative was to turn towards the enemy and try to sink the last boat in his line by ramming. We turned hard a-port and swung out of the line towards our target."

This is Sidebottom's reasoned explanation of a most gallant decision. With nearly all his guns out of action he had one remaining weapon—the stout stem of his ship—and he determined to go in and use it.

"It was only a short distance to cover, but to do so we had to turn at right angles to the enemy line, presenting almost a broadside target to his four leading boats, and we were raked by a concentrated fire. Just before the moment of impact, two shells hit the bridge, bursting and wounding everyone on it.[1] The coxswain collapsed, the wheel spun round, the ship's head swung to port and we passed under the R boat's stern, missing her by a few feet.

"As I was the only one on the bridge still standing, I took the wheel and put it hard to starboard. The boat swung round again, partly helped by the force of the enemy's wash, and her bows crashed into the R boat's port quarter some 20 feet from her stern. My First Lieutenant was thrown across the bridge and stunned by the impact, and the enemy's fire ceased immediately. She heeled well over to starboard, and both boats, locked together, swung to port out of the line. The starboard point-five gunner fired most effectively at the next ahead in the enemy's line, who was already under heavy fire from the other two gunboats.

"Our engines were still running at high speed, keeping our bows forced into the R boat, and as we had too many casualties to make boarding a possibility the only thing to do was to pull our bows out and let the water pour into the large hole we had made, which would, we hoped, sink her. I moved the engine-room telegraphs to stop, but she continued to go ahead; evidently the line had been shot away. An unwounded member of a gun's crew was sent with a message to the engine-room to stop engines. As we slowed, the R boat, whose engines were still running, wrenched herself clear and staggered off into the gathering darkness with smoke billowing out of her."

As soon as the leading boat had turned, with the obvious intention of ramming, the second M.G.B. had moved up into her place and continued to engage the remaining R boats with undiminished vigour. The last of these had been badly damaged in the first few moments of intense fire, but the enemy force was still powerful and the second M.G.B. suffered heavily. Two of the crew were killed and two more were mortally wounded. Her Commanding Officer (Lt. A. D. McIlwraith, R.N.V.R.), her Canadian First Lieutenant (Sub-Lt. L. B. McIlhagga, R.C.N.V.R.), her Navigating Officer and eight of the crew were wounded. But she fought on until the engine-room was hit and she was forced to disengage. As she did so, she struck some underwater wreckage which damaged the rudders and the propeller of the one engine which was still working.

The third gunboat then carried on the fight alone until her guns were put out of action and her Commanding Officer (Lt. N. R. Weekes, R.N.V.R.) was wounded; then she also disengaged.

[1] Including Sidebottom.

THE ATTACK ON THE ENEMY'S VAN

This ferocious battle had lasted only a very short time. While it was going on, Richards' two small gunboats had not been idle. They did not sight the enemy until Sidebottom was about to begin the fight.

They had been delayed by a steering breakdown in Richards' own boat, which had come off the slip after a refit only an hour or two before, and had not had time to complete all her trials. This breakdown could not be repaired, but Leading Motor Mechanic John Wibrin managed to steer the M.G.B., in the heat, noise and cramped space under the exhaust pipes in the after compartment, by moving the rudder bar against the full pressure of water on the rudders, so that it remained in line with the links actuated by the wheel on the bridge. He did this for seventy minutes, which included the period of the engagement. Thus the two small gunboats arrived upon the scene and saw at once that the larger M.G.Bs. were looking after the enemy's rear. Richards, therefore, decided to go for the van, and he roared in to attack the leader.

The two gunboats were much faster than the R boat they were attacking. They engaged it first to port, then turned and circled it, firing to starboard at a range of 150 yards. After two circuits, the enemy lost speed and a fire was seen amidships. Two more circuits brought the enemy to a standstill, and a few moments later she fired a six-star signal cartridge, three red stars and three green.

By now the whole area was enveloped in smoke, and several other six-star signals were lobbing into the air. Sidebottom was able to watch the two small gunboats delivering the *coup de grâce* to their victim because, after wrenching free from the rammed R boat, his M.G.B. lay stopped and licking her wounds. Two of his crew had been killed and nine others, including himself, were wounded. His steering and all his guns, except one pair of light machine guns, were out of action and incendiary bullets had started fires in six separate places. He records that the efforts of the remainder of the crew to get all these things under control " took some minutes."

" In the meantime, we were in the front row of the stalls for the rest of the action. It was noticeable that although we were stopped, the battle did not draw away appreciably. Dickie Richards' two gunboats passed close by firing at the enemy, who in turn was firing recognition or distress signals. If they hoped to bring their undamaged comrades to the rescue, they were unsuccessful, and all they did was to attract more fire from the two boats still in the fight."

At 9.45 p.m., eighteen minutes after it had begun, all firing ceased and Richards took his boat alongside the R boat, which he had silenced and stopped and set on fire. The second M.G.B.—commanded by Sub-Lt. R. M. Barge, R.N.V.R.—was ordered to stand by while he did so. Smoke was issuing from the enemy boat, although the fire which was at first started appeared by now to be extinguished.

As the M.G.B. closed in, the boarding party, which consisted of the First Lieutenant— Sub-Lt. P. G. Lee, R.N.V.R., and Leading Stoker R. Mackenzie—were in readiness.

Almost at once, however, an explosion occurred amidships, spreading flames from stem to stern, whilst the M.G.B. was showered with glass and burning debris.

Barge's boat had meanwhile picked up eight prisoners, six of whom were wounded, and later seven more were found, two of them being wounded. They were picked up by the light of the flames from their blazing ship, which according to Richards' report " rose to a height of 70 or 80 feet."

In this highly successful engagement the two boats suffered very slight damage and only one casualty. As they made their way cheerfully back with their fifteen prisoners, the German guns at Cap Gris Nez began to fire at the burning remains of their own vessel.

The damage to Richards' boat caused some flooding on the mess-deck, which necessitated a return to harbour, and by 11.30 they were alongside. Barge, however, reammunitioned his boat and proceeded to sea again at once to assume anti-E boat patrol until daylight.

The crew of Sidebottom's gunboat, after taking " some minutes " to rig the jury tiller, set course for harbour at slow speed. All the way home they fought the fires and the last one was extinguished as they entered. " As soon as we were alongside the jetty and the engines had been stopped, the whole engine-room crew staggered on deck and collapsed. One of the fuel tanks had been punctured and the fumes from the bilges had been asphyxiating them, but they had carried on without even mentioning their troubles. Of our other two boats, one was already in when we arrived and the third soon followed, limping in on one engine, so the whole force were safely home, though somewhat battered."

On the following night, as we shall see later, an M.T.B. picked up nine Germans from a raft. They were the survivors of a crew of twenty-six and they had been adrift for more than twenty-four hours since their R boat had been rammed by a British motor gunboat. Their boat had sunk, but they were certain that the British boat must have sunk too. The British boat, however, lay alongside in the harbour at which they were landed, although no one had the time or the inclination to show the prisoners how wrong they were.

Their High Command had apparently been equally deluded. Although prisoners had been brought in from two of their boats they only admitted to the loss of one. Their counter-claim was somewhat less optimistic than usual. Here is the communiqué:

" The Führer's Headquarters. 18th August, 1942.

" The German High Command announces:

" On the night of 16/17th August an engagement occurred in the Channel between German minesweepers and English motor torpedo boats, in the course of which an enemy motor torpedo boat was so heavily damaged that its loss can be assumed. One of our own boats has not returned. Long-range guns of the Navy sank an enemy ship which had been set on fire by minesweepers."

THE NEXT NIGHT

On the night following this great M.G.B. action came a great M.T.B. action, also fought by boats based at Dover. Under the command of Lt. C. L. G. Philpotts, R.N., they were trying out new tactics which were clearly needed after the last attack on a convoy in the Straits ten days before. On this occasion the attack was to be spread along the length of the Dunkirk channel, and boats were to lurk independently on the route, to attack as the enemy passed.

The plan succeeded to the extent that the first and the last attackers scored torpedo hits, one on an escort vessel and one on a merchantman. But a heavy price in casualties had to be paid. M.T.B. 43 (Lt. S. Butler, R.N.R.) was sunk by enemy gunfire though the crew were rescued. M.T.B. 218, the boat which Lt. Granlund had so skilfully brought back to harbour stern first in the previous December, now under the command of Sub-Lt. M. Ball, R.N.R., who had then been her First Lieutenant, was hit and badly damaged in the engine-room. In this condition Ball brought her in for a second attack, but she was making water fast and the attempt had to be abandoned. She began to struggle homeward, but finally the engines were flooded and she stopped. As she drifted helpless, she struck a mine and blew up. Unhappily her gallant captain and four of the crew lost their lives.

Nor were these all the casualties on that fierce night. Sub-Lt. P. Nicholson, D.S.C.,

R.N.V.R., who had for so long been Pumphrey's brilliant navigator and First Lieutenant, now commanding his own boat, was killed instantly on his bridge as he disengaged from his successful attack.

Sub-Lt. Arnold Forster made three attempts to get within range of the main target, but each was foiled. Between the first two, he steamed parallel to it on the seaward side. Quite close to him were two E boats which had been faring as badly as himself at the hands of the convoy and its close escort. If they were unaware of his identity as an enemy, it was no part of Arnold Forster's plan to disabuse them. The three boats steamed along in company until they had gained enough bearing for another attack. When this, in its turn, had failed and the M.T.B. was forced back to seaward, the E boats were there again to meet it, but they showed no more offensive inclination than before.

Philpotts was embarked as Senior Officer in an M.T.B. commanded by Lt. W. de Looze, Royal Netherlands Navy, and after firing torpedoes, which appeared to hit, he set off to hunt for M.T.B. 218 whose wireless silence was causing some anxiety. In the course of the search he came upon a raft containing survivors, and was at first delighted, but a moment later one of them raised his arm and shouted "Heil Hitler!" These were the survivors of the R boat rammed by Sidebottom more than twenty-four hours before.

Meanwhile Arnold Forster had also been carrying out an extensive search for 218, and in the early dawn he found her crew bobbing about in the thickest part of the minefield which had sunk their ship. With mines breaking surface all round him, he picked up the six surviving members, including Sub-Lt. Teekman, who was, so the story is told, swimming with his pipe still gripped firmly between his teeth.

While these battles were keeping the Dover flotillas fully occupied, a raiding expedition, in which the Coastal Forces were to take part, had been in preparation in the Channel. On the night after Philpotts' action off Dunkirk, it sailed from Portsmouth to carry out the raid on Dieppe.

CHAPTER VIII

To Implement the Threat

THROUGHOUT history one of the most valuable potentialities of sea power has been the strategy of holding down large land forces against the threat of sea-borne landing —forces vastly in excess of those required to implement that threat. The German air power during 1940 and 1941 had, to some extent, nullified our superiority at sea, but by 1942 the balance in the air had been sufficiently redressed for sea power to become once more the dominant factor in the Channel.

The object of this strategy, however, could not be achieved by threat alone. Raiding operations had to be put into execution from time to time in order that the enemy should be forced to maintain his defences at full strength; and in the summer of 1942, when the Russian armies were hard pressed on their southern front, it was more important than ever that we should stretch the German resources by every means that lay in our power. Moreover, although it was to be almost two years before our own resources would permit of a full-scale invasion of France, data on the technique of sea-borne landings and information about German defence measures were greatly needed for forthcoming operations in the Mediterranean as well as in the Channel.

These were the underlying reasons for the raid on Dieppe, and only those intimately connected with planning can know how much our successes on 6th June, 1944, owed to the experience gained on 19th August, 1942.

Like St. Nazaire, the raid was planned as a frontal assault on a heavily defended port, but there all similarity ended. This time much larger forces were involved; the shorter sea passage made possible the use of many of the new types of landing craft, some of them carrying tanks; instead of a night action, the landing was to begin at dawn, and, instead of a spearhead penetrating far up an estuary, the attack was to be made on 13 miles of cliff-girt coast. This time, too, the Coastal Forces had a relatively less important part to play than they had had at St. Nazaire. The main tactical objective of the raid was the capture and destruction of the harbour installations and other targets of military value in Dieppe itself. This was to be undertaken principally by troops landed on the mile-long beach which fronts the town. To protect the flanks of this operation, landings were also to be made on beaches a mile or two on either side—at Puits to the east and at Pourville to the west.

In addition to the Coastal Defence guns in the immediate vicinity of Dieppe, the approaches to the harbour were covered by two heavy batteries, one 5 miles to the eastward, at Berneval, and one 5 miles to the westward, at Varengeville. Since the raid was scheduled to last from dawn until about midday, during which time a great concentration of shipping would be lying off the port, it was essential that these batteries should be prevented from interfering, and to this end plans were laid for their capture and destruction by Commando troops landing near them. No. 3 Commando was to land on two beaches, one on each side of the Berneval battery, and No. 4 Commando was to land on two beaches, one in front of the Varengeville battery and the other to the westward, at the mouth of the River Saâne, whence they were to make a detour and take the enemy in rear.

The main assault was to be undertaken largely by troops of the First Canadian Army, although detachments of Fighting French and United States Rangers, as well as the British Commandos, all had their parts to play. They were all under the command of Major-General J. H. Roberts, M.C. The ships which were to carry these troops across the Channel, and

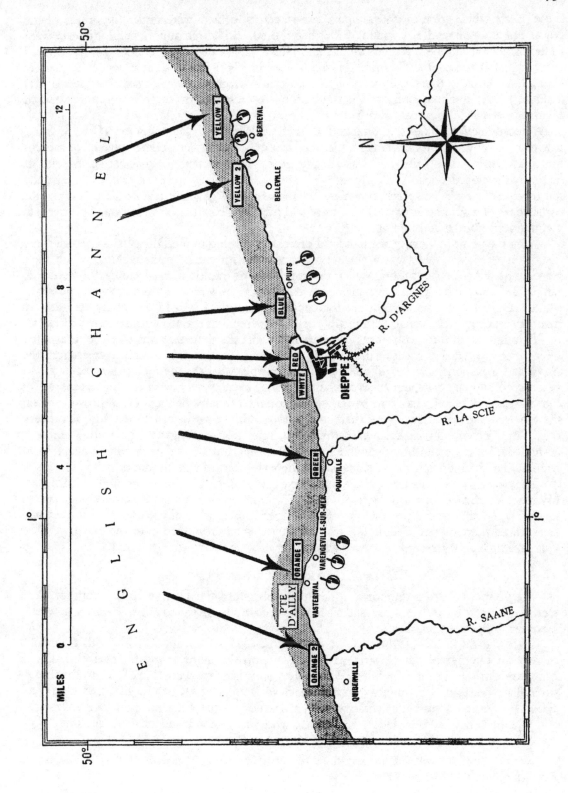

those others which were to give support and to act as escorts, were under the orders of the Naval Force Commander, Captain J. Hughes Hallett, R.N. He and General Roberts were to be together in the headquarters ship, the "Hunt" Class destroyer H.M.S. *Calpe*. Should anything befall her, another "Hunt," H.M.S. *Fernie*, had been equipped as reserve headquarters ship. In addition to these, the escorting and covering forces consisted of six other destroyers, a sloop, a river gunboat, and the Coastal Forces—represented by three steam gunboats and a number of motor gunboats and M.Ls.

Air co-operation, under the command of Air Vice-Marshal T. Leigh Mallory, C.B., D.S.O., was to be provided on a far greater scale than had ever before been contemplated for a combined operation. The Luftwaffe was already becoming reluctant to give battle, in spite of its newly developed Focke Wulf 190 fighter. It was anticipated, however, that it could hardly fail to accept the challenge laid down by a large assembly of ships off the French coast for eight hours of a summer's day. Plans were laid for the air battle for which our Spitfires had so long been waiting and hoping.

From the point of view of the Coastal Forces, the fighting in the Dieppe Raid was of three distinct types. First there was a normal night action with enemy surface ships, which took place an hour before the landing, when the spearhead of the left flank, heading for Berneval, ran, by bad luck, into a small German convoy escorted by trawlers. Then there were, throughout the raid, engagements with the enemy ashore in which the Coastal Forces only occasionally had opportunity to hit back. And finally there were frequent actions against enemy aircraft.

Throughout all this two aspects were predominant; the first, that this was a long-awaited opportunity to "take a crack at the Hun"; the second, that, in this combined operation, the Navy had a responsibility to discharge—a responsibility to the Army, to get them to the beaches, to support and help them in their fighting, even if only with smoke-screens or by drawing the fire of pillboxes and batteries, and to take as many of them off as possible when the time came to withdraw. And there was a responsibility to the Air Force, too, that every one of the airmen who came down in their parachutes from amongst the protective umbrella of fighters, or from the bombers and fighter bombers and smokelayers which swept in to support the landings, should be taken from the water with the minimum of delay.

The way in which these responsibilities were met is described in the account that follows. My new ship, S.G.B. 9, was in action for the first time on that adventurous morning, and so inevitably I can present the picture of this operation most easily from what I saw and experienced there myself, although it formed only a small cross section of the part played by Coastal Forces. My record of it was written down a few days after the raid.

DIEPPE: THE FORCE SETS OUT

They kept the steam gunboats in cotton-wool before the Dieppe Raid. Four of them were to be ready by 16th August, and since we were already on the top line, there was a week's leave for the crew of S.G.B. 9.

I received the orders for the raid five days before—60 or 70 pages of them with a portfolio of relevant photographs and charts, and I sat far into the night trying to form a picture of our particular jobs in the Combined Plan. Two days later we were "briefed" in the underground fastnesses of Portsmouth Combined Headquarters[1] by Cdr. R. E. D. Ryder, V.C. S.G.B. 9 was to support the landings at two beaches on the extreme right flank, Orange I and II, and I met Lt. Cdr. Hugh Mulleneux, who was in command of these landings. Our force was to be the 4th Commando led by Major Lord Lovat.

[1] It was a place with which I was later to become very familiar as a member of the Staff during the planning of the Normandy Invasion.

The preparatory signal for operation, " Jubilee," was postponed one day, but on the 17th the code word came through, and on the following day the executive signal, which meant that the expedition would sail that evening, set us into a ferment of last-minute preparation. The ship's company knew that time was short, but only the officers, the coxswain and the Chief E.R.A. actually knew that we were off that night until about four o'clock in the afternoon, when it became altogether obvious that the party was on. Soldiers were embarking in the Infantry Assault Ships ahead of us. Tank Landing Craft had already left to embark their tanks. Extra ammunition was taken on board and extra life-saving apparatus had to be stowed on the upper deck.

We slipped at 2037 and followed the great Infantry Assault Ships down Portsmouth harbour, whilst the siren sounded " All Clear." The German evening reconnaissance had been a few minutes too early to see the movement of the assembling ships. S.G.B. 8 (Lt. I. R. Griffiths, R.N.—Griff in this story) went down harbour ahead of us because he was escorting the leading group in the formation. There was a great feeling of elation to be started at last. " We're off, we're off, we're off." No. 9 slid so neatly and quickly into the adventure— followed so docilely behind the assault ships—past Fort Blockhouse and down the narrow channel to Spithead. We turned west there, along the Solent, to meet our group which was coming from Southampton, and found the *Prince Albert* in the dusk. " Are you P.A.? " we flashed and were told to take up our appointed station.

In the last light of a calm summer evening the force looked very impressive forming up to pass through the East Solent Gate. There were Infantry Assault Ships (L.S.Is.), destroyers, M.Ls., gunboats and the French Chasseurs of the " cutting out " party, who were to board and bring away any ships in Dieppe harbour. They lay stopped all round Spithead awaiting their moment to dive through the hole in their correct order. At one moment we were the unnoticed jam in a sandwich of *Prince Albert* and *Glengyle*, from which we only extricated ourselves with considerable agility and anxiety. After passing through the gate speed was increased to 19 knots and S.G.B. 9 took station on *Prince Albert* (Lt. Cdr. H. B. Peate, R.N.R.) with M.G.B. 312 (Lt. A. R. H. Nye, R.N.V.R.), and so to the channel through an enemy minefield which had been swept a few hours earlier by a special force of minesweepers.

" Now we really are off," I kept thinking, " really on our way." The Senior Officer S.G.Bs. (Lt. George Pennell, R.N.) was on board, as S.G.B. 3, his own boat was not ready in time. Since he was sleeping in the chart-house, I curled myself into the bridge sponson and tried to get some sleep there. This was so uncomfortable that I had a deck-chair brought up and sat at the after end of the bridge in that. It was a clear starry sky that moved gently round the foremast rigging. I lay wondering upon the outcome and thinking of many things past. The sea was calm but for the washes of the great convoy ahead.

Two lanes had been swept through the mid-Channel minefield and buoyed, but the entrance to the first through which we were intended to go was missed by the leading L.S.I., so that the first three groups passed down " B " channel. This did not make much difference, as the two channels were parallel and only a few miles apart, but it meant that we were sharing a narrow channel with a lot of slower craft. Near the entrance an M.L. made a determined effort to ram us (no doubt that because of our camouflage he could not see us), and later we overtook a row of L.C.Ps. (Landing Craft Personnel),[1] led by another M.L., and some Tank Landing Craft. Once through the minefield the various groups fanned out so as to arrive simultaneously off their respective beaches. Orange beaches I and II, to be assaulted by the 4th Commando, were the most westerly, one each side of Pointe d'Ailly; then came Green at Pourville, Red and White in front of Dieppe, Blue (which was supported by " Griff " in

[1] Known in those days as R boats, but much smaller and very different from the German R boat.

S.G.B. 8) at Puits, and Yellows I and II which were to be led in by S.G.B. 5 (Lt. G. H. Hummel R.N.R.) at Berneval—the extreme left flank.

A warm wind was blowing from the south, laden with the smell of hayfields, as, at 0258, the *Prince Albert* finally stopped in an estimated position 7 miles due north magnetic of Pointe d'Ailly lighthouse. While we were stopped we suddenly saw a light ahead. It flashed three times and then twenty seconds later it flashed three times again. The Germans had left their lighthouse burning to guide us. Then we *were* achieving surprise. There it winked at us— group flashing 3 every 20—just as shown on the chart. We wondered for a moment if it were a trap to mislead us. Perhaps it was not the Phare d'Ailly but a fake light 5 miles to one side of it to take us to the wrong beaches. Just as the landing craft were forming up the light stopped. Had the alarm been given? No. A quarter of an hour later the light popped up again and winked for three or four minutes.

After lowering, the *Prince Albert's* L.C.As. formed into two columns of four and kept close to port of Bob Nye in M.G.B. 312, who was leading the Orange force towards its beaches. We followed astern in support. Suddenly starshell went up away to port. It must be German starshell, because no one on our side would risk giving away the quantities of small craft that were approaching the coast. It was 0350, exactly an hour before the touch down, so it could not be the first of the landing. By the light of the starshell I could see a large ship, perhaps a German merchant ship (we suspected a German convoy must be passing because the Pointe d'Ailly light was on), perhaps the *Glengyle*—the largest of the L.S.Is. late at the lowering position.[1] Near it was a smaller ship, perhaps a destroyer. The starshell died and a tracer battle broke out, fierce white tinsel-like tracer being fired from the south and purposeful red tracer, much of it aimed far too high, from the north. This battle went on for twelve minutes and then subsided, and still the lighthouse winked periodically. Red and green lights on the port bow showed from the breakwater ends of Dieppe harbour. (These and the lighthouse were, in fact, no attempt to mislead us and prove one of two things: either the Hun was completely surprised, at least in the timing of the raid, or, if he had been forewarned, that the liaison between his Intelligence and the Authority which operates his lighthouses was not all that it might have been. Actually it is almost certain that the force of about ten large transports, eight destroyers and numerous Coastal Force craft approached to within seven or eight miles of the enemy coast totally unperceived, and that had it not been for the chance meeting of S.G.B. 5 and the boats for Yellow beach described above, the tactical surprise would have been complete. As it was, the battle was enough to send the Huns ashore to Action Stations.)

THE TOUCH DOWN

0450 was the moment for landing, when the first grey light would come into the clear eastern sky. Twenty minutes before this, we stopped a mile and a half off shore while Mulleneux transferred from 312 to the Support Landing Craft (L.C.S.) from which he was to direct the actual landing. Then our eight landing craft divided—three going off to the left to Vasterival with 312 in support, and the other five going towards the Quiberville beach with us in support. This included Lord Lovat himself and the L.C.S. with Mulleneux.

At 0442 the first aircraft appeared—Bostons and Hurricanes—and the streams of the same white tinselly tracer went up from the battery round the lighthouse, which seemed to consist of about five guns. To the eastward along the coast was more tracer, but all going upwards— still the landing craft were undetected. About a minute before the touch down a single white Very light or fireball lobbed up into the sky above the lighthouse. Then the pillbox at the

---

[1] This is what it was.

eastern end of Orange II opened fire along the beach, and the fire was returned by the L.C.S. The Huns behind the beach fired a six-star green firework—no doubt an invasion signal—and the party was on.

At a range of about 1,000 yards we opened fire with our 3-inch gun at the pillbox. One or two of the bursts seemed fairly near in spite of the fact that we had only open cartwheel sights. But, although we did not hit it, the pillbox ceased fire after we had fired about six rounds. Ten minutes later, however, it recommenced, so at 0515 we opened fire for a further three minutes' bombardment. The L.C.S. was firing most accurately with Oerlikon, and after that the pillbox was silenced for good. Unfortunately during this bombardment a non-flashless shell was loaded by mistake and the attention of a shore battery was drawn. It was not accurate fire, but since the pillbox was no longer giving trouble we retired behind smoke to a range of one and a half miles while the shells continued to fall short. The L.C.As. of the Orange landing party having landed their troops withdrew towards us while the shelling continued. We closed Bob Nye, who had also been shelled off Vasterival, apparently equally inaccurately. By now it was broad daylight, and at 0550 a new battery to the east of the lighthouse opened up and we had to draw yet farther off shore.

All this time there were explosions ashore from mortars, guns and bombs. At times there were great sheets of flame, at others very heavy detonations. All the while Bostons and Hurribombers kept coming in to attack the defences. One very loud bang was Lord Lovat's 4th Commando blowing up the ammunition dump of the 6-inch battery he had been detailed to destroy.

At about six o'clock we sighted S.G.B. 8 coming towards us through the smoke to the eastward. This smoke drifted to seaward like white mist on the light offshore breeze. Since there was no sign of S.G.B. 5 by 0615 (she had been badly damaged in the encounter with the convoy, but we had no knowledge of this until the evening), we told S.G.B. 8 to take station two miles on our starboard beam and set off on a course of N. 60° W. at 10 knots to carry out " Task I," a prearranged sweep fifteen miles to the westward in order to give warning of the approach of surface craft. (Five " T " Class torpedo boats were known to be in Cherbourg harbour.) Low-flying aircraft which passed near us at this time turned out to be first Blenheims and later Tac. R. (Tactical Reconnaissance) Mustangs. We steamed slowly along the enemy coast as bold as brass.

At this moment in the bright morning sunshine we were lulled into a most curious and entirely false sense of security. There, four miles away on our port beam, shone the cliffs and the brilliant summer green of the fields and woods. St. Valery-en-Caux nestled in its hollow, with a haze of chimney smoke above it. We remembered that we had been told that the Luftwaffe would be fully occupied elsewhere, and indeed we had seen the milling clouds of Spitfires arriving as we left. They had come, wave upon wave, in numbers the like of which I had never before seen. We forgot our own assessment, that unprotected ships outside the fighter umbrella would be exactly what the Germans were looking for. We did not imagine, as we might have done, the watchers on the cliff tops feverishly telephoning for the German Air Force to come quickly and bomb the two unprotected ships to the westward.

" Better send someone to get some breakfast for the ship's company, Number One," I said, and went on examining the coastline with glasses. A light westerly breeze turned the sea deep purplish-blue. Twelve Bostons flying in perfect formation passed inland high above us, shining in the early sunlight. Two aircraft slipped between us and No. 8 unseen until they were past, low over the sea. I got the glasses on them and saw the black cross on the side of one—probably F.W. 190s.

We altered course offshore to N. 75° W. We were not in a healthy place and we suddenly realised it. Two more square-wingtipped planes came back from the westward—the Tac. R. Mustangs. But a few minutes later at 0720 there were "Aircraft right astern." Two fighters were weaving about and working their way up into the sun. In a few moments it was evident that they had designs upon us, and as they turned their noses down I could see the bomb hanging under the first one. "Hard a-starboard," and I rang up the revs. to 28 knots. Off came the bomb just as the guns opened up. Not many fired, the pom-pom jammed, one of the point-fives had a misfire. The bomb fell in our wake close astern.

The second Hun was circling towards No. 8. Whether he misjudged the attack or saw that his mate had missed will never be known, but he transferred his attention to us, coming in on the port bow while we still turned to starboard. As he steadied up towards us in the shallow dive I saw splashes in the water short of us, and then our own guns opened up. The F.W. 190 was only firing machine-gun—not cannon—and he was himself enveloped in a haze of tracer. I saw his bomb take the water 20 yards short on our port beam. There was a pause and then a heavy shock and a huge waterspout—but the ship was still afloat and still steaming. I remember thinking it must have been a very small bomb not to have damaged us more, Then I looked at the F.W. A trail of wispy black smoke was coming out of it and it was losing height. But when it was nearly down to the water it picked up again and began to climb. I stopped watching it and became concerned with the fact that the ship would not steer, that the alarm bells were ringing continuously, that in fact we had been badly shaken. Those in No. 8, however, watched the damaged F.W. falter again, and crash head on into the bottom of the cliffs.

Meanwhile the Chief (Chief Engine-room Artificer O'Brien) had arrived on the bridge. " My vacuum's gone, I'd like to stop, but we *can* keep going slowly if we must."

I rang down, " Stop both," and told No. 8 to take us in tow. Griff came alongside with a rush and a bit of a bump, but five minutes later (and only fourteen minutes after the bombing) at 0739 we were under way in tow—very quick work.

At 0745 Jimmy Grout (Flotilla Engineer Officer) appeared grinning and sweating on the bridge, " We've found it—you can go ahead in a minute or two," and he disappeared again like a rabbit. Never was such a report more welcome, for our position was very sticky. We were still in full view of the coast—one F.W. had returned to base to report that we were disabled. It obviously could not be long before further aircraft were sent to complete the job and despatch us for good. At 7 or 8 knots we were still two hours from the fighter umbrella. But by 0755 the tow had been slipped and we set off at 30 knots to the eastward. A signal had just been received that E boats had been sighted southward bound from Boulogne. After a short stop a few minutes later for the engine-room to make an adjustment we proceeded at 25 knots, and at 0855 we were closing the assorted destroyers and small craft to the N.W. of Dieppe while hordes of Spitfires milled comfortably overhead. We breathed again.

Maintaining a Smoke-screen

Away to the east were three sources of smoke, over the horizon. We wondered what friendly craft would be making smoke right out there, and thought perhaps it was the E boats.

There was smoke, too, drifting idly north-east from Dieppe, and beyond it the battle spluttered and rumbled. Heavy fighting was going on by the sound of it. The westerly wind was now falling light as the sun blazed hotter, the sea was glass calm. Cloud upon cloud of Spitfires circled above between 3,000 and 10,000 feet. There were no enemy aircraft in sight at all. The Hun flak was still lively whenever our fighters or fighter bombers went low over Dieppe—especially to the eastward. Every twenty minutes or so a fresh bunch of

Hurribombers came in low from the sea and shot up and bombed the defences ashore. I saw one of these get hit and watched him circle very slowly before crashing into the trees.

Presently a Dornier came very low along the coast from the westward. It was spotted by some Spitfires and soon one was on its tail. Smoke came first from the Spitfire—probably smoke from his own cannon—and then from the Dornier, which at once caught fire and went straight down into the wood behind the Phare d'Ailly. A huge cloud of dark-brown smoke burst into the sky and curled up from the burning wreck.

We closed *Calpe* (the H.Q. ship), struggling with our loud-hailing equipment, which remained resolutely silent. She was lying stopped and was surrounded by L.C.As., L.C.Ps., M.Ls. and " C " Class M.G.Bs., L.C.Ts. and L.C.Fs. Some were alongside, others lay round the other destroyers, two or three of which (*Brocklesby, Bleasdale, Fernie, Albrighton,* etc.) were in sight. A smoke-screen began inshore of the assembled pool of craft and drifted sluggishly north-east, but to the south and south-west the coast, no more than a mile away, was clearly visible in every detail. No sign of opposition came from it. Lord Lovat's party had done their job well.

The feeling of peaceful inactivity was most strange and incongruous. The smoke itself was white and friendly—the protecting aircraft circled unmolested and the boat pool of perhaps fifty or sixty craft was equally unmolested. The sun was so hot and the sea so smooth that " Hands to bathe " would have seemed a perfectly appropriate signal. We leaned lazily on the bridge screen waiting for orders from the *Calpe*, while even the din of the battle to the eastward seemed to be muffled by the smoke.

The boat pool had drifted to the westward so that it lay between Pourville and the d'Ailly Lighthouse. How inviting looked the luxurious woods on top of the cliff and the brilliant fields, but the powers-that-be wanted them blotted out. " Maintain a smoke-screen half a mile inshore and to the westward " came over the loud-hailer from *Calpe*. We led off, with Griff following on our starboard quarter. The smoke-floats were ignited much more quickly than I expected after all the trouble we used to have with them in *Broke*, and before I could say knife, about five had been dropped in a bunch and far too near the boat pool. We steamed on up the coast and dropped more floats.

Half an hour later we were back beside *Calpe* with hardly any smoke left. She told us to take M.Ls. 309 and 190 under our orders and continue to maintain the screen. Both these M.Ls. had been damaged and were steering by hand with large tillers. 190 had a big hole in her starboard quarter. Our loud-hailer had been brought to life by the magic attentions of S.G.B. 3's leading telegraphist whom we had with us. With it we directed the M.Ls. when to drop their smoke-floats. As we went off a formation of three Dornier 217s unloaded their bombs in the middle of the boat pool from about 4,000 feet, without, as far as we could see, doing any damage. The Spitfires were on their tails before even the bombs were released and almost at once one was set on fire. The crew baled out and the aircraft crashed in the sea a few hundred yards off shore and two miles to the westward. The first two to bale out fell in the sea—the others drifted in over the cliffs before coming down, for the wind was beginning to blow from sea to shore now, such very light wind as there was.

Although the two parachutists who fell in the sea were about opposite Quiberville—a part of the coast which had not been attacked, we decided that to pick up the farther offshore of the two for interrogation was a reasonable risk as there was not much else to do, and we set course accordingly at 20 knots. Griff, however, came up on our starboard side and raced for the position, so we altered in, steering for the inshore airman—scarcely a mile from the cliffs. At last we sighted the bobbing head and slowed down. I overshot him a little, a heaving line was thrown and he grabbed it and was pulled along, his head submerged in his own bow wave. He let go and drifted a little astern and I began to go astern to get him when—whoosh crumph!—and a shell landed on the port bow close aboard. "Full ahead both, hard a-starboard." The pilot waved pathetically from the water, but his friends had sealed his doom. Another shell arrived within 30 or 40 yards. We made C.S.A. smoke and zigzagged sharply at 28 knots. For eight minutes the shells continued to arrive with remarkable accuracy for range but out for line. They all fell to port. I did not know whether to expect them to correct for line but kept altering to starboard, and it was as well that I did, for the shells kept falling to port. The last salvo was a two-gun salvo just ahead, after which we ran clear and reduced speed at 1035. We had got off a good deal lighter than we deserved, for it was, on the face of it, *not* a justifiable thing for which to risk a steam gunboat.

Twenty minutes later, when we were back amongst the boats and the smoke, a heavy air attack began. The log[1] reads thus:

1102 Opened fire on Dornier
1103   „   „   „
1104   „   „   „
1107   „   „   „
1110   „   „   „
1115 Stopped to pick up pilot

All these were separate engagements, and for a while the air was thick with enemy aircraft. Actually the first we saw was, I think, a Ju. 88, painted pale grey or silver. It was shot down, and we like to think we had a hand in it. A Dornier soon after kindled into a ball of fire immediately above us, when every gun was firing. Likely enough there was a Spitfire on its tail, and every other ship is convinced it was theirs—but again we like to think we had a share. One bomber blew up in mid-air and the bits fell slowly like autumn leaves. None of the bombs from these Dorniers seem to have troubled the ships at all.

We had just received a signal that the withdrawal was commencing, and the battle on the beaches seemed to increase in intensity as the landing craft went in to take off the troops.

At this time we were manœuvring in thin smoke. It was possible to fight the aircraft overhead, but most of the ships were hidden. When they did appear they looked enormous. "B" Class M.Ls. looked like vast transports. The effect was like a fog in a bad film. It was steamy and artificial, yet rather eerie and horribly real. Parachutes were coming down all round. Two fell near the *Locust*, which was dimly visible in the smoke. I thought it would be rude to race her to them, but a few minutes later she moved off again and signalled, "Pick up two pilots astern of me." We went ahead and began to pick them up. While we were doing it a fierce air battle was going on overhead, and whenever possible we engaged enemy aircraft that were in range. Once we opened up on a Boston, which came low directly at us out of the smoke. We managed to stop the gunners before it was hit. This and a few rounds unordered from one of the ·5 turrets at a Spitfire were the only times we fired at friendly aircraft. It was twice too often, but some of the other ships were much worse and sometimes the fire was general throughout the boat pool at an obviously friendly aircraft.

While we picked up the first parachutist, who was a Hun, the second one was shouting "Help—speed." We took rather a long time getting the first on board and he was finally hauled in over the transom. Picking up survivors with the air full of enemy aircraft and all our guns firing required a high degree of concentration, and I did not usually make a very good job of it. However, we finally got the second Hun on board (also over the transom),

---

[1] This log was most meticulously kept by my navigator, Sub-Lt. J. B. Henderson, R.N.V.R.—an indefatigable Scot who did magnificent work that day and in many other actions later.

LT. G. J. MACDONALD, D.S.O., D.S.C. AND TWO BARS, R.N.Z.N.V.R.

TRACER AT NIGHT

ENGINE-ROOM OF AN M.T.B.

LT. C. W. S. DREYER, D.S.O., D.S.C. AND BAR, R.N.

SEVENTY-FOOT M.G.B.
READY FOR
UNSLIPPING

Tractors driven by Wrens tow
her from the hangar at Felixstowe

NEW " D " CLASS
M.T.Bs. IN LONDON

FOR'ARD GUNS OF S.G.B. 8 (*GREY WOLF*)

S.G.B. 9 (*GREY GOOSE*) AT SPEED

THE DIEPPE RAID—
Chasseurs and landing craft off the beaches

On the seaward side of the smoke—Landing Craft (Personnel) alongside an M.L. in the " boat pool " during the raid

The destroyer H.M.S. *Berkeley* blows up. After damage by bombs she was sunk by a torpedo from H.M.S. *Albrighton*

LT. (NOW LT. CDR.) P. G. C. DICKENS, D.S.O., M.B.E., D.S.C., R.N.

SEVENTY-FOOT M.T.Bs. IN FELIXSTOWE BASIN

LOADING A TORPEDO IN FELIXSTOWE BASIN

LT. CDR. K. GEMMEL, D.S.O., D.S.C., R.N.V.R.

Lt. Cdr. R. P. Hichens, D.S.O., D.S.C., R.N.V.R. *(left)* and Lt. P. G. C. Dickens, D.S.O., M.B.E., D.S.C., R.N., at that time respectively Senior Officers of M.G.Bs. and M.T.Bs. at H.M.S. *Beehive*

Left to right: Lt. R. Saunders, D.S.C, R.A.N.V.R., Lt. G. D. K. Richards, D.S.O., D.S.C., R.N., Lt. B. C. Ward, D.S.C., R.N., Lt. M. Arnold Forster, D.S.O., D.S.C., R.N.V.R., Lt. M. Bray, R.N.V.R. Richards and Ward were at that time respectively Senior Officers of M.G.Bs. and M.T.Bs. at Dover

LT. (NOW LT. CDR.) D. G. H. WRIGHT, D.S.C. AND TWO BARS, R.N.V.R.

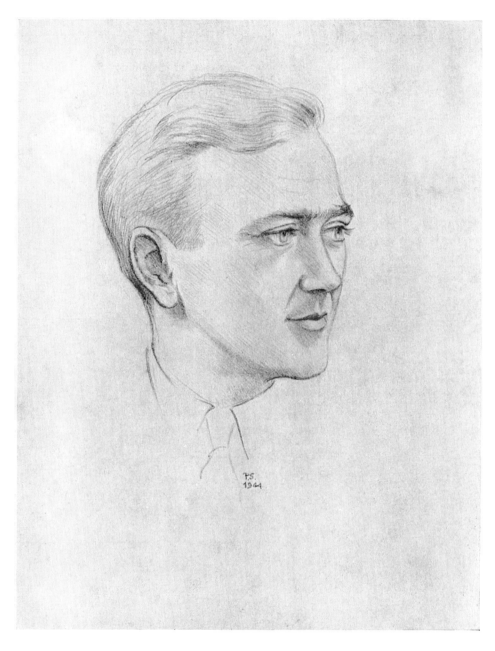

LT. CDR. (NOW CDR.) D. GOULD BRADFORD, D.S.O., D.S.C. AND
TWO BARS, R.N.R.

SEVENTY-FOOT M.G.Bs. AND A PATROL TRAWLER

SEVENTY-ONE-FOOT M.T.B. TURNING TO STARBOARD

LT. I. C. TRELAWNY, D.S.C. AND BAR, R.N.V.R.

LT. PETER DICKENS ON THE BRIDGE OF AN M.T.B.

LT. G. D. K. RICHARDS, D.S.O., D.S.C., R.N.

and he was almost drowned. We decided to transfer him, on the advice of the sick-berth attendant, to a ship with a Medical Officer. L.C.F. (L) 5 (a beach-protection craft flying a medical-guard flag) was nearby, and we went alongside and passed him across.

By this time (about 1215) the air attack was less fierce but fairly regular. The Dornier 217s—Germany's latest bombers—were coming in in formations of three. One of the three was always shot down, often two and once or twice all three. Once I saw three come in from seaward. The leader went into a steep dive, the other two only shallow dives. I could not see the target for smoke, but the Dornier who concentrated on the bombing run—a brave fellow—came out with six or eight Spitfires on his tail. He barely pulled out of his dive before he was heading down again on fire. On one occasion I saw a Dornier lining up for his attack. The Spitfires were elsewhere at the time except for one which was below and ahead of the bomber. This Spitfire turned up towards the Dornier and made a sort of lunge at it. The Dornier flinched and the Spitfire made a second lunge. The attack was spoiled—the Dornier jettisoned his bombs to escape a host of newly arrived Spitfires. We did not have time to follow his fortunes, but I doubt if he can have escaped. The Dorniers usually seemed to drop four bombs. Once or twice I saw more (six or possibly eight).

" Can We Help ? "

All this time it was very hard to know what was going on either ashore or afloat. From time to time signals came through calling for closer support. But how to do it, that was the question. How to know where our own troops were. The blanket of smoke between us and the shore was almost complete. Only occasionally glimpses of a silhouetted cliff showed in the gap between belching smoke-floats. At 1145 we had made a signal to *Calpe* (H.Q. ship), " We have plenty of 3-inch ammo but no smoke, can we help ? " to which we had received reply, " Closer support is required, offer of help appreciated." A few minutes later we signalled to *Calpe* again, " Can you give us a bearing on which to lob shells ? "; but got no answer to this.

There was a terrible feeling of helplessness at this time, and also a strange aloofness from the awful happenings so close to us but hidden by the thick white curtain. Every few minutes salvos of shells arrived on our side of the smoke, and occasionally there were plops from spent bullets and small shells.

About this time I first saw a signal to *Locust* timed 1112 which said, " Give support at rising ground at end of Green beach." It was a bad signal as Green beach had of course rising ground at either end, and without more precise instructions anything other than moral support was impossible. We called up *Locust* by lamp and made, " Can we help you support Green beach ? " to which came reply " Yes—go in." A general signal had just come through: " All ships. Make smoke. Executive signal." And then a most marvellous spectacle developed before our eyes. The destroyers were making clouds of brilliant white smoke which shone in the sun, crowned with deep chocolate billows of fuel smoke from their funnels. I took some photographs of this as we steamed in to " give our support," making the last dregs of our own white smoke as we went. Then we plunged into the fog of it and at last emerged with alarming suddenness on the other side. There was Green beach and the village of Pourville about six or seven hundreds yards away. We turned to port and opened fire at some defence works on top of the cliff at the left-hand end of the beach with our 3-inch gun.

There was no sign of activity on the beach. A light onshore wind had set in so that the smoke drifted slowly to the south-east over the front of Dieppe; heavy fighting was still going on at Red and White beaches, opposite the town itself. As we turned away from our bombardment bullets whistled around and Oerlikon shells plopped in the water beside us. But it was wild, desultory fire and none hit us.

All this time shells were coming from the cliffs to the eastward of Dieppe. They were not accurate but they were fairly constant, so that hanging about even in the thick smoke was not very restful. We closed *Berkeley* and shouted, "What is happening?" But Yorke[1] shrugged his shoulders. No one knew. That was the most difficult part. Help was undoubtedly needed, but no one could tell us where or how. We intercepted a signal from *Brocklesby* (Nigel Pumphrey)[2] saying she was aground, but it was evidently ancient history, as we saw her steaming out a couple of miles offshore.

At 1243 we suddenly saw three aircraft heading straight for us about 30 feet above the sea. We quickly saw that they were Bostons, but all the other ships opened fire. When they were quite close, suddenly a dense cloud of white smoke came from them and left a wonderfully thick screen. It was magnificent the way it was done, in face of so much fire from friendly craft.

Ten minutes later we headed in to carry out a further bombardment from closer—this time with pom-pom as well as 3-inch. We were receiving such signals as " Situation critical behind Red and White beaches, can you hasten close support as requested—1144," and later " Enemy holds all beaches."

As we came through the smoke-screen the coastline loomed up far closer than we expected. *Albrighton* (Tom Hanson)[3] was there, half shrouded in her own smoke and terrifyingly close to the shore. Her guns were firing and she seemed to be moving slowly ahead, and not, as we first feared, aground. We turned again to port, opening fire with 3-inch and pom-pom at the eastern outskirts of Pourville, which constituted the " high ground at the end of Green beach." We passed between *Albrighton*, who had ceased fire, and the shore at slow speed and turned back into the smoke. A good many shells and bullets were whistling both ways and plopping in the water all about us, but, miraculously, we were not hit.

Back on the offshore side of the smoke we engaged a Dornier—then another, and at 1308 a formation of three dived down. One of them pressed home this attack on the group of ships all bunched together, which consisted of *Calpe, Fernie, Berkeley, Albrighton* and *Bleasdale*, to say nothing of S.G.Bs. 8 and 9. The bombs came out and I saw one slanting down into the water close to the port side of *Berkeley*. Its slant took it right under the ship and when it exploded she reared like a bucking horse. The bridge went up and the fo'c'sle went down as if there were a hinge. Then for a few moments, as the ship subsided again into the water, the half-detached fo'c'sle waggled up and down. We turned at once towards the damaged destroyer (not knowing at the time that it was *Berkeley*). She was steaming at high speed in a circle, heeling over steeply and with steam escaping with a roar.

Griff was quite close—indeed, he had to go astern to avoid a collision—and as soon as she slowed up he laid his ship alongside the port side of the sinking destroyer and the crew trooped off on to his fo'c'sle. All the time that she had been steaming in a circle men had been falling off her steep decks and the wake was dotted with the heads of swimming survivors.

THE SINKING OF THE *BERKELEY*

As we closed in towards them we suddenly saw a bunch of three or four F.W. 190s coming at us with their nasty little bombs hanging underneath them. We were close to *Calpe* at the time, stern to stern, and one of the bombs fell between us—30 yards from us and 15 from him, but it must have been a small bomb. *Calpe* lurched but was none the worse, nor were we. Neither did any of the other ships appear to be damaged by this last attack, in spite of

[1] Lt. J. J. S. Yorke, R.N., her Captain.
[2] Lt. Cdr. E. N. Pumphrey, D.S.O., D.S.C., R.N.
[3] Lt. Cdr. R. J. Hanson, D.S.C., R.N.

the way in which they were all clustered together. We followed the circular string of bobbing heads and threw over two lifebelts and a rubber dinghy (to hold five). Then we went on to a Carley raft and collected half a dozen men from that. By this time the other swimmers had collected at the rubber boat and we were able to go straight to that and pick them up. This seems a good idea when there are many people to rescue.

Berkeley was now stopped and down by the bow, listing to starboard. Griff pulled away from her side with the last of her survivors and a signal came from Yorke, her Captain, now in No. 8, " Sink with torpedo," followed shortly after with a negative. Meanwhile *Albrighton* placed his stern opposite *Berkeley's* stern and took off the torpedo gunner's mate, who had been below and had been left behind. Then *Albrighton* lay off to the north of *Berkeley* and fired a torpedo. It hit under the bridge and blew off the bows, which sank immediately. The rest of the ship, however, relieved of the weight, floated more level. A second torpedo was fired and hit the after magazine, which blew up. A huge reddish-purple burst of smoke and flame belched out of the wreck and went up into the calm sky in a tall column with a mushroom of dense blackness at its top—an extraordinary and unforgettable sight. For a few seconds part of the ship floated so that we imagined she was resting on the bottom, then she disappeared altogether.

By this time the protecting smoke was thinning. *Albrighton* began to get a Chasseur in tow. The withdrawal from the shore was complete, no more boats were coming off. All who were left behind must now be taken prisoner. The *Calpe* turned back towards the beaches as the *Albrighton* came away. *Calpe* was firing her forward guns in a duel with a shore battery whose shells landed on her starboard side close between her and *Albrighton*. Under *Calpe's* starboard bow came an L.C.A. heading shorewards. (I heard afterwards that this was a last attempt to get a boat ashore to take off further troops.) It was a grand sight to see them nosing towards the shore with hardly any smoke cover. But it was quite evidently a forlorn hope. They could never have made it. They turned away and we turned away with them; and all the while 20-mm. shells plopped in the water round us.

All the destroyers were making black smoke, sometimes so diligently that flames belched from their funnels. I thought one of them must have a fire in the boiler-room, but it was only over-enthusiastic smoke-making. By 1341 the gallant attempt to get the L.C.A. ashore had been abandoned and all ships were withdrawing. The raid was over.

Another L.C.A. had appeared from somewhere and the two of them brought up the rear. We went to look after them and rounded up astern of them. A new battery was firing and the shells fell near the last destroyers just ahead. Meanwhile occasional single Dorniers managed to penetrate the fighter cover, and deliver fairly accurate bombing attacks on the destroyers farther out. Twice I saw them completely enveloped in splashes. The Germans afterwards claimed these as sunk, but in fact they were not even damaged, though they lurched and shuddered at the explosions of the near misses.

Calpe and *Albrighton* increased speed to outrange the new battery. The two L.C.As. chugged on slowly through the regular three-shell splashes while we brought up the rear. *Calpe* signalled, " Take one L.C.A. in tow," and at the same time a " C " Class M.G.B. dropped back to take the other. Actually she took both of them, and we watched *Calpe* go off to the S.E. in response to a Spitfire which was circling low and tipping its wings to indicate a pilot in the water. She made smoke as she went. A Dornier spotted her away from the Spitfires and did a shallow dive attack. We couldn't see *Calpe* at the time, only the pinnacles of the bomb splashes. A few minutes later another Dornier came out of the thin grey clouds which were now forming overhead. We fired a round from the 3-inch to warn *Calpe*. But the Dornier dived down unopposed by our Spitfires, which were all circling over the convoy of retiring craft three or four miles to the northward. Again the spouts of brown water appeared above the white smoke-screen. Surely the *Calpe* must be hit—and if she was hit there was only us to go to the rescue, and we knew she had many hundreds of wounded soldiers on board as well as the Headquarters Staff.

We increased speed and headed towards the smoke. There was no sign of the destroyer, but a breaking wave came out of the smoke across the glassy sea. That wave might have been started before the last bombing attack, the *Calpe* might still be sinking in the middle of the " fog bank " in front of us. Should we creep into it or skirt round it at high speed? I turned to port to keep to the north of it—the side on which the destroyer was most likely to emerge, and there at last she appeared steaming out at 25 knots. We all heaved a deep sigh of relief and made: " Interrogative O.K.," to which came back " Yes, thanks—please search two miles astern of me for five men in the water." Two miles! And we were little more than three miles off shore—with hardly any smoke left between us and Dieppe. We turned on to an opposite course and set off at 25 knots. Two miles back we still saw no sign of the missing men. The last of the smoke had gone and the sea was so completely smooth that I thought we could not possibly miss them. We turned to starboard in a wide sweep and suddenly something caught my eye—a flock of gulls on the water? No—five heads! As we approached, the swimmers waved and cheered from the water. We stopped amongst them and they were all on board in a surprisingly short time. It appeared that the first attack on *Calpe* in the smoke had caused a cordite fire on No. 2 gun-deck (the upper after mounting). Some of the men had been blown overboard, others had jumped to extinguish their burning clothing. The five were none of them more than slightly injured.

Although we must have been perfectly plain to see, the shore guns did not open fire. By now even the belated bombing attacks by our Bostons and Hurribombers, which had gone on after the withdrawal, had ceased. The shore looked peaceful except for some columns of smoke rising lazily above the town.

Five miles to seaward the Spitfires milled above the convoy, but only very occasionally did a small band of them circle out in our direction. Small parties of F.W. 190s circled there, too, so that every fighter had to be watched. There was a breathless urgency to get back to our protective umbrella, and every moment of delay caused an ever-growing impatience. As we increased speed to rejoin, I swept the port side with the glasses and saw an L.C.A. away inshore of us. At first I took it for one of two derelicts, one of which had been blazing half an hour before; but this one was under way. With a sinking feeling we turned once more towards Dieppe at 25 knots.

As we closed the boat I aimed a little to one side so that I could sweep round and take it swiftly in tow till we were clear of the shore and the guns, which must, we all thought, open fire as soon as we stopped. The L.C.A. turned towards us. I aimed the other side and the wretched thing turned and came for us again. Eventually I had to go straight to it and turn beyond it. As we approached we saw that it contained three soldiers, two of whom were completely naked except for their Mae Wests. One of them was semaphoring " S.O.S." After turning we passed them a rope and they managed to secure the eye. Then, miraculously still unshot at, although we were no more than a mile or so offshore, we set off again to rejoin. We increased to 12 knots, reduced to adjust the tow, stopped, and then set off again. The tow was chafing badly on our depth-charge gear, but we decided to go on till it broke, by which time we hoped to be a safe distance from the shore. So we increased to revs. for 20 knots and set course for the now distant convoy and its cloud of protecting fighters.

Five minutes later (at about 1500) I spotted two dots upon the eastern horizon. Two boats were approaching at high speed with bow waves easily visible at their range of six miles or more. E boats! Here was something right up our street. With an effort the immediate objective of the last half-hour—to regain our fighter protection with the minimum delay—was cast aside, as the gunners on the fo'c'sle cleared their mountings for low-angle fire.

The E boats were closing us. I thought it would be a mistake to chase them until they reached their closest, so we plodded on with our tow. M.L. 191 came back to meet us, evidently looking for a parachutist. He went past and turned half a mile astern. Meanwhile we made an enemy report: " Two unknown vessels bearing 045°, 6 miles, course 240°, my position 185° Dungeness 47 miles." Then we saw two destroyers heave out of the convoy to starboard and make out towards the E boats. This we thought would turn and disperse them. Now was our time. We slipped the tow, turned towards and increased to 35 knots.

It was just where we would have expected the enemy coastal forces to come in and harass the retirement, and here they were and we were going to have a battle with them. Spirits were very high as we sped eastward. But suddenly they were dashed by a signal from the destroyer 2 miles away to seaward, " Vessels are friendly." They were air/sea-rescue launches. Bitterly disappointed, we cancelled our enemy report and returned to the naked soldiers in the L.C.A. We took them off and put two of our own crew on board and were about to pass a tow when a Dornier appeared and headed towards us. We increased speed to take avoiding action, but the bomber went on to the convoy where it was met with such a tremendous barrage that it unloaded its bombs on the very outskirts 400 yards from any craft. As we returned to the L.C.A. one of the periodical air fights developed overhead and a pilot was seen floating down to the north-east of us. I decided that the L.C.A. was a secondary commitment and took off my crew, signalling to the M.L. to take it in tow, as we dashed off towards the pilot. Apparently the signal was not understood.

We found the airman sitting in his rubber boat; a large red flag with a white spot flying bravely over it. He was grinning and seemed perfectly well and happy. It was a striking contrast between our rescue equipment and that of the Germans. Their airmen had all been half drowned before we got them on board.

This lad—a Norwegian officer—was on board in a few moments, and we turned at once Dieppe-wards to collect another pilot whom we had seen descending. The M.L. made over towards the same pilot, so we signalled, " Suggest you rejoin at your best speed," which this time he understood.

We found the pilot without difficulty. He was sitting quite comfortably in his rubber dinghy in spite of a badly broken leg and an injured arm. With his good arm he caught and secured a heaving line to the dinghy. Being in a dinghy instead of in the water halved the time that it took to get him on board, and in a very few minutes we were off again on a course to rejoin the convoy. The second pilot was an American and was in some pain. We gave him an injection of one " Omnipon " ampoule ($\frac{1}{2}$ gr. morphia) to relieve him.

As we overtook the M.L. he signalled, " This is my best speed." It was 12 knots, so we made, " All right, we will stay with you." Just then a Dornier appeared out of the clouds. By now we were very familiar both with the appearance and tactics of these bombers. They were immediately recognised. This one came from right astern and dived down as we increased speed. We and the M.L. were the only unprotected targets—money for jam. All guns opened fire and I watched the bombs come out. At once I saw that they were travelling in the same direction as us and at about the same forward speed, perhaps a little more. They would fall just ahead, so above the uproar of the guns I yelled to the coxswain,[1] " Full astern, both." He didn't hear me the first time, but when he did the result was most striking. The

[1] Chief Petty Officer I. Stevens, D.S.M., who had been Gould's coxswain in all his battles in the Straits, and remained mine in many to come.

ship pulled up dead in her tracks and the bombs went on to fall about 60 yards ahead with four great spouting splashes. Meanwhile the guns had been doing well. The Dornier, which was about 2,000 feet up, was hit by a burst from the 3-inch gun under its starboard engine.[1] This caught fire and a thin stream of smoke came from it as the aircraft plunged almost vertically downward. There was great excitement on the bridge. "We've got him! We've got him!" and everyone danced with delight. But when he was a couple of hundred feet up he flattened out and, still burning, disappeared into the haze over Dieppe.

THE WAY HOME

Half an hour later as we gradually closed the convoy—our speed, limited by the M.L., was only three or four knots better than the assembled craft—two more Dorniers appeared. One remained half in the clouds, the other emerged below. They were headed perfectly straight towards us, and we increased speed to avoid the bombs. We and the M.L. were still obviously the best targets, separated as we were from the convoy's barrage and umbrella. The leader passed straight over us and a little ahead so that his bombs would have been exactly the right amount aimed off. I remember wondering what on earth I would do when I saw them released. A turn would be best, I thought. But as we watched we were amazed to see that no bombs came from him at all. He passed over harmlessly, and unharmed, for our fire that time was not very accurate. I did not see the second Dornier's bombs falling, but our increase of speed had tricked him, and the stick of four fell astern. The convoy put up a terrific barrage again by way of warning to the bombers, and the biggest danger seemed to be from their unexploded shells, which burst in the water all round us, some unpleasantly close.

At 1648, when we had almost caught up the destroyer, a parachute was reported two miles astern, and away we went again. The sea was now so completely glassy that we expected to see him easily, but after a search four miles in rear of the convoy we gave it up. Had he been one of ours we should have seen his rubber boat.

By now the Benzedrine tablet I had taken against fatigue was having a marked effect. I found myself singing away merrily and shouting exhortations to the Dorniers to do their worst.

At 1700 we came up with the convoy at last, just as it entered the southern end of the swept channel through the minefield. Since the sinking of the *Berkeley* enemy air attacks had been totally unsuccessful. An M.L. was stationed to mark the entrance to the lane of flagged dan buoys, the same M.L. that had so nearly rammed us sixteen hours ago.

We decided that close between *Albrighton* and *Bleasdale* was a dangerous place to be, should a determined Dornier turn up, so we crept past and up into the rearguard of the convoy. It was formed up into four columns with a speed of advance of 8 knots. Ahead were *Calpe* and *Fernie*. One of the centre columns consisted of Chasseurs towing L.C.As. The rest were M.Ls. and M.G.Bs. and one or two L.C.Ms., mostly towing L.C.As. Altogether there must have been between sixty and seventy craft, and it was most surprisingly orderly. Many of the motor craft were flying "Harry One" ("one of my engines is out of action"). Following the starboard column was the river gunboat *Locust* (with Ryder on board). Griff with the *Berkeley* survivors had long since gone on ahead to Newhaven.

As soon as we were through the minefield we gradually overtook the convoy so as to pass a signal to *Calpe*. We had a long signalled conversation with Tom Cartwright (Lt. Cdr. Cartwright, S.O. 14th M.G.B. Flotilla) in his " C " Class boat 316:

---

[1] The gunlayer of this gun at the time was Able Seaman J. Jones, who had served for two years with me in H.M.S. *Broke* before joining S.G.B. 9. For his work on this day, and for his unfailing good spirits, he was mentioned in despatches.

" How did you get on? " we asked.

" Our troops landed in face of strong opposition."

" Ours were luckier. Have you seen S.G.B. 5 ? "

" She was badly damaged. Wounded were transferred. Where is No. 8 ? "

" 8 did marvels and took off entire crew of *Berkeley* before she sank."

" When did *Berkeley* sink ? "

" 1308. Did No. 5 sink ? "

" Not that I know of," and so on by semaphore and later by light. We closed *Calpe* and told him we had collected five of his chaps.

While we were telling him, a single Dornier appeared and jettisoned his bombs some three miles away before making off with three or four Spitfires on his tail. The convoy put up a splendid barrage, much of which was closer to the pursuing Spitfires than the target. As an offensive act this attack was indeed pathetic, and seemed to be an interesting indication of the state of morale of what remained of the Luftwaffe at the end of their disastrous day. This was the last that we saw of the enemy except for a single bomber which passed over after dark. We obtained permission to tag on behind the destroyers returning to Portsmouth, and at 1928 we left the convoy heading for Newhaven and set off at 15 knots. Heavy dark grey clouds were coming up from the south-west and there was a menacing ruffle on the calm sea.

I went down to talk to the survivors and found one of the prisoners, a likeable youth who could speak no English, sitting between the Norwegian pilot and his guard (who was fast asleep with his head on the German's shoulder) with our black kitten on his lap. We had a short philosophical discussion on the senselessness of war to the limits of my German. He had apparently much impressed the ship's company by the way he had helped with the wounded. One of them told me that in spite of the blitzes, when he had vowed no quarter for any German he should meet, he could not help liking this one; " 'E's a gentleman, sir! " His reputation was the more remarkable as it was achieved without a word of the language.

The Norwegian told me he had shot down his first Jerry that day. It was the Dornier we had seen crash and burn on the cliff top early in the day. After that he had got home with a damaged plane, got another and come out again, only to be shot down himself by a F.W. 190.

We listened in the charthouse to the nine o'clock News giving details of the Raid, and I had half an hour's nap, from which I was roused by the alarm bell. When I emerged it was quite dark and raining hard, and the south-west wind was rising. A Dornier had just passed over low, and had been fired at by the destroyer ahead. It did not come back. Perhaps it was one of the force sent over to attack us at dusk or after, which owing to the change in the weather had not been able to find us and had gone on to unload their bombs somewhere inland —afterwards claiming great successes against the returning armada.

We turned up the Portsmouth swept channel half an hour later, and as we passed the Nab clouds of black smoke came from the funnel and we began to slow down. For more than twelve hours the engine-room staff had been fully extended, nursing badly shaken machinery. Now a combination of " stuck-up valves " and extreme fatigue was beating them. For the next hour and a half we proceeded in fits and starts in the inky darkness, having lost touch with the destroyers altogether. Finally, however, we found the gate at about midnight in spite of a steering compass that showed 15° difference from the standard and a completely unknown speed which varied between nought and 10 knots. We crept up the channel and groped our way into the harbour, turned and berthed alongside S.G.B. 3 at 0045 just over twenty-eight hours after we had left.

In a short while the 11 casualties, 5 survivors and 2 prisoners had been disembarked, an operation which was not made more easy by a failure of the shore lighting, so that the wounded had to be moved by torch-light. The prisoners were taken on board S.G.B. 3 and subsequently to the cruiser *Durban*, who lent us thirty blankets most promptly as all ours had been used by survivors and were wet or blood soaked. It was about three o'clock before we finally turned in to sleep late into the following morning.

CHAPTER IX

"WORKING-UP" WAS A STRENUOUS BUSINESS

THE Coastal Forces fitted only incidentally into the scheme of the Dieppe Raid, and it produced little fighting of their own particular type, with the exception of the twelve minutes of night action with the trawlers off Berneval. No torpedo targets offered themselves, neither did the E boats materialise, in spite of the reports that they were at sea. For the S.G.Bs. and the M.G.Bs. and the M.Ls. Dieppe was untypical.

For some time it had been realised, however, that the true Coastal Forces technique of night fighting had now become highly specialised. With increasing expansion in this branch of the Navy, it was clear that the facilities for training the crews must also be expanded.

The training of the individual (both officer and rating) which was carried out in H.M.S. *St. Christopher*, a shore establishment at Fort William, in Scotland (under the command of Cdr. A. E. P. Welman, D.S.O., D.S.C., R.N.), although excellent as far as it went, did not really go far enough. What was needed was for the whole crew to be trained together in their boat—a process known in the Navy as " working-up."

A " working-up " base for new boats soon after they were commissioned, and sometimes for old boats after they had been undergoing a long refit, had been envisaged some time before by Admiral Kekewich, the Rear-Admiral, Coastal Forces, and an officer was appointed to his staff in order to start such a base. Thus it was that the " working-up " base, subsequently named H.M.S. *Bee*, was established at Weymouth during the early summer of 1942, with the training in the capable hands of Cdr. R. F. B. Swinley, R.N.

H.M.S. *Bee* occupied an hotel, a theatre on a pier and a row of boarding-houses, as well as a number of sheds along the quayside; it was staffed partly by specialist officers in torpedoes, gunnery, signals, etc., and partly by Coastal Force officers whose long period of active operations qualified them for a rest and who usually remained at the *Bee* for about three months before returning to sea.

For those in training, " working-up " was a strenuous business. The day started with Morse flashing exercises, and lectures usually occupied the forenoon; then there were sea exercises in the afternoon and again during the night, often until three or four in the morning. The most valuable part of the training was at sea, and, when the weather was suitable, no opportunity for sea practices could be lost. During a long spell of good weather the boats went out night after night after night, so that it became a saying, towards the end of a work-up, that a boat would soon be going to operations for a rest.

It was eventually found that the syllabus took about thirty-five working days to complete. In summer this did not usually take more than the five weeks, but with winter gales sometimes seven or eight weeks were required before a boat was fully worked up. Many were the crews who spent even longer at H.M.S. *Bee*, because of engine troubles or other material break-downs in their boats.

This syllabus of exercises and practices was most exactly laid out in a standard sequence. Each type of lecture or drill or sea exercise was known by its initial letters and a figure. T.F.P. 5 was the fifth in the series of torpedo-firing practices. G.F.P. 2 was the second shoot in the series of gunnery firing practices. T.C.X. 1 was the first of the torpedo-control exercises, and so on. In spite of the standard sequence, however, there yet remained flexibility to meet the varying progress made by different crews. Therein lay the genius of Lt. Cdr. J. M. Matheson, R.N.V.R., who, as Lieutenant Commander, Administration, was responsible for the elaborate dovetailing of the daily training programme in which not only each crew but each part of each crew had its time exactly apportioned.

In most of the sea training the principle was to take one of the component parts of a successful attack and bring it to perfection, say the navigation for example, or the plotting, or the actual aiming and firing of the torpedoes. Not until nearly the end of the work-up were all these lessons combined in a full-scale C.F.X.—a Coastal Forces Exercise in which a complete attack was carried out at night with the maximum of realism.

Many of those passing through the *Bee* had already had wide experience of operations, and might well have claimed that they already " knew all the answers," but, in fact, this hardly ever happened. Those who really knew their job knew also that there is always more to learn, that one never quite catches up with the rapidly advancing material and tactical developments, that, but for a psychological staleness which occasionally develops, there is no such thing as too much training, if the training is good.

I myself passed twice through what was affectionately nicknamed " Swinley's Circus," before becoming one of the staff for my prescribed period. On each of those occasions I was impatient to be back on operations, but at the end of each work-up I tried to cast my mind back to the efficiency of the crew as a team when we had first arrived at Weymouth. Each time I thought, " Lord help us had we ever been called upon to go into battle in that state." As it was, we left each time confident that, if our team-work was not perfect, at least we were a fighting machine which worked.

At a later stage Captain the Hon. E. Pleydell-Bouverie, R.N., became Captain of the *Bee*, and when the preparations for the invasion of France were being made in the winter of 1943 and all the south-coast ports were required exclusively for that operation, the establishment moved to Holyhead in Anglesey to carry on the good work there. Cdr. J. L. Younghusband, D.S.C., R.N., who had wide experience of operating the Coastal Forces whilst on the staff of the Commander-in-Chief, the Nore, now became Training Commander; and the Tactical Commander was Cdr. A. V. de Labalmondiere, R.N.

For those who like to play a more active part in the war, a training job may well become irksome, but it is interesting to speculate on the direct effect upon enemy shipping which can be attributed to the teaching of such men as Lt. R. Hey, R.N., and Mr. S. Church, gunner (T), who were responsible for all the torpedo training at *Bee*; or Lt. Cdr. C. Russell Wood, R.N.V.R., the Gunnery Officer and Lt. Stratton Long, R.N.V.R., who with infinite patience taught so many guns' crews to shoot straight; or Lt. E. T. Smith, R.N.V.R., the Radar Officer. How many more interceptions were made, for instance, as a result of the meticulous care in navigation inculcated by Lt. P. N. Hood, R.N.V.R., who had been such a brilliant navigator in S.G.Bs. beforehand, and returned to sea later when he took over my boat, S.G.B. 9, then renamed *Grey Goose*. His work as Navigating Officer was taken on by Lt. R. G. Hudson, R.N.V.R., who later played an important part during the invasion of Normandy.

Amongst the officers who served for short periods on the staff of the *Bee* there are many names which appear elsewhere in this book: Jock Ritchie, Alan Gotelee, Ronnie Barge, "Boffin" Campbell, Mark Arnold Forster, Philip Lee, "Bussey" Carr, Peter Dickens, Basil Ward, Howard Bradford, Pat Edge, Lennox Cotton, John Best and John Mathias. It is a sad reflection that but for the action on the 13th April, 1943, the name of Robert Hichens would shortly afterwards have been added to the list.

The training at *Bee* set out to be basic and for the most part elementary, but, in the absence of any other Coastal Forces experimental centre, it was here that new tactics and new material were often given their first trials. But the solid achievements of the *Bee* meant that experience was no longer only to be gained in battle: and these solid achievements were reflected at once in the actions that were fought during that summer of 1942, when the first products of the new training were arriving at their operational bases. This flow of well-worked-up boats was, in itself, part cause of the greatly increased activity. We had improved our methods of bringing a reluctant enemy to action.

A Master of the Unhurried Approach

At the time of the Dieppe Raid the German programme of minefields in the Strait of Dover had not yet been completed. The E boats and R boats which were responsible for laying them had, as we have seen, already tried the ruse of coming out before dusk in order to forestall our night patrols. What more certain than that, with German thoroughness, they would explore the other extreme, coming out at dawn? For this the weather had to be carefully chosen when our aircraft could not take off because of mist over the airfields. Such a morning came on 23rd August, and another battle was fought in twilight, this time the morning twilight, against a strong force of minelaying E/R boats, supported, rather surprisingly, by an "M" Class minesweeper. Lt. N. K. Cale, R.N.V.R., was the Senior Officer of a unit of 70-foot M.G.Bs. which once more tackled odds of more than two to one in a close-range engagement in which Cale himself was killed. Although our force suffered damage, every boat returned from the engagement, in spite of the German broadcast claim that they had sunk four.

So the battles went on in the Strait. Meanwhile in the North Sea a new figure had appeared, an officer who was doing as much for the M.T.Bs. as Lt. Cdr. Hichens had done for the M.G.Bs. Now based on the East Coast, with the 21st Flotilla, consisting of sadly unreliable boats, was Lt. P. G. C. Dickens, M.B.E., R.N.

It has been pointed out how the spirit of a Coastal Force base depends greatly upon the leadership of the Senior Officers of the flotillas. This is so marked that those in Coastal Forces have come to connect particular periods at particular bases with particular names. Just as there was the Pumphrey-Gould era at Dover, so the Dickens era at Felixstowe was about to begin.

We have already seen at the very beginning of this book how Dickens was the master of the deliberate unhurried approach. His was a highly developed and scientific study of the technique of attack, combined with all the perceptions of a stalker. Since joining Coastal Forces he had fought one rather unsuccessful action, off Pointe de Barfleur, while operating from H.M.S. *Hornet* at Portsmouth, in the course of which the M.T.B. (under the command of Lt. R. G. Fison, R.N.V.R.), in which Dickens was embarked as Senior Officer, was set ablaze and lost, although the crew was skilfully rescued under fire by Sub-Lt. G. J. MacDonald, D.S.C., R.N.Z.N.V.R. Lt. I. C. Trelawny, R.N.V.R., commanding the third boat in the unit, also had a difficult time. " We found ourselves," he says, " all mixed up with the screen of the convoy we were trying to intercept. Hell was let loose, as the saying is. The Hun fired from, and in, all directions, and a searchlight played on the three M.T.Bs. present. My target was a largish merchant vessel at the tail of the convoy. Before long my steering was shot away, and the coxswain went off to steer from aft, leaving me alone on the bridge. Then the engines were hit, the engine-room crew passed out from carbon-monoxide gas poisoning, and our speed was reduced to 12 knots. My spare officer, Sub-Lt. Gill, and the gunner (the turret also being out of action), manned the engine-room, and we proceeded slowly and uncomfortably in the general direction of our target, being fired on from all sides, while one of our boats burned merrily in the middle distance. We got nearer and nearer and it looked as though we were going to make it, when suddenly a shell burst beside me in the bridge, knocked me down, and wounded me so that I couldn't get up again. Meanwhile we passed slowly under the stern of the target, who threw everything but the kitchen sink at us as we went by. Then No. 1 arrived on the bridge to take over, and found that we were so close to the beach, which was also joining in the proceedings, that the only way to get out was to go back the way we had come; which we did, while I lay on my back on the bridge and gave orders which No. 1 couldn't hear. Our torpedoes and firing gear were also damaged, so, after all that, we weren't able to inflict any damage on the enemy."

Trelawny's determination was to prove a good deal more damaging to the enemy in the months that followed, when he became Senior Officer of the 11th M.T.B. Flotilla, as we shall see in a later chapter.

PERFECT IN CONCEPTION AND EXECUTION

Dickens scored his first great success on 10th September, 1942, which was a busy night for the Coastal Forces. At this time he and his flotilla were installed at Lowestoft, and the tactics of combining M.T.Bs. and M.G.Bs. in one force were to be further developed. This time the two M.T.Bs., under the command of Dickens and Lt. J. P. Perkins, R.N.V.R., were supported by three gunboats led by Lt. E. D. W. Leaf, D.S.C., R.N.V.R. The attack on a small convoy off the Texel was perfect in conception and execution, and it was crowned with the success it deserved. A merchantman, and possibly one of its escorts as well, were quietly torpedoed while Leaf's gunboats " kept the party going."

Meanwhile several groups of E boats had been busy off the English coast and three 70-foot M.G.Bs., led by Lt. J. B. R. Horne, D.S.C., R.N., had intercepted one group as it retired. A long running fight followed as the M.G.Bs. pursued the E boats eastwards across the North Sea. With Horne were Lt. P. A. R. Thompson, D.S.C., R.C.N.V.R., and Lt. J. S. Price, R.N.V.R. For Horne and Thompson it was a satisfactory reversal of the occasion when, after their victory in March, E boat reinforcements had found them short of ammunition and fuel and with an engine breakdown in Thompson's boat, so that the pursuit had been in the opposite direction.

Lt. E. M. Thorpe, R.N., who had been waiting off the Dutch coast with a party of four " C " Class M.G.Bs., followed the signals from Horne with interest and plotted the reported positions of the enemy who would, he estimated, pass a few miles to the north. Like a cricketer in the deep field, he adjusted his position and waited for the ball to arrive.

By now it was getting light, and action damage had slowed up Horne's gunboats, so that the quarry had been lost. The point at which Thorpe was about to make contact was evidently a rendezvous for the E boats. Already two groups had joined, and when, in broad daylight, the " C " boats sighted the enemy the odds were already nine against four. Soon after the battle started M.G.B. 335 (Lt. J. A. Forbes, R.N.V.R.), which had turned out of line in order to close the enemy, was hit in the engine-room, stopped and set on fire. Two more " C " boats were hit, although the enemy also appeared to be suffering considerably. Evidently a further group of E boats had now joined in the action, as about twelve of them were formed in a semicircle round the disabled M.G.B. At bay, she was still firing back and the enemy remained four or five hundred yards away, but she was already a shambles and the casualties were mounting. It was at this stage that Thorpe decided to make a rescue bid. Under fire from twelve E boats at no more than 500 yards range in broad daylight, he laid his boat alongside 335 and took off most of the survivors: and then as he drew away he fired at the waterline in an attempt to sink her. Unfortunately the attempt did not succeed. Although he had been alongside her for some seven minutes, two of the crew, below in the wireless office and cut off by the fire in the chart-house, had been unable to get across to Thorpe's boat. These two and the burnt-out remains of the M.G.B. fell into the hands of the enemy. This unlucky conclusion, however, could not detract from the magnificent gallantry of Thorpe's rescue operation, for which he was awarded the D.S.O.

Less than three weeks later the German reaction to the combined M.G.B./M.T.B. attack had begun to make itself felt. On 30th September, Dickens led another such attack, with M.G.Bs. under Lt. J. S. Dyer, R.N. Once again Perkins showed his outstanding marksmanship in firing torpedoes. Two torpedo hits are believed to have been scored, but the battle was fierce and there were a number of casualties on our side. Amongst them Lt. M. T. C. Sadler, R.N.V.R., was killed instantly on the bridge of his boat. As usual, the German claim was over-optimistic. In their broadcast two days later they admitted that one of their patrol boats had sunk, but they claimed that no fewer than four of our boats had been destroyed and two others damaged. On the following day a long account of the battle was broadcast in support of this somewhat fantastic claim.

The loss of Tommy Sadler was a great blow to his flotilla and to the base at Lowestoft. He was typical of the eager and vigorous men who commanded the M.G.Bs. and fought night after night to maintain their initiative in the North Sea. The strain of this fighting is well described in a passage written of Sadler by his father, Michael Sadleir, the novelist:[1]

" On his last two leaves, when he was sitting alone with me and reading, or thought himself unobserved, he would sink into a sort of wistful brooding, and I feared that he was thinking of the many responsibilities of his command and of the danger and exhaustion of what for him and his friends had become the whole of existence. No outsider could intrude on a private unhappiness of this sort, nor could an ignorant civilian do more than guess at the strain under which the young men of the light coastal forces—for all the gaiety, comradeship and excitement of their job—were forced to live. One could only try to make the fleeting period of his leave fill the foreground of his thoughts, and so gain for him a short respite from the cruel apprehension laid on a whole generation of young people by a handful of evil men."

The particular tactics of the action on 30th September, however, had now been overplayed, and an attack launched against a convoy on the night of 3rd October was twice thwarted and finally proved unsuccessful, although Dickens had such names amongst his commanding officers that night as Trelawny, Weeden and Fraser in the M.T.Bs., and Thompson, Leaf and Lambert in the gunboats. Another fierce action two nights later resulted in the destruction of an E/R boat at the cost of one M.G.B. and one M.T.B. sunk.

But though the full-scale battle, with M.T.Bs. and M.G.Bs. in company, had lost, for the

---

[1] The passage is taken from a privately printed memoir.

time being, its element of surprise, there were still possibilities for " the unobserved attack," and Dickens, with boats whose so frequent breakdowns often left him with all too small a force when he reached his hunting-ground, now concentrated on the approach by stealth. The chances of an " unobserved attack " were, at that time, still sufficiently good, and the results so much more likely to be decisive, that it should, Dickens believed, always be regarded as the prime method. Briefly the principle of the " unobserved attack " was that the torpedoes should be fired before the enemy even knew that M.T.Bs. were in the neighbourhood, when they could be aimed without the distraction of dazzling starshells and flying tracer bullets, and when the enemy would be unlikely to alter his course or speed suddenly during the run of the torpedoes.

By regarding this as the prime method, Dickens, the greatest M.T.B. exponent of his time, indicated his full appreciation that surprise was still the most potent weapon of the Coastal Forces. Six days after the full-scale attack which had been abortive, he tried out a simple stalk which succeeded perfectly.

UNOBSERVED ATTACK

On the night of 9th November, 1942, two M.T.Bs. were approaching the corner of Holland. They were on their way to intercept an enemy convoy which their orders, based on the report of a reconnaissance aircraft earlier in the day, told them to expect near Terschelling, steaming northward.

The first of these two M.T.Bs. was commanded by Lt. J. L. Fraser, R.N.V.R., with Dickens on board as Senior Officer of the force, and the second by Lt. D. Felce, R.N.V.R. Soon after 10 p.m. the two boats reduced speed and began to creep silently in towards the coast and the route on which the convoy might be expected. As they did so they could hear our heavy bombers passing overhead in a continuous stream. Seven minutes later the convoy was sighted right ahead, and Dickens realised at once that the noise of his engines before he reduced speed must surely have been heard by the enemy but for the providential stream of bombers.

The night was clear but very dark, without any moon at all, and, as the M.T.Bs. closed in, they could see that the convoy was a large one. There seemed to be about eight merchant ships in two rough columns, with at least two, possibly three, escorts ahead of them. One of these looked like a " T " Class torpedo boat and another was an " M " Class minesweeper. Astern of the convoy came at least one more minesweeper. At 10.20 p.m. Dickens lay nicely ahead of the enemy and he stopped, so that the convoy would steam past at a range of no more than half a mile. As he waited he studied the approaching enemy in detail and decided that three large ships which were bunched together provided the best targets. The biggest of these was a ship of between three and four thousand tons with its bridge and funnel aft, which he took at the time to be a tanker. The other two were only slightly smaller and of the normal one-funnel, two-mast, three-island type.

For twelve minutes the two boats lay stopped while the convoy steadily advanced and the suspense mounted. Still the Germans were unaware of their presence. Dickens gave his instructions to the other boat through a megaphone, then slowly the two M.T.Bs. moved in again, to deliver their " unobserved attack." Two minutes later four carefully aimed torpedoes had leapt from their tubes and were speeding on their way towards the enemy. The suspense was ended.

Both the boats started up their main engines to disengage, and as they did so a column of water and smoke shot up the side of the enemy ship. One torpedo had hit. Three seconds later there was a flash and a loud explosion as a second torpedo hit, and it is possible that a third one also found its mark.

" After an appreciable interval," writes Dickens, " fire was opened on the M.T.Bs. by the convoy and escort, starting with light automatic weapons, until later starshell and 4-inch joined in. The fire was wild, however, and no damage was caused except to our aerial, which collapsed as the initial enemy report was being transmitted. The M.T.Bs., disengaging at high speed to the west, were soon out of range. During this time the enemy ships were seen to be firing at each other and large numbers of starshells were put up. At 10.46 p.m. I cut engines in order to discuss the action, and when I started up again the battle astern was re-doubled in intensity and continued intermittently until 12.15 a.m., when starshells could only just be seen over the horizon."

" On 9th November the steamer Abisko, 3,085 tons, bound for Stockholm with a cargo of coal, was hit by a torpedo in No. two hold, but jettisoned 800 tons of coal and reached Emden."—
Swedish Newspaper.

No mention is made of any ship or ships that may have sunk.

SHIPS THAT PASS IN THE NIGHT

Not so successful, but no less exciting, was an adventure of Dickens' a few nights later, on the 15th November, 1942. His force was again two M.T.Bs.—one, commanded by Lt. Felce, in which he was embarked, and the other by Lt. Perkins. The two boats were lying in wait for a convoy off the coast of Holland, on a dark night with a fairly strong north-west wind. The visibility was very poor and it was drizzling.

Soon after a quarter to two in the morning, Dickens sighted two ships on his starboard quarter coming towards him:

" I shouted to the other boat, but she could not hear owing to the wind; it appears, however, that she sighted at much the same time as I did. My first impression was that the enemy were trawlers, and I decided to attack. I therefore carried on on a northerly course so as to increase my distance from the line of advance of the enemy. Very shortly after this I observed that the range had decreased considerably, and this showed that the targets were moving fast. Then I saw that they were destroyers. They were steering to pass about 100 yards astern of me, and I tried to decide whether I had been sighted and they were preparing to ram, in which case I had better disengage, or whether I was still unobserved. As they were not coming straight at me I chose the latter alternative, put the wheel over to port and hoped I could turn in time to get the sights on before it was too late."

By this time the leading destroyer was right on top of the second M.T.B. " He passed close astern of us," says Lt. Perkins, " at a range of about 40 yards, alarm bells and shouting being heard. Then I saw another destroyer about half a cable astern. As I was facing in completely the wrong direction, I knew I would have no time to turn before they were both past, and I thought there was considerable chance of being rammed by the second destroyer." So Perkins made a crash start and moved out to gain a suitable attacking position.

Meanwhile Dickens' boat had turned to port and was in a good position to fire torpedoes at the incredibly short range of 150 yards. There was no time to set the torpedo sight, and the torpedoes had to be fired by eye.

" I was too concerned," Dickens' report goes on, " with the danger of missing astern, having judged the enemy's speed to be 25 knots, and gave the order too early. Both torpedoes ran straight and were seen to pass very close ahead. I was too close to the enemy to disengage in the normal manner and therefore started main engines and passed through their line. The second ship altered course to port as I came through; perhaps she thought I was a torpedo. It was only when I was about 200 yards away that the enemy started firing, but even then it was wild. I made smoke and was soon clear. It was obvious that they were not at action stations and not even alert and keeping a good lookout."

Perkins having gained bearing turned in to attack, but at once he saw he was in a bad position for a torpedo attack. Again he moved out, but again when he closed in the firing position was hopeless. While he was trying a third time he lost contact altogether. The two destroyers had vanished into the night.

AN IMPORTANT TARGET

By the autumn of 1942 Lt. Cdr. Hichens had left the West Country and returned with his flotilla to Felixstowe; but his experiences in the Channel had been sufficient to indicate that here was a fruitful field for the expansion of Coastal Forces activity. From this time until the Channel was virtually cleared of enemy ships by the reconquest of France, M.T.Bs. and M.G.Bs. were based at Dartmouth under the control of the Commander-in-Chief, Plymouth, for defence against E boats, and for offence against coastal shipping between Cherbourg and Ushant, and amongst the Channel Islands.

By comparison with the North Sea, the Channel, being deeper, had a lesser mine risk for such ships as destroyers, and it was west of the Straits that tactics were developed which involved sweeps along the occupied coast by destroyers and M.T.Bs. in company. One such sweep was carried out in the autumn of 1942 when the Germans were trying to take an important ship through the Channel and out into the Atlantic. This was a new fast ship of about 4,000 tons, heavily armed and equipped as a commerce raider and supply ship.

In the earlier stages of its passage through the Straits and down Channel it had evaded all attempts at interception, and on the evening of the 13th October[1] it sailed from Le Havre towards the west. From its escort of four or five "T" Class torpedo boats it was evident that the enemy attached great importance to its safe passage.

It was not certain whether this next stage of the journey would be the normal leg to Cherbourg or whether in view of its speed it would strike on past the Channel Islands towards Brest.

A strong force had been assembled to destroy it, consisting of H.M. destroyers *Cottesmore*, *Quorn* and *Albrighton* with the Norwegian destroyers *Glaisdale* and *Eskdale* (constituting Group A) and two flotillas of M.T.Bs. (Groups C and D). Owing to the fast speed of the enemy ship, there was not time to intercept it before it could reach Cherbourg, and so the British force, hoping that the Germans would decide to run the gauntlet of the whole danger area in one night, lay in wait farther west near Cap de la Hague, the westernmost point of the Cherbourg peninsula. Meanwhile, in case the enemy was able to slip past the main force, four more destroyers, *Brocklesby*, *Fernie*, *Tynedale* and the Polish *Krakowiak* (making up Group B) were sent to wait in the neighbourhood of the Channel Islands.

Fortunately the enemy was spotted early in the night by Coastal Command aircraft in the middle of the Baie de la Seine, and his speed was estimated at 16 knots. At this speed, however, it was necessary for the main force to make for the intercepting position off Cap de la Hague with all despatch. It was a very dark night, with a moderate westerly wind, and

[1] About a month before the two actions of Lt. Dickens just described.

unfortunately Group C consisted of M.T.Bs. of the very oldest type. They were following astern of the destroyers, and in the prevailing conditions they were unable to keep up. The other flotilla (Group D) was following astern of them, so that all the M.T.Bs. became separated from the destroyers. A few minutes before one o'clock the enemy was first sighted from H.M.S. *Cottesmore*, and two minutes later the destroyers fired starshell to illuminate him. The battle had begun.

The enemy force consisted of a large vessel " of modern cargo design " with one funnel and two masts apparently screened by four " T " Class torpedo boats. Lt. Cdr. J. C. A. Ingram, R.N., the Captain of the *Cottesmore* and Senior Officer of the force, reports that " the enemy appeared to have been taken completely by surprise, and it was only after several salvos had been fired that any counter-action was taken, and consisted partly of the torpedo boats engaging each other with green and red ' Flak.' "

The five " Hunt " Class destroyers passed on opposite course at about 4,000 yards range, firing principally at the main target, which was very soon set on fire. The " T " Class torpedo boats of the screen were also being engaged. They retaliated by firing torpedoes. *Cottesmore* heard one of these approaching and was able to alter course in time to avoid it and see it pass harmlessly up the starboard side. But the escort was being overwhelmed. Two of them were on fire and the remainder, pursued by the destroyers, turned towards the land and the protection of the shore batteries, which had begun to fire with considerable accuracy by now.

It was at this juncture that M.T.B. 236 came upon the scene.

THE *COUP DE GRÂCE*

A few days before, the Commanding Officer of M.T.B. 236 had gone sick and the First Lieutenant—Sub-Lt. R. Q. Drayson, R.N.V.R.—had been appointed in command. This was his first operation in that capacity, and, being the junior Commanding Officer of Group D, his place was at the end of the line of M.T.Bs.

Soon after midnight he received a signal by shaded blue light from the next ahead to stop. He reduced speed, but the boats ahead seemed to increase speed, for they were immediately lost to sight. So he increased speed again, but he was unable to regain contact. Actually he probably overshot them, for the leader *did* stop at about that time to tell the Senior Officer of Group D, who was following him, that he had lost touch with the destroyers and to discuss what they should do. What they decided does not concern the story, because owing to a failure of wireless signals and the slow speed of the older boats they never made contact with the enemy. What does concern the story is that M.T.B. 236, a faster boat, had become detached, and her Captain reports that he " decided immediately to proceed direct to Cap de la Hague."

After a while he saw starshells and tracers ahead as the action began, and he increased speed. He decided to slip in towards the shore and intercept anything that might be trying to slink away in the smoke and confusion of the battle.

Suddenly he sighted the main target silhouetted in the starshell. She was being heavily engaged by the destroyers and she was firing astern, but she was still making more than 15 knots. The M.T.B. was ahead of her and crept in unseen at very slow speed. At about 500 yards she fired her two torpedoes and then immediately turned away to starboard, " crash-started " her main engines and made off under cover of a smoke-screen. Drayson says in his report: " As soon as torpedoes were fired the gunfire from the target's stern guns swung round and eventually passed across my stern. The after life-line was severed but no casualties were suffered. A few seconds later the torpedoes hit the target with two distinct explosions, the target burst into flames and blew up, showering fragments of burning material past my ship. The flames spread rapidly and were capped by a thick pall of rolling smoke."

This is how the Senior Officer of the destroyers described it: " . . . a violent explosion took place, followed a fraction of a second later by another which dwarfed the previous one. Flames shot up at least four hundred feet, the ship blew completely to pieces and burning oil spread over about a square mile of sea; a great pall of smoke rose to a height of several thousand feet. The explosion was an ammunition one aggravated by oil fuel and took place at 0116."

The supporting force of destroyers (Group B) were more than thirty miles away at the time, but the Commanding Officer of the *Brocklesby* reports that " a bright flash followed by a huge column of smoke was seen over the top of Guernsey—changing into a deep dull red glow and then to the normal glow of a fire."

Drayson describes how the stern of his M.T.B. was " lifted out of the water by the force of the explosion," and how as a result his centre engine broke down and the port engine was damaged so that his speed on the homeward journey was limited to 15 knots. " Just before she blew up," he wrote afterwards, " the merchantman *was* becoming rather accurate, but my greatest fear was, after she had been hit, that some of the bits in the air might land on us."

Thus the little M.T.B. after losing contact with the next ahead—one of the deadly sins in Coastal Forces—was able, through the admirable initiative of her Commanding Officer on his first operation in command, to retrieve the situation by arriving in time to deliver the *coup de grâce*, a feat for which Drayson was subsequently awarded the Distinguished Service Cross.

" The situation now," Lt. Cdr. Ingram's report goes on, " was that slightly to the right of the blazing remains of the merchantman one torpedo boat lay blazing from stem to stern and to the left one lay stopped emitting black smoke. Fire was shifted to the latter and it finally was covered in flames. It is considered that both of these vessels must have been lost."

Although they were only a mile or two from Cap de la Hague, these fires could be seen from the English coast, sixty miles away.

There is some doubt whether these burning torpedo boats did actually sink, but there is no doubt whatsoever that they were badly damaged and left well and truly on fire.

GREAT CONFUSION AMONGST THE ENEMY

Meanwhile the four " Hunt " Class destroyers of Group B were speeding up between the Channel Islands and the coast of France. When they were abeam of Sark they could see three distinct fires in the Race of Alderney ahead of them and suddenly a nearby puff of smoke was silhouetted against the glow; below it a line of ships could just be seen.

It was now 2.15 a.m., about an hour after the destruction of the raider, and the shore batteries farther to the northward were still firing intermittently. Group B was on an opposite course to the new enemy force, which consisted of four escort ships, and a brisk engagement followed at close range. The Commanding Officer of H.M.S. *Brocklesby*[1] describes how, about a mile astern of the main force, another enemy vessel was being heavily engaged by its own shore batteries. The whole of the enemy force appears to have been surprised. As our Group B completed its first run, the Senior Officer reports that: " Great confusion took place in the enemy astern, multi-coloured rockets were fired in all directions and a continual stream of tracer was exchanged amongst themselves."

By now a general alarm had been raised amongst the islands, and since the fire of the shore

[1] Lt. Cdr. G. Blackler, R.N.

batteries was becoming accurate the destroyers disengaged. The Commanding Officer of the *Tynedale* [1] reports that he " ceased fire with the remainder at 0234, and it was then seen that the enemy were engaging one another with good effect." What self-inflicted damage the enemy suffered cannot be known, but the primary object of the operation had been achieved. The raider had been destroyed and at least two of the escort had been seriously damaged.

Although this action was fought close under the heavy coastal batteries, our whole force suffered no damage at all and only two slight casualties. The enemy, however, could not stomach such a loss without a counter-claim. The German communiqué on the following day contained this passage:

" During the night of 13th/14th October, a Naval encounter took place in the Channel between German escort vessels and a superior enemy formation consisting of two groups of destroyers and several M.T.B. flotillas. In hard fighting a British motor gunboat was sunk and five M.T.Bs. were damaged or set on fire by artillery hits. One of our own vessels was lost."

Rather, if one might be allowed to add, a valuable vessel.

---

[1] Lt. J. J. S. Yorke, D.S.C., R.N., previously Commanding Officer of H.M.S. *Berkeley* when she was sunk off Dieppe.

CHAPTER X

FRESH FIELDS

THE " D " Class Fairmile had by now proved itself in battle as an efficient motor gunboat. It was capable of keeping the seas in much heavier weather than the smaller boats, it had a greater range, and it packed a heavier punch. With the addition of torpedoes the boats could be made even more formidable, and it was realised that as winter approached they would be suitable for making the passage from the north of the British Isles to Norway. Accordingly, a flotilla was equipped with torpedoes and manned by personnel of the Royal Norwegian Navy, under the command of Lt. Cdr. R. A. Tamber, R.Nor.N., and the curtain was raised in a new theatre of operations for the Coastal Forces.

The first success was scored in the early morning hours of 27th November, 1942, when two M.T.Bs. penetrated the Skjaergaard and found two large merchant ships, lying at anchor together with three trawler escorts, in the anchorage of Askevold, which lies between Bergen and Stavanger.

There was a brilliant moon, but in spite of that surprise was complete. The enemy was quite unprepared for the possibility of such an attack, and the two M.T.Bs. approached to 700 yards. The first merchant vessel was estimated at between 5,000 and 7,000 tons, and appeared to be heavily laden. The leading M.T.B. fired both torpedoes at her and reports that " the starboard torpedo struck amidships and a column of water was seen to rise 300 feet into the air. The port torpedo ran inaccurately and either struck a jetty or another ship alongside it. The merchant vessel sank very rapidly; four minutes later her upper deck was awash on the port side, and when last seen only her stern was visible above the water."

The second M.T.B. was following 20 yards astern of the first and she had to make a very sharp turn—going astern on the inside engine—in order to bring her sights to bear on the second merchant ship lying to the south of the first. " She was a heavily laden vessel of 6,000–8,000 tons; an anchor light was burning forward. She was an old ship, probably of the Taurus class. One torpedo struck under the bow and the other amidships. Her bows seemed to lift out of the water and fall back, and then she settled by the bows and when last seen, as in the previous case, only her stern was visible."

" As soon as the last two torpedoes had struck, both boats increased speed to 25 knots. One of the escorts fired three rounds of tracer shell which passed ineffectively overhead."

More than an hour later flares were seen to the eastward, probably dropped by aircraft searching for the M.T.Bs. These and the three tracer shells were the only signs of enemy activity that were observed. By 7 a.m. our force was well on its way home, but the south-west wind was steadily increasing, and by 11 in the forenoon it was blowing a full gale—Force 9—sea very rough. The two boats became separated in the gale, but they struggled on and reached harbour during the afternoon.

This was the first of a series of highly successful operations carried out in the fjords of the Norwegian coast. More and more ambitious schemes were conceived, until on 23rd January, 1943, with the co-operation of Commando troops, the destruction of an iron pyrites mine in the island of Stord was undertaken. The raid was completely successful. The mine was put out of action for at least a year, a merchant ship of 2,000 tons was sunk, and a number of installations round the harbour were wrecked. Many enemy gun positions were destroyed—four of them with demolition charges—and prisoners were taken. Finally, a Ju. 88 which attacked the force on the return journey was hit and exploded in mid-air. This destruction was wrought at the cost of one Commando killed and a few minor casualties.

In winter the long nights in these northern latitudes greatly assisted operations in this new area, but the Norwegian M.T.B. Flotilla was not content to interrupt its activities during the summer months even though there was no true darkness at all. One of their most notable successes was an attack by two M.T.Bs. on a 7,000-ton merchant ship and its escorting "M" Class minesweeper, on the 4th June, 1943, off Traelso. All four torpedoes hit their target and the ship sank immediately. As she went down she pulled the balloon she had been flying down towards the water until finally it remained just above the surface to mark her grave. The escort minesweeper was engaged and heavily damaged by gunfire, before the M.T.Bs. disengaged with casualties of two killed and five wounded.

These battles amongst the fjords and the islands were very different from the more usual Coastal Force actions off the coasts of France and the Low Countries, but they were a part of the struggle to interfere with enemy transport routes and to attack enemy shipping wherever it might be found.

THEY NEVER KNEW WHAT HIT THEM

So successful were the operations of the M.T.Bs. on the coast of Norway that this Norwegian flotilla was later reinforced by a British flotilla under the command of Lt. Cdr. K. Gemmel, R.N.V.R., but in the spring of 1943 this officer was making his name as a cool leader in the "D" Class M.T.Bs. operating from H.M.S. *Midge* at Great Yarmouth against the convoys off the Dutch coast. The greater range of the "D" boats made it possible for them to hunt round the corner of Holland, where the enemy was less likely to expect them. In March he made a successful attack on a large tanker which, together with two of its escorts, was probably sunk, but in the course of the action one boat, commanded by Lt. F. W. Carr, R.N.V.R., was destroyed. All the other boats returned with no more than superficial damage, in spite of the German claim:

"Off the Dutch coast a formation of British M.T.Bs. attacked a German convoy. The escorting forces repelled the attack, sank three enemy M.T.Bs. and shelled and set on fire two others."

Three days later, on 12th March, 1943, Lt. Cdr. (then Lt.) Gemmel brought off perhaps the most perfect unobserved attack of the war.

"Although this attack eventually proved to be completely unobserved," writes Gemmel, "and no rough house developed in consequence, I think I voice the opinion of most of those present, that the nervous tension was greater than that experienced during a 'free for all.' Perhaps this was due to the fact that three nights previously we had attacked a similar convoy in this area, which resulted in the magnificent bag of a 6,500-ton tanker and two escorts. On this occasion destroyers had severely mauled us and we witnessed one of our flotilla mates sink in a raging inferno of flames. The memory of all this, I think, created no small amount of reaction—it did for me, anyway.

"Visibility was good and our quarry was sighted at fairly long range. Yes, there it was— quite a large convoy, including at least three big merchant vessels and a hell of a crowd of escorts. A repetition seemed imminent.

"The three M.T.Bs. were stopped and plotting the enemy course. 'See the bastards,' came a voice floating across the water. 'A big 'un for each of us,' came another. 'All right, let's go,' I said in a voice I hardly recognised as my own. 'Take a merchant vessel each—I shall not give you any signals—only the executive to attack. Good luck.'

"We moved off and commenced the stalk. The enemy came nearer and nearer, and at an approximate range of 3,000 yards, I gave the executive signal. The M.T.Bs. turned as though on a pivot. I glanced down the line and saw everyone in perfect station on the beam. It was a thrilling sight as these ferocious little boats closed the range and jockeyed for a good firing position. We could see them plainly now, and fully expected all hell to be let loose at any second. 'I hope there's no bloody destroyers this time,' said someone. 'Have a shot from here, sir. You can't possibly miss,' suggested my coxswain. 'For God's sake, stop yapping,' I snapped—I felt awful. My sights were slowly coming on a large rather old-fashioned cargo vessel with a tall thin funnel. I overheard a stage whisper that the others had fired their torpedoes. The target crossed the sight—swish! and away went mine.

" Still no opposition as we turned to port, steadied and disengaged slowly away. An age seemed to pass by as we anxiously peered at our target. Bill and Johnny, my two officers, were beside me. 'I'm afraid I've missed, boys,' I remarked, and felt like crying. Almost as I said this we felt a great thump, closely followed by another. 'Two have been hit,' yelled someone, and the crew cheered. It was right enough—our target had broken in half and was settling fast. Ahead of her another merchant vessel belched black smoke and tongues of flame—she was sinking by the stern. Even now our opponents failed to realise our presence and we drew farther away to safety. We noticed a certain amount of inter-signalling and presently up went one solitary starshell—no use, it was fired in the wrong direction and plainly illuminated the stricken vessels. The other two M.T.Bs. rejoined us and cheered lustily as they ran alongside some yards away. 'What a bleeding picnic,' someone shouted. I gazed silently astern—a voice at my side said, 'Try one, sir.' 'Thanks,' I replied. The raw spirit burned my throat."

CO-OPERATION IN THE STRAITS

That night was an expensive one for the Germans, for at the same time as Lt. Gemmel was sinking ships off the coast of Holland, the Dover M.T.Bs. were doing great work off the coast of the Pas-de-Calais. By this time enemy activity in the Strait had become greatly reduced. The efforts of our M.G.Bs., although they had harassed and upset it, had not been able to prevent the minelaying programme of the previous autumn, and their mid-Channel minefield was regarded by the Germans as complete. But they realised, nevertheless, that the risk to their coastwise convoys was still great, and so they had substantially reduced the number of ships passing through the Narrows. As usual, those which did pass were surrounded with a massive escort, and the fighting was as fierce as ever, but at this period the M.T.Bs. working from Dover were seldom in action more than once a month, and not always so often.

New tactics, too, were being developed, involving the co-operation of Fleet Air Arm Albacores and the heavy-gun batteries on the Kentish shore. How successful these tactics could be is shown by the following account of that same night, told by Lt. B. C. Ward, D.S.C., R.N., who had lately become Senior Officer, M.T.Bs., at Dover.

On the 12th March, 1943, a striking force consisting of M.T.Bs. 38 (Lt. M. Arnold Forster, D.S.C., R.N.V.R.), 35 (Lt. R. Saunders, D.S.C., R.A.N.V.R.) and 24 (Lt. V. F. Clarkson, R.N.V.R.) was lying at short notice in Dover Harbour. Ward was the Senior Officer of the Force.

" I had just gone to bed, thinking it was a bit late for anything to happen that night," he writes, " when, at about 1 a.m., the Duty Officer rushed in to say that I was wanted on the telephone by the Operations Room at the Castle. I dashed to the phone, shouting like mad, as I went, for the boats to start main engines, and was told that an enemy merchant vessel had been spotted leaving Boulogne, and that we were to go to sea and intercept it.

" Lt. B. Easton, D.S.C., R.N.V.R., of M.T.B. 221, whose boat was at long notice that night, had been woken up by all the noise and implored me to let him come too; if only we could hold on for five minutes he would get his boat ready. He was told that we couldn't wait, but that, if he could catch us up, he could join in the party.

" Our three boats got to sea in very quick time and we proceeded at once up Channel towards Dunkirk. A supporting force of M.G.Bs. led by Lt. G. D. K. Richards, D.S.C., R.N., joined us and we all stopped for ten minutes while Richards and I discussed our tactics. Then we set off again for the interception. The wind was fairly fresh, and with a nasty choppy sea we were all getting miserably wet. The big guns at Dover had opened fire on the convoy and the enemy was replying. The enormous white flashes from both sides of the Strait as the guns went off were difficult to distinguish from the bursting of shells, which take over a minute to arrive at the other side.

" As we approached the convoy we could see starshell being fired, and shortly afterwards tracer at the Fleet Air Arm planes that were already going in to attack. In the light of the enemy's starshell, I suddenly caught sight of the merchant ship and shouted out to Arnold Forster, who was beside me, ' Can you see her, Mark?' Just at that moment, to our intense annoyance, the starshells went out, but that glimpse had given us a good idea of the position of the enemy and we crept ahead at 10 knots to get into a good firing position. ' Tin-hat time,' said someone, and we all put on our tin-hats. At last Mark sighted the main target through his binoculars and I shouted out to the other M.T.Bs., ' Enemy in sight.'

" We continued to close in until we were on the enemy's beam at 700 yards range, and Mark fired his torpedoes as the target steamed across the sights. Dick Saunders, the next boat in the line, had also seen the enemy and fired his torpedoes less than half a minute after us. We were sighted by one of the escorts almost immediately after firing torpedoes and the party started. We disengaged at full speed with considerable fire coming at us. Frank Clarkson in M.T.B. 24 had not seen the target and, although he tried to get closer, he was driven off by the escorts. About forty seconds after Mark had fired there was a beautiful explosion amidships of the merchant vessel and a column of water shot up to a hundred feet. Saunders told me afterwards of his disappointment and rage when he saw his torpedoes running perfectly to hit, only to pass just ahead as Arnold Forster's torpedoes stopped the target before his two arrived.

" Meanwhile Dicky Richards and his gunboats had gone in at full speed and were attacking the escort, as we had previously arranged. He was most gallantly taking a lot of the enemy's fire off us, but not before all the M.T.Bs. had been hit.

" ' Teek ' (Lt. H. Teekman, D.S.C., R.C.N.V.R.) was out with us, as he always was when he thought there was likely to be a battle. He shouted up to the bridge from down below, saying there was a fire forward. Sub-Lt. H. G. Bradley, D.S.C., R.N.V.R., the First Lieutenant of M.T.B. 38, gathered his fire party and staggered down below to put out the fire. It was pitch dark down there, as the lights had been put out by a shell coming in through the ship's side, and he saw a yellow glow coming from a pile of blankets. The blankets were flung away to disclose that the ' fire ' was an ordinary miner's lamp that had fallen down owing to the bouncing of the boat in the rough sea. Its light had been shining up through the blankets which had fallen on top of it. We got back to harbour with three minor casualties and only slight damage. The M.G.Bs. had had a very spirited action with the escorts, of which there were about a dozen, and having done their job of diverting the fire of some of the enemy from the M.T.Bs., they retired on receipt of a signal from me, as the enemy was by this time fully awake and the odds were at least twelve against three.

" Barry Easton in 221 had left harbour in very quick time some ten minutes after us, but he was just too late to catch up with us before the action started, and had the mortification of returning to harbour without having taken part. It took a lot of explaining to him on our return that we couldn't have waited a bit longer for him to join up.

" A most excellent dinner was provided for us all on the following evening by the Commanding Officers of the M.T.Bs. at a neighbouring base, as the result of a bet, made shortly before, on which flotilla would be the next to sink a ship."

The enemy account, which follows, of the two battles fought that night takes a somewhat different, and, for them, more optimistic view of the results achieved. It will be recalled while reading it, that Gemmel's force was not engaged with gunfire, and therefore suffered no casualties whatever, and that Ward's force returned to harbour with only slight damage and three minor casualties.

HEAVY NIGHT FOR OUR PATROL BOATS IN THE CHANNEL
FIVE M.T.BS. SUNK, FOUR SET ON FIRE AND ONE DAMAGED

By War Reporter Hans Mänz-Junkers

" As reported in the High Command communiqué of 13th March, a total of five M.T.Bs. was sunk off the Dutch coast and in the Channel by German patrol boats; four more were set on fire and one damaged.

" It was a heavy night for our patrols, with bad visibility and, what is more, the convoy was up against heavy seas. Our patrol-boat crews knew that they had to expect something from Tommy. It was a valuable convoy that had to be escorted through the Channel. Soon the vanguard of the convoy had reached the Channel's narrowest part, at Cap Gris Nez. The wind dropped, the sea calmed down. The look-outs doubled their vigilance. Now the place was reached on which Tommy is wont to focus the fire of his shore batteries. And sure enough, here he was. Fire! Now they all knew where we were. One shell after another burst near our convoy, sending up huge columns of water, followed, sometimes, by a shower of splinters over the boats. And now, flashing up from starboard, the fire of our own batteries, which immediately opened up on the enemy batteries. It was certainly a relief for our patrol-boat crews when the British, handicapped in their firing, lowered the intensity of their salvos and had to let the convoy go.

" ' Noise of aircraft astern ! ' the cry resounded over the deck of the leading boat from the look-out post aft. The noise diminished, then came again. Suddenly the surface of the sea was bathed in glaring light. No bombs were dropped; now our patrol-boat men knew where they were. ' Look out for shadows on all sides,' said the Commander. There were bound to be motor torpedo boats in the vicinity. A few seconds later: ' Shadows ahead ' came the cry from the fo'c'sle to the bridge. ' Let go a fan of starshells,' the Commander ordered. But even before the shells lit up the black night, one could hear quite plainly the drone of the motor torpedo boats and gunboats which had lain in ambush here, and which now took up fighting position at high speed.

"When the tracer shells first lit up the scene one could see the long black shapes which were now speeding along parallel to the convoy sending over the first tracers in a running fight. Then came the clatter of our automatic weapons. Ever more starshells lit up the great darkness. Then the leading boat scored the first hit on a passing shape. A flame leaps up. The attacking motor torpedo boats alter course to starboard. There are hits on our boats, and the first wounded. Again a glaring flame leaps up, astern this time, where our other boats are situated. So they are attacking there, too. The convoy leader sees to it that the formation is kept, that the patrol-boats' defensive chain is not broken, but none of the attacking boats had access to our convoy steamers. One shot follows another bursting on the enemy boats trying once more to break through. A huge detonation drowns the inferno of our ships' artillery. A Tommy has received a direct hit, apparently in his ammunition store. Yet one of the attackers has scored a hit. One of our boats has been hit by a torpedo and sunk.

"Soon afterwards there followed another great explosion. Another of the attacking boats trying to break through astern had been hit, blown up by the 8·8 cm., and gone down. 'Load and fire'—that was the slogan of our patrol-boat men. When the convoy had safely arrived at the port of destination, the convoy leader was able to report to his escort division: 'Convoy brought in, two enemy motor torpedo boats sunk, two set on fire. One of our boats sunk, the crew saved. Casualties low.'"

ORGANISATION ASHORE

Each of the three Coastal Forces Bases in East Anglia—H.M.S. *Midge* (Cdr. M. A. Brind, R.N.) at Great Yarmouth, H.M.S. *Mantis* (Cdr. K. M. B. L. Barnard, R.N.) at Lowestoft, and H.M.S. *Beehive* (Cdr. T. Kerr, O.B.E., R.N.) at Felixstowe—was responsible for the administration and maintenance of the boats operating from it. The operations, however, were controlled from the Headquarters of the Commander-in-Chief, the Nore (Admiral of the Fleet Sir John Tovey, G.C.B., K.C.B., K.B.E., D.S.O., R.N.) at Chatham. In short, the affairs of the Coastal Forces on the east coast, which were mostly occupied with the same sort of work, were dotted along a hundred miles of coast. Early in 1943 it was felt that a co-ordinating authority was required, particularly to develop training along the lines of a common doctrine suitable to the conditions in the Nore Command. In February Captain H. T. Armstrong, D.S.O. and bar, D.S.C. and bar, R.N., was appointed as Captain Coastal Forces (Nore) with a small staff to assist him, which included Lt. Cdr. W. D. F. B. Muspratt, R.N., as Torpedo Officer, and Lt. Cdr. F. H. Dunlop, R.N., as Signal Officer. With great energy Captain Armstrong organised much more specialised and advanced training than had been possible in the time available at H.M.S. *Bee*, and his influence on the achievements of our M.T.Bs., M.G.Bs., and M.Ls. was very soon apparent. Later his work was carried on by Captain H. Browning, O.B.E., R.N., and later still by Captain W. G. Robson, D.S.O. and bar, D.S.C., R.N.

In the early days the Coastal Forces had been little understood. They had even been nicknamed in some quarters "the Costly Farces." The officers and men serving in them had struggled hard with unreliable boats and indifferent material when all too little was known of the dash and spirit of their fighting. They had the reputation of being individualists and pirates, and although their courage was admitted, their technical skill was too often called in question. If, through no fault of their own, they had had to teach themselves in those early days (because the C.M.B. tradition had been thrown away after the last war), things were very different now. The standard of training and fighting experience, particularly of night action, in Coastal Forces had, by 1943, become second to none in the Navy, a position which was perhaps finally established for them by Captain Armstrong serving as Captain Coastal Forces (Nore).[1]

At the Admiralty two departments were responsible for the Coastal Forces, one for the material side and one for the operations. The Director of Coastal Forces Material when the department first came into existence was Captain F. H. P. Maurice, R.N., who had been on the staff of the Rear-Admiral Coastal Forces and had been connected with M.T.Bs. for many years. He and his staff were responsible for the development of the boats and their equipment.

It was the Deputy Director Operations Division (Coastal)—Captain D. M. Lees, D.S.O., R.N.—who, with his staff, co-ordinated the operational use of the boats and organised their allocation to the various Commanders-in-Chief who operated them.

To his staff, in 1943, came Cdr. O. C. H. Giddy, D.S.C., R.N., who undertook, amongst other duties, the publication of a monthly review of the activities of Coastal Forces. He had taken part in the historic C.M.B. attack on Kronstadt harbour in 1919, and in this war he had been First Lieutenant of H.M.S. *Beehive*, the base at Felixstowe, during the time when Hichens and Dickens had done so much to formulate the offensive tactics of Coastal Forces. No one therefore could have been better suited to make a comprehensive study of the trend of this kind of warfare and to advise upon the " staff requirements " for our boats and their equipment.

In 1943, when Captain Lees, after two years at the Admiralty, was appointed to command a new cruiser, his place as D.D.O.D. (C) was taken by Captain H. Geary Cooke, R.N. And in 1944 Captain W. L. G. Adams, O.B.E., R.N., who had been Captain of H.M.S. *Wasp*, the base at Dover, followed Captain Maurice as Director of Coastal Forces Material.

PROWLING UP FROM BEHIND

In a book of this kind it is impossible to describe every engagement, or indeed every important engagement which took place in the Narrow Seas. It is only possible to select and record actions which have special significance or a direct bearing on the development of the story of Coastal Forces. Such an action, however, was fought off the Dutch Coast on the night of 15th/16th March, 1943, by a unit of three 70-foot M.T.Bs. under the command of Lt. D. G. H. Wright, R.N.V.R.

It was an interesting action for two reasons. First it was highly successful; and secondly Wright, who had been in M.T.Bs. since very early in the war and had been First Lieutenant of one of the boats in the successful attack on Flushing Roads in December, 1940, was scoring his first success as Senior Officer of a unit—the first of many.

Let us turn for a moment to one of the technical reasons which made this action successful. To give a torpedo the best chance of hitting it must be aimed accurately a certain exact distance ahead of the target, so as to allow for the distance travelled by the target during the run of the torpedo. This distance ahead is influenced by two main things—the speed of the target and the course of the target. The two are interdependent because, for example, the

---

[1] Captain Armstrong, serving as Captain (D), was lost soon after leaving the Nore Command, when the destroyer H.M.S. *Laforey* was torpedoed in the Mediterranean.

aim off will be less if the enemy's speed is less, and it will also be less if the enemy's course is oblique instead of at right angles to the track of the torpedo. In the dark these two key items of information—the enemy's course and speed—are very difficult to assess at any given moment, but by plotting the enemy over a period of time, both course and speed can be accurately determined. From now on this plotting became an integral part of stalking an unsuspecting enemy.

On the night in question Wright spent nearly an hour and a half stalking his convoy, during which he crept round from its port quarter across its wake and up on to its starboard beam, so as to get the advantage of the moon, and at five past midnight the enemy could be seen clearly up the silver track. There were three merchant ships with what looked like a destroyer ahead, though it may have been an " M " Class minesweeper, and ahead of that was another escort vessel, whilst a flak trawler guarded the rear of the convoy. On the seaward side there were other escorts which could scarcely be made out, though they soon disclosed their presence when the general mêlée broke out soon after. At twelve minutes past midnight the three boats turned in to fire torpedoes, and Wright and Lt. N. G. Kennedy, R.N.V.R., fired before the dazzle of starshell and tracer filled the air. The third boat, M.T.B. 230, under the command of Lt. Perkins, was unable to get her torpedoes away before the dazzle made aiming impossible.

As the first two boats disengaged a hit by at least one torpedo was observed on one of the first two merchantmen, which were overlapping each other at the time. For a further twenty-five minutes Perkins continued to stalk the convoy, which, from going north, had now turned sharply east. When he closed in he found only two merchant ships—with a trawler in close company, and he had not yet been observed. His torpedoes were fired while he was still unmolested, and when the shooting began the enemy was already too late. " The jarring of a large underwater explosion was felt after about twenty seconds," he reports, as he turned hard a-port to disengage. The thoroughly satisfying battle was over.

Wright, in his report, commends the service of Sub-Lt. P. Knowles, R.N.V.R., one of the Base Maintenance Officers, who, like Lt. Teekman at Dover, went to sea whenever there seemed to be a chance of action. In this way he was involved in more fighting than almost any other officer working from his base. It was his own conception of his duty which forced him to go so often and earned him the award of the D.S.C.

The M.G.B. did not Succeed in Passing the E Boat

In E boat alley the defence was now well ahead of the attack. In the spring of 1943, a sortie by the E boats had become a hazardous undertaking for them, even if its object was the laying of mines, and if they came to attack a convoy it was even more dangerous. Still, they had a nuisance value to the Germans, by holding down our fairly strong defensive forces, although the toll they took had become almost negligible.

When they did come over to our convoy route, they came usually in strength and spread out on their hunting-ground in order to keep as many of our patrols occupied as possible.

On the night of 28th/29th March they came over with the apparent intention of attacking a southbound convoy in the neighbourhood of Smith's Knoll, a shallow patch in the North Sea at the north end of E boat alley.

Amongst the forces that were waiting for just such a move were two " C " Class M.G.Bs. under the command of Lt. Donald Gould Bradford, R.N.R., a name which was later to become well known in the M.T.B. battles off the Dutch coast and in the Channel during the invasion of Normandy.

How he dealt with the situation that night is best described by his own account:

" We were lying on patrol, two boats, waiting and listening. It was the type of night that we had learnt to associate with E boats—pitch black with a few stars, visibility very low— a hundred yards or so. We had rocked and rolled for three hours when we suddenly heard the whisper of engines on our starboard bow, growing louder.

" I crash-started, went to full-action stations and moved off on what I worked out as a probable intercepting course, with the other boat following close astern. I increased to 16 knots and steered to cut across the course of any possible E boats approaching the convoy route. After a few minutes of tenseness the port lookout shouted, ' Object on the port bow.' I put the glasses on it and saw three white streaks on the water—three wakes. Frank, my No. 1, had been in the chart-house doing the usual plotting and signal routine. I called him up on to the bridge and told him to flash a warning to the boat astern. The guns had already swung on to the bearing—we could all see them plainly by that time. I kept the glasses on the streaks of white and suddenly counted five of them—they couldn't be anything else but E boats.

" They were going slow—about 12 knots, I reckoned—and we closed them rapidly. They were like ghost ships, I couldn't see any men on deck—just the boats gliding through the water in a seemingly effortless way. I decided to risk them opening fire first, and altered course to close the boat next to the leader so that my partner would also have a choice of targets. I closed to about 40 yards, indicated the second boat as target and ordered ' open fire.' We did; a hell of a blast—at 40 yards they couldn't miss. The gunners just smothered Jerry. We had one small squirt of light machine-gun fire returned, but that nearly started something— it hit the magazine on the Oerlikon and the rounds started burning and exploding. I saw the flash out of the corner of my eye and realised that something was wrong; however, there was nothing. I could do about it whilst we were actually engaging. I concentrated on getting closer. The other guns were all going full blast, and I could see large chunks flying off the E boat and could see the deck lifting as our heavy stuff went into its side. Frank was enjoying himself—there were two light machine guns just behind me and he was squirting these into the E boat's bridge as fast as the loading number could replace the empty pans, and all the empties were spattering over me—down my collar—everywhere. We closed to about 20 yards and suddenly I heard the Oerlikon gun come into action again. The gun's crew had torn off the magazine, thrown it overboard and put another on. That gunner was annoyed— he just pressed the trigger and poured the whole magazine into the deck of the E boat just abaft the mast—in the light of the gun flashes I could see the deck of the E boat as if a search-light was flooding it. The crew of the enemy's after gun were lying on the deck flaked out in awkward positions—dead. Then it happened—there was a sudden belch of flame from the E boat and the deck seemed to rise in the air and fold back. I think the Oerlikon must have hit the warhead of a spare torpedo. We were deluged with bits of metal and wood falling from the air.

" Meanwhile the leading E boat was about 50 yards away, ahead, and I suddenly realised that he was firing at us and the stuff was whistling over the bridge. The other E boats had gone, and so had my partner—after them. I risked a depth charge and cut across the wake

of the leader, opening fire on him as I went across. He was altering course to port, trying to get out to the east again. I increased to full ahead and drew up his port side about 40 yards away. My guns were hitting nicely—shells plunging into the deck amidships.

" I suddenly decided to ram him and rang ramming stations on the gun bells. The wheel went hard over and we bore down upon him. I could see someone on the bridge of the E boat waving his arms and shouting to some men on the after-deck and a ' wag ' of a gunner on my bridge said, ' He's telling them to put a fender over,' and at the same time poured a full pan of ammunition into the bridge. We saw him curl up and fall.

" We hit her, about 20 feet from the stern, and I felt my boat rise up and ride partly over her—and then the E boat broke. The stern came off and slid down my starboard side and the remainder passed along my port side—we had gone straight through. The after-gunner continued to pour shells into the remains as they passed him and then everything was over.

" I circled back through the area, looking for some definite evidence and found nothing but two large pieces of wreckage about 400 yards apart. I left them and chased off to the eastward, hoping to contact other E boats. We did—we found three of them stopped in a group, and I opened fire on them at about 70 yards, but no luck that time. They saw us and were away at full speed. My gunners hit the last one several times, but not enough to slow him down, and we were left well behind, going flat out with one engine developing a severe attack of asthma."

This is how the German propaganda machine handled the same engagement:

" Oslo in German for German soldiers in Norway. 5 p.m., 30th March, 1943. Berlin: In the course of an operation of German M.T.Bs. against the English convoy routes in the Channel, a group of German boats met with British motor torpedo boats and motor gunboats (Kanonenschnellboote) at dawn yesterday. Visibility was outstandingly good. An exchange of fire followed in which both sides used all artillery at their disposal at a very close distance, in parts only 30 metres. The following details have come in about the dramatic course of the battle.

" After both sides had opened fire, while the boats were approaching one another at full steam until they were within hand-grenade range of each other, a large number of hits was scored, in particular on two English gunboats: one of these was set on fire. At the same time a German boat on which the entire artillery of the enemy had been concentrated received several hits so that part of the crew was put out of action and the working of the machinery impaired.

" Meanwhile, the two English gunboats were seriously threatened. Owing to the tactical skill of the German M.T.Bs. they were exposed to the full firing power of the German vessels so that they had to suspend operations temporarily. While they were trying to get away at full steam, one of them did not succeed in passing the damaged German M.T.B. which was sailing slowly. [*Surely this is the most ingenious phrase ever devised to describe being rammed.*] This English boat suffered severe damage. The crew of the damaged German boat, most of whom were wounded, succeeded in driving the enemy boats away by defying death and danger, and afterwards were able to retire with their severely damaged boat. At dawn their boat was met by its own formation, which had sustained no losses whatsoever. After the dead and wounded, arms and other equipment had been taken over, the boat was sunk.

" Another group of German M.T.Bs. had thrust into another area off the English Channel coast during the same night. In spite of their long search and excellent visibility, however, they did not sight any enemy coastal escort vessels or steamships; they turned back at dawn without having sighted the enemy."

"INDEED A MISFORTUNE OF WAR"

Since his return from the West Country Hichens had been operating regularly in the North Sea again, with his flotilla based once more at H.M.S. *Beehive*, Felixstowe, and as usual he had been thinking hard about the development of his boats. Recently the M.G.Bs. had often found themselves with perfect opportunities for a torpedo attack, had they only carried torpedoes, and he came to the conclusion that, with certain minor modifications, torpedo tubes could be fitted to these boats without seriously jeopardising their existing capabilities as gunboats.

Although the numbers of Coastal Force craft had now greatly increased, we had not yet so many that we could afford to set aside M.G.Bs. exclusively for anti-E boat work and M.T.Bs. exclusively for the attack on enemy convoys, which would perhaps have been the ideal plan. In 1943 it was still necessary for the two to be mixed, and in these circumstances Hichens realised the advantages of an all-purpose boat. He believed that such a boat could be achieved fairly easily on the British Power Boat Company's " seventy-one-foot-six " hull, and to this end arrangements were made for his own boat—M.G.B. 77—now due for a refit, to be fitted with two 18-inch torpedo tubes, as an experimental prototype.

The action which most forcibly convinced him of the desirability of torpedo tubes on M.G.Bs. was fought on the night of 27th/28th February, when he was acting in support of M.T.Bs. under Lt. Weeden and Lt. N. S. Gardner, R.N.V.R., in an attack on an escorted southbound merchantman off the Dutch coast. The M.T.Bs. never got into position to attack, but Hichens shadowed for some considerable time, during which he could easily have fired torpedoes had he had them. Eventually he decided to attack with guns as the enemy was about to enter harbour. With him that night was M.G.B. 79, commanded by Lt. D. James, R.N.V.R., who although he had been on a great many operations with Hichens had, by an extraordinary chance, never yet taken his boat into action. In the middle of his first battle his boat was disabled and set on fire close off the harbour entrance. She lay stopped and surrounded by a group of the convoy's escort, but for some incredible reason they allowed Hichens, and Lt. T. J. Mathias, R.N.V.R., who was following him, to begin the work of rescue. For more than five minutes they withheld their fire, uncertain perhaps of the rescuers' identity. When at last the battle started up again only a few of the crew remained in the water, but amongst them was the Captain. It was necessary, of course, for the M.G.Bs. to get under way at once, otherwise they would have shared the fate of 79. A heaving-line was thrown to James, and for a while he was towed astern, but as the speed increased he had to let go. He was struck by Mathias' boat following astern, and the blow pushed him far enough down to clear the screws as she passed over him. In a somewhat battered condition he was later picked up by a German trawler and became a prisoner of war. In due course he escaped and was at large for a week in Germany, but was recaptured, only to escape a second time and finally to reach England.

Hichens himself had a narrow shave one night when the boat in which he was embarked as Senior Officer had been damaged in a heavy engagement off the Dutch coast. On the way home it quite suddenly burst into flames from end to end. It was impossible to get the fire under control, so the crew abandoned ship on a tiny raft. Whilst they were clustered on and around the raft, the boat drifted away with the wind. Finally the lashings of the depth charges burned through, the depth charges went down and blew up immediately beneath the wreck so that the petrol showered out and blazed on the surface of the sea, gradually spreading out across the water. As the circle grew larger the flames came closer and closer to the party round the raft. About 50 feet short of them it stopped and the fire began to subside; but not before it had been sighted by two other M.G.Bs. returning through the same area. They came to the rescue, after Hichens and his crew had been in the water for about an hour.

On the 12th April, 1943, which was a very dark night, four M.G.Bs. were acting as close escort for a force of minelaying M.Ls. It was a routine job which was not especially likely to lead to action, but flak trawlers and " gun coasters " had recently been interfering with the operations of our Coastal Forces in that area, and Hichens, whose orders gave him a free hand on completion of the minelay, was determined to seek out, attack, and beat up any such patrols that he could find.

As the M.Ls. were finishing their job, a green flashing light was sighted and, as soon as he was free, Hichens set off to discover its origin. He was embarked that night in the boat commanded by Lt. D. C. Sidebottom, who had lately joined his flotilla. A long stalk ensued, a stealthy approach was made, and finally the enemy was recognised as a trawler and a small ship of a different type, probably a Dutch *schuyt*, a number of which had recently been converted by the addition of a heavy armament into what had become known as " gun coasters." The M.G.Bs. effected complete surprise, creeping up on the enemy's port quarter until the range was no more than 100 yards. Then suddenly they increased speed and opened fire simultaneously, running past the two German ships on a parallel course.

The gunnery was accurate and a large explosion was seen to blow the engine-room hatch off the trawler. Hichens remarked on this to Sidebottom as they began to draw ahead, but the enemy was still firing back. Most of his shooting was wild, but suddenly as the leading boat turned away to reload for the next run, a stray and solitary burst of cannon shell came directly in at the back of her bridge. Hichens was killed instantly; Sidebottom was gravely wounded, and so was the First Lieutenant, Midshipman D. Okey, R.N.V.R. Wing Cdr. T. H. E. Edwards, R.A.F.V.R., who was on board as an observer was also injured, but he was able to take the boat clear of the action under the direction of Sidebottom, and then Lt. S. J. K. Edwards, R.N.R., who was also on board as a passenger and had been controlling the fire of one of the guns, was summoned to the bridge, where he took command. The boat had scarcely been damaged, and he brought her safely back to harbour. Lt. Cdr. Hichens was the only fatal casualty in the battle and, as the Commander-in-Chief, the Nore, says in his letter to the Admiralty, " It was indeed a misfortune of war that he was killed by what appeared to be a stray shell." He had been on 148 operations, which included fourteen actions. He had been awarded the D.S.O. and bar, the D.S.C. and two bars, and was three times mentioned in despatches. That proportion of actions to operations clearly shows the hard slogging at uneventful patrols which made up the bulk of Coastal Force activity even in the most offensive type of craft.

The following passage was the conclusion of the Sunday-night Postscript which I broadcast a fortnight later on 25th April (from which I have already quoted in Chapter IV) : " The officers and men who fight these battles will not forget Robert Hichens. He left a rich legacy— the fruits of his energy in the development of the boats, and the fruits of his experience in the way they should be handled and fought, and then that other thing—that example of courage that makes people think, as they go into action, ' This would have been a mere nothing to Hitch.' "

CHAPTER XI

"The Four Horsemen"

THE loss of Lt. Cdr. Hichens was not only a heavy blow to the Coastal Forces, it was a particular blow to the officers and men working from H.M.S. *Beehive*, because of the direct relationship between the spirit of such a base and the spirit of the leaders who go out from it to fight. *Beehive* was lucky at this time to have Dickens as Senior Officer, M.T.Bs. In addition they had Lt. I. C. Trelawny, D.S.C., R.N.V.R., who, after a spell serving as Staff Officer (Operations) there, in order to recover from the wounds he received off Pointe de Barfleur in the previous autumn, had now returned to sea in command of the 11th M.T.B. Flotilla.

Under these two officers the technique of M.T.B. warfare was destined to make great advances during the spring and summer of 1943. The defensive patrols of enemy trawlers which nightly took up their appointed stations along the German convoy route had recently been strengthened to meet the continuous and increasing pressure exerted by our M.T.Bs. These flak trawlers usually kept company in parties of four, and the four which were nearly always to be found off Ijmuiden became so familiar to our forces that they were nicknamed "The Four Horsemen of the Apocalypse." As targets they did not compare in value with the merchantmen of the convoys, or even with the larger escort vessels and "M" Class mine-sweepers, but they played their part in the balance of power in the enemy's waters at night, and for this reason it was always considered important to harry, and if possible sink them. Gun actions against "the four horsemen" were frequently fought by the "D" Class M.G.Bs. based at Great Yarmouth, but the most decisive results were obtained with torpedoes. "You can knock things about with guns," Dickens used to say, "but if you give it half a chance, a torpedo will do the job for you, suddenly and completely." Twice in April, 1943, Dickens proved the truth of this precept, by blowing up patrolling flak trawlers when he could find no better target.

But it was Trelawny's good fortune to come upon bigger game when he was hunting off the Hook of Holland on the 19th April with a unit of three M.T.Bs. During the early part of the night the light of the full moon was diffused by thin scurrying clouds, but later when they cleared the night became almost as bright as day. The battle which developed under these difficult conditions was at that time the longest that had ever been fought by the Coastal Forces.

"We sighted a convoy," writes Trelawny, "with its usual strong escort, well to the south of us, proceeding south at what was practically our maximum speed on silent engines. They were too near the Hook for me to risk going silently out to sea, then racing down the coast to a position south of them, and creeping in on silent engines again; so it had to be a long, long stern chase at full speed on auxiliary engines. The moon was to seaward of us, and in the worst place it could have been.

131

" We crept slowly up the seaward side of the enemy, oh, so slowly, but gradually gaining bearing. The slower boats could not keep up with the pace I was setting, but there could be no waiting, and my line got longer and longer and tactically more and more unsound. The excitement of the chase was intense. The Hun should have seen us years ago—we were only a thousand yards off him; at any moment that moon might come bursting through and bathe us in brilliant light. To add to my personal excitement, it was the first operation I had been on since coming back to work after being shot up.

" Finally, when I was level with the leading ship, and about 800 yards on his beam, the dreaded thing happened—out came the moon and played on my foredeck like a spotlight. Almost immediately the leading Hun opened fire, the convoy woke up, and in a matter of seconds they were all firing everything they had in our general direction—what a party!

" I decided it was a matter of ' now or never,' gave the order to attack, and turned in and fired my fish at the second ship in the line, a medium-sized merchant vessel. At first I thought I had missed him—it always seems ages before your torpedoes get there—but then suddenly a glow like a bonfire started on his waterline, no enormous flash, no huge column of water, nothing dramatic at all. And then slowly he seemed to disintegrate, puffing out steam like a puff-ball puffs out dust when you tread on it. Maybe disintegrate is the wrong word—he seemed to deflate more than anything.

" When the others rejoined I found that owing to the length of my line most of my team hadn't been able to get in an attack, so back we went again for another shot. For two and a half hours we fought the convoy, trying every trick we knew and discovering a lot of new ones. They knew a few tricks too, though, and by the time dawn came and we had to give up and come home we could only claim one more ship. Jack Saunders got that, and it was a beautiful sight. He found a dark patch, crept up it, and slammed both his fish home. They hit with an enormous orangy-red flash, and a great column of water soared slowly up into the sky, tastefully coloured by the multi-coloured tracer and illuminated by starshell. It looked very pretty and very satisfying."

This action came just one week after the loss of Hichens. " The fact that we were successful and had no casualties," concludes Trelawny, " acted as a fine tonic and started a series of successes."

"Down Below Two Crumps were Felt"

It was not until the following month that an equally interesting opportunity came the way of Dickens' flotilla and the series of successes continued. On the evening of 13th May four M.T.Bs. under his command set out for patrol on the enemy convoy route off the coast of Holland, and this is his account of what happened.

" It was a lovely night for M.T.Bs., calm, dark with the visibility not too good, and if we met anything we should stand the greatest chance of getting right in close before the enemy would know what was going on. We left Felixstowe some time before dark with orders to patrol between the Hook and Ijmuiden and inflict violence on anything that happened to be around. There was a possibility of a convoy materialising and also a division of ' T ' boats, young destroyers which make splendid torpedo targets; these had been spotted by aircraft during the afternoon, but of course there was no knowing whether they would stand on during the night or nip into one of the many small ports on the Dutch coast. We were rather on our mettle, last time had not been as successful as we thought it should have been and we were going to show the world what we were really capable of.

" Besides my own, there were three boats running from the flotilla that night, one

HIT IN THE MAGAZINE

"ATTACK COMPLETED—ONE HIT"

As the starshells burst overhead and float down on their parachutes
they leave a trail of brightly illuminated smoke above them

commanded by MacDonald, a stout-hearted New Zealander and veteran of about a dozen actions who has an uncanny knack of always doing the right thing; then Ohlenschlager, who had taken his own boat into action only once before but who had already proved himself to be the right type, and Hartley who was brand new and, though perhaps not quite sure of himself, it was obvious to everyone else that he was going to take to the business like a duck to water.

" For four hours after we left the Sunk Lightship we ran at cruising speed over the flat sea until we approached near enough to the enemy coast for there to be a possibility of our being detected. Then we reduced speed to a crawl and continued to close the coast. At any time now we might sight what we were looking for. However, we had to wait. We got to a good central position about three miles north of the Hook and stopped. Nothing was in sight, not even the coast, as it is very low lying in this part and you have to be very near indeed to see it. Our position, therefore, was found by dead reckoning from a point about 90 miles away and, in the absence of a check, I could only hope we were where we thought we were. We set hydrophone watch and I was mentally congratulating the engineers on keeping the engines of all four boats heaving round all this time when I was startled by the sight of Leading Stoker Clarke emerging from the engine-room and lurching his way up to the bridge as if he were very drunk indeed. His report was alarming, to say the least. One of the exhaust-pipe junctions had worked loose and the engine-room was filled with poisonous gases. The seamen dashed below at once and fished out the other two who, not having Clarke's extremely robust constitution, were already unconscious. All three were laid out on the upper deck, and gradually they came round with splitting headaches and violent nausea. After about ten minutes Cuthbert, the motor mechanic, felt he could go below again, and did so with the third officer; the atmosphere was still very bad and they just managed to get the leak repaired before having to come up again, feeling much the worse for wear. On the upper deck everyone was straining his eyes and hoping to goodness nothing would turn up yet awhile with the boat practically immobile. Luck was with us, though, all through this night, and we were able to let the engine-room crew lie on the upper deck inhaling the ozone and gradually coming back to life.

" While waiting for this, and as we were in a nice central position to catch enemy traffic coming either north or south or going into the Hook, we abandoned the idea of sweeping up the coast. For nearly two hours we waited with nothing happening nor indeed any sign that there might have been shipping about, when, over the hydrophone there came a soft but distinct murmur, growing very gradually in volume. We manned the engine-room; they were still shaky and the stoker was not yet in a fit state to go below. The other two just managed it and were helped by Sub-Lt. Natusch and the gunner who, like the seamen they were, could turn their hands to anything. As a result, the engines ran perfectly throughout the action which followed.

" All the boats started engines and we got under way at slow speed towards the sound we had heard on the hydrophone. Nothing was seen for five minutes, but then, quite suddenly, there they were. Only a few blurred shapes could be seen at first, and we carried on closer to get a better view. Now it appeared that it was a convoy, as there were about four large ships surrounded by several smaller ones, all quite a distance away. We were in a good position on their beam, they hadn't seen us and we thought we had time to attack according to our prearranged plan. Hartley and I went on and MacDonald and Ohlenschlager hung back so as to be ready to attack through the same hole as us after we had finished, because the enemy's attention would then, we hoped, be riveted on us.

" Quite suddenly the range, which we had thought was about 2 miles, turned out to be 500 yards. The target ships were not big merchantmen but warships surrounded by R boats.

We thought at the time that they were the 'T' Class torpedo boats, but actually they were 'M' Class minesweepers. This collection, which packed quite a heavy punch as far as an M.T.B. is concerned, could not be at sea for any reason but to ruin us. This we realised at once but, if we made the most of the few seconds left to us, we might still get the upper hand; they had not seen us and we continued to close the range.

"In a moment everything happened at once. The enemy challenged MacDonald, who was separated according to plan, and he, while flashing a phoney letter back which confused the Hun, let drive with all his guns at the nearest R boat. This was a splendid move, as the enemy fire, spluttering into life from all along the line, was chiefly directed at him, leaving Hartley and I more or less free to do our torpedo attack in peace. This took about ten seconds more, and four torpedoes were then on their way towards the second ship in the line. The gunnery really started then, the air was brilliant with tracers of all colours, and you could hear them whistling overhead, exploding all round and hitting the boats with a sharp and ominous crack.

"This was the end of the first half, as Hartley and I had got rid of our torpedoes and MacDonald had been unable to make a torpedo attack owing to his surrender of surprise. He therefore disengaged to starboard under smoke and we went to port, doing the same thing. But Hartley's steering had jammed and he had to continue on a course parallel to the enemy about 200 yards from them. I was on his starboard side, so I could not turn either, and we were both heading for the shore at about 40 knots with nothing to do about it. This lasted for an eternity of a quarter of a minute and then his steering came free. I found out afterwards that the cause of the jam was the strap of his binoculars which had caught up on one of the spokes of the wheel. Hartley was half strangled every time the coxswain tried to turn it. As we turned behind the blanket of smoke a terrific explosion lit up the scene from the ship we had fired at, and down below two 'crumps' were felt. Once behind the smoke the firing ceased, and we watched the glow of the ship we had torpedoed and tracer going straight up into the air, which must have been her ammunition exploding, or perhaps a distress signal.

"This was satisfactory so far, but it was only half-time, as 'Mac' and 'O' had still got torpedoes left. Very soon we saw them again and joined company, where we heard each other's stories of what had happened since we last saw them—five minutes before. There were plenty of small bullet-holes in all the boats, but there were sighs of relief when we heard that there was only one very slight casualty in Hartley's boat. The torpedo hit was definite, which was another good point. We gave the enemy a little time to quieten down and stop shooting starshell all over the place, which incidentally was not doing him any good, and then we formed up again and went back to the field of play. Very soon we were rewarded with a sight of something I had half expected we might find. An 'M' Class minesweeper in very poor shape indeed, right down by the stern and with her bows blown clean off. This certainly confirmed two hits, but why she had not sunk we couldn't understand. The main point, however, was that another, perfectly whole, 'M' Class was steaming slowly round and round the wreck and, if ever a ship deserved to be torpedoed, it was she. From the Hun's point of view there were half a dozen R boats who should have picked up the survivors, and the 'M' Class should have decided whether they wanted to go back to harbour or engage us; anything but present a target. However, there she was and, after a momentary qualm, while I considered whether it was exactly the most humane thing to do, 'Mac' was despatched to finish off the second ship. He went by himself with orders, if he missed, to disengage in some direction away from the rest of us, so that he would draw the enemy's fire and 'O' could have his crack. Unfortunately 'Mac' did miss, and it is possible that his fish ran under, owing to the small draught of the target. When it was obvious to the watchers in the grandstand that this had happened, it was ' O "'s turn, and off he went. He was spotted, unfortunately, at about 600 yards from the target, and he was surrounded with tracer so that we could not see him. I did not think it would be possible for him to get a good sight of the target and fire his fish in that concentration and, indeed, it looked as if he would be lucky to get away at all. However, he held straight on until the range was 400 yards, got his sight on and fired. Only one fish went, owing to a missfire, but this was enough. Up went the target in a terrific sheet of flame, the firing ceased as if it had been turned off with a tap, and she appeared to break in two. As luck would have it, there was another sweeper coming up from the landward, but, without torpedoes, there was nothing for it but to let her be and wend our cheerful way back home to Felixstowe and breakfast."

At daylight the Germans sent four Focke Wulf 190s to attack our returning unit. Dickens reports that they " carried out a very feeble attack on the M.T.Bs. They dived till the range closed to about 2,000 yards and fired their cannon in the general direction of the boats. Sometimes splashes could be seen some way off, but by no means always. . . . Gunners were allowed to open fire for practice, but the range was at all times too great for effective shooting."

This very successful night's work entailed slight superficial damage to three of the boats and only one casualty, a rating who was very slightly wounded by shrapnel in the arm. The enemy were thought at first to have been ' T ' Class torpedo boats, as these, according to the aircraft report, were believed to be at sea. It was only later that it was found that they had been ' M ' Class minesweepers—a vessel of much the same size. The Germans, however, made good use of our misidentification of the target. Two days later they broadcast the following account from Berlin:

" Yesterday the British Admiralty spread the false report that during an engagement between German and British Naval Forces off the coast of Holland two German torpedo boats had been sunk. It was declared officially that on the night of 13th/14th May no German torpedo boats were either attacked or damaged and certainly not sunk.

" This is what actually occurred off Scheveningen: a formation consisting of six British M.T.Bs. attempted to operate on the German sea routes off the Dutch coast and was, before reaching its destination, spotted by forces of the German Naval Coastguard and engaged. During this short-distance engagement the British M.T.Bs., whose gunnery was inferior, received several direct hits. Two boats caught fire, which soon spread over the entire length of the British boats. A third boat capsized owing to heavy damage received below the waterline, having been fired at heavily both sides. In clear moonlight it could be seen that she sank. Apart from a number of losses of personnel, the German boats suffered no damage and were able to remain in position until daylight. They have reached their base at dawn on 15th May in full numbers."

Since the action took place only 3 miles from the Hook of Holland in the early hours of 14th May it is interesting to speculate upon how the enemy ships spent the thirty hours from then until dawn on 15th May, and on how they managed to avoid damage in spite of three torpedo hits.

"THIS ENGAGEMENT LASTED FOR THREE HOURS"

Dickens and Trelawny worked together in a long and rather confused action on the night of the 24th/25th July, 1943. They spent three hours attacking a southbound convoy near Ijmuiden, which was forced to turn back to the northward half-way through the battle.

Our force consisted of seven M.T.Bs., but they made their presence felt to such effect that the German communiqué reported them as fifteen, and the German propaganda machine enlarged upon the details with their usual fertility of imagination.

Undoubtedly the enemy was very wide awake that night, and exceptional phosphorescence made it almost impossible to approach unobserved. After about two hours Dickens' boat suffered a direct hit on the stern. " Despite a very large hole," he says, " which allowed the sea free access to the compartment, and splinter holes in the petrol tanks, the propellers, rudders and steering-gear were intact and the boat was able to continue the action." Thus, at the seventh attempt, just as dawn was breaking, he and Sub-Lt. G. J. MacDonald were able to fire their torpedoes.

The boat commanded by Lt. T. Neill, R.N.V.R., had also been hit and set on fire, and his First Lieutenant, Midshipman R. H. Jones, R.N.V.R., and his turret gunner, Able Seaman C. M. Paddick, had been killed. When all the extinguishers had been exhausted, the fire was subdued but not out. Neill had to slow down so as to fill buckets with sea-water with which finally he quenched it, and returned safely to harbour.

Meanwhile Sub-Lt. A. J. Lee, R.N.V.R., whose boat had been following Neill's, pressed home a most courageous attack on what was either a merchantman or a large escort. At 350 yards he fired torpedoes and they were running to hit, but he disengaged in such a welter of tracer that he could not observe the result, though miraculously he escaped from it with only minor damage and no casualties at all.

Two killed and one wounded were the total casualties in all our force during those three eventful hours; and, though most of the boats were superficially damaged, only Dickens' and Neill's were seriously hit, and all returned to harbour under their own power. So great was the enemy's confusion that at one time the leader of two E/R boats began to signal by light in plain language to Trelawny. " Können Sie . . . " the message began, before the firing broke out afresh amongst the convoy escorts and Trelawny's attention could no longer be devoted to reading the Morse.

Now let us observe the tale which appeared two days later in the *Völkischer Beobachter*, under the heading : " Two British M.T.Bs. sunk. The successful naval battle off the Netherlands Coast."

" Berlin, 26th July, 1943.

" Following on the beating off, with heavy losses to the enemy, by German defence forces, of a number of British M.T.B. attacks during the night 22nd/23rd July, the night of 24th/25th July brought the British a further considerable defeat. During this night, as announced in the High Command communiqué of 25th July, two groups of British M.T.Bs. attacked a German convoy, in order to torpedo the valuable cargoes. Due to the watchfulness of our crews, however, the attacking enemy vessels were recognised in such good time that the first attack was beaten off.

" The night was lit up over a wide area by the starshells fired by the escort boats, so that the silhouettes of the M.T.Bs. could be clearly recognised. Almost at the same time a barrage was put up by all weapons of the German boats. More than 1,000 shots of all calibres were fired at the attacking M.T.Bs. within the space of a few seconds, so that they nearly disappeared under the hail of missiles. The British at once turned away, but first fired all their torpedoes at the convoy. While turning away, one of the enemy boats sustained a direct hit. She emitted a huge tongue of flame, and an explosion followed. Wreckage from the boat was flung everywhere, and shortly afterwards the boat had disappeared. She had been literally blown to bits.

" Almost at the same time as the first attack, which was from the starboard, another group attacked the convoy from aft. Torpedoes were also fired, of which one hit one of our patrol boats and caused her to sink. A few British M.T.Bs. proceeded towards the hit boat, to pick up prisoners. However, before they were able to reach the sinking boat, two

German boats had already reached the spot, and covered the enemy boats with a hail of fire. While one of the German boats picked up the crew of the sinking vessel, the other boat set two of the British M.T.Bs. on fire. One of the boats hit sustained such a severe hit, that a violent explosion followed. Some seconds afterwards, the tongue of flame had vanished and there was nothing more to be seen of the British boat. The other boat which had been hit disappeared from sight, developing considerable smoke, so that her sinking could not be observed.

" In the course of this battle, therefore, two of the attacking British M.T.Bs. were certainly sunk, not only one, as reported in the High Command communiqué of 25th July. A number of other boats were set on fire, and our crews were able to ascertain that two of the burning boats remained stationary. Due to the selfless action of their comrades, the greater part of the crew of the sunk German boat were rescued."

On the following day an even more colourful version of the story was broadcast by an eyewitness:

VIOLENT ENGAGEMENT WITH BRITISH M.T.BS. LASTING SEVERAL HOURS
TWO BRITISH BOATS SUNK BY GERMAN COVERING FORCES OFF IJMUIDEN

By War Reporter Helmut Peterson

" The commander of a coastal vessel stands on the bridge. Shadows are made out, low silhouettes. A starshell is sent over. It tears the dark veil that night has spread over a large group of British M.T.Bs. All the guns are fired at them at once, they are damaged and, making a smoke-screen, they turn away. But almost simultaneously another German covering force farther away begins an engagement. As the first group turns toward it, it is suddenly faced by four enemy M.T.Bs. Hit after hit is scored on them and they turn off rapidly north-west.

" There must be several groups of M.T.Bs. operating around here. The sea is lit up almost ceaselessly. In the magnesium glare a British torpedo boat is seen coming up, believing itself to be unobserved. It zigzags and fires a torpedo. Its track races towards the coastal vessel, which takes evading action.

" The M.T.B. has hardly disappeared from sight when three M.G.Bs. turn up. They reply to the steady fire of the coastal vessels with a 4-cm. rapid-fire gun. But they aim badly to-night. As they have received several hits, they retire. The four M.T.Bs. which attack almost at the same time that the gunboats disappear are met by a curtain of tracer bullets. Zigzagging wildly, they turn away.

" To-night the British don't succeed in their attack on the other group either. One M.T.B. is so violently fired on at a favourable distance that it is set on fire. Then the M.T.Bs. regroup for another attack. Burst after burst is aimed at them. They fire back with all their guns. Steady fire from the heavies forces them back north-east. They must have suffered a good deal of damage, because two boats fall behind to the south and four try to save themselves by going back home. We evade their torpedoes. One boat is fired on by a heavy gun. A sheet of flame roars up, then the boat sinks on an even keel. The others get out of sight in the mist of the early morning. This engagement lasted for three hours."

"HIT IN THE SMALL OF THE BACK"

Since he had come to Coastal Forces in the summer of 1942, Lt. Peter Dickens, handicapped with a flotilla of boats that were none too reliable, but ably supported by a team of first-class officers whom he had trained himself, had turned in one success after another.

In the summer of 1943 he was awarded the D.S.O., and in the autumn he left *Beehive* to serve for a period on the training staff of H.M.S. *Bee*, so that his doctrines might be even more widely spread.   Subsequently he returned to sea in command of the "Hunt" Class destroyer *Blencathra*, which worked in conjunction with the Coastal Forces off the Normandy coast during the summer of 1944.

The tradition which he had founded at Felixstowe, however, was upheld by Trelawny, who with the newer boats of the 11th Flotilla continued to take regular toll of the German ships moving up and down the Dutch coast.   But, as he points out, the excitements do not all happen in the successful actions.   " In my opinion," he says, " there are just as many heroes in the ones that don't get into the papers.   For instance, last October my crowd were operating off Scheveningen when we ran into a patrol, the very patrol we had been told to avoid.   We wanted to save our fish for another customer, so we retired, closely pursued by a lot of hot metal.   One of these objects had our number on it, for there was suddenly the most enormous explosion just behind me, the boat skidded to a stop like a police-car on the films, and we began to sink rapidly by the stern.   We had been hit in the small of the back by a 4-inch brick, and had suffered very severe damage.   There was nothing we could do for the poor old girl, and the Hun, elated by his success, was coming up rapidly, preceded by a hail of fire from everything he could bring to bear.   So we yelled to the next boat, commanded by Lt. Peter Magnus, who had seen our plight and stopped : he brought his boat neatly alongside and we transferred, with only three casualties and hardly a wet foot.   A few moments later our own boat blew up and sank.

" Just before we were hit our leading telegraphist, Hulme, had been given two signals to transmit.   He had just got the first through when he was ordered to abandon ship.   He quietly packed up all his confidential books, transferred them and himself to Magnus' boat. went straight down to their W/T office, sat down, and transmitted the second signal.   There were many other similar occurrences on that occasion."

Trelawny seemed to specialise in Coastal Force actions of unparalleled length.   He spent most of the night of the 9th/10th December, 1943, harrying a very strongly escorted convoy off the Hook, in the longest battle that was ever fought by our M.T.Bs. in the narrow seas.

The convoy consisted of three fair-sized ships screened by eight or nine trawlers and several E/R boats.   Trelawny describes how his division went in to attack first.

" We were met with an absolute storm of abuse from the Hun, who appeared to be putting down a barrage at about 1,200 yards range and about 200 yards deep.   In that area the surface of the sea was absolutely seething with bullets like a puddle in a hail-storm.   It wasn't much fun going through, but once we got there the shower eased off a bit, though it was still hard to pick out the target in the dazzling tracer.   However, there was one really big fellow spitting tracer at us along his entire length, so we closed in and let him have it.   As soon as we had fired we turned away, and had a very nasty few minutes getting out of it.   They were very angry.   The gunfire was so intense that I did not myself see the result of our attack, but when we rejoined the others they said they had observed two definite hits.

" Then we went off to harry the Hun again while the other division tried to get in an attack.   While we were stooging around inside the convoy, to my amazement I suddenly saw something that looked like a Thames barge under full sail.   We went over to have a look and found it was an enormous black bow sticking out of the water, a bow we'd last seen on the front end of our target.   Nearby were four trawlers pooping away with their guns at anything and everything they saw.   They weren't shooting at any of our people, so we left them to it."

"APPROACH BY BLUFF"

Although Gemmel had made a successful " unobserved attack " in March, the " D " Class M.T.Bs., because of their larger size, had a correspondingly smaller chance than the 70-foot boats of getting in to torpedo range unseen. More often than not they were detected during the approach, and many of their actions became a whirl of flying tracer at all too early a stage.

On the morning of 1st May, 1943, however, an unopposed approach was successfully made, though it cannot have been unobserved, for it took place in daylight. During the night two units of " D " boats under the command of Lt. Cdr. H. M. Duff Still, R.N.V.R., had been operating in adjacent areas off the coast of Holland. Each unit consisted of four boats—two M.G.Bs. and two M.T.Bs., and, if they had encountered nothing by dawn, it had been arranged that they should rendezvous and return in company.

As day broke Duff Still sighted, about 4 miles away, what he supposed at first to be the four boats of the other unit, but in a few moments he realised that these were German patrol ships. One appeared to be an " M " Class minesweeper and the other three were evidently gun-coasters. All were much larger and more heavily armed than the " D " boats, and in day-light their superior fire power must surely tell. The only chance, if they were to be engaged, was to get to close range by bluff, when it was just possible that good shooting might smother the enemy's guns before they had recovered from the surprise. The other alternative—to regard them as too tough a proposition in daylight, to leave them alone and proceed to the rendezvous—was immediately rejected, if indeed it ever passed across the Senior Officer's mind.

To pass themselves off as E boats there must be no half measures and no needless delay. Duff Still turned towards the enemy and increased speed to 24 knots. He led his force under the stern of the German formation, and having, as it were, completed his reconnaissance of their disposition, he rounded up on to a parallel course at a range of 400 yards—with still no reaction from the enemy. When all guns had been brought to bear, the unit opened fire, and for one vital minute they had the field to themselves. " It was impossible to miss," writes Duff Still, " at such close quarters in broad daylight." In that minute many of the enemy's guns must have been put out of action and one gun-coaster was set on fire without returning a shot. The other three, however, joined in the battle, though two of them were quickly subdued. Whilst Duff Still and Lt. W. Harrop, R.N.V.R., commanding the second M.G.B., continued to engage the enemy on parallel courses, Lt. P. A. Berthon, R.N.V.R., who was leading the two M.T.Bs., turned in to fire torpedoes; he was not satisfied with his first run, however, and turned a complete circle in order to come in again and make his attack, but one torpedo had been damaged by gunfire and the other probably ran under the target. At all events no results were observed. The second M.T.B., under the command of Lt. G. A. Guthrie, R.N.V.R., also turned in towards the enemy. Whether he intended to fire torpedoes or make a depth-charge attack will never be known, for as he approached he was killed by a shell which hit the bridge and struck down everyone upon it. With no one to steer it, the boat went on towards the German ships until it was in the centre of their formation and less than 100 yards from each. Under such conditions heavy casualties were inescapable. Besides the Commanding Officer, two ratings were killed and seven others wounded, and the First Lieutenant, Sub-Lt. F. M. J. Goddard, R.N.V.R., was so seriously wounded that he afterwards died. It was at this stage that the Navigating Officer, Sub-Lt. W. G. Dalziel, R.N.V.R., himself wounded, reached the bridge and took charge. From this desperate situation he was able to extricate the boat under cover of a smoke-screen.

By 5.45 a.m. the action had been in progress for half an hour and all our boats had sustained some damage. The Senior Officer decided that the time had come to disengage. "At 0600, writes Duff Still, " the unit re-formed and stopped about one and a half miles from the enemy, who had ceased fire. During this time one ship was observed to sink, with two more still on fire and stopped."

All our boats returned under their own power in company, arriving at 4.45 p.m., eleven hours after the action. Despite the wounds in his back, Dalziel, who had assumed command of Guthrie's boat, remained on the bridge continuously during the whole of this period, and brought her safely into harbour. Apart from the heavy casualties in this boat, only one other casualty was sustained in the whole force.

This had been the most striking *daylight* action against surface ships in the Narrow Seas since the passage of the German battle cruisers up the Channel in February, 1942.

"Having Lots of Fun, Come and Join Us"

Amongst the most brilliant and outstanding leaders in Coastal Forces the name of Lt. G. D. K. Richards, D.S.C., R.N., one of the greatest of them all, has so far appeared only incidentally in this book. This is perhaps because his highly individual achievements did not conform to the more usual pattern I have described. They stood alone as an example of originality and thoroughness brought, in combination, to a rare perfection.

For more than two years he had been training his M.G.B. flotilla, based at Ramsgate, for the specialised fighting of the Dover Strait. His boats had been in action dozens of times, few flotillas had wider experience or more extraordinary adventures, and few were more ably or more courageously led.

Take for example the hectic occasion described by Lt. M. Bray, R.N.V.R., who was in Richards' boat one night for a minelaying operation. "Having completed our job, the three M.G.Bs. were beating a rather hasty retreat from some 'T' Class torpedo boats and E boats, going pretty fast, and chased by the usual assortment of whizzbangs, tracers and starshells. Dick was worried lest we should lose the other two boats and told me to keep my eye on them. I could see a boat on either quarter, following us in nice station, so I reassured him. Just at that moment the telegraphist passed up a signal from Tom Fuller [1] saying he had engine trouble and required immediate assistance, and giving a position some distance astern. This produced a tricky problem: which of the two boats in station on us was friend and which foe? However, one of them started spouting tracers at us, and after a brief exchange we lost him and turned to look for Tom. Over in the distance was a terrific concentration of fire, all of which seemed to be directed on one spot where we thought we could see a boat. " Poor old Tom," we said, " he's had it. There won't be anything left by the time we get there." The telegraphist interrupted us with another signal from Tom, " Engines O.K. Having lots of fun. Come and join us."

Richards' most usual adversaries were flak trawlers, and the technique he had developed for dealing with them was bold in conception and devastating in effect.

One of his greatest successes in this field, and one which earned him the D.S.O., was on the night of 4th/5th April, 1943, when he destroyed a trawler off Nieuport and returned with a load of prisoners.

This was the second time that Richards had returned triumphantly with prisoners on board. Last time it had been an R boat's crew; this time it was a trawler's. Bray describes how he had only one prisoner in his boat, whom he had rescued from the water, very miserable and cold. " On arrival in harbour, where a large armed guard was waiting, I led my sorry-

[1] Lt. T. Fuller, R.C.N.V.R., Commanding Officer of one of the three M.G.Bs.

looking specimen up to the Petty Officer in charge, explaining that he had been soaking wet for five hours and should be fixed up with dry clothes as soon as possible. The Petty Officer did not at first recognise him as one of his charges and proceeded to explain in great detail how if he doubled down to the end of the road, turned right and went into the second office on the left he would find the Master at Arms who would fix him up in a jiffy. When I explained that he couldn't understand a word because he was German, the guard gripped their rifles tightly, surrounded him and marched him off as if he had been Al Capone at least."

On the 29th May, 1943, Richards' flotilla was ordered to act in support of a minelaying force led by Lt. Basil Ward. They were to wait off Gravelines to assist the minelayers if they were molested and to return to harbour on completion of the lay at 3 a.m.

Four M.G.Bs. were to take part, though Lt. Philip Lee, D.S.C., R.N.V.R., the Commanding Officer of one of them, records that there was some doubt whether repairs to his boat would be completed in time for him to sail.

"Richards wasn't very concerned. 'Three boats will be enough,' he said at dinner, 'but come if you can.' He was never very enthusiastic about operations like this one; it was just a routine job with little prospect of action. All the same, I felt unnaturally keen to go. I have always suspected 'routine jobs' of being the most likely time for the startling to happen. Besides, it was a lovely, still, warm night; after a winter of cold, wet, protracted flogging across the Channel with very little result, the atmosphere was suddenly poignantly reminiscent of the active summer before. It felt as if the 1943 season was just opening, and I did not want to miss the first shoot."

The repair was completed, and Richards in M.G.B. 110 led his force of four boats to sea at half-past ten in the evening.

"Watching an Unsuspecting Enemy"

"We had only just cut our engines at the patrol position off Gravelines," continues Lee, "and the cocoa was only just warming up when the first signal from Ward's minelaying party came up from the wireless office. He had got nearly up to his lay, to find some ships apparently stopped right in his track, about 5 miles to the east of us. Our four boats were lying very close together, quite still on an undistinguished-looking piece of glass-calm sea, with darkness 200 yards away in every direction. Some shouting, sounding very loud, from bridge to bridge; yes, we'd all had the signal, and were plotting the position given. I went below to look at the chart and smoke a cigarette. I looked at our sailing signal: 'To remain until 0300 then return to harbour.' I looked at my watch: 0115. Then another signal from Ward and the cocoa coming up the hatch from the galley. The enemy ships were still in the same place. Trawler patrol, probably. I thought of Ward watching the unsuspecting enemy stopped between him and his laying position. I thought of Richards in 110's chart-house 20 yards away. He would be rocking a pair of dividers thoughtfully over the chart, one point on our position, the other on the enemy's, plotted from Ward's signal; looking at his orders: 'return at 0300.' I remembered his reply to a signal from Dover, the previous summer, ordering him to return: 'Returning via Calais,' and then I felt quite certain that there was going to be a lot of fighting soon after three o'clock this night.

"A long time to wait, though, with no light, no movement, no sound except the high-pitched Morse coming from Ward, waiting, still reporting the enemy obstructing him, and the slight rustle from the chart-house as Midshipman Barlow plotted their position on the chart. 'Still there, sir,—same place.' Then nothing but the occasional lapping of water under the chine and the gunners shifting in their turrets.

" We didn't have to wait until 0300. At half-past two a few green tracers floated across the blackness away to the eastward, and then stopped. Richards' voice, very clear in the still air, called ' Start up '; the boats shuddered in quick succession as the muffled exhaust burst through the water and the little group moved off in line ahead towards the Dunkirk channel.

" We were already a mile nearer to the enemy when Ward's next signal came to the bridge. Determined to attempt his lay before the limiting time, he had moved in on the chance of getting past unobserved, but he had been sighted and engaged, turning skilfully away with his mines to leave the enemy for the gunboats. His signal addressed to Richards was concise and adequate: ' Three trawlers '—implying, it seemed, ' Yours if you want them, old boy.' No doubt about it now, I thought: I shouted to the gunners, telling them what I thought was going to happen, and we all put on our tin-hats. The hours of anticipation, and now the slow deliberateness of our approach, were quite unlike any Coastal Force action I'd ever known. I thought how different it had been, for example, that evening last summer when I had been Richards' First Lieutenant. We had pulled our boat off the slip at six, sailed at eight, engaged R boats at twenty past nine, and were back in harbour by eleven with a cargo of German prisoners. This was somehow much more cold-blooded. Barlow called up from the chart-house to say we should sight them pretty soon on the starboard side, and immediately the darkness seemed to be filled with darker objects as the eyes strained for Ward's ' three trawlers.'

" Suddenly three of them really *were* there, and the nearest one flashed a Morse lamp at 110. Richards was still answering when we turned in—probably sending a rude message in his mock German, I thought; bluffing the already roused enemy for a few precious seconds. The first manœuvre was just what we expected, the attack we had been specially exercising, and we had had hours in which to think about it. It should be a copy-book attack.

" The bluff didn't last long. One thin streak of tracer from a machine gun, and then sheets of it—at this stage, thank God, in no particular direction. Richards roared straight at the nearest trawler at 35 knots, the rest of us abreast of him to starboard, all forward guns firing: a sharp turn to port when 100 yards off, broadsides at point-blank range, and the trawler was heavily on fire.

" ' Stick to the S.O.,' ' Follow father '—all the slogans of the gunboat pundits came to my mind as I concentrated on the vital job of station-keeping, hanging on to the leader's plume as he turned in a wide circle for a second attack. There were plenty of distractions too; a trawler burning furiously astern; tracer still floating towards us, but not very annoying at this range; the ever-recurring concern for the high-bred engines; for the health of the gunners and their guns. Some reassuring shouts from each turret; just time to send a hand to investigate the damage on the starboard bow, where I had noticed a particularly vivid flash, and to be wanly amused at the precision of the report in unhurried Cockney, ' 'Ole eighteen inches wide, three foot from the water, sir.' Commendable accuracy, I thought; the crew were evidently enjoying themselves."

At this point the third M.G.B. (Lt. M. O'Mahoney, R.N.V.R.) was forced to haul out of line owing to a stoppage in her principal armament, and this unfortunately caused the last boat to lose contact with the other two. Lt. R. M. Barge, R.N.V.R., her Commanding Officer, proceeded single-handed to attack the last trawler in the line, which he was able to silence.

While he was doing this Richards and Lee came in again on the two leading trawlers, and this time they closed to even shorter range. The Germans were still firing back briskly.

" I didn't like the flashes which came from 110's hull as the shells hit her," continues Lee, " but she never reduced speed. Nobody noticed the explosion of the shell which hit our mast and spattered four of us with splinters. Running in for the third time, I noticed, with a shock, blood on the bridge and then the quickly rising pain and felt furious that this should happen to me at this moment. The leading trawler, which happened to be right ahead, became the object of all my spite, and in concentrating my attention on her I committed the major blunder of losing touch with the leader on a sharp turn. A few seconds later the trawler blew up with a roar, which was some consolation at the time."

Of the three enemy vessels at this stage, one had blown up, another was stopped and silenced and the third was damaged.

With both her officers and two of her crew seriously wounded, however, Lee realised that his boat was in no condition to continue the action, so he set course for harbour and, dangerously wounded though he was, remained on the bridge until she reached harbour at dawn, an action which very nearly cost him his life.

Engage the Enemy More Closely

Meanwhile Richards found Barge, whose stopped and silenced trawler the two M.G.Bs. closed in upon, with the intention of boarding. Already survivors could be heard shouting in the water. It was at this moment, when the battle had been in progress for almost an hour, that German reinforcements appeared on the scene.

Six E boats approached at their best speed from the west, to the assistance of their hard-pressed comrades in the trawlers. Faced with this new development after an hour of action, in which much ammunition had been expended, Richards might well have considered withdrawing, but nothing was farther from his intention, and it was then that he made Nelson's favourite signal: " Engage the enemy more closely."

Straight for the six new-comers went the two M.G.Bs., and a most violent and ferocious battle followed. Richards led down the line, the two boats taking the enemy's full broadside, and although our shooting was good, the M.G.Bs. were forced to turn away. On disengaging close together, Barge saw that 110 was taking heavy punishment and she immediately burst into flames. The fire was extinguished, but the next moment she disappeared. Observation was difficult due to severe enemy fire, and Barge turned back to look for her. A group of enemy boats and two burning craft were seen ; one no doubt was enemy but the other was probably 110. Close approach being impossible, he waited, and after a fruitless search at dawn, Barge joined O'Mahoney and they returned together.

Survivors from Richard's boat were taken prisoner, but he was not amongst them. The German account which follows cannot be regarded as of any historical significance. Not until the official German records are available will the true details be known of the final stages in this gallant action.

D.N.B. in German for Europe. 1.9 p.m. 30th May, 1943.

" Berlin (*International Information Bureau*): According to the latest reports on the naval engagement off Dunkirk on 29th May, British M.T.Bs. suffered a heavy defeat. The latest reports available make it clear that, apart from the news of the sinking of two M.T.Bs. already reported, the British lost altogether five M.T.Bs., which were sunk by vessels of the German coastguard service. Apart from these five boats sunk, another two were heavily damaged and left burning, and it may be assumed that these boats were also lost.

" During the engagement one of the enemy boats attempted to ram a German vessel, although the former was in a completely hopeless position. Before she succeeded in doing this, a direct hit was obtained upon her and she blew up. It was possible to rescue some of her crew. Other enemy boats attempted to get out of their desperate positions by use of boarding apparatus. This caused them heavy losses in lives. From this dramatic engagement the German crews and their numerically inferior boats emerged with only small losses, which represents a remarkable tribute to their fighting spirit. All German vessels have meanwhile reached their base."

Borkenau. German Home Service via Luxemburg, in German for Germany. 7.15 *p.m.* 31st *May,* 1943

"Encounter between German coastal units and British M.T.Bs. near Dunkirk in the morning of 29th May. Five English M.T.Bs. sunk; two more set on fire. Some prisoners taken. No losses on the German side.

"The commander of one of the German E boat flotillas engaged in the encounter tells his story: 'The whole thing developed so rapidly that the English were as surprised as ourselves. Certainly two English boats found themselves at 20 metres from us and were so flabbergasted that at first they forgot to fire. We blazed away as best we could, and the English, who in amazement sailed across our whole front-line, got hits from one of our boats after another. The two boats caught fire quickly and one sank. The other veered round sharply and disappeared in flames. Shortly afterwards I saw something burning in the distance, and guessed it was one more M.T.B. I moved near, attempting to encircle it. But when my circle was starting to form two more English boats broke into it, firing in all directions and getting fire from all sides. One of the boats broke through my ring, and a fight at close quarters ensued. Hand grenades were thrown; that boat also started to burn and disappeared in flames. The other boat could not break through, and finally, as a last resort, attempted to ram one of my boats. But it got very heavy fire from that boat and from another one near by, and just before it could ram there was an explosion. Its magazine was blown up; it caught fire and sank. We succeeded in saving five survivors and took them with us. We ourselves went safely back into harbour.' "

It seems that the two British boats made their presence felt.

Many tributes have been paid to Richards' brilliant leadership. His determination, his sheer courage and, above all, his enthusiasm were of the order which constitutes greatness.

"Life was one huge adventure for him," wrote one of the officers of his flotilla. "He never got flustered and, even at sea, regarded everything as highly amusing. I can remember one night in the summer of 1942, sitting beside him on the bridge whilst we crept about, rather too near the French coast, looking for shipping. Dick was enjoying every moment of it, singing '*Sur le pont d'Avignon*' and suggesting mad schemes. He ought to have lived in the days of Drake."

CHAPTER XII

In the Baie de la Seine

EARLY experience with the steam gunboats had shown that they required some fairly extensive modification before they could be regarded as really efficient fighting machines. This involved a long refit, and it was during the refit that I took over command of the 1st S.G.B. Flotilla. It was discovered at this time that S.G.Bs. came just within the limiting length which entitled them to names instead of numbers, and the Admiralty agreed to a proposal that they should be called after a series of animals beginning with the word Grey. There were six boats in the flotilla, and they were called *Grey Goose*,[1] *Grey Wolf*, *Grey Seal*, *Grey Fox*, *Grey Shark* and *Grey Owl*. These names had been selected by the Commanding Officers of the boats, and the Admiralty gesture in approving the proposal was received with pride and delight by the whole flotilla.

The S.G.Bs. did not all complete their refits simultaneously; one of them, *Grey Shark*, was ready for action some time before the rest. A number of operations were therefore undertaken in the spring of 1943 in which she led a force of mixed Coastal Force craft. One defensive patrol of four boats consisted of the S.G.B., a " D " Class M.G.B., a " C " Class M.G.B. and a 70-foot M.T.B.

In April *Grey Shark*, of which I was temporary Commanding Officer while Lt. Howard Bradford recovered from a broken arm, accompanied by two " D " boats, was in action in the Baie de la Seine against the local equivalent of " The Four Horsemen "—though in this case there were only three trawlers, and by comparison with their North Sea counterpart they were considerably less sophisticated. In moonlight that was almost as bright as day we fought a brisk gun action with these trawlers which ended after eight minutes when *Grey Shark's* steering-gear had jammed hard a-port. One of the M.G.Bs. had by this time stoppages in its main armament and one gun had a shell jammed half-way up its barrel. In this condition I regarded her as a liability, and instructed her to wait for us at a prearranged rendezvous, though, as it turned out, this was probably a wrong decision. Then, when our hand steering-gear had been engaged, we set off again to find the enemy, with the other M.G.B. following astern. This M.G.B. was commanded by Lt. J. H. Hodder, R.N.V.R., with whom, at Dover a year before, I had had my first introduction to Coastal Forces.

The trawlers were probably, we guessed, heading for Le Havre, for while we had been stopped, repairing our steering and signalling to each other by light, they had lain no more than a mile to the southward, also signalling to each other, before disappearing in a south-easterly direction. After various detours in order to regain the advantage of the moon we " suddenly sighted them right ahead about $3\frac{1}{2}$ miles with terrific bow waves, obviously legging it at speed." (I quote from the account I wrote a few days after the action.) " I must own to a sinking feeling on sighting. The moon was so bloody bright. While there was a doubt about finding them, the cowardly subconscious was saying hopefully, ' Perhaps you won't '; although the conscious went on working out every possibility to make sure we did find them."

In the battle which followed, the leading trawler was silenced and stopped. Boarding was considered, but by now dawn was not far off and we had a long way to go. There did

---

[1] *Grey Goose* was my own boat. It was a name which held many associations for me, not only with memories of surely the most romantic birds that fly, but also with the first boat I ever owned, a duck-punt which was so christened.

not seem to be time. So we ranged up opposite the silenced enemy and about 150 yards away, slowed down and raked her from end to end with gunfire, in an attempt to sink her, but unfortunately our 3-inch gun was irreparably jammed. Under a hail of machine-gun bullets, which could be heard clanging up and down her metal hull, the enemy very bravely brought one of his 20-mm. cannon into action, and the first burst came into the bridge, knocking us all down, but only slightly wounding the Navigating Officer (Sub-Lt. John Harris, R.N.V.R.). This burst also set fire to a magazine under the bridge, and it became necessary to draw away to extinguish the flames; Hodder's Oerlikon gunner, however, replied to the trawler and silenced its fire. By the time that our magazine conflagration had been extinguished, the approaching dawn forced us to start for home. And so the battle was once more indecisive, although we had undoubtedly given more than we received. Damage to our force was slight, the S.G.B. had one killed and two wounded and the M.G.Bs. had no casualties at all. In such a battle, however, the personal bravery of the British seaman is just as likely to be demonstrated as in a clear-cut victory. Indeed, it is usually in defeat and adversity that the greatest qualities of mankind come to the surface. (So it had been on this occasion with the German gunner who brought his gun to life under that hail of bullets.)

Thus paragraph 28 of my official report to the Commander-in-Chief, Portsmouth, reads as follows:

"I should like to bring to your notice the conduct of Able Seaman Norman Clegg, Official Number D/JX 237892. Early in the action this rating was wounded by two bullets which broke his left arm, causing severe bleeding and great pain. In spite of this he continued as Oerlikon loader, lifting the heavy magazines with his good arm until the end of the action some half an hour later, and refusing all suggestions that he should be given first-aid."

In this action the enemy mistook the S.G.B. for a destroyer, and on the following day a detailed account of the proceedings was broadcast from Berlin under the headline "Motor Gunboat Sunk."

"In the first morning hour of 16th April there was a dramatic battle between a British destroyer, accompanied by two motor gunboats, and boats of the German Coastal Defence off Northern Brittany. In spite of the enemy's superiority in arms, the skilfully manoeuvring German vessels succeeded in forcing aside one of the motor gunboats, so that they were enabled to fire on it at a range of 400 metres. This led to a violent fire. The vessel, which had been rendered immobile, was lost from sight in the further course of the battle. Its loss can be assumed.[1]

DESTROYER'S BOARDING ATTEMPT REPULSED

"During a renewed thrust of the enemy ships there were losses in arms and to the crew in one of our own boats, so that the enemy Commander of the destroyer believed it possible to make an attempt at boarding. As there were no other means of defence which had remained intact, close combat arms and hand grenades were used against the approaching destroyer. Only at the very last moment a Petty Officer succeeded in repairing one quickfiring gun which had been damaged by the enemy fire. He fired at a range of a few metres on the boarding party climbing up the side of the ship and dealt it heavy losses.[2] The immediate danger of boarding thus being removed, the bridge of the destroyer was heavily fired on from a very close range of a few metres: the destroyer thereupon fled."

[1] In the first part of the battle our force was practically unscathed and neither of the M.G.Bs. was set on fire or immobilised at any time.

[2] At no time was the S.G.B. ever closer to the trawler than about 100 yards.

THEY LOOKED LIKE A FLOCK OF WIDGEON

By the summer the S.G.Bs. were working as a flotilla, though at this time there was all too little enemy shipping for them to harry, except for the standing patrols of the German Coastal Defence. There was, for example, a flotilla of R boats which were often to be found off Pointe de Barfleur. In the early hours of 27th July an Albacore of the Fleet Air Arm came across them, and attacked them with a stick of bombs. As a result a force of four S.G.Bs. was soon steaming at high speed to intercept them before they should return to Cherbourg. This force was under my command, and I was leading the line in my own boat—*Grey Goose*.

By the time we had reached the reported position, the short summer night was almost over. It was ten minutes to four when the enemy was sighted ahead about 3½ miles north of his harbour.

The action which followed was very fierce and violent. It was not a victorious battle, but its thirty-six minutes were full of adventure and misadventure, and, for those who fought in it, there was peril and opportunity.

Here is the account of it, which I wrote a few days afterwards.

" When I saw them I turned slightly to starboard so as to engage them on the port side, firing to southward. There seemed to be no end to the Huns. They looked like a flock of widgeon with two or three geese amongst them. The sea was so glassy calm that you could see the reflections of stars. The last-quarter moon had only just risen, but what little light it gave was almost directly behind us, and behind us, too, was the faint glow of dawn over the north-eastern horizon. The geese—two or three trawlers—were on the left, and the widgeon—R boats—were sitting still and all clustered together. All told, there seemed to be too many Huns to count—about a dozen it looked like—before things started to happen.

" We were intent upon bringing the enemy to action before he entered harbour, and we had no time to work round to get the advantage of the light. We soldiered in at 20 knots, and when the range was 500 yards one of the R boats challenged with a blue light.

" When it is very calm it is hard to judge range, but I do not think it was more than 300 yards and possibly a good deal less when I said, ' Open fire.' Then it started. Some fifteen ships all opened fire at once and the air was as thick with tracer as I have ever seen it, red and green and white. It ripped away from our guns towards the enemy line, it fanned out of the enemy ships and whipped over our heads, it criss-crossed ahead and astern, it ricochetted off the water and popped as it exploded in the air, and it thumped into us from time to time with a shower of sparks. There were also some big splashes caused by heavy shells, probably from the trawlers or perhaps from the shore. I suppose the enemy was blinded by the tracer as much as we were because, considering how close we all were to each other, it is odd that more damage was not done on both sides.

" The R boats must have got under way fairly quickly because, by the light of sudden flashes which I took to be hits—but which may have been gun flashes—I could see them creaming along on a parallel course about 300 yards away. Too many of them seemed to be shooting at my boat, and we could not fire at more than two of them at a time. I looked back and could not see any of the other three following. In truth I could see very little at all as the tracer was completely blinding.

" I remember seeing the leading R boat on our beam and shooting at us and thinking, ' Thank God, there aren't any more to pass.' We had overtaken at least six—one at a time and quite slowly as we were only going about 5 knots faster than they were. They had hit us several times and we were burning aft, with a lot of smoke. A report came to the bridge that ' Y ' gun was out of action and some of the crew had been laid out, but we kept on on a steady course still, because the other guns seemed to be firing quite well. The fire aft died down, but then suddenly flared up very bright again, and all the Huns started shooting at us alone. A 20-mm. shell hit the mast and splinters flew amongst us on the bridge. One very small one hit me on the nose and the wireless aerial descended in coils round our necks.

" I decided that we should have to disengage. A long way astern and on the starboard quarter I could see two of our boats, but at the moment we seemed to be tackling the line of R boats single handed. No. 1 (Lt. J. B. Henderson, R.N.V.R.), although he was wounded, beetled off aft, and together with Able Seaman Wendon and Stoker Clelland put the fire out very quickly, with a hail of bullets whistling round their ears. (Wendon was given the D.S.M. for it and for his general conduct that night.) It was a ' Ready Use ' locker full of ammunition which had been blazing so brightly. Another locker full of pom-pom ammunition had vanished in one ' poof ' and left the locker looking like a tulip.

" After turning north, I reduced to 10 knots as soon as the worst of it was over, in order to let the others catch up. From time to time some hopeful German would direct a burst at us, and the tracers would come lobbing towards us. I planned to wait until the others had joined up, then re-form and go in again. As I looked back I saw a line of the other three boats in the light of some starshell which the Hun had just put up. This was the first starshell which had so far appeared. I watched the line go in to attack and then, when the starshell had gone out, I suddenly saw one ship get the most terrible pounding. I hoped it was one of them, but I feared it was one of ours, because it was very near where I had seen them in the starshell. For about twenty seconds shells were bursting and sparkling all over it, so it seemed. The battle roared on very fiercely and then rather suddenly ceased. There was a pause of a couple of minutes and then a distress signal from one of our boats. I said to the Coxswain, ' Starboard thirty—steady on south,' and my heart sank into my boots.

" Now—to go back to the others. Early in the action Howard (Lt. H. O. T. Bradford, D.S.C., R.N.V.R.), in *Grey Shark*, which was second in line, had his steering shot away. Before the hand steering could be brought into operation the boat had turned 90° to starboard and lost contact with the leader. Griff (Lt. I. R. Griffiths, D.S.C., R.N.), in *Grey Wolf*, which was third in line, did not know that Howard was not following me. Indeed, so blinding was the tracer that he found it almost impossible to follow anyone. So the line was broken, and for a bit Griff and Jimmy (Lt. J. S. Southcott, R.N.V.R.), in *Grey Seal*, which was the last boat, took on the trawlers. This was the stage when we had been trying to cope with the R boats by ourselves.

" As soon was Howard's steering was fixed up, he saw me burning brightly and decided that I must be in a very poor way and must be protected from the rough Germans. So without hesitation he plunged into the mêlée between me and the R boats, announcing to his First Lieutenant[1] his intention to ram. Before he could so so, however, he passed within 25 yards of about four of them, getting a horrible pasting as I had seen. He managed, however, to give a pretty fair return, I gather, and saw a lot of hits on the enemy. Some of his crew also think they saw two men in the water clinging to some wreckage. They wondered if they were some of our blokes as they quite thought that we had sunk by now (and so did the Germans, according to their communiqué). They also reckon they saw a ship very low in

[1] Lt. " Sandy " Bown, R.N.V.R.

the water which looked as though it was sinking, although I have my doubts about this myself.

"Howard's engines were hit and he came to a standstill. Griff was too blinded by the tracer and starshell even to see that Howard had been stopped. All he knew was that he couldn't see the next ahead and that he was being shot at by ships at Red 30° and at Red 130° and at every ten degrees in between, so it seemed. He could still see me burning on his starboard side and decided to follow round. His bridge had been hit, his First Lieutenant and Navigator and Coxswain all slightly wounded, and he was at the wheel and coming round to north. The Coxswain had been cracked on the head by a large piece of Perspex wind-screen dislodged by a two-pounder shell which hit the bridge just below it. He picked himself up from the deck and took the wheel again and went a little past the course, altering back to port.

"Meanwhile Jimmy had seen Howard stop. He stood on for a few seconds and then said to himself, ' Oi, you can't leave old Howard there,' and turned back hard a-starboard. Half-way round his turn he suddenly saw Griff on his starboard bow, and as Griff altered back to port on to his course he suddenly saw Jimmy. There was nothing to be done. They both went full astern, but they hit pretty hard. Griff's for'ard mess-deck was holed very badly, a hole about 15 feet long at the upperdeck and going down to a point about 3 feet below the waterline. Fortunately, the bulkhead abaft it was undamaged and so, although he thought at first he was going to sink, he was in fact quite well able to keep the damage under control.

An Exercise in Towing

"All those things had happened pretty quickly while we had been trying to put out our four fires—two for'ard and two aft—and before the distress signal had been made to summon us to Howard's assistance. The position was now that, of our four boats, one was lying stopped without prospect of repair some $3\frac{1}{2}$ miles off Cherbourg breakwater, another was still on fire and the remaining two had been in collision.

We steered south towards the distress signal, and then in the binoculars I saw *four* ships lying more or less stopped, and a dozen possibilities went through my mind. Were they all Huns? Were three of them Huns, mustered round the damaged boat and waiting perhaps to board her? Two of them looked German in silhouette. The first moved off slowly, passing quite close to us, and not until it had gone did I realise that it was the only enemy one, for the second turned out to be Griff down by the bow because of his flooded mess-deck. He made off to the northward, informing me by signal, and I closed the other two and circled them. Jimmy was passing a tow, and in the incredibly short time of four minutes the tow was secured. While this was being done, some of Howard's crew report that they saw and heard a German shouting in the water about 50 yards away.

"I had followed the single R boat with my glasses, and, sweeping to the westward, I suddenly picked up a whole bunch of enemy ships—at least seven of them. They were clustered against the darkest part of the horizon, while we were completely silhouetted against the dawn, and it rapidly became apparent that they were closing in at slow speed to try conclusions with us. Still our two boats lay stopped. I could distinguish now which was ' tower ' and which was ' towee,' and suddenly I saw the ' towee ' start to pivot round: the strain was on the tow: they were under way. For me it was a moment of supreme relief and renewed hope.

"By this time, however, the enemy were less than 1,000 yards away, and the only course was, obviously, to lay a smoke-screen to cover the tow. I increased speed and started to make smoke and immediately the Hun saw what was happening and opened fire. But I had already passed between him and the tow, and the thick billowy white clouds of smoke had hidden it perfectly. The R boats' fire was very poor and our 'B' gun, which had had a stoppage in the first part of the action, was in particularly good form. MacAlistair had once been Hitch's pom-pom gunner and now was firing in short but admirable bursts.

"We reckon we hit the second R boat in line, and the towing party reckon they saw the flash and glow of it through the smoke. The first R boat turned towards, and I expected him to come through the smoke after us, but the second one turned away and the others seemed to follow. Some starshells were fired and several big splashes appeared about 50 yards away, but the crisis seemed to be past. Meanwhile the tow was proceeding at 10 knots. With excellent judgment, Jimmy refused to attempt anything faster, realising that all would be lost if the tow were to part. We dropped astern of them again so as to be able to repeat the smoke run, and we did in fact make another puff of it for good measure. A few minutes later we ran into what we took to be natural fog. Actually it was some smoke which Griff, with admirable foresight, had made ten minutes earlier with the object of providing cover for us.

"After that we ran through several patches of real mist, so that I began to feel more sanguine about the likelihood of enemy air attack. By now it was broad daylight, and I did not think that enemy ships would dare to follow in face of our air support, which they would expect.

"About half-way home we were met by *Bleasdale* and *Stevenstone*, two 'Hunt' Class destroyers, and we stopped to transfer the casualties. Howard, wounded in the leg, was still hopping about on his bridge, but Johnny Harris, his Navigator, was very badly wounded and the Midshipman died on the way home. His Coxswain, himself badly wounded, had to amputate the mangled remains of another man's leg (with a razor blade) in order to dress the wound. The Coxswain (Petty Officer Hicks) went on working till they got back to harbour nine hours after the action, when he collapsed. (He was awarded the D.S.M.)

"Griff had joined up with the destroyers before we did and transferred his casualties too. One of them—Able Seaman Gray—had had his leg severed by a shell bursting on it. Standing on one leg and supporting himself on his gun, he had taken over breechworker and gone on fighting the gun for six minutes, until the boat had disengaged, when he collapsed and died soon after.

"So in the early afternoon our battle-stained force entered harbour. We had suffered casualties and damage; we believe we inflicted more; and all our boats were safely home."

This is how the Germans described the action in their broadcast account:

D.N.B. in German for Europe. 12.41 *p.m.* 27*th July*, 1943

CHERBOURG NAVAL ENGAGEMENT THIS MORNING

" *Berlin (International Information Bureau)*: This morning, 27th July, German naval patrol boats encountered, north of Cherbourg, a British formation of M.T.Bs., which they engaged. The enemy formation, consisting of five gunboats, lost one boat immediately after fire was opened, which was set on fire and sank, having been hit heavily on the waterline.

" HEAVY BRITISH CASUALTIES :

" During a renewed patrol by our vessels three enemy boats were spotted doing rescue work. Since, apart from the boat already sunk, there were only these three boats about, it is to be supposed that another enemy boat had been sunk. Fire was opened immediately on these boats, which were lying close to each other in bright moonlight. Hits were scored. The enemy barely returned the fire and our vessels were able to approach them closely without much risk. Damage inflicted on the enemy was accordingly heavy. Heavy losses amongst the British crews were observed in the moonlight : piles of killed or wounded were seen lying at the various guns. The German vessels had only small losses in men and suffered negligible damage ; they have all returned to their base meanwhile."

TIME AND THE PHOSPHORESCENCE CONSPIRED AGAINST US

Although, as we have seen all through this book, stealth was the essence of a torpedo attack, there were times when our Coastal Forces, and particularly our S.G.Bs., because of their relatively large size, could not approach undetected, yet *still* they had to try to fight their way through to a decisive torpedo range. One such battle began in the Dover Strait on the evening of 4th September, 1943.

On that night the enemy's high speed and the sea's phosphorescence made it impossible for our boats to creep in unseen. Although the night was dark and calm, the bow wave and wake of a moving vessel shone with pale-green luminosity, so brightly that the phosphorescence, even at slow speeds, could be seen at far greater distances than the dark lump of the vessel itself.

Soon after 9 p.m. an enemy force left Boulogne and steamed southward along the coast of France. Four S.G.Bs. (again under my command) were at sea on the way to their hunting-ground when wireless signals reporting the enemy's position began to come through. As soon as the high-pitched Morse messages were received they were passed to the chart table on the bridge of *Grey Goose*, where the Navigating Officer worked feverishly, with roller ruler and dividers, plotting the enemy's course and speed and laying off a course to intercept.

The speed necessary to make a successful approach produced too brilliant a phosphorescent wake, while the speed at which the wake would not be sighted was too slow to make a good approach, for the enemy was hurrying along at little less than 15 knots. Time and the phosphorescence conspired against us; and so it was that when we were still a mile and a half from the enemy, and trying to manœuvre into an attacking position, we heard the sound of distant gunfire.

" Damn and blast," I said, " that'll be starshell "; and a moment later, hopelessly, " It is! "

Suddenly a brilliant light burst overhead, and then another and another. We were bathed in a dazzling white glare while the starshells floated lazily down on their parachutes. Tracers and the heavy shells followed, streams of green and white shimmering out across the calm sea and great shell splashes spouting up all round. The tracer seemed to be a barrage, for it criss-crossed about in a tangled network of flying sparks. Very little of it came directly towards us. Nevertheless the tactics had to be changed, and as the German force hurried down the coast we yapped round its heels like terriers waiting for a chance to bite. Once we passed through the enemy's wake in order to try to gain bearing for an attack on the landward side in the mouth of the River Somme. There was a strong smell of smoke as we passed astern, and we pitched and rolled for a moment as we met the waves thrown up by the enemy formation. Three times we closed in to attack, but each time the starshells went up, followed by cascades of tracer and the leaping waterspouts of heavy shells. Once a single white flare went up far away over the coast, and by its light the enemy force was perfectly silhouetted—seven "M" Class minesweepers in line ahead.

"Two of the middle ones," to quote from the account I wrote a few days after the action, "were old-type sweepers with tall, thin Woodbine funnels, the others seemed to be of the squat-funnelled kind. They were all smoking like hell and obviously legging it as fast as ever they could go.

"Seven 'M' Class minesweepers—solid great ships of six or seven hundred tons with 4·1-inch guns and a large number of automatic weapons—were fairly formidable opposition for four S.G.Bs., but the night was still young and we decided to keep on trying.

"Next time their starshell went up when we were still 3,500 yards away, and the high explosive arrived shortly after, but we soldiered on in at 20 knots. I remember looking astern and seeing the rest of the force snaking after us amongst the tall pillars of the shell splashes. All round it was as bright as day, or brighter, and it was an extraordinarily beautiful spectacle. The sea was a brilliant unreal green under the starshells; some of them burned through their parachute strings and fell into the water, where they went on burning as they sank, with a wonderful luminous greenish glow. Above, the sky was full of curling question-marks of smoke left by the flares as they floated down. I thought one flare was going to land on the fo'c'sle, but it fell just clear ahead. There were still torrents of tracer trickling and streaming away from the enemy ships, and our boats were occasionally hit. The Huns were using a multiple 20-mm. gun, which put down a strip of bursts in the water that would have been most unhealthy to be in. There were also some bursts of self-destroying stuff which exploded in a neat little row in the sky.

"We fired back very little at this stage, for it would have been wasted in the dazzle, and we were concentrating on the torpedo attack, but it soon became apparent that that was not going to be possible. Four-inch shells were arriving thick and fast and getting rather accurate. I saw the next astern spattered by a near miss. Another fell directly ahead of us and many whistled narrowly over. I had another look with the glasses. Was there a hope of seeing the target and firing torpedoes? My impression was no, so we turned away in order to try another plan. The 4-inch followed us out to about 5,000 yards, and I don't quite know why none of us got a direct hit, considering the average accuracy. At last the starshell stopped and there was a sudden darkness—the after-dazzle darkness which seems darker than the night.

"New tactics were necessary, and we set off to get into position. On the way we ran full tilt into a new German patrol which was lying to seaward of the convoy route. We tried to slip past unobserved so as to continue our efforts to torpedo the minesweepers, but at less than a mile it was impossible, and the new enemy, who must have been watching the fireworks for some time, now joined in the battle. At once starshell came up again and immediately after it the streams of tracer.

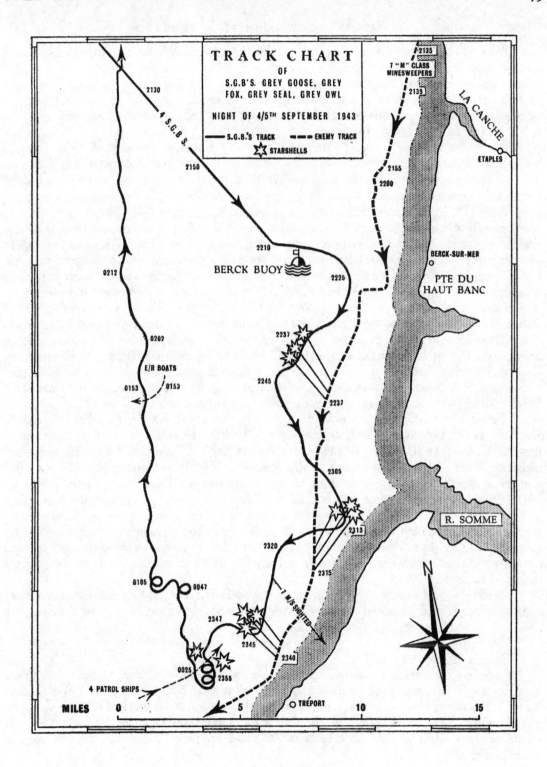

TRACK CHART
OF
S.G.B'S. GREY GOOSE, GREY
FOX, GREY SEAL, GREY OWL

NIGHT OF 4/5TH SEPTEMBER 1943

S.G.B.'S TRACK ——
ENEMY TRACK ----
STARSHELLS ✦

A WILLY-NILLY TURN TO STARBOARD

" Here was a sudden opportunity, and I decided to take it. We were already close to some enemy ships, and it seemed we had a better chance of doing them down than we had of getting at the minesweepers. I came hard round to port and opened fire, and again the tracers began to buzz about like purposeful red bumble-bees, the smaller machine guns burst forth in tinselly white and yellow showers like Golden Rain, and all the while the scene was lit by the bright white starshells hanging overhead.

" As we closed in to 500 yards and came round in an arc, we seemed all to be firing at the centre. I have never seen nicer shooting—there was nothing wild about it, just deliberate bursts ploughing straight into the targets. We took the right-hand one, and in a matter of seconds the stream of tracer from him had dwindled to nothing.

" Peter (Lt. P. E. Mason, R.N.V.R.), who was next astern in *Grey Fox*, was putting up some prettily placed starshell, and by its light Jimmy (Lt. J. S. Southcott, R.N.V.R.), who was following in *Grey Seal*, picked out a Hun going from left to right. With amazing quickness he turned out of line, reduced speed and fired torpedoes, one of which apparently hit. I didn't see the explosion myself, but all the other boats did. Meanwhile the enemy we were engaging was firing only spasmodically but still steaming fast, and we were converging on him and fairly raking him with everything we had. Clouds of smoke were coming out of him, and a fine red glow showed under the bridge aft, apparently through a hole in the ship's side. He was about 150 yards away. If only we could illuminate him our fire would be twice as effective, but we had run out of starshell. I shouted for the searchlight, and Dearing, my leading signalman, jumped up to man it. But, before he could switch on, a 20-mm. shell had mown him down. He was badly wounded in both legs. As usual, the wireless aerial fell in coils all round us on the bridge, the result of a hit on the mast.

" We were overtaking the enemy, and I got a good view of him by the light of starshell. He was one of the converted landing-craft type known to the enemy as an A.F. boat and to us as a T.L.C., type III. The sloping bow and stern and the little high bridge aft were very distinct. When he had fallen just abaft the beam he suddenly got one of his 88-mm. guns going and clocked us a couple of times in quick succession. They made a terrific ' bonk.' I felt sure the first one had got the engines and was not surprised to feel the ship lose speed. It was a very curious feeling. I knew for certain that these two hits were 88-mm. shells, for they pushed the ship over quite a lot when they hit. I remember thinking that if he hit us a couple more times he would finish us; and then miraculously we were still going—and not only that but increasing speed again and turning away to starboard. It seemed almost too good to be true.

" ' Midships, and steady as you go,' I cried hopefully. But no, we turned to starboard and to starboard, and I realised that the steering had been shot away. In a few moments we should be heading straight back towards the Hun.

" ' Stop both.'

" Telegraphs shot way, sir.'

" I pressed the engine-room bell, but all the lighting and electrical circuits had gone. The seaman torpedoman popped up beside me, ' Port tube badly holed, sir.' We did not realise in the din of the battle that a direct hit on the firing mechanism had actually fired the torpedo without our knowing it. By the time a messenger could get to the engine-room it would be far too late to stop the ship before she had completed her circle and was back in action again.

" Many of the guns' crews had been hit (for we had been under fire on and off for two hours) and one gun was jammed, but we would have to tackle the Hun with what we had—including the starboard torpedo; not a very good chance perhaps for a torpedo attack with the rudder jammed hard a-starboard, but it seemed likely to be the only chance.

" During our turn away both Peter and Jimmy had gone past making a smoke-screen and, so far, the enemy was invisible, but a few moments later we were through the smoke and there was the Hun. I set 7 knots for his speed on the sight, and as we swung on I pulled the starboard firing lever and yelled ' Fire Sugar.' The lever came back freely in my hand. The connections had been shot away, but a couple of seconds later the torpedo went off, fired from the tube. I could see by then that the slight delay would be enough to make it miss ahead as the ship was still swinging to starboard. The fish jumped once and then went away straight, and it passed well across the bows of the enemy, making a bright phosphorescent wake as it went. The range on firing was about 400 yards and we closed to about 250 in turning, engaging with all guns that were still working. If it was the same Hun as before, he had put out the fire in between whiles, but I think it may have been a different one. He scarcely fired back at all, and continuing our willy-nilly turn to starboard, we plunged back into the smoke again.

" At last we had established a sort of ' bush telegraph ' between bridge and engine-room and had stopped engines. This seemed the only way to end our mad gyrations. The Chief (Chief Engine-room Artificer W. Bird) got the rudders amidships and reported to the bridge that although there were two gaping holes in the engine-room he thought he could keep the ship going, but we should have to steer by main engines.

" It was evident that we were in no case to undertake any more fighting, so we came round to northish and rigged a jury wireless aerial to find out how the others had got on. At first we could not get through to them and we were rather anxious, but later we found that Jimmy and Richard (Lt. R. M. Hall, R.N.V.R., in *Grey Owl*) were all right, although, in disengaging, they had been illuminated by what appeared to be a third enemy force to the westward. As we went we had the greatest difficulty in keeping the rudders amidships. From time to time they worked over until the ship was circling again, and for a while we progressed in a series of loops.

" Sometime later we had a quick brush with some E/R boats which appeared on our starboard beam. We couldn't do much about it, as we couldn't steer to pursue them, and the problem of identity was rather acute, as Jimmy and Richard had just joined up with us. The E boats crossed astern of us and were lost almost at once. They were the fourth enemy force we had encountered that night.

" On joining up Jimmy had signalled with a blue light ' My fish hit,' which was the first we knew of his torpedo attack, and splendid news it was. But we had also received a signal from Peter Mason which was too weak to read. We could only make out a part of it, but that said, ' . . . require assistance,' and we were immediately in a ferment of anxiety. I planned to send Jimmy or Richard back to look for him, but before doing so we asked for a repetition of the signal from Dover. When they answered I went down to the wireless office and we decoded it feverishly, ' My position . . . ' and we knew that it ended ' . . . require assistance.' The position followed, and there was one more group before ' require assistance '; it was sure to be ' disabled ' or ' broken down '—it was neither—it was simply ' interrogative require assistance.' I have seldom felt a more delightful glow of relief.

" Towards dawn the wind began to rise, but in spite of the two big holes and the many small ones in our ship's side, the engine-room crew managed to keep the ship going under her own steam. The work of improvisation that they did down there in the darkness and the heat (for the fan circuits had been shot away) was beyond all praise.

" At daybreak we found that Peter Mason was about 4 miles ahead of us, and he got into harbour first, followed a few minutes later by the other three. Amongst all four boats one man was killed, one died of wounds and eleven others were wounded. My ship was the only one that was damaged, except for the superficial bullet and splinter marks with which each was liberally spattered."

The German claim was quite a different story:

D.N.B. in German for Europe.   10·47 a.m.   *5th September,* 1943.

" *Berlin*: The International Information Bureau reports that during last night German coastal covering forces engaged two British motor torpedo boat formations off the west coast of France. During the first action about midnight, two of the enemy boats were sunk by direct shell hits. One hour later a second engagement took place in the waters off Le Treport, in which another two motor torpedo boats were sunk and a third one was set on fire. Thus the British light surface fleet lost four of its boats and probably lost a fifth within a few hours, in an attack against the German convoy routes off the coast of Western Europe. This was the first attack for a considerable time. The German vessels suffered only a few casualties in wounded. There was some superficial damage which did not affect the manœuvrability of the boats."

" What Ships ? "

After Richards was killed Lt. R. B. Rooper, R.N., became Senior Officer of the M.G.B. Flotilla at Ramsgate, and not long after his arrival, on the night of 24th/25th July, he met two E boats of the Cherbourg flotilla which were on passage through the Strait of Dover on their way to Germany. On being attacked the E boats became separated, and Rooper, with two M.G.Bs., engaged the second E boat, and was lucky enough to score a hit on one of its spare torpedoes, with the result that the boat blew up at once and was destroyed. Four of the crew were taken prisoner, and from these it was learned that the Commanding Officer had been the first to jump over the side, and that as a result of this he was not amongst the survivors. From prisoners taken some time later it was also learned that the Commanding Officer of the other E boat had been court martialled for deserting his companion.

The tempo of the autumn of 1943 from the Coastal Forces point of view was not so swift as that of the year before. The reason for this reduced activity was partly that the enemy had fewer ships at sea, as he was not now engaged in the extensive minelaying which had led to so many engagements during the previous autumn, and partly that the weather was much less favourable. So fierce, for example, were the gales at the beginning of August, that, on the night of the 7th, one of the older 70-foot M.G.Bs. broke her back and foundered while returning from patrol, though her crew was safely rescued.

The length of occupied coast lying within reach of Newhaven, which had not seen very much Coastal Forces activity before 1943, was now being exploited by three flotillas: S.G.Bs., "D" Class M.G.Bs., and 70-foot M.T.Bs.; but owing to the development of Radar by the enemy, and the high cliffs of Normandy, which gave it the best possible conditions, it became rather an unhealthy stretch off which to lie in wait. One night an M.G.B. commanded by Lt. H. W. Paton, R.N.V.R. (who was known, for no particular reason, throughout Coastal Forces as " the Colonel "), was hit in the bows by the very first salvo from the Radar-controlled shore batteries, at a range of more than 4 miles. Although she had suffered no casualties Paton's boat could not proceed forwards because of the damage to her bows, so, having come all the way across the Channel to be struck smartly on the nose as soon as she arrived, she then steamed slowly home again—backwards. Her speed of advance (backwards) was, to begin with, no more than 3 knots, though Paton was able gradually to increase it. But for more than an hour—until he was 10 miles offshore—the batteries continued to shell him, and the rest of the unit who were standing by him. It is interesting that having scored a hit with their first salvo they could not repeat their success, and the M.G.B. returned safely to Newhaven.

The smaller M.T.Bs. were not so regularly shelled, and it was on this same beat that they scored a notable success in a skilful little action on 7th September, 1943. On that night three M.T.Bs. of the 14th Flotilla were creeping stealthily in towards the coast of Normandy near the village of St. Valery-en-Caux. The Senior Officer of the unit was Lt. Donald Rigg, R.N.V.R.

"When we were running in to start our patrol," he says, "some misguided person on the French coast turned a searchlight on to a ship steaming along close inshore. We all thought this was a very good thing, as it saved us the trouble of waiting all night for something to come along."

Through binoculars Rigg saw that the ship was coming westwards towards him, but it was still more than 3 miles away. The presence of our Force was evidently suspected by the enemy—perhaps that was why the searchlight was originally used, although it had inadvertently disclosed the whereabouts of his own patrol. A few minutes later there came a challenge from the shore and a single red tracer shell passed high overhead. Again the searchlight came on and this time swept towards our boats, but they were not seen. After another ten minutes starshell burst overhead, but still the enemy was bewildered and uncertain. If he saw anything, it was not enough to warn him of the impending disaster so soon to overtake his ships.

The Senior Officer planned his stalk most carefully and waited for half an hour so that the moon should have set before he came to attack. At midnight the force reached its prescribed position near St. Pierre. The sea was very calm.

"We stopped," says Rigg, "and I shouted across to the other boats to ask them if they could see the ships and tell them which to attack. The reply from one of them was 'What ships?' It appears that Sub-Lt. J. G. Hubbard, R.N.V.R., the last in line, had not seen the enemy ships in the light of the searchlight, and he had followed the recent manœuvres without the least idea of their object or the least idea that the enemy was so near.

"When he had grasped the situation, the M.T.Bs. crept in towards the five enemy patrol ships. Two of them fired their torpedoes within a few seconds of each other, aiming at two enemy ships which were almost abreast of each other, and looking like one long target in the sights.

"It seemed ages before anything happened, then suddenly there was a frightful explosion and a huge flash shot upwards from the nearest vessel. All that remained to be seen was a large column of smoke. About seven seconds later a second explosion was heard and felt but no flash was seen."

Rigg was embarked in the M.T.B. commanded by Lt. N. W. G. Taylor, R.N.V.R., and the second boat was commanded by Sub-Lt. P. Aspinall, R.N.V.R., who relates how he was engaged by gunfire from the third ship in the enemy's line. "This, though fierce, was very wild, all the tracers passing well overhead. I crash-started all main engines, disengaging to starboard, and as the fire became progressively more accurate, I increased to full speed to open the range as quickly as possible. One hit from a 20-mm. shell was received on the bridge, but the only injuries sustained were very slight, being caused by splinters from the woodwork. When the enemy fire was becoming rather troublesome it ceased most abruptly, and in his position appeared a column of black smoke as if he had been hit by a torpedo."

" It looked," says Rigg, " as though the enemy's fire, which was streaming out as if from a hose pipe, had suddenly been cut off with a knife."

This remarkable and satisfactory phenomenon was caused by the timely intervention of Sub-Lt. Hubbard, in the third M.T.B. He heard one of the other boats firing, saw the flash of the first explosion and a few sparks and heard the second explosion. He guessed that the other two had both hit and felt that for that very reason he was bound to miss.

" However, at this stage," he says, " the third chap in the enemy line—a large trawler— turned to port and came inshore, guns blazing at the other two M.T.Bs. as they disengaged. This seemed an excellent opportunity for me, as he would pass within about 500 yards. I turned and closed in towards him with considerable anxiety lest I should miss, and fired when he came, of his own accord, into my sights. Actually, I believe that both torpedoes hit, one forward and the other amidships. When the smoke cleared, in a matter of about fifteen seconds, the vessel had sunk. I passed through the area of the attack and spent about fifteen minutes looking for survivors (without success) and to assure myself that the other two M.T.Bs. had not been damaged."

The two leading enemy ships had stopped about a mile to the westward, not far off Fécamp. Not for half an hour did they dare to return and search for the survivors from their three torpedoed companions under the light of starshells, flares and searchlights. Meanwhile the three victorious M.T.Bs. were speeding back towards their base. Seldom has stealth and surprise been exploited with more devastating effect.

The German account, which appeared more than twenty-four hours later, was skilfully worded so that the casual reader might suppose that only one, or at the most two, of their ships had sunk. This is the text that was broadcast in German for Europe at 7.43 a.m. on the 9th September, 1943:

" *Berlin* (*International Information Bureau*): During Tuesday night, shortly after one o'clock, there was a clash between German Coastal Patrol Forces and British M.T.Bs. just off the French coast in the area of Fécamp. During the fight, which the Germans conducted with artillery and automatic weapons fired from close range, the enemy fired about ten torpedoes.[1] One of them hit a German vessel, while several of the enemy boats simultaneously received a number of well-aimed hits on the water-line.

" By an unlucky chance, the ammunition, lying ready for use on one of the German ships which was hit, caught fire, and the subsequent explosions caused such severe damage that the vessel could no longer be kept afloat and had to be abandoned by its crew, who were picked up by the other boats."

[1] Actually six.

CHAPTER XIII

EXTRAVAGANT CLAIMS

DURING the six months ending 30th September, 1943, the Germans claimed to have destroyed 27 M.T.Bs. and 6 M.G.Bs. for certain, and " so badly damaged that their loss can be assumed " a further 14 M.T.Bs. and 2 M.G.Bs. in the waters of the Channel and North Sea. In fact, during that period and in those waters the only losses were M.G.B. 110, which was sunk, as we have seen, when Richards was killed off Dunkirk on 27th May, and the old 70-footer lost by stress of weather on 7th August, in which the enemy could claim no part. So the claim of 33 boats sunk for certain, and 16 more assumed, shows perhaps a trace of optimism.

A careful study of the German broadcasts clearly shows how embarrassing to the enemy had been the activities of our Coastal Forces, and what efforts his propaganda found it necessary to make in order to encourage not only the home front but the crews of his escort and patrol craft. He consistently made wild claims, supported by picturesque details quite unrelated to fact. Perhaps the officers and men of the vessels concerned were encouraged to give full rein to their imagination, but any feelings of respect for the enemy seamen who have shown skill and courage in battle entitle us to hope that the stories originated in the offices of the Propaganda Ministry.

Here, then, for comparison are the British and German accounts of the same action. It was an S.G.B. action, and I wrote this account of it before I had seen the German versions, which follow it.

" It was a night of brilliant phosphorescence and heavy storms, with lightning but no thunder. The four of us had been down to Le Havre and drawn blank, and we swept northward again towards Cap d'Antifer. Just before 2 a.m. we found the enemy and stalked him for about an hour. I wondered if he would sight us in the lightning flashes, but I finally came to the conclusion that, unless someone happened to be looking directly at us at the moment of the flash, he wouldn't.

" There was a very black storm approaching from the nor'-nor'-east, and we decided that there was a good chance of an unobserved attack if we could time it to coincide with the arrival of the storm. Gradually we worked our way round until the black cloud of it was behind us, and then we turned in to close the enemy as the storm broke. The hail pattered down on our tin-helmets and the night was inky black.

" We came down the wind so that it was at our backs; all sight of the enemy ships was blotted out, and it was useless to try to use glasses because of the rain. Peter Mason, the Commanding Officer of the boat (*Grey Fox*), was at the torpedo sight and I stood just behind him. Rather impatiently I kept asking, ' For Heaven's sake, can't you see them yet,' for I knew we must be getting close. Suddenly he saw them and said very calmly, ' Yes, I can see them now—port ten,' in order to bring his sights on. The range was less than 600 yards when he fired both torpedoes. The enemy had been unable to keep a lookout upwind into the driving hail, and he seemed to be taken completely by surprise.

" We disengaged to starboard and fired a spread of starshells. By their light we saw two trawlers quite close together. The First Lieutenant, John Erskine Hill, put the guns on to the second one and opened fire at once. From that time on the illumination was continuous, partly supplied by our second in line and partly by the Germans. Although the rain restricted the area of starshell illumination, the scene directly below the bright white light seemed to be quite as bright as day. The two trawlers were so unready that they did not reply at all and all our guns ripped into the second one, which was about 300 yards away. A small fire appeared to start at once, just forward of the bridge.

" Suddenly I saw a third trawler right ahead, and as we turned to starboard it came down the port side at very close range. Just as John, without a moment's delay, made all his guns change target to this trawler, there was an explosion on the after end of the leading trawler as our torpedo hit. A vivid flame of bright cherry red, with streaks of blue and green in it, shot out of her—not vertically, but sloping to the right, and after it had gone there was a white column of either smoke or spray, which must have been at least 100 feet high. At the same time all guns engaged the third trawler, now no more than 60 yards away. I think that one small machine gun was firing back at us, but that was all, and everything we had was going into her. The gunners couldn't miss. There was a roar of escaping steam, and suddenly a white cloud came out of the ship's stern. Whether this was steam or white smoke, I don't know. At the same time she altered course to port round our stern. Bits were flying off the upper works as every gun hit. At that range and with bright starshell illumination, it was quite impossible to miss.

" As soon as we had passed this third trawler, two more ships began firing at us out of the rain. The fire was not very accurate, although we were hit twice by 20-mm. shells in the port torpedo tube. The torpedo had already gone, and so these two hits did practically no damage, although a splinter scratched the midshipman's ear. We increased speed and disengaged.

" We were 3,000 yards from the cliffs of Etretat, we had achieved complete surprise and fired our torpedoes, we had emptied our Ready Use ammunition lockers into the third trawler, but the Hun was now fully roused. The starshells burst continuously overhead and the shore batteries joined in with a vengeance. I collected the flotilla together, and found that two of them had not fired their torpedoes yet. Richard Hall, in *Grey Owl*, was still away, and from his signals it appeared that he was still manœuvring to make his attack. It seems that he had missed us in the thick of the hailstorm (he had also narrowly missed a collision with his next ahead), but by the light of the starshell he had seen the enemy ships and gone in to attack on his own in spite of the shore batteries. He saw two larger ships, probably " M " Class mine-sweepers close under the cliffs and fired his torpedoes at them, nearly three-quarters of an hour after our attack. That he was able to approach to within 900 yards, under the continuous glare of starshell, can only be attributed to misidentification. In some way the Germans must have thought that he was one of them, returning perhaps from the pursuit of the rest of us. It seems likely that the Hun was either stopped or nearly stopped at the time, and the torpedoes probably missed ahead. At any rate, no result was observed.

" Richard then disengaged, still unshot at except by the shore batteries. He could still see a ship burning to the westward, which was presumably the trawler we had shot up fifty-five minutes before. It was after 4 a.m. by the time he joined up with the rest of us. The wind had freshened to about Force 5 from the north, and the sea was rising. I thought the time and weather were not very promising for another attack, so we set off home. The Germans kept firing their starshells for another half-hour, by which time we were well on our way to Newhaven.

" We all four entered harbour in company at 7.20. The only damage whatever suffered by the whole force was the two 20-mm. holes in the port torpedo tube and the only casualty was Peter Platt, the midshipman, with a scratch on his ear. He was most annoyed when I insisted he should go to the sick bay and have the blood washed off it before he came in to breakfast."

" TWO SUNK, THREE HIT—A TOTAL OF 5 OUT OF 4

" The International Information Bureau learns that two large British E boats were set on fire and sank," said the German communiqué in describing the action next day. " Three other British vessels received hits and had to break off the engagement . . . "

The story was amplified in the German European Service in English: " *Matters of Moment*." 5.30 *p.m.*, 1st October, 1943. *News from the Front*—" Here is a recording we have just received from one of our reporters on the Channel coast :

" *Reporter:* ' On September 28th the German Supreme Command announced the destruction of two English motor gunboats. Just now the patrol boat flotilla arrived at its base on the French coast, and we received first-hand information. The flotilla is one of the most successful ones in the Channel area. So far, one man has received the Knight's Cross of the Iron Cross and ten others the German Cross in gold. These high decorations are only awarded to men who have accomplished something extraordinary.

" ' Well, this night was again a night full of action. The crews had to stay on board, for orders had arrived to leave the port to take up positions. While the formation was on the way, the starlit sky changed very soon into a pitch-dark night. The flotilla leader, a Commander, was on board one of the boats, and this boat was the one which received the wireless message that in square XY enemy ships had been made out. Immediately orders were given to the crews to keep careful look-out in square Y.

" ' For about half an hour nothing happened, but all of a sudden several look-outs reported wakes of torpedoes. What that means only a man who has been on board a torpedoed boat knows. With great skill the torpedoes were out-manœuvred, and a few moments later the shadows of several English motor gunboats appeared out of the rain squall. The concentrated fire of the German patrol boats, steaming in line ahead, covered the enemy boats, but they had made up their minds to fight this time, and for a few minutes it was just a free-for-all affair. One of the motor gunboats stopped, developed smoke and fire, and sank very close to the German boats. Another enemy boat wanted to make an especially dashing attack. It tried to break through the German line-up. A leading seaman, the gun captain of the fo'c'sle gun, on one of the German boats had noticed this. With his automatic gun he commenced to rip the enemy boat apart, even though a shell splinter had caused a wound on his forehead. Blood was trickling into his eyes, but all he did was to wipe his eyes a few times with his elbow, and fire till the enemy boats disappeared, leaving nothing but a cloud of smoke behind. This was too much of a dose for the remaining English seamen. They turned their boats and disappeared into the dark of the night.

" ' The patrol boat had also suffered casualties. A 4-cm. shell had entered the chart-room. A leading seaman in the room, as well as the helmsman, was badly wounded. The mate, who saw the helmsman sink down on the wheel, jumped over and kept the boat on the right course. Again, German seamen and German weapons proved to be unequalled in skill and quality.' "

A further account of the same action appeared in the German Home Service. 2.30 *p.m.*, 2nd
    October, 1943.

" The German Navy does not limit itself to defending the immediate vicinity of the coast; on the contrary, light German naval forces carry out daily thrusts into the Channel to attack the enemy wherever possible. The little ships of the German Navy remain victorious in numerous encounters with enemy naval forces and bombers. Only a few nights ago a naval action took place at night in the Channel, and was mentioned by the High Command.[1] The

---

[1] This was an unhappy choice in view of the opening sentence of this broadcast, as the action took place within 3,000 yards of the cliffs of Normandy.

fighting is usually severe, and demands real men and cold blood. This being in constant contact with the enemy, the necessity for bitter fighting which often leaves no alternative than either to destroy the enemy or perish oneself, has marked them. They are not easy to bring to the microphone, because they claim that they were doing nothing special, and in their modesty they believe that the other fellow has done more. This is also the case with the Commander of one of the patrol boats which played a major part in the sinking of the two M.T.Bs. reported in the High Command communiqué of 28th September.

"I am now in the Commander's cabin, and he sits opposite me with members of his crew. The Lieutenant tells his story:

"*Lieutenant :* ' It was one of those encounters we have fought out so often, except that it was the most recent one, and, therefore, we all remember it well. It was typical Channel weather, a light sea and squalls of rain. Suddenly we saw torpedoes racing towards us out of the darkness of a thunder cloud, but we were able to turn away. In the glare of our star-shells I saw an English " Gun Speed Boat " (in English) quite close, about 50 m. to port. I immediately gave orders to open fire, but the British opened up at the same moment. I received a direct hit in the wheelhouse and was thrown down. As both my legs were stiff I thought at first that my spine had been injured. I dragged myself up by the compass, and was surprised to find that my boat was still manœuvrable. The man at the wheel had been mortally wounded and was groaning heavily. His place was taken by the quartermaster. I was especially pleased with the performance of the gun served by Ordinary Seaman 1st Class Börzer, who calmly poured one round after the other into the English boat.[1] He had better continue the story ':

"*Börzer:* ' There is really not very much to tell. I saw an M.T.B. quite close to us to port, trying to turn, and opened fire. There was a short but severe exchange of fire, in the course of which we received several hits as well, and several guns became total losses. After that the M.T.B. directed the fire of its front gun at me, and I aimed at it in return, silencing it. After that the M.T.B. just lay there, its engines stopped, and it became an easier target. I then directed my fire at the bridge and at the stern gun, and suddenly, after several hits which I had been able to score, there was much smoke and then an explosion, and the boat was no longer to be seen.'

"*Lieutenant:* ' We too, however, had received several more hits on the water-line and the Mechanician 2nd Class had better continue the story to tell us what happened below.'

"*Mechanician:* ' When the noise started I was just working on the engine. We received several hits in the stoke-room as well as on the hull. These leaks were immediately stopped. The artificial-fog boxes (Nebelkannen) had been hit and when we started manœuvring the fog got into the engine-room through the ventilators. It was very difficult to continue working in the biting smoke, but when the Commander asked whether we were all right, we had put everything in order and were able to continue on our way.' "

M.T.B.s. of the Royal Netherlands Navy

On the same night another and even more successful action took place farther up the Channel, just south of Boulogne. It was fought by Dutch M.T.Bs. supported by British M.G.Bs., and it resulted in the sinking of a large laden merchant ship with a particularly strong escort. It was all the more remarkable, therefore, that it should have been achieved without a single casualty on our side.

The whole force was under the command of Lt. E. H. Larive, Royal Netherlands Navy,

[1] This may be literally correct as, in fact, two rounds hit *Grey Fox.*

the Senior Officer of the Dutch M.T.B. flotilla at Dover (who reached this country after his fifth escape from the Germans), but the successful torpedo was fired by Lt. H. G. Jörissen, R.Neth.N.

When Lt. Jörissen first reached England some months previously, he was sent for a short time to H.M.S. *Bee* for training, and he came out with me, for experience, on a day torpedo-firing practice in my boat. The torpedo missed ahead of the target ship and I turned to Jörissen, to whom, as I thought, I was demonstrating the first principles of torpedo firing, and said, "I always have a tendency to miss ahead. I think I shall aim at the target's stern in future."

"I have always found that, too," said Jörissen. "The last time I made a torpedo attack I aimed at the stern of a Japanese cruiser and hit it amidships." He had, I discovered, lately returned from Java. His deadly aim with torpedoes was fully maintained in the Channel: on this occasion the target was hit just abaft the funnel and sank almost at once. This success was only one of many which built up a great reputation for the M.T.Bs. of the Royal Netherlands Navy.

"A BIT OF 'GUMSHOE WORK'"

Donald Gould Bradford, who, as a Lieutenant R.N.R. in a "C" Class M.G.B., had destroyed an E boat by ramming in March, 1943, was now, as a Lieutenant Commander, leading a flotilla of "D" boats. This was a powerful fighting force well suited to his temperament, for it seemed that fighting was in his blood. He had served as an adjutant in the Bolivian army during the Gran Chaco war, and as an ensign in a cavalry regiment of the International Brigade in Spain, and in both he had been wounded. Before coming to Coastal Forces he had escaped from a prison camp in Vichy French West Africa. There were great opportunities in the North Sea for such a fighter—opportunities he was not slow to take.

On the night of 19th September he was lucky enough to come upon the 17,000-ton liner *Strasbourg*, which had run aground just off the entrance to Ijmuiden harbour. The Germans had made some attempt to protect this vessel by describing her as a hospital ship, but the Allies had refused to accept this device, and so she remained a legitimate target for our M.T.Bs. Bradford describes how the combined force of four M.T.Bs. and two M.G.Bs. slipped and set off from Yarmouth in the early afternoon in flat-calm weather.

"At Brown Ridge[1] we found that we were ahead of time, so we stopped and tied alongside each other—six boats, beam to beam. We had an hour to waste and spent the time drinking tea and coffee and yarning on the bridges, speculating on what we might find when we did arrive on the enemy coast.

"We started sweeping up the coast from the Hook of Holland towards Ijmuiden just after dark. There was a bit of moon occasionally peeping from behind the clouds and quite a little phosphorescence in the water, making it imperative to keep our speed low so as to avoid being seen from the shore.

"At 11 p.m., as we were approaching Ijmuiden, we came upon a very large ship apparently lying stopped off the harbour entrance with an outer and inner screen of escorts disposed to seawards. I couldn't believe it at first, it seemed altogether too big. I held on, on a northerly course, until we were able to see that the vessel was a very large passenger liner. The larger escorts—'M' Class—were to the north of the target and two trawlers were lying roughly a mile to the westwards. There were also four E/R boats lying close to the liner. It seemed a case calling for a bit of 'gumshoe work,' so I determined to try to creep in from the south, closer to the shore, and turning, reduced speed to 8 knots to stalk round.

[1] The bank of shallows about midway between East Anglia and Holland.

" As we approached for the attack, the E/R boats for some unknown reason moved out to the westward, leaving us a clear range. The trawlers were now the only remaining danger to a successful sortie, so the gunboats were detached and placed so as to screen us from any interference from that quarter. The whole unit closed the target in this disposition, and I was so fascinated by the sight of the terrific mountain of a ship, that almost before I realised it, we were 300 yards away and, by a real stroke of bad luck, right on top of a sandbank that reduced the depth of water below that which was safe for the discharge of the particular type of torpedo we were carrying at the time. I therefore had to turn the whole force round and creep out again, with a beautiful crop of goose pimples up my spine and suffering absolute agonies of apprehension in case we had been detected and I had lost the chance of an attack. However, at 1,500 yards we turned again and came in to the kill from a slightly different position in order to avoid the bank. At 1,000 yards I fired two torpedoes, and feeling confident of them hitting, turned the whole unit towards the trawlers, re-forming them into single line ahead and preparing for a gun battle. As the boats re-formed we heard two loud explosions and saw the torpedo target completely obscured by water, spray and smoke—the two ' fish ' had hit and we had chalked up the biggest target ever seen off the Dutch coast.

" By this time we were getting close to the two trawlers, who were apparently quite unconcerned. However, when we were about 500 yards away the leading trawler challenged us with a lamp and we opened the ' party ' immediately. The combined fire from the six boats was terrific, and the leading trawler gave up the ghost right from the start—he was just smothered. It must have been absolute hell on board: the shooting was beautiful to watch, real King's Cup marksmanship."

Lt. D. G. Dowling, R.N.V.R., who, as Divisional leader, was in charge of the M.G.Bs., describes his feelings when, as he says, our force " let these two unfortunate blighters have the works. I was, as usual, all tensed up for the return fire, but suddenly I realised that for once we had caught them on the wrong foot, and they would not be despatching much from their end. The feeling of relief was terrific and it was one of those moments when life seems a bed of roses."

Bradford had approached most skilfully, so that the leading trawler blanketed the other's fire. " We had the time of our lives," he says, " using this ' Northern ' Class trawler for target practice. We were using 2-pounder pom-pom starshell for the first time that night, and it acted as the perfect incendiary. Within one minute the target was ablaze from stem to stern, listing to port and settling rapidly by the stern. By this time the range was about 200 yards, and as I watched I saw a 6-pounder shell hit the trawler right behind the bridge and the funnel sailed up into the air and disappeared over the side. She was sinking before our eyes, belching steam, fire and smoke like a stricken dragon.

" I then checked fire and shifted the guns on to the other trawler whose range was now clear, and we proceeded to administer the medicine as before. She was a little tougher, biting as well as growling, and one or two of the boats got hit once or twice. While this was going on two R boats came tearing out of harbour and closed us from astern, evidently out for trouble—they got it. The last two boats in the line shifted target and gave them a few well-placed squirts which registered and caused them to return whence they came at a much reduced speed, remarkably like a couple of chastened puppies.

" By this time the ' M ' Class to the north had come to the conclusion that everything in the area wasn't satisfactory, and down they came, four in number, at a rate of knots, firing everything that their gunnery people had given them. Bob Harrop[1] in one of the boats got a nice-sized shell through his tank space, causing a fire, but he maintained his station and place

[1] Lt. W. Harrop, R.N.V.R.

Able Seaman J. WITH and Signalman R. A. CLEGG, members of the ship's company of S.G.B. *Grey Shark* after the action described on page 145

Sub-Lt. B. H. GERRARD, R.N.V.R., First Lieutenant and Navigator of an M.T.B., working at the chart table

THE AUTHOR ON THE BRIDGE OF S.G.B. *GREY GOOSE*

LT. CDR. E. H. LARIVE, D.S.C., R.NETH.N.

THE CREW OF THE DUTCH M.T.B. 240. The Commanding Officer was Lt. F. Visee, R.Neth.N. *(centre at back)*, known in Coastal Forces as " Happy "

H.R.H. PRINCE BERNHARD OF THE NETHERLANDS, WITH LT. CDR. E. H. LARIVE, D.S.C., R.NETH.N., ON THE BRIDGE OF A DUTCH M.T.B.

GERMAN E BOATS

M.Ls. 150 and 145 after the engagement described on opposite page, in which they rammed and sank the E boat S.96. M.L. 145 on the extreme right is very much down by the bows

COMMANDING OFFICERS OF LT. CDR. BRADFORD'S FLOTILLA AFTER THE ATTACK ON THE LINER *STRASBOURG*

(see page 163)

Left to right : Lt. W. Harrop, R.N.V.R., Lt. C. S. Claydon, R.N.V.R., Lt. P. C. Wilkinson, R.N.V.R., Lt. Cdr. D. G. Bradford, D.S.C., R.N.R., Lt. D. G. Dowling, R.N.V.R., Lt. J. A. N. Whitby, R.N.V.R.

ABLE SEAMAN LAMONT—AT 60 THE OLDEST RATING IN
COASTAL FORCES

LT. E. D. W. LEAF, D.S.C. AND BAR, R.N.V.R.

Remains of a German destroyer ashore on the Brittany coast after the anti-salvage operations of Lt. Cdr. CARTWRIGHT's flotilla (see page 182)

" A " Class M.Ls. loaded with mines in Dover Harbour. The outside boat has ground mines and the inside one moored mines

Lt. R. T. Sykes, R.N.V.R. (*centre*), on the bridge of his M.G.B. with his First Lieut., Sub-Lt. R. J. W. Timms, R.N.V.R. (*right*), and Lt. P. G. Lee, D.S.C., R.N.V.R. (see page 193)

The bows of the " D " boats of Lt. Cdr. Bradford's 55th M.T.B. flotilla were painted with sharks' teeth and a red "mouth," which, if it did not spread terror amongst the enemy, acted as a useful identification mark for the flotilla

Lt. Paul Berthon, D.S.C., R.N.V.R. (*left*), and Lt. (now Lt. Cdr.) C. A. Law, D.S.C., R.C.N.V.R., who led the Canadian Flotilla with such outstanding success during the invasion of Normandy

THE MULBERRY AT ARROMANCHES

The Coastal Forces anchorage was at the extreme right of the picture, where two M.T.Bs. can be seen

HASLAR CREEK IN PORTSMOUTH DOCKYARD, JUNE 1944

" D " Class M.T.Bs. berthed at *Dolphin*, a " C " Class M.G.B. proceeding towards *Hornet* and a trot of H.D.M.Ls. at extreme left

H.M.S. *HORNET*—THE ASSEMBLY FOR THE INVASION OF NORMANDY

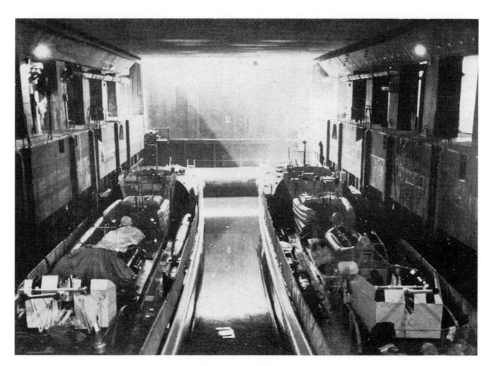

E BOATS IN THEIR PENS

TEN FEET OF REINFORCED CONCRETE OVER THE E BOAT PENS AT LE
HAVRE, PIERCED BY BRITISH BOMBS

H.M. THE KING VISITS THE INVASION BEACHES SOON AFTER D DAY
The Royal Standard at the masthead of a " B " Class M.L.

GERMAN E BOAT

CAPTURED GERMAN EXPLOSIVE MOTOR BOATS
Note the hoop mounted on springs which actuates the explosive mechanism when the boat hits
the target. This secret weapon was a complete failure

LT. P. G. LEE, D.S.C. AND TWO BARS, R.N.V.R.

Lt. Cdr. J. H. Coste, D.S.C., R.N.V.R. (*left*), and Lt. Cdr. A. R. H. Nye, D.S.C., R.N.V.R.—both Commanding Officers of " C " Class M.G.Bs. who became Senior Officers of flotillas—the former of a " C " Class flotilla, the latter of a flotilla of M.T.Bs. designed and built by Messrs. Nicholson of Gosport

Lt. J. F. Humphreys, D.S.C., R.N.V.R., who led a unit of two M.T.Bs. supported by the frigate H.M.S. *Stayner*, which destroyed an entire unit of three E boats (see page 215)

Lt. G. J. MacDonald, D.S.O., D.S.C., R.N.Z.N.V.R., Senior Officer of the 21st M.T.B. Flotilla

in the battle. His Motor Mechanic attempted to put out the fire, and indeed succeeded, being held over the side by his heels while he stuffed rags into the hole to keep out the air. Just as he finished he was struck by an Oerlikon shell and killed.

" The fire from the ' M ' Class was both heavy and accurate, so we turned away and made smoke, leaving the remaining trawler in a very sad and sorry plight, on fire and listing, and quite definitely upset at our ungentlemanly treatment."

Dowling described as " very pretty work " the way the Senior Officer was manœuvring the force under fire. " I remember, even at the time," he says, " thinking that it was pretty to watch the six boats all performing ' blue turns,' and making smoke to order—doing the job as if it was a night station-keeping exercise off our own coast."

Bradford concludes the story: " We played around in the smoke for a few minutes and then tried to cut back to make sure that the last trawler was sunk, but we noticed four more ' M ' Class leaving harbour and steering west to try to cut us off. I decided that eight ' M ' Class escort ships were just too much of a good thing, so we too turned west and hared out of it, stopping 6 miles out to count our holes and check on the casualties. These totalled two killed and two wounded: and they had to be set against 17,000 tons of liner torpedoed, one Northern Class trawler probably sunk, one trawler possibly sunk and two R boats damaged."

Since she was already aground, the *Strasbourg* could not actually be sunk beneath the waves, but the damage was such that she became a total loss and remained as a wreck upon the sand.

" BUYING A PACKET "

Bradford did not always have such good fortune. Less than two months later he was involved in a fierce affray which entailed the loss of one of the " D " boats. Dowling was the Commanding Officer of this boat, and the following is his description of the misadventures which attended her destruction:

" I suppose most of us have, from time to time, wondered what it would feel like to ' buy a packet,' and when I ' bought it ' on the night of the 3rd/4th November, 1943, it came right up to expectations. Being just out of dock after a refit, we were not down for operations that night. A show was laid on and one of the boats detailed from the 55th M.T.B. Flotilla fell over at the last minute; ' Operations ' wanted a boat from the 50th Flotilla to make the number complete. I detailed another boat, but, on the spur of the moment, changed my mind and said I would go myself. I liked working with Don Bradford, who was leading the party. As it turned out, this change of mind was ' Bad Joss,' as I had all my gear on board after leave and I had intended to sort it out that night and put some of it ashore.

" The job was a small Commando landing on the other side, with a proviso that, if any trouble occurred on the way over, the landing was to be abandoned and an offensive sweep made instead. Trouble did occur, for we ran into E boats on the way over, knocking them about a bit before they got away; but the secrecy was gone, and Bradford decided to send the Commandos back in his own ship, while he himself transferred to me. I had been leading the second division, whose job it was to guard the landing on one side, and Lt. J. R. H. Kirkpatrick, R.C.N.V.R., with the first division, was to have guarded it on the other.

" We re-formed into two divisions with Bradford in my boat leading, and set course for the Hook, intending to sweep north and see what we could find. We were ' stooging ' in quietly when we sighted some ships almost ahead, at rather too close a range for an immediate torpedo attack as we did not yet know their course and speed. Bradford quickly decided to wade straight in and wipe off the leading escorts with gunfire. I saw two trawlers off my port bow and opened fire on one, fairly knocking her for six, as she did not fire back. Then I saw what looked like a medium-sized merchant ship, and shifted fire to her, hitting her pretty hard, as the shells were bursting all along her side. At about that time I felt very happy, thinking we were getting on top and that the enemy were in for a thin time. The thought was premature. An outer screen of escorts came in to play ball with us, and I suddenly found myself on the deck with hell going on all round. We had been hit by a fair-sized shell on the bridge, which came in behind me, killing my signalman, wounding Bradford and myself, wrecking the bridge controls and communications, and generally putting the bridge out of action. Two more shells had hit either end of the engine-room, knocking out both port engines, and so damaging the two starboard engines that they would only run for a few more minutes without major repairs. The Chief Motor Mechanic and a stoker were killed, the engine-room and the after petrol compartment were on fire, the steering compartment had also been hit and the rudders were jammed hard aport. Several more of the crew on deck had been wounded, and the ship was slowly circling towards the enemy in a very shaky condition.

" Life from then on was sheer hell, and as I picked myself up from the deck and grabbed the telegraphs to try to steer the ship with the engines, not realising for a moment the state of things in the engine-room, I thought, ' This can't be happening to me, it must be a particularly nasty dream.' However, it was soon painfully obvious that it was not a dream, as I saw a large trawler bearing down on us, looking as if she was going to ram us fair and square. Luckily she had been hit very hard in the opening round, and she too was in a shaky state. Listing to port, she passed slowly astern of us without firing a shot. My Oerlikon gunner got his guns into hand operation and ' filled her in ' as she passed, which cheered us up a bit, but after that happy moment we had no occasion to feel cheerful for quite a time, as we performed two complete circles in the middle of the opposition, getting all they could give us the while. I managed to stop the engines by sending the First Lieutenant to the engine-room when we were on the outer circle, and all hands worked like blazes to rig hand steering and sort things out. After a pause we got under way again with the two remaining engines which would only run for a few minutes each before having to be stopped to go off the boil. The only way out was through the enemy, so we had to face it. I was steering aft with the Cox'n, and Ivan Kinross,[1] the Navigator, was assisting nearby with the bridge compass which he had wrenched off the bridge. Tubby Hewitt,[2] my First Lieutenant, was fighting fires and generally looking after the engine-room; Don Bradford on the bridge was shouting directions to avoid the enemy, meanwhile dodging armour-piercing shells which were coming through the bridge screen, and Freddie Dunlop,[3] who had come with us for the trip, was doing monumental work in the wireless cabin, getting in R/T touch with Kirkpatrick and the rest of the party to get them to take us in tow.

" We broke through the enemy line but were still only a few hundred yards from the Hun when the fires in the engine-room got out of hand, and we had to evacuate it and pull the methyl-bromide extinguisher plugs to save the ship from blowing up. This, together with the damage to the engines, soon stopped them and we lay stationary, waiting for the *coup de grâce*. Most of us really felt then that we'd had it. However, Freddie Dunlop had been in contact with Kirkpatrick, who was searching for us, and after a while we saw some shapes ahead of us crossing our bows. We hoped like hell it was our chaps, and Bradford and I fell over each other on the bridge to try to find a lamp or a torch, as all the lights in the ship had gone and the bridge was in such a mess we could not find a thing. Just when we thought they would go by without seeing us, Bradford found a torch in his pocket and

[1] Sub-Lt. I. Kinross, R.N.V.R.
[2] Sub-Lt. F. L. Hewitt, R.N.V.R.
[3] Lt. Cdr. F. H. Dunlop, R.N., Signals Officer to Captain, Coastal Forces, Nore.

signalled to the leader. He turned towards us in a suspicious manner, then recognised us and came up to take us in tow. He ordered the others to make smoke and generally screen us, as the enemy were re-forming to come back, and the firing, after a brief lull, had started up again. We began to get hit once more, and while trying to pass the tow we had to duck pretty often.

"I dived for shelter during one nasty burst, when I was feeling very naked on the bows, and a shell hit the base of the forward gun, blasting me right over the dinghy which was on deck and down to the side of the bridge. This sort of thing did not help to get things going smoothly, but in the end 'Kirk' got us in tow and started off. Unluckily our bows had been hit, and the tow pulled away. 'Kirk' came round again and Bradford decided that we should have to 'abandon ship,' as one big shell had just hit the base of the bridge, loosening all the armour plate, and she was getting low in the water forward. The fires were starting up again in the engine-room and aft, and the escorts were closing in for the 'kill.' 'Kirk' came alongside, we evacuated the wounded, grabbed the books, ditched all the necessary stuff and hauled down the ensign. The other officers and myself quickly searched the ship to see that all hands were away, set the scuttling charges and pushed off. It is a nasty moment when you realise that you will have to blow up your own ship—rather like having to destroy a favourite dog, only worse. I think I can understand why many captains have, in the past, elected to go down with their ships.

"Odd little details of that night have stuck particularly in my memory. For example, when we were pulling away from the ship and standing on 'Kirk's' bridge looking back, a rating came along with a jar of water. That drink was the finest I have ever had. I suppose we had all been working pretty feverishly for the last half-hour or more; I know I myself felt physically exhausted, and that water was like nectar. Another was, when we were in the wardroom on the way back; Kirkpatrick had a moment to leave the bridge and he came down to see us. During the taking in tow, I had cursed 'Kirk' lustily for not being quicker, which considering we were under fire was very unreasonable. I had also cursed his First Lieutenant, Alan Yates,[1] for chucking over a smoke-float which flamed for a while and drew the enemy fire as if by a magnet, though it did good work later, when it started smoking. When Kirkpatrick came down, he put his head inside the door and said, in a very mild manner, 'I suppose you are very angry with me.' Considering he had just saved our lives, this so flabbergasted me that all I could manage was a weak, 'Of course not, old chap! Whatever for?'"

AN E BOAT SORTIE

The operations of the E boats were by this time much reduced both in quantity and achievement, but the German High Command, still well aware of the importance of holding down our defensive forces, were turning their attention to the tactics of mass attack.

[1] Sub-Lt. A. Yates, R.N.V.R.

On the evening of 24th September, 1943, six E boats of the 4th Flotilla, under the command of Korvettenkapitän Werner Lützow, set out from Rotterdam on a minelaying and torpedo sortie against the British east-coast convoy route. Outside the harbour two further flotillas joined company, and the combined force proceeded westward.[1]

At about the same time a number of Coastal Force craft, as well as destroyers and trawlers, were taking up their anti E boat dispositions on the Z lines—the standing patrol positions which protected our shipping lane. Amongst them were two "B" Class M.Ls.—150 commanded by Lt. J. O. Thomas, R.N.V.R., and 145 commanded by Lt. R. F. Seddon, R.N.V.R. For nearly two years these M.Ls. had been carrying out monotonous anti E boat patrols, and had listened with envy to the tales of their more fortunate comrades in the gunboats and torpedo boats, who appeared to be having all the fun. "All we seemed to get was lots of sea time and more than our share of bad weather." But to-night their triumph was at hand. Their luck was about to turn. Even to-night, however, the wind was beginning to freshen, with promise of dirty weather before dawn.

The freshening wind was a source of anxiety to the E boats, too, as they approached our coast. At one time it seemed likely that they would have to abandon the operation, but they decided to carry on, and finally divided up into groups in order to lay their mines.

At about 1 a.m. one group, consisting of three E boats, came suddenly upon a patrol of two trawlers. Their presence was almost immediately detected by the trawlers, one of which, as she turned towards, saw a torpedo passing down her port side, no more than 6 feet clear. Another torpedo was on its way, however, and this time the aim was true. H.M. Trawler *Franc Tireur* was hit amidships and sank within a few seconds. The first torpedo had been fired by the E boat *S.88*, in which the Senior Officer, Korvettenkapitän (Lieutenant Commander) Lützow was himself embarked. The second and successful attack had been made by *S.96* commanded by Leutnant-zur-see Wilhelm Sander. Sander was new to E boats, but he had with him a more experienced officer, Oberleutnant Wilhelm Ritter Von Georg, the Commanding Officer of an E boat that was refitting at the time. *S.99*, the third boat of the group, did not get into position in time, and did not fire torpedoes at all.

When the E boats had disengaged they stopped to discuss the battle.

"Who hit the trawler?" shouted Lützow.

"It was us, sir," replied von Georg.

"Nice work—congratulations! We'll keep together now."

The three boats formed up in line ahead and retired to the eastward at 30 knots.

At the same time M.Ls. 150 and 145 were steering south from their patrol line at full speed to cut off the enemy's retreat. It was a very dark night, but at 1.20 a.m. the M.Ls. sighted phosphorescent bow waves 500 yards away on the starboard bow. Thomas knew at once what he was going to do. His maximum speed was so low that the E boats would outrange his guns in a few seconds. They might be damaged during that time, but they were not likely to be destroyed. The only way to *sink* an E boat was to ram it, so Thomas held his course for *S.96*, the second E boat in the line. He writes:

"My immediate reaction—and there was only time for reaction, not for reasoned thinking —was 'This is the moment I've been waiting for for a very long time.' We'd been putting in a lot of hard training, and my actions from then on were almost instinctive. Something like 'This is it' flashed through my mind, and I just made straight for him. We hit him with a terrific crash just for'ard of his bridge, and there was an awful rending crunch. It threw my crew flat on the deck, and bits of wood and metal flew round our heads on the bridge.

[1] The movements of the enemy described in this chapter are reconstructed from statements made by German prisoners of war.

The E boat bounced clear with a lot of smoke coming from it, and my port gunner got in a crack at him. He vanished in a cloud of smoke, and I stopped my engines because my bows by then were not all that they should have been."

When two fast boats are approaching each other at right angles, split seconds make the difference between ramming and being rammed. Thomas had judged it well but, in spite of that, at this stage the M.L. had received greater damage than the E boat. Her bows had been carried away to the forward side of the wheelhouse, and she was in some danger of sinking. But the E boat's speed had been reduced. As it rebounded clear of the M.L. and went off slowly into the darkness, S.99 overtook it and dashed on after the leader, being subjected to a flood of abuse from everyone on S.96's upper deck for leaving them in the lurch.

Meanwhile M.L. 145 had plunged into the engagement, firing with all guns that would bear. The sea was too rough for accurate gunnery, however, and Seddon had also decided that the only way to make certain of the E boat's destruction was to ram it. "When I saw him breaking away from Jimmy Thomas's possessive embrace, I thought I might be able to ram him again before he knew what it was all about." At the first attempt, Seddon missed narrowly, but, firing all the while, he gained bearing for a second attempt. The E boat was returning the fire fiercely, but she was too badly damaged to escape. It was some twelve minutes after the initial contact that M.L. 145 turned in again to ram. The enemy seemed to anticipate the manœuvre and also altered course—towards the M.L. The two boats met almost head on with terrific impact at a relative speed of approach of more than 25 knots.

"We seemed to climb on top of him," writes Seddon, "then heeled over to port as we slid off again and scraped right down his starboard side. Our speed was too great for the boarding party to get away, but all the guns opened fire at a range of approximately 1 yard. As we rubbed alongside we could see several fires, but little sign of activity on his upper deck." The M.L. was badly holed forward and making water rapidly in the forepeak and mess-deck, but the watertight door and the bulkhead were holding, and she was still manœuvrable with difficulty.

"At 0140," continues Seddon in his report, "the enemy was stopped about half a mile away and burning fiercely. I tried to close him, steering by engines, but the wind and the heavy sea made this extremely difficult, and I had to approach stern first."

S.96 had been trying feverishly to make radio contact with her S.O., to inform him that the two British boats were damaged and to summon aid, but it was of no avail. Korvettenkapitän Lützow had turned back to the rescue, but it appears that his look-out reported the presence of *four* British boats and against such odds the attempt was abandoned.

Oberleutnant von Georg finally seized one of the machine guns on the bridge and fired a burst of tracer vertically into the air as a last effort to obtain assistance. Seddon, wrongly interpreting this distress signal as an indication of surrender, sounded the cease fire and began to close in, but von Georg, who by now had taken command of the situation, was still determined to fight, and a burst of fire greeted the M.L. as she closed. "Not quite cricket," was how one of Seddon's crew described it afterwards, though, in fairness, it must be said that there was no reason whatever for supposing that a burst of vertical tracer was the equivalent of a white flag. Von Georg called for hand grenades and was bitterly disappointed when they could not be found. In his own boat he would have known where to look for them, but in S.96 everything was stowed differently. The E boat was heavily on fire aft, and for a short period complete confusion reigned. Von Georg left the bridge and tried to bring one of the forward guns into action, but they were all jammed and by this time most of the crew were casualties. Turning to Sander, he shouted, "We must scuttle."

The order was given to abandon ship, and the scuttling charges were fired in the engine-room. Then the crew jumped overboard and were kept as far as possible in one group by von Georg. " Shortly afterwards," says Seddon, " there were some minor explosions and the E boat disappeared amid a shower of sparks."

Meanwhile M.L. 150 was in a bad way, and indeed Thomas's chief concern was the safety of his ship in the rising sea. A quarter of the ship had gone altogether, but the bulkhead was shored up and the pumps were controlling the water in the galley flat. The rudders had jammed hard a-starboard, so that under way the ship could only make circles. Finally, however, Thomas found he could steer west by engines alone, stern first at about 3 knots. " By then," he continues, " we could hear the E boat survivors shouting in the water. It took us at least an hour to pick them up, because of the sea that was running. I was able to manœuvre close to a raft, and then to drift down on to it. There were three ratings on the raft, one of whom was laid out, having swallowed a lot of oil. When the raft was fairly near me the two Germans who were up and doing jumped into the water and swam towards us, leaving the third man to his fate: but the yells of my infuriated crew sent them back for him, and eventually the three were hauled inboard. I could not leave the bridge, but ordered an armed guard to take them down into the wardroom for medical attention. A few hours later, when I was able to visit them, I found the Germans turned in, in my blankets, with the armed guard playing them my records on my gramophone.

" M.L. 145 rescued thirteen Germans, including two officers. One of these attracted attention to himself in the water by blowing steadily on a referee's whistle. When the search-light beam found him he was seen still to be wearing his cap at a very rakish angle, and it appears that he kept it so until he was landed at our base.

Soon after 6 a.m. two M.G.Bs. arrived on the scene. M.L. 145 proceeded homeward under her own power, but M.L. 150 was taken in tow stern first and finally reached harbour at 2 p.m. On the way, Thomas describes " a very tricky piece of seamanship carried out by the gunboat that was towing us. We had had to extinguish the galley stove because of the petrol which had leaked into the bilges. In that sea it was impossible for him to come along-side, and we were all badly in need of a hot drink. So tea, gallons of it, was floated down to us in ' safari jars ' lashed to a small Carley float. The float was secured to a grass line and by slight alterations of course they were able to manœuvre it alongside us so that we could haul it inboard with boat hooks. Never has tea tasted better."

POSTSCRIPT

German Telegraph Service (DNB European), 11.30 a.m., *26th September*, 1943. *Berlin (International Information Bureau. Midday)*: " Yesterday morning German E boats attacked British patrol vessels with torpedoes off the English coast and sank one of the British vessels. Visibility deteriorated. British M.T.Bs. came to the aid of the hard-pressed British patrol vessels, but were unable to make a successful attack. There was a heavy fog, and a German E boat tore off the bows of a British M.T.B. near the bridge so that the vessel sank at once. The German E boat also sustained considerable damage, so that her crew was no longer able to keep her afloat and scuttled her."

ANOTHER MASS ATTACK

It was exactly one month before the E boats ventured forth again. On the evening of 24th October, 1943, they came over in strength to make a concerted attack on a northbound convoy near Smith's Knoll off the Norfolk coast. The night was calm and, to begin with, moonless; for E boat activity conditions were perfect. It seems likely that more than thirty E boats took part, and the expedition led to a complicated series of actions spread over many hours and a large area of the North Sea. No less than sixteen separate encounters took place during the night between the German boats and our patrols of destroyers and Coastal Force craft.

Eight boats of the 4th E boat Flotilla were taking part in this mass attack. They had left Ijmuiden at about 8 p.m., with their Senior Officer, Korvettenkapitän Lützow, embarked, as on the previous sortie, in S.88, commanded by a Chief Petty Officer, Obersteuermann Heinrich Rehbiger.

The flotilla had proceeded in line ahead until about midnight, when it was some twelve miles off the convoy route. Here it split up into two divisions with four boats in each. Kapitänleutnant Albert Causemann, an officer of fairly wide E boat experience with several successful operations to his credit, led the second division in S.120 and proceeded to the westward, while Lützow turned south-west with the first four boats—S.88, S.63, S.110 and S.117.

Half an hour later Causemann's party was in action with the destroyer H.M.S. *Worcester* (Lt. J. A. H. Hamer, R.N.). "The E boats returned a heavy fire," reports Hamer, "with light weapons, apparently at the Commanding Officer's white cap, which he forthwith exchanged for a steel helmet. No hits were scored on *Worcester*, but several Oerlikon shells were seen to hit the second E boat in the line . . ."

This battle had been sighted by Lützow as he crept in towards the convoy route. A quarter of an hour later his own unit was in contact with "the Tommies." He sighted a bow wave directly ahead, coming straight towards him, and he realised at once that it was a destroyer. The E boats turned and ran for it, making smoke and dropping delayed-action depth charges as they went. H.M.S. *Mackay* (Lt. Cdr. J. H. Eaden, D.S.C., R.N.) engaged them and encountered a "heavy but very wild return fire." During the ensuing chase S.63 was hit in her engine-room, so that her speed was reduced to 20 knots. S.88's port torpedo was fired accidentally and ran harmlessly away. There was no time to reload the tube. As the E boats retired at the speed dictated by the crippled S.63, they did not know that Unit Y had been "fleeted" into the path of their withdrawal. Two "D" Class M.G.Bs. under the command of Lt. R. M. Marshall, R.N.V.R., made up Unit Y, and they were watching the approaching battle with interest and anticipation. Soon after two o'clock the E boats outstripped the *Mackay*; a few minutes later the M.G.Bs. fired starshell to illuminate them, and action was joined at once.

What followed is confused, for the enemy, who was taken by surprise, immediately made smoke. Korvettenkapitän Lützow, however, did not intend to leave the damaged S.63 to her fate. He attempted to hold off the British boats while she made good her escape, but in doing so S.88 took terrible punishment from the concentrated fire of both M.G.Bs. One engine was damaged and a stoker killed. The telegraph of another engine broke down and the compressed-air bottles were hit, making it impossible to restart the damaged engine. Almost simultaneously a direct hit on the bridge killed Korvettenkapitän Lützow himself, as well as the Commanding Officer of the boat and the boatswain's mate. Then a raft just abaft the bridge was set slight and the fire spread rapidly for'ard.

Marshall swept round ahead of S.88, looking for more E boats, and almost at once he found one appearing out of the smoke of the battle, close on his port bow. This E boat altered to starboard towards the M.G.B., perhaps to break through the line or perhaps to ram, though her chances of survival after ramming, so far from her home base, would not have been very great. Marshall anticipated the move and altered sharply in to port. In waters comparatively near our coast, the advantage in a ramming match was clearly his. As the two boats approached each other the E boat's guns scored a devastating burst on the M.G.B. a few moments before Marshall rammed her amidships "at practically full speed."

The two boats bounced clear of each other and the M.G.B. stopped to survey the situation. Her casualties were heavy. Five of the crew had been killed and six more were wounded, most of the guns were out of action, but the damage to the hull was not so serious as Marshall had expected.

Lt. F. R. Lightoller, R.N.V.R.,[1] commanding the second M.G.B., had been engaging a third E boat and had momentarily lost contact with Marshall after the ramming, but he now rejoined company to stand by his leader. During this time the rammed E boat was burning slightly and soon after she was seen to sink, the fire being extinguished as she went.

S.88 was burning much more fiercely, and Lightoller reports that while he was passing her close abeam to starboard " she blew up with a colossal explosion, throwing debris some 200 feet in the air. When the smoke and debris cleared away another glow was seen a mile away to port, which shortly after being sighted blew up at 0242, though without quite such a violent explosion as the first."

Half an hour later nineteen of S.88's survivors were rescued by Lightoller. After picking them up he returned to stand by Marshall's boat, which was making water fast.

With Odds of Six to One

At 3.45 a.m. it became necessary for the damaged M.G.B. to be taken in tow, and by four o'clock they were under way at 6 knots, but ten minutes later a fresh party of E boats was approaching from the westward. Lightoller requested permission to slip the tow and go in pursuit, and Marshall gave this at once, although it meant leaving his boat unescorted with most of its guns out of action, half waterlogged and scarcely manœuvrable.

At 4.13 Lightoller went off to intercept the enemy, and by 4.20 a party of six E boats were close abeam to starboard. The single M.G.B. had not been detected, and her gunners were able to take a careful and unhurried aim before opening fire. " We were only quicker on the draw by a matter of seconds," writes Lightoller, " for all six E boats replied almost at once."

The M.G.B. then made smoke to confuse the enemy, and after a running fight lasting two minutes she turned away to take breath. Three minutes later she closed in to attack again, one against six. She worked round so as to gain the advantage of the waning moon which had lately risen; but the E boats had had enough. They turned and fled to the eastward at full speed. Lightoller pursued them for ten minutes, but they outstripped him, and he returned to the assistance of Marshall, who had been making 3 knots astern towards home in his absence. He took the damaged boat in tow again, after two small M.G.Bs. had taken off the wounded, and brought her safely into harbour.

Those were the adventures of Unit Y followed through to their conclusion, but meanwhile many other battles were taking place. Soon after 1 a.m., for example, H.M.S. *Worcester* was in action again, this time against three E boats.

Simultaneously a very brilliant tactical game of fox and geese was being played by Unit R, which consisted of two M.G.Bs. under the command of Lt. P. N. Edge, R.N.V.R. A few minutes before 1 a.m. the M.G.Bs. detected the presence of E boats on their hydrophones. The E boats were to the north-east. The convoy was a few miles to the south-west. Unit R lay directly between the two. Here was a case for stealth. If he turned to the attack, Edge realised the danger of the E boats breaking past him on one side or the other. His duty, in these circumstances, was clearly that of a half back, not a centre forward.

For forty minutes they prowled along almost on parallel courses, north-westward—the

---

[1] He was killed ashore a year and a half later when the German garrison in the Channel Islands carried out a Commando raid on Granville in March, 1945.

convoy and the E boats, and the M.G.Bs. in between. The E boats increased speed, the M.G.Bs. increased speed; the E boats stopped and the M.G.Bs. reduced speed. Then the E boats turned in as if to pass astern of the M.G.Bs., and the M.G.Bs. turned back to cut them off. It was no good; the E boats couldn't break through; they turned away to the north again, and the gunboats, following like their shadows, turned north with them. As the enemy eased round again towards the convoy, Edge held his course. The two forces were converging—on the one side five E boats, on the other two M.G.Bs. A moment later the battle started. The M.G.Bs. concentrated their fire on the second E boat in the line, which almost at once was heavily hit and forced to turn away. As it went, a brilliant red flash was seen which lasted for nearly thirty seconds. The remaining E boats also decided to break away to the eastward, and disappeared into a cloud of smoke.

After H.M.S. *Pytchley's* original contact before midnight, the first of the night's actions, this was the only E boat attempt which seriously threatened the convoy. It was frustrated by sheer tactical skill. Whether the thirty seconds' flash indicated the destruction of an E boat or not, the threat to the convoy had been removed. The enemy had been out-manoeuvred.

Whilst this battle was going on, however, another group of E boats farther to the south-ward scored their only success of the night's operations. They came upon H.M. Trawler *William Stephen* and sank her with a torpedo. Fifteen survivors were picked up by the E boats and made prisoner.

Meanwhile, when the Commander-in-Chief, Nore, first learned of the E boat activity just before midnight, he ordered additional patrols to sea. One of these was Unit J, consisting of two seventy-one-foot-six M.G.Bs. under the command of Lt. C. A. Burk, R.C.N.V.R., of Toronto. These M.G.Bs. proceeded at once to a patrol position near Brown Ridge, in the middle of the North Sea, there to await the returning E boats. At 3 a.m. they were in position and fifty minutes later the whirr of high-speed propellers was heard on the hydro-phone. It was six minutes past four when three E boats appeared out of the gloom at a range of 700 yards. The leading E boat was engaged and turned sharply to pass astern of the gun-boats. Burk circled round and came up on a parallel course, firing briskly at the second and third E boats. Then he settled down in station on the port quarter of the second E boat, and a high-speed running fight ensued. The E boat put on a burst of emergency speed and drew out of range, but it evidently could not be maintained, and when it reduced the M.G.B. came up with it again. Five times it drew ahead, but each time Burk caught up again when it slowed. Each time the E boat was under heavy fire until at 4.40 an armour-piercing 20-mm. shell struck the M.G.B's. forward gun and caused a stoppage. For ten more minutes contact was maintained in the hope of clearing the stoppage and bringing the gun back into action, but it could not be done. Meanwhile, a hit on the bridge killed the First Lieutenant, and Burk and the Coxswain were knocked down, so that for a moment the enemy was lost. The mess-deck was rapidly flooding, which reduced the gunboat's speed, and a fire on the after-gun platform was started at the same time. In consequence chiefly of the damaged forward gun, Burk says in his report: " . . . it was considered that our capacity for causing further damage to the enemy was so restricted that course was set for Lowestoft." The chase had lasted forty-four minutes.

That eventful night, with its sixteen encounters, was the greatest concerted E boat operation that had, at that time, ever been launched. The results of a night action are notoriously difficult to assess with accuracy. Damaged and burning vessels remain afloat with extra-ordinary tenacity. Crippled boats creep back to harbour after they have been given up for lost by their own side and claimed as sunk by their opponents. Many of the fantastic German claims may have been made in good faith, and some of our claims, made in good faith, may prove to have been over-optimistic. But it seems possible that at least four E boats failed to return to their harbours on the morning of 25th October, 1943. It was unfortunate that fog over the aerodromes made it impossible for the Royal Air Force to follow up the many E boats which must still have been limping home long after daybreak. But even as it was, the price they paid for the sinking of a single trawler was a heavy one. The defence had definitely drawn ahead of the attack in the East Coast E boat war.

"In the Spirit of the Greatest Sailor of All"

By the beginning of 1944 some of the E boats had been rearmed, and they began to show a more offensive spirit. It was for the time being short lived, as we shall see, but although their operations against our convoys were crowned with less and less success, a hitherto almost unknown phenomenon made its appearance one night in February. E boats deliberately sought contact with our Coastal Forces.

When they made a sortie against our east-coast route on the night of 14th/15th February, they were driven off by our destroyers without interfering with our convoys. As they withdrew, two units of Coastal Force craft were racing to a point in mid-Channel to cut off their retreat. The Senior Officer of these boats was Lt. E. D. W. Leaf, D.S.C., R.N.V.R., and when he reached the prescribed position in the vicinity of Brown Ridge he felt sure that the E boats were already ahead of him; but he was not to be cheated of action. At once he decided to push on towards Ijmuiden and wait on the doorstep for the returning Germans, a decision which the Commander-in-Chief, Nore, described in the report to Admiralty as " entirely correct."

As Leaf approached the Dutch coast he came upon a defence patrol consisting of a medium-sized flakship and two trawlers, and he made up his mind at once to attack, putting into operation a prearranged plan. In his force he had five seventy-one-foot-six boats, one of which was fitted with torpedo tubes. This boat was detached to attack with torpedoes while the four gunboats went in to draw the enemy's fire. It was the old combined attack, only on a smaller scale, and it was entirely successful. Both M.T.B. 455's torpedoes hit the target, and a few moments later her guns scored hits on the leading trawler, while Leaf engaged the rear trawler at 100 yards and left it silenced and burning. When the shore batteries joined in our force withdrew to re-form, reload and attack again. As they did so, steering north-west at high speed, they ran straight towards another enemy ship which they did not see until the range was very short. Leaf's boat was heavily hit and suffered serious casualties. The rest of the force made answer as they went past, apparently to good effect, but it was too late to save their leader. Leaf himself and three ratings had been killed and two others wounded.

It was 4.15 when the force re-formed. Neither the damaged boat nor 455 were in company, but Lt. C. A. Burk, R.C.N.V.R., immediately took charge of the rest of the Unit—three boats—and set off to look for Leaf. Almost at once a party of six E boats was detected shadowing on the port quarter and gradually closing in. Two more groups of E boats were detected ahead, and so Burk decided to tackle the first lot first. He turned hard a-port at full speed and crossed ahead of the E boats at a range of 100 yards—a manœuvre known as crossing the enemy's T. As each of our boats passed ahead of the enemy line with all guns firing, only the forward gun of the foremost E boat could fire in return. As a result, the first two E boats were hard hit, and the leader turned to port, ceased fire and stopped, with a fire burning aft. Unfortunately the last of our boats lost touch during this action, but the other two sighted the next group of E boats, six more, closing from right ahead. Once more Burk led across the enemy's T, and once more the first two E boats suffered. The M.G.Bs. were heavily outnumbered, and now broke off the engagement to the westward, meeting two more E boat groups and engaging each as it passed. These two boats had been in action against no fewer than seventeen E boats, yet Burk's boat had sustained no casualties or damage, and the second in his line had only three men slightly wounded.

"During last night," said the Germans on their radio, "German E boats, in spite of enemy destroyer attacks, carried through an operation off the English coast according to plan and without loss. At the same time German outposts off the Dutch port of Ijmuiden intercepted British light coastal craft, sank three of these vessels in a fierce engagement and forced the others to turn away. The returning E boats attacked this battered enemy formation, by their fire destroyed another two boats and damaged several others. The enemy suffered heavy casualties. All our boats returned to their bases; damage to them was slight."

So once again out of a force of five boats the enemy claimed to have sunk them all and damaged several more, and it is hard to believe that a medium-sized flakship could survive two torpedo hits. Leaf's force had certainly made its presence felt. But the loss of so brilliant and dashing a leader was indeed a setback. Derek Leaf had already achieved so much since the early days of which he wrote in his diary. How much more could he not have achieved, had there been time? It has been written of him that "boyhood shone in his face after manhood came, as loath to 'fade into the light of common day'; and his courage was the untroubled courage of a boy. If events furnished no occasion for daring, he would make them for himself in manœuvring his ship; and in action and out he chose the most aggressive course, and reduced caution to its irreducible minimum. His fire-eating so impressed the lower deck that, it is said, superstitious sailormen would cross themselves as they passed his ship, for luck for him and for themselves. He served in the spirit of the greatest sailor of all, and died, like him, conscious of victory."

CHAPTER XIV

The Less Lucky Ones

THE dashing battles were for the M.T.Bs. and the M.G.Bs., although rare enough even for them amongst so many hours at sea. But for most of the M.Ls. round our coasts there was little prospect of action—for some flotillas scarcely any at all.

Consider for a moment the M.Ls. which had to operate from the North of Scotland and the Northern Isles. They were held ready as anti-submarine striking forces, but few U boats dared to operate in their area after the early days of the war, until the use of the Schnorkel[1] in the summer of 1944 came to change the pattern of the U boat war.

" One feels very much cut off from the rest of the world," wrote the Senior Officer of one of these flotillas based in Scapa Flow, " and particularly the Coastal Forces world. How tremendously thrilled we are to hear of our pals down south doing so well in action. But how envious! How we wish *we* could have a smack at some E boats for a change. If only Jerry would even fly over us occasionally, what a difference it would make. It is extremely difficult to keep on the top line when the enemy always seems so far away."

The crews of these boats lived a very different kind of life from the Coastal Force crews in the south; a lonely life in which all their provisions and stores were waterborne, and they must cruise from ship to ship in the anchorage to get food and water, fuel, coal, ammunition and canteen goods. Often they were tucked away in some remote corner of the Flow, the boats moored to a buoy in twos and sometimes threes; often they were very much on their own for a week or more, waiting at immediate notice for the emergency which so seldom arose.

In the summer the conditions were not so bad. There is little darkness in those regions— only a short twilight while the sun dips shallowly behind the horizon for an hour or so either side of midnight. The patrols, too, were short, and the boats lying in out-of-the-way places could be relieved regularly. For recreation there were long walks across the barren, treeless islands and long sails in the dinghy to visit friends, maybe, in ships lying a mile or two across the Flow, and returning, tacking laboriously back in the sunrise, at two in the morning. But the summer was all too short. In the autumn the gales began again, and followed one another with almost ceaseless regularity week after week, month after month. In mid-winter there was scarcely more daylight than there was night in summer. But winter or summer the patrols and sweeps had to be carried out if there was any suspicion of U boat activity in the area.

The winter-time was indeed grim for the northern M.Ls.; often they had to put to sea in appalling conditions of wind and sea if there was " a U boat flap." On a pitch-black night of sleet and rain, for example, with half a gale blowing, they often had to steam for 5 miles through three anchorages crowded with mooring buoys and darkened ships. There were no shore lights to help them, there were strong tides to contend with and violent back eddies. The sweep itself might have been ordered near one of the sounds connecting the Flow with the open sea. Here the tidal currents run sometimes as fast as 10 knots, and should they be running against the wind they will raise a short, steep, vicious sea for which a " B " Class M.L. is little suited. Here the battle was not against the enemy but against the elements. One slip and both the boat and her crew might have been lost in a matter of minutes. Running

[1] The Schnorkel tube enabled a U boat to charge its batteries and freshen its air without coming to the surface, thereby greatly reducing the chance of being sighted by aircraft.

aground meant smashing the hull to matchwood on a sharp outcrop of rock or at the foot of a precipitous cliff.

These flotillas were indeed less lucky than those fighting in the Channel, with the constant stimulus of imminent battle, for who would not exchange boredom for danger and count himself lucky for the choice!

THE TASK OF MINELAYING

But although the vast majority of the M.Ls. were principally occupied with the defence of our merchant shipping and with standing patrols, there was, for some of them—a more fortunate few—a task that was adventurous enough, the task of minelaying in enemy waters. It was unspectacular work which went on year in, year out, a routine job which was, however, often exciting and always nerve-racking. It required a great deal of training, a high degree of skill in station-keeping and faultless navigation.

The mines had to be laid at night in the enemy shipping lanes, many of which ran close under the cliffs of their coastline; and close inshore the minelayers had to go to deposit their load. If they were discovered, not only did the shore batteries and coastal patrols engage them, but the lay was worthless, for the enemy was forewarned. He could send sweepers to the area to deal with the minefield and route his shipping clear of it until it had been swept. For the minelaying M.Ls. as for the M.T.Bs., but more than ever, the keynote was stealth.

Many of the lays were carried out without incident, though the nervous strain of operating in a comparatively slow type of craft right on the enemy's doorstep was always intense. Often our minelayers arrived to find their chosen stretch of the enemy channel occupied either by a convoy or a patrol. Sometimes they were able to wait until the enemy had passed by, sometimes they had to turn back for a while until "the coast was clear." (Indeed the minelayers, creeping in surreptitiously towards the shore, had much in common with the smugglers who originated the phrase.)

These encounters when minelaying called for great presence of mind and coolness on the part of the Senior Officer. Loaded with high explosive, his boats could ill afford to be engaged by the enemy. Contact had always to be avoided if possible, and to avoid it required instant decision and action. On one occasion a force of M.Ls. led by Lt. Cdr. T. Ashdowne, D.S.O., R.N.R., ran straight into a convoy on a very dark night. Before anyone was aware of it, the M.Ls. were all in amongst the enemy ships. The Germans of the inshore screen challenged, the Germans of the seaward screen replied correctly. The enemy was satisfied, and the M.Ls. sailed nonchalantly through the convoy to lay a successful minefield. This was the second time within a few months that just such a bluff had been successfully worked.

Ashdowne's flotilla were not always so lucky, however. One night in February, 1943, they had a narrow escape. Three of his " A " Class M.Ls. were operating with four " B " Class M.Ls. of a flotilla manned by personnel of the Royal Norwegian Navy. They were to lay mines in two positions well up the lit channel into Dunkirk—the " A " boats in the easterly position and the " B's " a mile or so to the west. The night was exceptionally dark.

Lt. G. D. Olivier, D.S.M., R.N.V.R., who commanded one of the " A " boats, describes how they steamed up the channel in starboard quarterline with the buoys winking at them on either side, expecting trouble at any moment.

" When trouble did arrive, with rather unexpected suddenness and ferocity, the third boat in our line had completed her lay. I was the second boat and I had laid all my mines but one, and the obstructor (a device for interfering with the enemy's sweeping apparatus), when suddenly a light flashed a challenge at us from our starboard side not more than 200 yards away. I yelled to my No. 1 to get rid of the last mine and the obstructor, which he did with commendable despatch, and turned at once to watch the leading boat carefully so as not to lose contact. He turned swiftly to port, at the same time dropping his mines off as quickly as he could all in a cluster. The boat astern turned to port too, but I had to follow round the outside of the curve in order to avoid running on to the leader's mines, which were plopping into the water just ahead of me.

" The enemy apparently consisted of two ' Narvik ' Class destroyers with a third ship two or three cables astern—probably an ' M ' Class minesweeper. The destroyers turned towards us and I found I had one on each quarter. I think my boat was the first they saw. A few seconds later starshell turned night into day, and then came as nasty a cross-fire from cannon and heavier stuff as I hope ever to experience. I could feel the blast of the guns in my back. By this time we had all cracked up to maximum speed and were making smoke as hard as we could. I thought ours would never make itself felt, and for what seemed hours (actually only four or five minutes) the inferno continued. The enemy was luckily shooting high, but I had a sort of hopeless feeling that it was too good to last, and that at best it would be some sort of prison camp for most of us.

" We had all been pretty quick off the mark, however, and I reckon I managed to put the leading boat's smoke between me and the destroyers just in time. Amazingly enough, my boat was practically undamaged and we suffered no casualties. The other two boats had only superficial damage and three or four casualties. After something like ten minutes the enemy destroyers gave up and continued on their way. I don't think at any time they can have worked up to anything like their full speed. The Norwegian flotilla, pushing off home some 2 miles to the west, had a front-row view of the proceedings, which I have no doubt gave them food for thought. With their slower speed things would undoubtedly have been unpleasant had they been with us. We heard later that an ' M ' Class sweeper stumbled on to the little bunch of mines early that morning."

One of the most effective lays ever made was a double event. Ashdowne's M.Ls. were assisted by a number of M.T.Bs. also carrying mines. Eleven boats set out to lay a field about 2 miles from Calais. By 11 p.m. all the boats were back in Dover. Two hours later the M.Ls. had been reloaded with mines and at 1.30 a.m. they sailed again. A second field was laid successfully a few miles to the west of the first, and the boats returned to their base at 7 a.m. The whole double operation had occupied twelve hours. Next day a special congratulatory signal addressed to the flotilla was received from the Admiralty.

In common with so many jobs in this war, it was not usually possible to observe the immediate results of successful minelaying. Occasionally a new wreck was sighted by reconnaissance aircraft or details became known to our Intelligence Service. But whether enemy ships were sunk or not, minelaying continued. Large numbers of enemy sweeping craft were kept occupied, enemy shipping routes were menaced and the resulting inconvenience to the Germans fully justified the strategy.

Lt. Cdr. J. S. Cambridge, D.S.C., R.N.V.R., Lt. Cdr. T. N. Cartwright, D.S.C., R.N.V.R., Lt. Cdr. H. T. Kemsley, R.N.V.R., and Lt. C. Kitson, R.N.V.R., are some of the officers who led their flotillas time after time on successful minelaying sorties in the narrow seas. Under them and many others the stealthy work went on until the Channel and the Straits were cleared of enemy ships.

ON THE INSIDE OF THE TURN

Amongst the slower types of boats in Coastal Forces there was always a danger when they were operating in enemy waters of being run down and destroyed by German destroyers or torpedo boats with a higher speed than their own. The minelaying M.Ls. had been lucky to escape on that night in February, 1943, in the Straits. Lt. Arnold Forster had an even narrower escape in the following November. He had a boat which would have been fast enough to escape but for a breakdown which led to a most unpleasant experience. With two 70-foot M.T.Bs. of his flotilla (M.T.B. 211, commanded by Lt. N. Taylor, R.N.V.R., with whom he himself was embarked, and M.T.B. 207, commanded by Lt. D. Morrison, R.C.N.V.R.), he was lying in wait off Cap d'Antifer for two German destroyers which were expected to be moving westward down the Channel. It was just after half-past three in the morning when the two destroyers were sighted, and since they were heading to pass at an excellent torpedo range from him, Arnold Forster stayed where he was. At a mile, however, the enemy altered course directly towards, increased speed and fired starshell. "This," as Arnold Forster remarks in his report, "placed the M.T.Bs. in an impossible position for torpedo attack." They had no alternative but to make off at best speed, which, owing to an engine failure, was, in the case of 211, no more than 18 knots. The destroyer which was pursuing her tried to ram. It passed about 100 yards astern and 211 turned sharply to starboard. The enemy also turned to starboard, but his turning circle was slightly larger than that of the M.T.B., and in the words of Arnold Forster's report, "he then kept station on the port quarter at ranges between 150 and 250 yards. The enemy was compelled to use a large amount of rudder in order to do this. At the speed at which he was moving this gave him a considerable list to port and prevented most of his starboard guns from depressing sufficiently to hit . . ." M.T.B. 211 was damaged by 20-mm. shells, but by the use of smoke she finally managed to get out of this unpleasant vortex, and disaster was averted.

The beginning of March, 1944, was a productive period for our M.T.Bs. off the Dutch coast, in spite of the bright moonlight. On the night of 6th/7th a particularly bold and colourful attack was made by a flotilla of "D" boats—the 53rd—under Lt. Cdr. D. H. E. McCowen, R.N.V.R., right in the entrance to the harbour of Ijmuiden, where complete surprise was achieved.

There was no excuse for the enemy to be surprised, for only the night before Macdonald, the New Zealand leader, had blown up a trawler in a characteristically neat and decisive operation off the same port. McCowen, however, had the good fortune to arrive just as a convoy was forming up outside the harbour mouth, and his six boats were evidently entirely undetected as they approached, picking their way between the patrols, the escorts and the convoy itself. McCowen sighted two merchant ships and detached two boats to torpedo them while he led the others to a point only 500 yards from the harbour breakwaters. Here he was all in amongst the still unsuspecting German ships. Nearest to him was a gun coaster with a party of R boats in company, and when he was almost on top of them he turned and poured his broadsides into the enemy ships. "We held the stage," he writes in his report, "for perhaps fifteen seconds, and then the enemy opened a heavy and sometimes accurate, but mostly wild, fire on the unit from all directions, with the exception of the coaster, which was heavily hit by our initial burst." The gun coaster and an R boat were left on fire from stem to stern, and the gun coaster was seen to be settling down, so that she probably sank.

On the opposite side were some trawlers to which our boats then turned their attention. The enemy was now fully roused but thoroughly confused, as McCowen slipped away to the southward. The shore guns had joined in the fray, and the trawlers and R boats, from between which he had vanished, proceeded to fire at each other. "For the next ten minutes," he writes, "the enemy continued the contest among themselves. A most spirited encounter was observed between two enemy vessels, and it was most gratifying to see that the standard of shooting had improved considerably; both sides seemed to be scoring a satisfactory number of hits."

Meanwhile the larger of the two merchant ships had been hit by a torpedo, and also by the guns of one of the detached boats. The other's torpedoes had evidently missed the second merchantman, but as the M.T.B. disengaged she was accurately shelled from the shore. As the fountains of water rose up all round her, two R boats were sighted trying to head her off. A few moments later she also had the satisfaction of seeing these two open a brisk fire upon each other. All six of our boats escaped serious damage, and the casualties, for so bold a thrust, were amazingly light, although unhappily one boat was hit by a shell on the bridge, killing the Navigating Officer, Sub-Lt. J. W. G. Morrish, R.N.V.R., and Lt. D. T. Wickham, R.N., who had recently become Gunnery Officer to the Captain, Coastal Forces, Nore, and was on board one of the boats for experience. The Coxswain, the First Lieutenant and the Commanding Officer, Lt. D. L. W. MacFarlane, R.N.V.R., were wounded by the same shell, but for the whole of the return trip of five hours MacFarlane did not leave the bridge. " He brought his boat alongside," McCowen's report goes on, " and refused medical attention until the other wounded members of his crew were attended to. He then collapsed from loss of blood and great pain."

Three days later Lt. Cdr. D. G. Bradford's flotilla was at it again off the Dutch coast near Ameland, where he scored two hits on a 400-foot merchant vessel of the tanker type. While he was doing this his second division under Lt. W. S. Strang, R.N.V.R., sank a large tug and rescued its Dutch crew. The German guard had already jumped overboard and were not found.

It was less than a week after this that the other Bradford—Lt. Cdr. H. O. T. Bradford, R.N.V.R., began a series of successes in the Dover Strait. These two men of the same name, each commanding a flotilla of " D " boats, were not related. It was Donald Bradford, the north countryman, who had fought in Bolivia and in Spain, who had rammed an E boat with his " C " Class M.G.B. and was credited in the newspapers with having " the toughest crew in Coastal Forces," who had torpedoed the liner *Strasbourg* and had later had a " D " boat sunk under him. Later still, as we shall see, it was he who had the honour of leading the very spearheads of our Normandy invasion, thereafter fighting for many weeks in that fierce corner of the Channel off Le Havre.

Howard Bradford, an architect in peace-time, had earned a D.S.C. in trawlers during the Norwegian campaign, fought E boats in a 70-foot M.G.B. in the early days, and had then commanded a steam gunboat in which, as I have already described, he came to my assistance one night off Cherbourg and was badly wounded in doing so.

Now he arrived at Dover at a time when German defence measures had more than once defeated the efforts of our M.T.Bs. Rooper, who succeeded Richards, had himself been killed when his boat and her crew were lost; an attack on an east-bound convoy on Christmas Eve, 1943, had failed, and although no boats were lost there had been heavy casualties. Another convoy attack in January had been no more successful. The enemy passed his shipping through the Narrows very seldom now; and when he did so it had a fantastic array of escorts. From the time it left one harbour till the time it reached the next its way was almost continuously illuminated by starshells from the shore, turning night into day. There did not seem to be an answer, but somehow Howard Bradford found one. On the night of 14th/15th March, 1944, he tackled one merchant ship with a close escort of two auxiliary vessels and ten to twelve R boats. True it was only a single small merchant ship, or it would no doubt have had a larger escort, but one of Bradford's unit of four boats sank it with a torpedo and the other three set about the R boats, leaving one on fire. The leading M.T.B.

was slightly damaged and its wireless was put out of action, so Bradford transferred to another boat and made another attack on a further enemy group of six R boats and three trawlers. Once again an R boat was left burning and once again the enemy were left firing at each other, while the M.T.Bs. withdrew without a single casualty.

AMONG THE LEADS

Meanwhile arrangements had been made to exploit more fully the prospects opened up off the coast of Norway by the Norwegian flotilla. The British 58th Flotilla under Lt. Cdr. Gemmel was sent north to join them in this very different type of Coastal Forces fighting among the main fjords or " leads " as they are called by Norwegians.

It began to operate in November, 1943, working in close co-operation with the Norwegian flotilla. Although at first the new job was regarded, according to Gemmel, with mixed feelings by many in the flotilla who generally voted that it had " no future," as time progressed they settled down and learned thoroughly to enjoy these excursions. " I myself," he writes, " will always consider that we possessed the choicest job in Coastal Forces. Perhaps our chief enemy was the weather. This was ever, or so it seemed, bloody, and sea-sickness raged in consequence. Even the most hardened generally succumbed to this malady, and I well remember my Coxswain, after indulging in a good bout at the bucket, turning to me and saying, ' You know, sir, I've been lovesick, homesick and booze-sick, but, my God, I never thought I'd be seasick.' "

Just what an enemy the weather could be was demonstrated in February, 1944, when two " D " boats were returning from an uneventful patrol amongst the leads. The wind was S.S.W., Force 5 to 6, with a confused sea, which is uncomfortable but not dangerous, when they set off for home, but by the following forenoon it had veered and was blowing Force 11 to 12—a strong gale—with sea very rough. Meteorological stations in that area recorded occasional squalls at well over 100 miles an hour on that day, as the two " D " boats struggled into it. Inevitably they became separated, and at one time they were making good 1 and 2 knots respectively. Gradually they became flooded until one of them, M.T.B. 625, was so full forward that she had only 6 inches freeboard. She was rolling dangerously and almost unable to steer. The torpedoes had to be jettisoned, and eventually she reached the shelter of the land.

M.T.B. 666 was in little better case. She continued to fill up steadily and to develop a list, until the water came up to the sparking-plugs of the starboard outer engine. Gear was shifted to try to counteract the list, but to no avail, and finally the starboard torpedo was fired. In this way the starboard outer engine ran for another four hours before it was again flooded by the steadily rising water. Of the four engines only the port outer was now working. When the water had risen so that it was splashing one bank of plugs on this last engine, the port torpedo was also jettisoned, and the engine continued to run just long enough for the boat to reach shelter, where with the help of another vessel she was pumped out, repaired a second engine and finally reached her base under her own power. It is a tribute to the " D " boat that these two craft survived this storm. The bare account of what happened can give no idea of the hell of apprehension and sheer discomfort which must have been suffered for hour after hour by the crews.

Gemmel himself was lucky enough never to be caught out in so heavy a gale, but he had many adventures of other kinds. " There is, for example, the story of the Christmas trees," he writes. " We had occasion to be waiting in one of the ' leads ' near a slope on which grew scores of fir trees, and the crew were particularly anxious to possess one and decorate it for the mess-deck. Although it was perhaps unwise to cut them down and possibly betray the fact that someone had been nosing around this district, I decided to risk it and willingly entered into the joke; and so, like a lot of schoolboys, we hacked down five. It was remarked that, like Kensitas cigarettes, we should have ' four for our friends.' On arrival at our base a few days later the prizes were produced with great pride. It was then suggested that, as a gesture, one should be sent to King Haakon of Norway. This was done, the tree being flown to London, and it was, I am told, decorated and displayed in the Norwegian headquarters there."

AN ANTI-SALVAGE OPERATION

While these two flotillas were operating against the German shipping in Norway, at the opposite extremity of the British Isles Coastal Forces in the Plymouth Command had been fighting regularly off the Brittany coast and in the Channel Islands ever since Hichens left Dartmouth in the autumn of 1942.

After the sinking of the enemy raider off Cap de la Hague by a combined force of M.T.Bs. and destroyers in October, 1942, this type of attack was further developed in the western channel, and used successfully a few weeks later by an international combination in which the Polish " Hunt " Class destroyer *Krakowiak* led the British " Hunt " *Tynedale* and a mixed Dutch and British unit of M.T.Bs., commanded by Lt. E. H. Larive, R.Neth.N., to attack a convoy near the Roches Douvres, and sink a merchant ship and a trawler.

Later, when the Dutch M.T.Bs. left Dartmouth, their place was taken by a Free French flotilla of 70-foot boats, commanded first by Capitaine de Corvette Meurville, F.F.N., and then by Lt. Ièhle, F.F.N. The flotilla scored many successes amongst the Channel Islands, often in company with the M.G.Bs. of the flotilla which Hichens had commanded, and which was now under Lt. T. J. Mathias, R.N.V.R. Later still came a flotilla of " D " boats under Lt. Cdr. Cartwright. All these fought often amongst the islands, amongst the treacherous rocks and the sluicing tides. As Cartwright remarks, " To play anywhere round the Minquiers at night would have been thought the height of folly in peace-time, unless you were a native." And yet round the Minquiers was where they often did play, and an indication of their success was given to me during the summer of 1944 when I spoke to a Dutch merchant captain who had escaped into the Allied lines at the fall of St. Malo. For many months the inter-island traffic in which his ship had taken part had been known to the Germans as " the suicide run."

Cartwright was much occupied with minelaying during most of his time in the West Country, as we shall see in the next chapter, but in the spring of 1944 he was given the interesting and unusual task of preventing the salvage of a German destroyer.

As a result of an action between our own and some enemy destroyers at the end of April, an " Elbing " Class destroyer was driven ashore on a rock near St. Tregarec, on the north Brittany coast, by the Canadian " Tribal " Class destroyer H.M.C.S. *Haida*. The stranded vessel was subsequently attacked by aircraft which encountered flak from newly set-up positions ashore, and reported that " camels " for refloating her could be seen alongside. The air attack had been indecisive and two aircraft had been lost. The Commander-in-Chief, Plymouth (Admiral Sir Ralph Leatham, K.C.B.), decided to attempt the final destruction of the wreck by M.T.Bs.

Three " D " boats were to take part—673 (Cartwright's own boat), 677 (Lt. A. Clayton, R.N.V.R.) and 717 (Lt. B. H. C. Robinson, R.N.V.R.), with three of Mathias' M.G.B. flotilla as a support force, because enemy trawler patrols had been sighted in the area.

When Cartwright made his plan of attack, he had to reckon with the following problems. First of all, the target was aground on a rock less than half a mile from high-tide mark. Secondly, within a radius of 1,000 yards of it there were no fewer than twenty different rocks or shoals either awash or dry at some state of the tide. The torpedoes had to be fired from a position where they would neither hit the bottom during the initial dive nor run into a rock on their way to the target. The selection of such a position was not helped by the fact that the only available aerial photographs had been taken from such a height that it was extremely difficult to pin-point the exact rock on which the enemy ship was aground. Lastly, there was no time to be lost. The operation had to be carried out at once, and there was a full moon. To reach a firing position under these conditions without being sighted either from the target or from the shore seemed, on the face of it, an almost impossible task. Cartwright planned to detach the M.G.Bs. 3 miles north of the target to deal with any patrols that might come along. M.T.B. 717 was also to be detached to approach from the north-east, abaft the destroyer's port beam, while 673 and 677 approached from the north-west, attacking on the enemy's starboard beam and quarter respectively.

"In the event," writes Cartwright, "and most surprisingly, the tactics worked out exactly as planned. We saw the target two and a half miles away; it seemed at first sight to have several ships and two high-speed craft near it. On longer inspection, however, these were all recognised as rocks—the high-speed wakes we had seen were caused by the swell breaking heavily on the half-submerged rocks. We closed at 8 knots, bows on to the beach and the moon, and almost bows on to the target—nothing happened although it was as light as day.

"717 reported 'in position' just as 673 and 677 turned to an easterly course to close the target between two shoals; I was certain we were now bound to be spotted, as we were beam on to the beach, and to the moon as well—but again nothing happened. The target was between two and three cables distant and was listing far more heavily than shown in the aerial photograph; also she appeared to be farther on the rocks. In view of this, and things being still quite quiet, it appeared to me to be a pity to fire six fish at this 'sitting bird' (business man's instincts coming out!), and I decided to fire one myself, ordering the remaining boats to keep their sights on and fire in case of trouble only. (This caused a certain amount of 'drip' on the R/T.)

"After a little more manœuvring to clear shoals in the intended torpedo track, I fired the port torpedo, which ran clearly visible in the moonlight straight for the target, hitting abaft the bridge superstructure. There was a satisfying explosion and the after superstructure disappeared in showers of debris and burning ammunition. We turned short round between the shoals and were heading out on a northerly course before the enemy opened up from the shore with searchlights and guns, which we managed to evade after ten minutes of zig-zagging and 'near misses.' We had no casualties or damage, and air reconnaissance later showed the destruction of the target to be complete. The sight of breaking water on the rocks all round us had not been pleasant, but it was not half so unpleasant as that of my Echo sounder trace which looked like a silhouette of the Cuillins; I was full of sympathy for my wretched 'pilot' who had had to sit and watch 'the bottom getting very near the top.'"

CHAPTER XV

PLANS FOR AN INVASION

WHILE for three years the nightly skirmishes had continued in the moat round Britain, the main forces within the castle had been building up their strength and preparing to sally forth. The greatest combined operation of all was in preparation.

In the plans for the landing in Normandy the Coastal Forces had many important parts to play, and in the event they played them supremely well. Hitherto, because London had to be supplied by convoys using the East Coast route, and because the area off the Dutch coast was the busiest part of the enemy's convoy route, the activity of our M.T.Bs. and M.G.Bs. had been centred north rather than south of the Dover Strait. Now the position was to be reversed. Large reinforcements were to be brought to the south coast, where already the ports were crowded with landing craft, and extensive redisposition of the flotillas would be necessary in order to accommodate and maintain them in the harbours of Newhaven, Portsmouth and Portland.

On the east coast the appointment of a Captain Coastal Forces (Nore) just over a year before had produced excellent results, and now it was clear that a similar appointment on the south coast would be needed for the planning and execution of the Coastal Forces' part in the invasion. Thus it was that on 8th March, 1944, Captain P. V. McLaughlin, R.N., was appointed to the staff of the Commander-in-Chief, Portsmouth, as Captain, Coastal Forces (Channel) and took over the organisation and operation of all the M.T.Bs.[1] and M.Ls. in the Portsmouth command, from which the invasion was principally to be launched.

To help him in his work, Captain McLaughlin had a small staff of which I was lucky enough to be a member. Lt. C. W. S. Dreyer, D.S.O., D.S.C. and bar, R.N., was also on this staff, having returned from great successes in the Mediterranean, where his flotilla had been operating in the Straits of Messina. [His most notable achievement there came one night when a U boat on the surface suddenly bore down on him and passed 20 yards ahead, too close for him to fire torpedoes although he was going full astern. He was about to give chase when he saw a second U boat following the first. Still going astern, to get far enough away, he fired one torpedo at a range of scarcely 100 yards, and the submarine blew up. Further torpedo attacks on the leading U boat failed, though it may have been damaged by depth charges. Then it was that he made his classic signal to the Commander-in-Chief, Mediterranean (Admiral Cunningham): "Two U boats in position so and so. Regret only one sunk."]

Christopher Dreyer and I had worked together as Senior Officers of our respective flotillas at H.M.S. *Aggressive* at Newhaven in 1943, and our association together on the staff of Captain, Coastal Forces (Channel) was equally happy throughout the spring, summer and autumn of 1944.

Also recently returned from the Mediterranean to join this same staff, with wide experience of Coastal Forces problems in a seaborne landing, was Lt. Cdr. (E.) R. S. Bickerton, R.N.,

---

[1] By this time the conception of a dual-purpose boat had become universal in Coastal Forces. The distinction between M.T.B. and M.G.B. had been almost entirely removed, all newly constructed boats were fitted with torpedoes *and* guns, and a torpedo armament was being added to all but a very few of the oldest M.G.Bs. The official title "M.G.B." was replaced by "M.T.B.," except in the case of two flotillas of "C" Class boats and the few old 70-foot gunboats which remained in service for special jobs such as despatch-boat work. A small number of the oldest "D" Class boats changed their title but were not converted, and found themselves in an anomalous position as M.T.Bs. without torpedoes. From now on in this book the term M.T.B. must be taken in the wider sense.

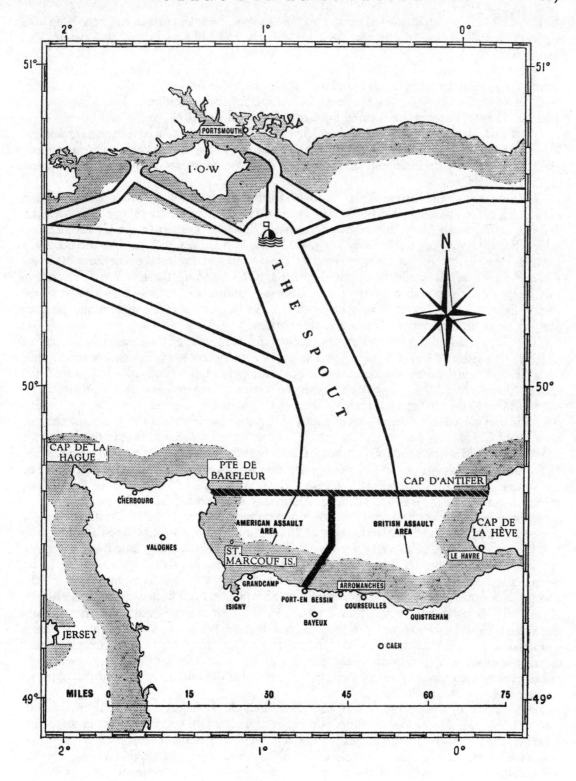

as Engineer Officer, upon whom fell the organisation of the maintenance and repair facilities to meet a concentration in one area of more M.T.Bs. and M.Ls. than had ever before been assembled.

From H.M.S. *Bee*, where the working-up of new boats had, of necessity, to be curtailed at this time, came Lt. Cdr. J. M. Matheson, R.N.V.R., who from the intricate dovetailing of training programmes, took on the intricate dovetailing of operations. From the staff of Captain, Coastal Forces (Nore) came Lt. Cdr. F. H. Dunlop, R.N., as Signal Officer.

Lt. D. J. Long, R.N., who had been Senior Officer of a flotilla at Lowestoft, was the Staff Torpedo Officer, and as such was responsible also for the detailed arrangements in connection with M.T.B. minelaying, which, as we shall see, was one of their most important functions at this time.

In its broad outline the naval plan had been formed some time before by the Allied Naval Commander, Expeditionary Force (the late Admiral Sir Bertram H. Ramsay, K.C.B., K.B.E., M.V.O.). The most likely threats had been assessed, and it was up to the Commander-in-Chief, Portsmouth (Admiral Sir Charles J. C. Little, G.B.E., K.C.B.), to take the necessary measures for the defence of the spearhead of our attack and the subsequent flow of cross-Channel traffic which would be required to supply and build up the landing. The part in this defence plan to be taken by the Coastal Forces—and it was a very large part—was the responsibility of the Captain, Coastal Forces (Channel). Captain McLaughlin and his staff had just under three months to make the preparations.

The Navy's task in this operation was mainly (and in the case of the Coastal Forces almost entirely) the defence of an offensive. A landing was to be made on the shores of the Baie de la Seine, and thereafter the route between that bridgehead and England—as it were " the spout " down which the supplies and reserves would be poured—must be protected on either flank. Protected against what? That was a question of vital importance to every staff officer involved in preparing these plans. On paper the Germans had a certain number of weapons which could be brought to bear. There was still a German fleet in being, though it did not seem likely that they would bring it into the confined waters of the Channel in spite of the successful passage of the *Scharnhorst* and *Gneisenau* two years before. The balance in the air had gone too much against them since then, unless the Luftwaffe was really holding back and waiting for the invasion to start. The heavy ships would be more likely to stage a diversion elsewhere. But there were destroyers and torpedo boats and "M" Class minesweepers in good force, both on the Atlantic coast of France and in the Low Countries. Both flanks of " the spout " could be menaced by these. There were E boats, too, based at Cherbourg to the west, and farther up the Channel to the east. Again, both flanks would have to be defended against them. There were large numbers of U boats which might come up the Channel from their bases at Brest and Lorient and St. Nazaire, or all the way from Germany. If they tried to get through at night on the surface, like their colleagues in the Messina Strait, there might be a chance for our M.T.Bs. Besides all these, there was the possibility of secret weapons. It was not likely that the flying-bomb or the V2 rocket would have a direct influence on the war at sea, but there were indications that midget submarines, human torpedoes (such as had already been used at Anzio), and explosive motor boats might well be launched against our shipping.

The reaction of the Luftwaffe was also problematical. It might attack with bombs and guns or it might use torpedoes or glider bombs, or again it might concentrate (as in the event it did) on the laying of mines. Mines. They, too, were an unknown quantity. Already the waters off all the occupied coasts were thick with them, and it was certain that amongst them, and amongst those yet to be laid, there would be new types requiring research and experiment before they could be swept. The planning of the operation had to include measures for defence against all these possible weapons.

It was too much to hope that the assembly of so vast an armada on the south coast, and principally in the Isle of Wight area, could remain entirely hidden from the enemy's reconnaissance. How much surprise could be counted upon in the " initial stages "? It was only safe to say " very little," although when D day came it turned out to be unbelievably complete.

The Coastal Forces fitted into this defensive plan in various ways. First and most important, they were to take up patrols flanking " the spout " on either side to prevent the penetration of enemy surface craft or secret weapons, and also to carry out offensive sweeps off the enemy's harbours in order to cut off such attacks at source, or at least give warning of the enemy's activity. There were some areas, however, particularly close to those parts of the French coast that would still be enemy held after the landings, where it was thought that M.T.Bs. would not be able to patrol because of the coastal batteries. Here, therefore, in the weeks before D day, they were to lay minefields, and these had to be laid unobtrusively so that the laying would give no clue to the position of the landings to come.

In the early and critical hours of the invasion, while a foothold was being secured, it was important to exploit any doubt that might exist in the enemy's mind of the whereabouts of the main landing. For this reason various diversions were to be staged, using Coastal Forces craft—notably H.D.M.Ls.—which, behind smoke-screens, were to give the impression to the enemy that a major landing was about to take place.

Besides these jobs M.Ls. were to carry out normal escort duties with the spearheads and the build-up convoys, acting as navigational leaders and sheep-dogs as well as defenders. Other M.Ls. were equipped for minesweeping, and yet others, together with a few M.T.Bs., were to be fast despatch boats, running a regular service across the Channel.

Those briefly, then, were to be the functions of the Coastal Forces in this momentous operation.

THE PORTSMOUTH PLOT

During the months of preparation, however, the normal work of Coastal Forces had to go on in the Channel, where the E boats were more than usually active. Evidently uncertain of the time when the invasion would be launched, and insufficiently supplied with intelligence and aerial reconnaissance, the German High Command was using E boats regularly during April and May to reconnoitre the approaches to the Solent area, as well as for their more normal functions of minelaying and attacking our assembling ships with torpedoes. Although these may have been their objectives, the E boats met with very little success. The pendulum had now swung against them. Our defence was on top and, although the enemy's high speed usually made it possible for him to escape, it was seldom enough that he was allowed to achieve what he set out to do.

The nerve centre of these operations was the Headquarters of the Commander-in-Chief, Portsmouth. These headquarters were situated in the bowels of the earth. In a tunnel deep in the chalk hillside was the Naval Plotting Room, the centre of a vast network of underground tunnel-shaped, air-conditioned offices known as Portsmouth Combined Headquarters, where Navy, Army and Air Force were able to work in close co-operation.

It was from this plotting-room, usually called for short " the Plot," that a complete picture of the naval part of the invasion was continuously made available to the Allied Commanders, and it was from here, too, that the Channel war against E boats and enemy shipping was conducted during the months before.

Only once in that time did the E boats achieve anything of consequence. That was during an invasion exercise when they got in amongst a convoy of landing ships in Lyme Bay and wrought serious devastation and heavy loss of life; it was their sole success although they were at sea night after night.

There were two flotillas of them based at Cherbourg, the 5th, under the command of Korvettenkapitän Bernard Klug, and the 9th, under the command of Korvettenkapitän Götz von Mirbach. From the German wireless and newspapers and from prisoners of war we learnt much about the personalities of these two men, who were fighting continuously, with great courage, in an area where the defence was consistently ahead of them and the initiative was hardly ever theirs.

Klug was the senior of the two, tall, dark, handsome and brilliant, always immaculately dressed, even at sea, where he wore his Ritterkreuz (the Knight's insignia of the Iron Cross) round his neck. Less loved than admired by his men, he was said to be rather conceited, but by this time he had very wide experience, and he was undoubtedly a leader of exceptional ability. Von Mirbach was a different type, short, slight and fair. Not perhaps so brilliant, he was a man of unquestioned coolness and courage. He had been in action more times than any other E boat leader, yet never lost his appetite for battle, and for this reason, if for no other, he was most popular with his men.

The Cherbourg E boats, like all the other E boats in the Channel and North Sea, were under the direct control of the Führer der Schnellboote (F.D.S. for short), Kapitän zur See Petersen, himself once the Senior Officer of a flotilla, who had his headquarters at this time at Scheveningen in Holland. There, no doubt, he had a very similar organisation to our Naval Plotting Room at Portsmouth, and in planning our operations, both then and later during the invasion, we were always conscious of the personal battle of wits against these men.

DEFENCE AND OFFENCE

In these last months, when the Allies were poised ready to spring, the activity in the Channel was sharply divided into two spheres. First, defence against E boats on our convoy routes, and more particularly the approaches to our harbours, for with more freedom the enemy might well have attempted to " mine in " our invasion armada; and secondly, the preparation for offence—the laying of the minefields which were to protect the flanks of " the spout."

In the defensive field the Coastal Forces were often in action, but never for long enough to encompass the destruction of an E boat. Only two were sunk during this period—both by the Fighting French " Hunt " Class destroyer F.S. *La Combattante* under the command of Capitaine de Corvette A. Patou. The efficiency of this ship, and particularly the outstanding accuracy of her gunnery, enabled her to score direct hits in the very brief time that a 40-knot E boat remains within range of a destroyer pursuing a little more than 25 knots. Each time prisoners were taken, though the son of Admiral Dönitz, Chief of the German Naval Staff, who had been on board the unlucky E boat as a passenger on the second occasion, was not amongst the survivors.

On the night of 18th/19th May a large-scale exercise was held in which the Naval Commander, Eastern Task Force (Admiral Sir Philip Vian, K.C.B., K.B.E., D.S.O. and two bars, R.N.) tried out off the English coast the defence measures he was going to employ off the French coast when the invasion had begun. It was a complex exercise in which certain M.T.Bs. were to represent E boats and attempt to penetrate a defence line and reach an " anchorage " off Worthing. Outside the whole exercise area was another defence line to prevent the real E boats from getting mixed up in the exercise. The real E boats came out and were intercepted by the very outermost fringe of the patrols. Two S.G.Bs.—*Grey Owl* and *Grey Wolf*—

engaged them, and they turned tail at once and fled. Meanwhile the sham E boats continued their exercise attack, and it is interesting to note that they penetrated more deeply into Admiral Vian's defences than, when the time came, any genuine E boat ever managed to do.

The work of minelaying, although unspectacular, is, as we have already seen, not lacking in excitement and tension. The preliminary minelaying for the invasion was no exception. It was carried out by two flotillas of 70-foot M.T.Bs.—the 13th, under the command of Lt. Arnold Forster, and the 14th, under the command of Lt. D. A. Shaw, D.S.C., R.N., and one flotilla of "D" Class M.T.Bs.—the 64th, under the command of Lt. Cdr. D. Wilkie, R.N.V.R. Between them they laid 562 mines, principally in two fields—one off Le Havre and one off Cherbourg. To complete such fields required a large number of sorties, laying a few mines each time, and incidentally running the gauntlet of the shore batteries. With these, however, Lt. Shaw was lucky. "For reasons unknown to us," he writes, " the guns remained silent, although on occasions the boats were only a few hundred yards from their muzzles. It was on these occasions that the risk of running ashore was sometimes greater than that of being shelled, as any errors in navigation or the failure of instruments could result, as it nearly did once when there was a coastal mist, in a unit motoring quietly ashore in enemy territory. But the flotilla was lucky; in its first twelve minelaying sorties in this preparatory period, the only casualty was a man who took the skin off his hand in his endeavours to release a mine which had got stuck."

The other flotillas did not always meet with so little opposition. One night when, amongst other things, the weather was particularly rough, a unit led by Lt. P. M. Cohen, R.N.V.R., was heavily shelled while approaching the laying position, and forced to turn away. As he closed in for a second attempt the shelling began again, but Cohen was determined to complete the lay. Under a hail of heavy shells lasting for more than half an hour, he went straight in and laid his mines exactly in position, withdrawing, by well-deserved good fortune, undamaged.

Weather was one of the minelayers' worst enemies, for the mines they carried on deck were so heavy that in anything but a fairly calm sea they affected the sea-keeping qualities of the smaller boats. The "D" boats, of course, could stand up to more, but the laying of forty-four mines off Cherbourg by Lt. Cdr. Wilkie's flotilla on the night of 20th/21st May in a north-westerly wind of Force 6 to 7 was a notable achievement.

In addition to the minefields off Le Havre and Cherbourg, the Commander-in-Chief, Plymouth, had been undertaking, over a period of several months, an extensive programme of minelaying off the coast of Brittany and in the Channel Islands. Only in its later stages was this programme linked with the plans for the invasion, in order to take a toll of any reinforcements which might be sent to the Seine Bay from the French Atlantic ports.

The Coastal Forces which took part in this series of operations were Lt. Cdr. Cartwright's flotilla of " C " Class M.G.Bs., specially equipped as navigational leaders, followed later by his flotilla of " D " boats, and a flotilla of " B " Class M.Ls.—the 10th—under Lt. Cdr. H. T. Kemsley, D.S.C., R.N.V.R.

"We laid our eggs in the approaches to several harbours and anchorages," writes Cartwright, " one being Lannion Bay. This was a tricky piece of navigation as, having got into the bay, we had to start the lay close to a rocky shoal projecting out from the beach on the south shore and finish close to a similar shoal on the north side. At one time, as we made the final approach, the course was such that land was ahead and continuous all round us except for an arc well abaft each beam which was clear to seaward. This gave rise to some amusing remarks which stick in my memory; a stoker in one of the boats came up from below to pass a message to the bridge and saw the high cliffs close ahead and on either beam. Having delivered his message to the C.O., he turned to the signalman and said, ' 'Ere, Ginger, where the 'ell's the ——— sea gone.' The signalman jerked his thumb astern and said, ' There you are, chum, and tell the motor mechanic we'll be wanting the shore lighting rigged in about five minutes.' The shoal on the south side of the bay was marked by a beacon tower at its end, and since it was low water it looked not unlike a small pier in the darkness. We passed no more than 30 yards from the beacon, and as it swam suddenly into the field of vision of the midship's gunner he was heard to give a startled oath followed by ' Blimey! Brighton pier an' all! ' The lay was completed by the six boats without interference.

" The closest shave we had was during a lay on the convoy route south of Guernsey and east of the Roches Douvres. It was after a spell of bad weather, and as we were chafing at the inactivity we had suggested we might do the operation on a fairly moonlight night. As a result, it was decided to give us a close escort of four ' C ' Class M.G.Bs.—a total force of twelve boats, which was a hell of a lot to control. I was in Bobby Nye's[1] boat that night, and, as we steamed towards the lay in two columns with the moon almost astern of us, Bobby and I spotted through the glasses two enormous bow waves, gleaming nicely in the moonlight and approaching down the convoy route dead ahead of us. I ordered a ' red ' turn to port and watched the bow waves with ' the wind up absolutely vertical.' We had been warned that there were two " Elbing " Class destroyers in Cherbourg, and these bow waves looked very like them. The one thing we were frightened of at that time was the chance of destroyers running into these parties; the ' B ' boats hadn't the speed to get away and we hadn't any torpedoes. The turn was executed slowly; we were only doing 10 knots, and two columns of six boats each take some time to get round. How they didn't see us I shall never know, for they had all the advantage of the moon. But they didn't, and four minutes after first sighting the two destroyers were abaft our starboard beam and opening—though they passed not more than eight cables away.[2] Nothing happened, and half an hour later we returned to the position and laid our mines.

" We made so many landfalls on the Roches Douvres in these operations that the ratings began to know it as well as we did by the ' characteristic ' of its light or, when that was not lit, by its silhouette. One night I picked it up in the glasses, and had the sighting confirmed, as usual, by my signalman, who was a *very* fine night look-out. The following conversation then ensued:

" Signalman: ' There she is! '

" Bridge Messenger: ' There who is? '

" Signalman: ' That smashing blonde.'

" Bridge Messenger: ' Don't be ——— silly! There ain't no parties around here.'

" Signalman: ' Do you mean to say you're so ——— blind you don't recognise the lighthouse-keeper's daughter after all these trips.' "

In all, twenty-four minelaying operations were carried out by this team (representing 168 " boat-lays "), and neither Cartwright nor Kemsley, the two Senior Officers, missed a single one of them. It was the last eleven which were planned in preparation for the invasion.

Besides laying mines and chasing E boats, Coastal Forces fought a few of the more typical offensive actions against enemy coastal shipping during this period along the whole length of the Channel from Brittany to the Straits. For example, Lt. Cdr. I. D. Lyle, D.S.C., R.N.V.R.,[3] whose " D " Class flotilla had not yet been equipped with torpedoes, made a

---

[1] Lt. A. R. H. Nye, D.S.C., R.N.V.R., was Commanding Officer of M.G.B. 312.

[2] Four-fifths of a mile.

[3] Known throughout Coastal Forces as " Spud " Lyle, he had been Senior Officer of a " D " Class M.G.B. flotilla at Newhaven at the time that I was based there with the S.G.B. flotilla.

whisker-singeing attack on a convoy within a mile or two of the harbour at Dieppe at the end of March.

In April Lt. Cdr. Donald Bradford, who had brought his flotilla round from the east coast, lost one of his boats when it was run down by three " Möwe " Class torpedo boats which had come out from Cherbourg. Five or six of these vessels had been working from bases in Normandy for some time, probably helping to lay anti-invasion minefields, and it had been noticed, whenever our forces came into contact with them, that they had much more of the offensive spirit than any other German ships.

One night in May, however, we were able to hit back at them when a party of five torpedo boats together with three or four " M " Class minesweepers moved from Cherbourg to Le Havre. It was a disastrous passage for them, for on the way one was sunk by aircraft, one—an " M " Class—was sunk by M.T.Bs. under Arnold Forster, two were induced by Shaw to fire at, and hit, each other, and one hit a mine. It was the remainder, based at Le Havre, which were to figure prominently in the early days of the invasion.

As D day drew near the maintenance organisation was in full swing at our bases, particularly in Portsmouth harbour, where H.M.S. *Hornet*, the Coastal Forces base, had overflowed into H.M.S. *Dolphin*, the submarine base, and H.M.S. *Vernon*, the torpedo establishment. This table shows the admirable work which these base staffs did, together with those at H.M.S. *Attack* at Portland and H.M.S. *Aggressive* at Newhaven, to get every possible boat ready for the great day.

Date						Total No. of M.T.Bs.	No. Available for Operations	Per cent. Availability
1st May	..	..	..	..	..	47	26	55
8th May	..	..	..	..	..	48	31	64
15th May	..	..	..	..	..	64	39	61
22nd May	..	..	..	..	..	67	45	67
29th May	..	..	..	..	..	73	55	75
5th June	..	..	..	..	..	76	74	97

The figures for M.Ls. were almost equally impressive, and on D minus one day only eight M.Ls. were defective in the Channel ports out of a total of more than a hundred and forty.

D DAY

On the night of D–1/D day, the 5th/6th June, 1944, the Coastal Forces were out in full strength in spite of the strong wind and heavy sea. The spearhead of the assault convoys and the minesweepers which preceded them were escorted by M.T.Bs., M.Ls. and H.D.M.Ls., some of them acting as navigational leaders, others as smoke layers; the patrol units were in position on either flank. The diversionary forces sailed on their dangerous mission of attracting attention to themselves and distracting it from the real assault, and in addition the last of the protective minefields had to be laid off Cap d'Antifer to the north of Le Havre.

" The weather was bad," writes Lt. Shaw, who was to carry out this last task, " too bad for us, in fact, but the operation had been put off once, and was not likely to be postponed again, although the oft-perused weather reports showed little improvement, and so, as the long-awaited time drew near, the crews prepared for a dirty trip.

" It was indeed a great moment when, having left the base and its waving inhabitants and having received the farewell message from the Captain, Coastal Forces, the unit slipped through the inner boom and saw the vast armada under way. The crews stood and stared as we threaded our way through line after line of landing craft which stretched as far as the eye could see, and it did not need General Eisenhower's personal message, which was given to them on leaving harbour, to tell them that they were part of the greatest military undertaking in history.

"When we reached the open sea, it was obvious that this operation was going to be one of the most uncomfortable that we had experienced, as the boats, made heavy and sluggish by the mines, were soon shipping quantities of water, and the enthusiasm of the crews in watching the ships which stretched from horizon to horizon soon waned as one by one they were overcome by sea-sickness. When the time came to decide whether we should turn back or go on, knowing that if we decided to go on we were not allowed to turn back, come what might, it was somehow amusing to think that by all the rules we should go back and yet know perfectly well that we were going on."

The risk that was run by the Allied Commanders, however, in launching this great invasion in such doubtful weather was more than outweighed by the increased chances of achieving surprise. As it turned out, these chances were fully realised. The enemy was, in fact, surprised. The minesweepers swept channels leading into the Seine Bay, and the long streams of landing craft followed, to arrive next morning off their respective beaches. The enemy had offered no serious opposition to our assault until the landings began, and then the opposition was only by his land forces.

Visibility was not very good on the morning of D day, and when the Germans became aware that the invasion had begun a force of the "Möwe" Class torpedo boats in Le Havre put to sea. But our forces were strong, and although the "Möwes" carried out one torpedo attack, they saw warships so much larger than themselves that it was not long before they retired again into the harbour. One of their torpedoes had hit the Norwegian destroyer H.M.N.S. *Svenner*, which subsequently sank; but their brief sortie did not affect the progress of the landings in the very smallest degree. It was learned later that the E boats in Cherbourg also put to sea, but they too achieved nothing. Indeed, they were not even in action against our ships.

So the first naval objective, the safe arrival of the spearheads at the appointed time, had been achieved. This time there was no such interference as that which so deeply affected the landing at Dieppe nearly two years before. But once the whereabouts of the supply channels of "the spout" became known to the enemy, it was to be expected that some counter-attack would develop; German reinforcements would surely soon arrive, and the advantages of the initial surprise would fade. In the weeks which followed, these counter-attacks did develop, and fell into a regular pattern based upon the two ports so closely adjacent to our bridgehead—Le Havre to the east and Cherbourg to the west.

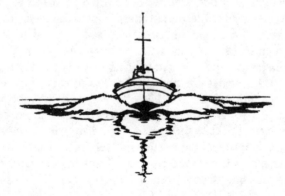

THE FIELD OF BATTLE

The Seine Bay was divided by a north and south line of Command limit, to the west of which was the American area under Admiral Alan G. Kirk, U.S.N., and to the east the British area under Admiral Vian. North of these assault areas, the flanks of the spout were defended by the Home Commands—on the east side the Admiral Commanding, Dover (Admiral Sir H. D. Pridham Wippell, K.C.B., C.V.O.), and on the west side the Commander-in-Chief, Portsmouth. The areas bounded by these imaginary lines became, as it were, separate stages, on each of which the fighting developed in its own characteristic pattern. Thus, for example, the waters north-east of Cherbourg, near Pointe de Barfleur, became the scene of fierce fighting between the E boats working from Cherbourg and the M.T.Bs., supported by frigates and destroyers, working on the west flank of " the spout." This began on the night after the landings, and went on for many nights in spite of the continuous strong winds and rough seas. On the night of 7th/8th June, for example, our M.T.Bs. made contact with the E boats no less than seven times, supported by the frigates H.M.S. *Stayner* (Lt. Cdr. H. J. Hall, D.S.O., D.S.C., R.N.R.) and H.M.S. *Retalick* (Lt. J. S. Brownrigg, R.N.). An M.T.B. unit under the command of Lt. Neil Watson, R.A.N.V.R., was almost continuously in pursuit or in action during the whole night, and engaged a number of E boats with good effect. Battles on this scale continued night after night in spite of the attacks on the frigates by German torpedo bombers and the perpetual activity of the shore batteries. On the 10th/11th, Lt. R. T. Sykes, with a unit of the 35th M.T.B. Flotilla, discovered a party of E boats lying stopped. He plunged with great determination into their midst and passed through the enemy's line, dealing destruction all round him at a range of only a few yards, and dropping a depth charge which must have shaken up one of the E boats, if it did nothing worse. In the course of it, a burst of 20-mm. fire hit his boat at the water-line, perforating, as it were, the edge of the ship's bottom. As he increased speed the bottom tore out and the boat began to sink. There was only one fatal casualty—a Press Correspondent travelling on Sykes' bridge as a passenger. The remainder of the crew were rescued and put on board *Stayner*. Nearly an hour later a unit under Lt. Cdr. D. H. E. McCowen, D.S.O., R.N.V.R., attacked the same E boats which had been lying stopped since their engagement with Sykes. They made off into Cherbourg, and McCowen went off to intercept a different enemy group. He managed to cut off the last of five E boats which were being engaged by *Stayner*; he set it on fire and eventually destroyed it, rescuing six survivors.

The co-operation of the frigates and M.T.Bs. was assisted by experienced Coastal Forces officers, who went nightly to sea in the frigates. Notable amongst these at this time were Lt. P. G. Lee, D.S.C. and bar, R.N.V.R., who had played a large part in the pre-D day training, and Lt. H. A. J. Hollings, D.S.C., R.N. Lt. R. G. O. Hudson, R.N.V.R., was doing the same work in the Dover Command.

The E boats did not suffer only at the hands of the M.T.Bs. and frigates and destroyers. One night off Pointe de Barfleur those on the bridge of *Retalick* saw a big explosion as a party of E boats passed through the area of the minefield which Lt. Cdr. Wilkie had laid before D day. Next day survivors were rescued in the American area—whither the tide had swept them—and they reported that not one but two E boats had been destroyed by mines that night.

So effective was the defence on the western flank that the enemy seldom managed to break through into the American area. In the east activity was centred near Le Havre itself, which lay within the British Assault Area. The enemy torpedo boats were there, based almost within sight of our anchorage off the beaches. It was a more difficult problem here than in the west. Admiral Vian's flagship was the cruiser H.M.S. *Scylla* (Captain T. M. Brownrigg,

C.B.E., D.S.O., R.N.), and his staff officer, who co-ordinated the M.T.B. operations, was Lt. P. N. Edge, D.S.C., R.N.V.R. The 55th Flotilla under Lt. Cdr. D. G. Bradford, D.S.C., R.N.R., and the Canadian 29th Flotilla under Lt. Cdr. A. Law, D.S.C., R.C.N.V.R., were the two which bore the brunt of the early fighting in this ferocious corner.

Bradford has vividly described his first meeting with the enemy on the flank of the invasion, which came on the night after the landing:

" I had a unit of four boats," he writes, " and we had been assigned a patrol on the east flank of the landing about 10 miles due west of Le Havre and just on the edge of a mined area. Tony Law, with the Canadian unit, was lying about 3 miles to the north of us.

" About midnight six craft approached us from the east at fairly slow speed—obviously enemy. We got under way and steamed to the north for half a mile to wait on their line of advance, and I warned Tony that things were beginning to happen. They were five R boats and a T.L.C. obviously out on a mine-laying sortie. The visibility was moderate—a damn dark night, but no mist. I led towards them and formed into quarter line for a gun battle. They must have seen us practically as soon as I fired rockets to illuminate them. We opened fire at about 500 yards' range, closing rapidly, and the return fire was pretty close and hot, though a bit straggly, as if their hearts weren't in it and their Senior Officer couldn't make up his mind what to do. I don't blame him. There they were—caught with six or eight mines in each boat—some five tons of highly temperamental explosive set on deck, where it wouldn't do the least good if it was hit. They scattered as we charged in, altering round to the east and going up to full speed. The T.L.C. altered to the south to make for their occupied coastline and I let him go, wishing to concentrate on the R boats, which were the more important.

" Our guns were hitting them, and we could see the flashes as the Oerlikon shells tore in. One R boat got a direct hit with a 6-pounder shell and started to fall back crippled. They commenced making smoke to try to cover themselves, but we were on their windward quarter and it only served to silhouette them. They were jettisoning their mines as fast as possible— we could see the splashes as they went over the stern.

" In the excitement I had forgotten the minefield—but not so my navigator. He suddenly howled up the voice-pipe, ' Sir, we are a mile inside.' However, the R boats were there too, so there couldn't be more danger for us than for them. They stopped making smoke when it was obvious that it only helped our shooting—but two of them were smoking involuntarily —showing flame and noticeably slowing down. I thought we had them cold and was quite chirpy—the first scrap with our German counterparts in the assault area, and we were caning them in no mean manner. Suddenly there were a couple of tremendous explosions in the water quite close to my boats—mines. Life was starting to be difficult. I could slow down and lose the R boats, or go on and risk it, taking a chance with all my boats. More mines started to go up, some around the R boats, and then suddenly the last R boat in their line exploded in a vast sheet of flame—either we had detonated a mine on board by gunfire or it had hit a submerged mine. That decided it. I altered course hard over to starboard and reduced speed, content with our victory and thinking in terms of ' We'll play again another day.' We picked our way out, slowly and daintily, everyone talking in whispers and walking around on tiptoe. Even so, we detonated mine after mine, some quite close, others farther away being apparently countermined by the near ones. We got out, shaken up a little, but still whole, having set off twenty-three mines. Our Gods were certainly with us that night!

" The following night we were out again. As we went to the same patrol position we came upon an unknown vessel and steamed up to investigate: I illuminated, and we were surprised to see one of our own landing craft peacefully at anchor with some ratings standing on deck waving their arms. We closed them and took off the ratings, who were under the command of a Petty Officer. Their story was simple: they had been coming across on D day with others, when their engines broke down, and they had drifted until seeing land, when they thought it better to anchor. As we were preparing to take them in tow we received a signal telling us of a sortie of enemy craft to the northward. We set off at top speed to intercept and were then informed that the enemy were probably destroyers. Now this was different meat to the episode of the previous night; we had a score to settle with the German destroyer men. The loss of Larry Toogood[1] and practically all his officers and men off Cherbourg about six weeks previously was still fresh in our minds.

" We formed up for torpedo attack and reduced speed to try our beloved tactics of sneaking in. We picked them up—three of them—and closed on a good bearing to attack. We were nearly within range when we suddenly picked up the outline of another ship to the north of us. We were steaming in between two units—we could see the destroyers to the south by this time, an ' Elbing ' Class leading two ' Möwes.' They were moving slowly up towards the north-west, apparently closing the ship which was to the north of us: I couldn't understand the set-up at all. Suddenly the chap to the north opened fire with starshell and illuminated the destroyers; without more ado they illuminated him and opened fire in return. It came in a flash; the chap to the north was one of the corvette escorts to an Allied convoy, and he was attempting to take on three destroyers at once.

" It was obvious for the moment that both sides didn't know we were there—our chance. We went in, and then the Germans saw us: they swung to the southward, altering course away from the corvette and firing torpedoes at him as they turned. We fired and away went six torpedoes, a tricky shot as the destroyers were turning away and were firing at us. For a moment I thought we had been beaten, but suddenly a plume of smoke and spray went up just behind the bridge of one of the ' Möwes.' We had hit. The ' Elbing ' started to turn back towards us, and got hit on his forward gun turret and bridge by a burst of gunfire from the boats. But we had shot our bolt—it was time to disengage. Both the remaining destroyers could run circles round us with their superior speed, so I turned away, up towards the corvette. The German boats went back towards their crippled comrade, and we saw no more of them. I believe they did manage to tow the cripple back.

" When I got within hailing distance of the corvette I received bitter complaints for having fired torpedoes at him; but when I explained that ours had gone the other way and the ones he saw going past his bow and stern were fired by the destroyers, the Commanding Officer calmed down a bit. He was a very belligerent officer."

One of the most serious problems which faced our night patrols at this time was recognition. There were great crowds of landing craft and other ships in the area, and amongst them there were bound to be errors in navigation. But any ship found outside the anchorage at night was in grave danger of being attacked by its own side, for, with the enemy harbour so close, our patrols had to be " quick on the draw." A number of our ships did stray from their proper positions, so that there was sometimes doubt of the identity of ships which the patrols were ordered to investigate. A great opportunity was lost in this way on the night of D plus three. The six " D " boats which formed the second division of the 55th M.T.B. Flotilla were on patrol under the command of Lt. W. S. Strang, R.N.V.R. (known in Coastal Forces as " Biscuits " Strang). They were investigating what was believed to be a stopped E boat some distance to the eastward of the area. " Just as I was on the point of giving the order to open fire," writes Strang, " he switched on his navigation lights, and I saw he was

[1] Lt. L. E. Toogood, R.N.V.R., Commanding Officer of M.T.B. 671, whose boat was sunk in the early hours of 25th April, 1944.

a 'B' Class M.L. The *Scylla* still could not believe it, and Pat Edge kept saying over the R/T 'Sink him, sink him,' until I told him that the target was M.L. 243, that we were speaking to him, and that I recognised the C.O. (Even afterwards when I met the C.O. ashore he could not believe how near destruction he had been by cheerfully anchoring outside the anchorage.) No sooner were we finished with him than off we were sent to investigate some L.C.Ts., which turned out to be our own again, anchored out of position. They gave us rather a warmer reception by firing (over us, fortunately) till we closed them and identified ourselves.

"After this we went northwards to intercept a group of three destroyers which had been reported, and I was told to carry out an attack if possible. Almost immediately three destroyers were sighted and we estimated that they were either stopped or proceeding at very slow speed. At this moment *Scylla* came up again and told me to 'Negative attack' as our own duty division of destroyers was about. So I proceeded at 12 knots round the stern of the destroyers, which were lying practically stopped, in line ahead at a range of 600 yards. They certainly did not look like any of our own, so I asked *Scylla* to confirm they were the duty division, and Bill Beynon[1] came up on R/T and said, 'None of ours has a raked bow like that first one.' Before *Scylla* could reply the destroyers opened fire over our heads, as a form of recognition I should think. By then my suspicions were aroused, and I turned towards them again. *Scylla* had at last raised the duty division on R/T, who confirmed that they were not at that minute firing, and so we were ordered once more to attack. By that time, the element of surprise had been completely lost, and the enemy came at us firing with everything that would bear. We had to disengage to the westward under smoke, and after a short fierce chase, during which we dropped depth charges, they gave up. We were lucky to escape with only two wounded and a few holes.

"Thus through bad ship recognition on my part, and the confusion caused by friendly ships getting out of position, one of the finest sitting targets ever presented to a unit of Coastal Forces was allowed to escape unscathed. It was agreed afterwards that the targets had been one 'Elbing' Class destroyer and two 'Möwe' Class torpedo boats."

Nevertheless, the Coastal Forces were playing a vital part in the defence of the eastern flank. That this was realised at once by the Naval Commander was shown when Admiral Vian made the following signal:

"The Coastal Forces operating in the Eastern Task Force Area are doing fine work. M.T.Bs. have intercepted each night. It is largely due to them that the Assault Area has been enjoying immunity from surface attack. The M.Ls. have performed an essential if less spectacular task. The 55th M.T.B. Flotilla, under Lt. Cdr. Bradford, have particularly distinguished themselves."

THE AIR-RAID

The enemy destroyers and E boats menaced the eastern flank of our landing so closely, however, that on the night of D plus eight, which was the 14th June, Air Chief Marshal Sir Arthur Harris agreed to devote a heavy bomber raid to the harbour at Le Havre; 2,000 tons of bombs rained down on to the port, and at one sweep the whole balance of the naval war in that area was changed. All the torpedo boats were sunk or damaged beyond repair and thirteen E boats were destroyed. The bomb-proof shelters, in which they would normally have been housed, were occupied at the time by the much less valuable R boats, of which, therefore, a good number survived the raid. The "Elbing" Class destroyer also survived, but was considered unlikely to be in a condition to cause us any anxiety. It was learned much later that the E boat commanders had all been at a party on board one of the torpedo boats

---

[1] Lt. W. Beynon, R.N.V.R., Commanding Officer of M.T.B. 682.

RANGE 60 YARDS—S.G.Bs. AGAINST TRAWLERS OFF CAP D'ANTIFER,
27TH SEPTEMBER, 1943

DISENGAGING UNDER COVER OF SMOKE

when the raid began. It was a party in celebration of the award, that morning, of the Oak Leaves to Korvettenkapitän Götz von Mirbach, the leader of the 9th Flotilla,[1] and the Ritter-kreuz to Korvettenkapitän Johannsen, who had taken over the 5th Flotilla from Klug soon after D day. He claimed to have sunk a cruiser in the American area (this may have been the U.S. Destroyer *Nelson*, which was torpedoed by an E boat, as no cruiser was ever attacked there), and it was for this exploit that his decoration had been awarded. When a bomb fell on the torpedo boat and sank it, there were only two casualties amongst the E boat officers at the party, Johannsen was killed and von Mirbach was wounded in the neck and knee.

E boat reinforcements were not long in arriving at Le Havre from the eastward after the raid, but they were never able to regain the initiative, although they hardly ever missed a night at sea in these early days. Occasionally they broke through our defence lines and into " the spout," but here they had still to face the convoy's escorts, although often enough they were not very strong. On one occasion, for example, M.L. 903 (Lt. J. C. Lewis, R.N.V.R.) put up a gallant and spirited defence against a group of E boats which succeeded in attacking a convoy of fourteen " Landing Craft Tank " and three " Landing Craft Infantry," of which M.L. 903 was the sole escort. One L.C.T. was sunk, one L.C.I. had to be abandoned and later sunk, and one other L.C.T. was hit by a torpedo, but remained seaworthy. " By his action," comments the Commander-in-Chief, Portsmouth, in his report to the Admiralty, " Lt. Lewis undoubtedly prevented greater losses being suffered."

When the invasion had been in progress for a week most of the E boats had left Cherbourg and gone to Le Havre, to be caught, on arrival, by the air-raid. The German attempt to reinforce the attack on the west flank with destroyers brought up from Brest had failed disastrously when a force of them was intercepted by our " Tribal " Class destroyers off the north coast of Brittany. One of their number was sunk, another driven ashore and the remainder fled back to Brest.

Meanwhile the American armies under General Omar Bradley were closing in on Cherbourg from the south, and the fall of the port was imminent.

Our M.T.Bs. were waiting for the final evacuation convoy to leave the harbour, which the Germans had heavily mined before their departure. This convoy consisted of a hetero-geneous collection of small coasters, tugs and Type III T.L.Cs. Outside the breakwater two units of Lt. Shaw's 14th Flotilla were lying in wait. Lt. G. H. Baker, R.N.V.R., with three boats of the second division (the other two commanded by Sub-Lt. N. G. Oldfield, R.N.V.R., and Sub-Lt. J. McC. Morrish, R.N.V.R.), caught the convoy as it was forming up, immedi-ately outside the breakwater, and scored three certain and one possible hit with torpedoes. The targets were two small coasters, a trawler and a large tug. Scarcely had the remainder of the convoy extricated itself from the resulting confusion when Shaw himself attacked with the first division. His three boats (the Commanding Officers were Lt. D. Rigg, D.S.C., R.N.V.R., Lt. P. Aspinall, R.N.V.R., and Lt. A. W. B. Hawkes, R.N.V.R.) had been lurking in the smoke which was blowing to seaward from the fires in the town. Two more torpedo hits were scored for certain, possibly a third, and one ship was seen to sink.

How much of the convoy remained after these attacks it was difficult to ascertain; only one ship—a small coaster—stood on to the westward, though it is possible that others crept in close under the shore to derive what benefit they could from the coastal batteries, which were as active as ever. Three " D " Class M.T.Bs. under Lt. Cdr. McCowen found what was

[1] Not until after VE day was it learned that von Mirbach claimed to have torpedoed the British battle-ship H.M.S. *Nelson*. While returning from the Assault Area *Nelson* was damaged by what was believed at the time to have been a mine. When all reports and details have been correlated von Mirbach's claim may be substantiated.

apparently the sole survivor. Under continuous shelling from the shore they manœuvred to attack with torpedoes, but the coaster, aware of its danger, was looping and zig-zagging about, so that eventually McCowen decided to destroy it by gunfire. This was expeditiously achieved, and fourteen minutes after he had opened fire the vessel sank.

CHAPTER XVI

ONE FLANK SECURE

WITH the fall of Cherbourg the threat of attack by surface craft on the west flank of the spout disappeared. The remaining E boats made their escape by running the gauntlet to the eastward, and the enemy destroyers were contained in the French Atlantic ports, whence they dared not emerge to risk another meeting with our destroyers or our aircraft. There were, however, still U boats coming up the Channel, some of them fitted with the new Schnorkel device, the tube through which the Diesel engines could be run to recharge the batteries while the submarine remained submerged. With the E boats gone, only the anti-submarine patrols had occasion to remain in the western Channel, and it was now possible to dispose them entirely against U boats and without thought of attack by surface ships.

For the most part the Coastal Forces were not concerned with U-boat hunting, and the M.T.Bs. were moved at once to reinforce the eastern flank off Le Havre. There was one flotilla of " D " boats, however, under the command of Lt. Cdr. J. A. C. Findlay, R.N.V.R., which had been specially equipped for anti-submarine work and which spent the latter half of the summer in the Channel working mainly from H.M.S. *Attack* at Portland.

One other task remained for the Coastal Forces at Cherbourg: it was the sweeping of the mines which filled the harbour by M.Ls. of the 5th M.L. Flotilla under the command of Lt. A. B. McArthur, R.N.V.R., a hazardous though unspectacular job which they performed most excellently well.

When the Continental bridgehead had been firmly established in Normandy, Admiral Vian, according to plan, turned over the command of the British Assault Area to a new Flag Officer, Rear-Admiral J. W. Rivett-Carnac, C.B.E., D.S.C., with headquarters ashore at the village of Courseulles not far from Caen, and soon afterwards I found myself working at these headquarters as Staff Officer, Coastal Forces, providing the liaison with the boats on the one hand and with the Captain, Coastal Forces at Portsmouth, on the other.

A small 'plot' was set up in a dug-out in the orchard of a modern château, where we worked nightly in our shirtsleeves (for we were crowded and the dug-out was hot and ill ventilated), while the A.A. barrage against German minelaying aircraft clattered overhead.

With the west flank cleared of the enemy, the defence of the east flank against surface craft was organised in three ways. First and foremost there was a close blockade of Le Havre ; but in case this could not entirely contain the enemy, defensive patrols had also to be maintained round the anchorage off the beaches. Both these two functions were undertaken by forces working under F.O.B.A.A. (the Flag Officer, British Assault Area) for which we, in our dug-out, were responsible. In addition, a defence line was manned to protect " the spout " from E boats which might come down the Channel from Boulogne or Dieppe, or might break out of Le Havre in a northerly direction before turning west. This function, which had been the responsibility of the Dover Command in the early days of the operation, was now undertaken by forces under the Commander-in-Chief, Portsmouth, which had been released by the fall of Cherbourg.

Amongst the flotillas working for the blockade of Le Havre were still the original two—Bradford's 55th (" D " boats) and Law's 29th (the Canadian-manned " seventy-one-foot-six Power Boats "). They were carrying the fight right on to the enemy's doorstep in the old Coastal Forces tradition.

" The first night we tried the close blockade," writes Bradford, " I was out with a unit of only two of my boats. My own boat was in England for repair, so I used M.T.B. 632, Charles Ford's boat, as my flagship, and 650 (Jimmy Fulton) was the other. I had been given the much coveted position closest to the harbour as my patrol, and approached it from Cap d'Antifer, sneaking down close inshore, hoping to meet the E boats coming out. About half-way down we received a message that a bunch of E boats were coming towards us. We prepared for a scrap. The E boats were coming up inshore of us, so I slowed down and altered in towards them in line abreast. They were moving slowly, about 10 knots, and it suddenly struck me that we were in perfect position for a torpedo attack, though a risky thing to try. They were small targets—very small for that form of attack, and their Lordships view with horror the complete waste of such expensive ammunition as torpedoes. But I had always longed to give E boats a touch of their own medicine—the torpedo. So I told Charles to stand by. I felt that luck was with us. When we were 1,000 yards away I ordered " Illuminate," and up went the rockets from both boats. There they were, nine of them. The first five in line were big R boats followed by four E boats. Evidently Jerry had decided that his E boats needed escorting. They were the perfect torpedo target, in very close order, so close that they appeared as one unbroken line of boats to us. I tapped Charles on the shoulder and away went the torpedoes, and then we opened fire, closing in on their beam. The Hun was prepared, all his guns opened up as one, and the fight was on. It was fierce and obviously couldn't last long. We concentrated on the E boats with our guns, and the last one in the line got a succession of bad hits—one of them a 6-pounder shell which seemed to tear off part of the deck amidships. I had almost forgotten about the torpedoes, and we were roaring in when all at once the third R boat disappeared in a terrific sheet of flame and smoke and a couple of seconds later the fourth boat exploded in the same manner. We had done it—two R boats with two torpedoes. The idea had paid the maximum dividend.

" By this time another E boat had been slightly hit and we were beginning to feel the weight of the odds. We disengaged, making smoke and pulled out to the west—roaring out to the world on W/T that we had sunk two R boats by torpedo and damaged two E boats by gunfire. The remaining E and R boats returned to Le Havre and we were ordered back on to our patrol position.

" We hadn't been sitting there long when we picked up two minesweepers leaving harbour. They were either ' M ' Class or large trawlers. From our plot of them it seemed that they were sweeping the inshore channel up to Cap d'Antifer, so we moved off to attack. The visibility had reduced to about 800 yards. We had a fair chance of sneaking up on them. Jimmy Fulton still had torpedoes, so I told him to sneak in on the seaward bow while we came in on the quarter—the idea being that we would rush in and open up with guns, thus attracting their full attention, leaving, as I hoped, the chance for Jimmy to get in an unobserved attack with torpedoes.

" In we went, and as we moved in we saw and felt a large explosion astern of the sweepers —they had swept a mine. As soon as we got inside visibility range we illuminated and opened up, scoring two hits with our 6-pounder with the first two shells. Back came the reply thick and fast, they were ' M ' Class all right. We stuck it out, hoping to see one of them go up in a cloud of smoke and flame from Jimmy's torpedoes, but it wasn't to be; *they* weren't to be caught napping. As soon as Jimmy poked his nose in sight, he caught it just as we were doing. He made a quick short attack and fired his torpedoes, but missed. Then we both settled down to a gun action. The gunners were giving of their best that night. We went in for a last run and found them both stopped and in a pretty bad way, but still with plenty of fight. As we went in 632 got a hit in the forward petrol compartment from a 40-mm. shell—trouble in no small way. We turned round to the west to make a dash out of range of the shore batteries, who were then starting to be fairly accurate. Jimmy was also in a bad way, having been fairly severely damaged, and he disengaged with us.

"It seemed as if 632 was on her last legs. The bridge and engine-room were smothered in clouds of black smoke, and we could see flames down in the forward petrol compartment and forward end of the engine-room. The motor mechanic was performing miracles of engineering and fire fighting, nursing along the engines, two of which were damaged, and at the same time directing the attempts to quell the fire in the engine-room. We steered west at the best speed possible until it seemed that she was on the point of blowing up, and then cleared the engine-room, having stopped the engines, and pulled the petrol-compartment fire-extinguisher plug. The fire went out and the smoke dispersed. We were safe enough, and after inspection of the damage we got going and struggled slowly back to the anchorage. M.T.B. 632 was a shambles and had to be sailed back to pay off—a severe loss to the flotilla.

"The next night but one I was out again, but in strength this time. I had four boats on patrol, R. R. Smith (M.T.B. 629), Stewart Marshall (624) and John Whitby (621), while I led in my own boat (617). We repeated our patrol—down the coast from Cap d'Antifer to Le Havre. Just north of Cape de La Hève we received a report of ships leaving harbour, and prepared for an attack as soon as they got round the corner. We turned in towards the coast in line abreast ready for either torpedo or gun attack, and soon picked up the enemy patrol moving slowly along the coast. We closed at slow speed, hoping for some measure of surprise, but when we got to within approximately 1,000 yards range I heard the single bang of starshell going up and knew we were detected. I ordered all the boats to illuminate and stand by with 6-pounder guns, and away went the rockets. When they burst we could see a long line of ships, two larger ones leading—either 'Northern' Class trawlers or corvettes followed by five or six big R boats tailed by another trawler or 'M' Class.

"I gave the order to open fire at the second in line and real salvos of 6-pounder shells flew on their way. The results were completely unexpected and far beyond our wildest dreams. The target received four shells as one. I watched them curve over leisurely and hit— there was a magnificent gout of flame and smoke and the corvette blew up, debris flew high into the air, and she was left with no upperworks and completely smothered in flame from stem to stern. I shifted the boats on to the next target, the leading R boat, and within a few seconds the same thing happened—she exploded in a vivid sheet of flame—cocked her stern in the air and sank before our eyes. This was the thing our gunners had been dreaming about. We swung into line ahead and raced down the line of enemy ships at about 500 yards' range, pelting them with all guns. We were starting to get hit but not seriously, though the shore batteries were beginning to bother us.

"The Hun seemed completely shattered by the spectacle of two of his ships exploding within a few seconds. We rather suspected that they had loads of mines aboard—nothing else could explain the fury of the explosions. The battle started to reach a crescendo as their gunners got our range and the shore batteries added their full weight. We were outgunned; 8-inch shells from the shore batteries were falling all round us. We had one last quick run in and saw that two more of the R boats were smoking and damaged, and then I led off—it was time to go. As we disengaged, making smoke and zig-zagging, Stewart and 'Stinker' Smith received bad near misses and then Stewart had real bad luck. An 8-inch shell from the shore batteries plunged underneath the stern and exploded under his boat. I believe she took off and flew for a few yards. Certainly when the noise and smoke had subsided the boat was a veritable wreck. Everything in her was shaken loose; engines, petrol tanks, all the fittings had broken loose from their mountings. Stewart didn't seem dismayed. The usual calm voice over the R/T reported a near miss and on he struggled and, what is more, made it. We all got back, bits missing here and there, but in the best of heart. We were making our mark at last, forcibly and frequently."

Bradford and Law had been strongly reinforced in the assault area. Shaw's 14th Flotilla had been switched to the eastern flank after its triumphs off Cherbourg. Lyle's 51st—the "D" boats without torpedoes—and two flotillas of "C" Class M.G.Bs. under Lt. Cdr. J. H. Coste, D.S.C., R.N.V.R., and Lt. Cdr. D. M. Probert, R.N.V.R., also arrived. Later three more flotillas joined the fray under Lt. P. Magnus, D.S.C., R.N.V.R., Lt. Cdr. G. C. Fanner, R.N.V.R. (who had up till then, with the S.G.B. flotilla, been attached to the American "Western Task Force") and Lt. Cdr. D. Wilkie, R.N.V.R.

This was not quite such a great force of boats as it might appear, for already the pace had begun to tell and the wonderful figures for availability which had been achieved for D day were beginning to fall off rather rapidly. That they did not fall off much more rapidly was the result of the establishment at Arromanches, within the great artificial port or "Mulberry," of a Mobile Repair Base called C.F.M.U. 1 (Coastal Forces Mobile Unit) under the command of Cdr. M. A. Brind, R.N. (previously the Commanding Officer of H.M.S. *Midge*—the base at Great Yarmouth). When C.F.M.U. 1 began to operate in late July most of these flotillas could be maintained by it from day to day, and it was only for major repairs that they had to return to England (or, as it was always called in official abbreviation, the U.K.). The maintenance staff of this base lived under canvas in a field at the back of the village of Arromanches, with a signal station on top of the cliff overlooking what was to me the eighth wonder of the world—the huge man-made harbour set up in a few weeks upon the sandy beach of the Seine Bay. Even with the C.F.M.U., breakdowns amongst the M.T.Bs. became more and more numerous as week after week went by of the hardest running that the Coastal Forces in the Channel had ever had. The crews were willing to take their boats on patrol if 60 per cent. of their full speed was available, and provided that the main engines could produce this they went out no matter what other gear in the boat was defective. The engine-room crews of the boats themselves, as well as the maintenance staff of the Mobile Unit ashore, worked unceasingly to keep their engines running, and often enough they had no more than a few hours' sleep for days on end. In a huge operation of this kind it is important to realise the sheer technical skill which plays so large a part. The repair of some tiny piece of mechanism in these engines meant the difference of one M.T.B. more or less on the night patrol, and that very possibly meant the saving of ships and convoys carrying thousands of tons of supplies to the armies ashore. It was, perhaps literally, an example of the tiny cog which enabled the great machine to keep turning.

"THE NIGHT TRAIN"

To describe in detail the nightly battles fought in this corner of the Channel would double the length of this book. The trend of the fighting was that the E boats under Zymalkowsky, Obermaier and Opdenhoff, and later Müller, came out almost every night, and almost every night they were intercepted by the M.T.Bs., frigates and destroyers. Here again, experienced Coastal Forces officers went to sea each night in the larger vessels in order to improve the liaison and co-operation between them and the M.T.Bs.   Lt. H. A. J. Hollings, M.B.E., D.S.C. and bar, R.N., Lt. R. G. Fison, R.N.V.R., and, until he was killed, Lt. Cdr. G. E. Bailey, D.S.O., R.N.V.R. worked night after night throughout the fierce struggle off Le Havre.

Besides the E boats there were regular patrols of R boats supported by " M " Class mine-sweepers and trawlers, which steamed nightly northward for a few miles from Le Havre and back again, like the party which Bradford had so successfully tackled. This party was so regular that it became known as " the night train." Sometimes it seems that it laid mines, sometimes it swept out the channel for the E boats and for the final evacuation of German shipping, which even now their High Command must have realised was inevitable. Whatever " the night train's " duties, it was fair game for our boats, but it was a tough proposition, for it never forsook the protection of the shore batteries and all its ships were very well armed.

This did not deter our boats, and some extremely courageous and determined attacks were launched against it. Wilkie tackled it within less than a mile of the Le Havre entrance. The Canadian flotilla under Law, and his divisional leader Lt. C. A. Burk, had more than one exchange with it, but perhaps the most spectacular fight was the one in which Lt. F. P. Standley, R.N.V.R., led in a unit of the 30th Flotilla for a second attack through the smoke-screen he had made during his first attack. On the far side of the smoke he plunged in amongst a group of R boats, engaging them at 15 yards' range, an opportunity which he used to good advantage.

" The night train " was slower and less manœuvrable than our M.T.B. units, but by the very nature of the fighting it always outnumbered us, for in an offensive action there is a well-defined limit to the number of craft which can be handled together as one unit, while the defence is not so limited.

In addition to the E boats and " the night train," the enemy now sprang the first of his surprise weapons against the invasion anchorage. Suddenly one morning a number of curious dome-shaped objects made of Perspex were seen bobbing about in the defence lines off the mouth of the River Orne, and almost at the same time two of the defending ships were torpedoed. The M.Ls. which had for so long been helping to guard these lines—interspaced amongst a variety of other types of ships—now had their chance. They and the M.T.Bs. returning from the approaches to Le Havre set about mopping up the first of the human torpedoes. These consisted of two ordinary torpedoes mounted one above another, but instead of a warhead in the top one, there was a pilot sitting under a Perspex dome. He was able to aim and release the bottom torpedo and then set course for home, but his speed was so slow that, once seen, he had no chance of escape. It is extraordinary how little was achieved by these contraptions considering how small was the visible part of the dome and how many objects of various kinds were floating about amongst the hundreds of ships in the anchorage. Although they were launched on several occasions their success was always limited, and it may be that the small proportion which returned from the first attempt broke the spirit of their crews in much the same way that the almost inevitable interception had taken all the fight out of the Le Havre E boats.

Some weeks later the second German surprise weapon was launched, simultaneously with another human torpedo attack and an E boat sortie. This was the explosive motor boat, and it turned out to be even more of a fiasco than its predecessor. The principle was that three very small motor boats with a speed of about 25 knots made up each team. The centre one navigated and directed the party and the other two had large explosive charges in their bows. After aiming these two at the target each driver deposited himself in the sea on a little raft, later to be picked up by the directing boat, while the explosive boats were intended to run on and destroy themselves and the target they hit. This whole enterprise could not have failed more completely. The M.T.Bs., the " C " Class M.G.Bs. and the M.Ls. dashed hither and thither destroying the explosive boats one after another, without, of course, any return fire. Never had they had such admirable target practice. They even managed to take a number of them in tow. Exactly how many E.M.Bs. (explosive motor boats) set out on this first occasion is not known, but of those which made any attempt to attack no single one returned to tell the tale. Such an overwhelming defeat must again have had its effect upon those called upon to carry out the next E.M.B. attack. At any rate, amongst the great invasion armada off the beaches of Normandy not one Allied ship was even damaged by these craft, and our Coastal Forces could claim another notable victory, which, if easily won, was none the less important at that time.

With aircraft which laid mines at night the enemy had managed to make the assault area an unhealthy place, and one or two of our M.T.Bs. were unfortunate enough to put up these mines. In this way a few were destroyed and others damaged, though often the damage was not very serious, for an underwater explosion raises a small boat bodily where a larger vessel might break its back.

One boat on its way to the Mulberry detonated a mine so close ahead that it ran underneath the column of water as it came down. The First Lieutenant and the engine-room crew had some nasty moments when, convinced that the boat was sinking, they found the water pouring down on them so hard that they could not force their way up on deck to escape. A good deal of minor damage was done, but through the efforts of the C.F.M.U. the boat was ready for operations again next day.

The commonest type of damage to our M.T.Bs. was the bending and breaking of their high-revving propellers caused by pieces of floating debris with which the whole surface of the Seine Bay was strewn. Some idea of how serious this became is given by the fact that one flotilla of twelve 70-foot M.T.Bs. required 102 new propellers in two months. These could only be fitted by hauling the boats out of the water on to the slip, for which they had to return to the U.K. Lt. Shaw describes the spectacle of three boats of his flotilla lashed together and chugging slowly across the Channel on the only two usable propellers out of the nine which between them they possessed.

THE WESTERN AREA

During the early days of the invasion there had been few actions with enemy surface craft in the American area to the west. Two of our flotillas—the S.G.Bs. under Lt. Cdr. P. Baker, R.N., and Lt. Cdr. Fanner's " D " Class flotilla—had been attached to Admiral Kirk's Western Task Force to reinforce three and a half squadrons of U.S.P.T. boats. These " patrol torpedo boats " were the counterpart of our 70-foot M.T.Bs., and they were under the command of Lt. Cdr. John D. Bulkeley, U.S.N., whose exploits in the Philippine Islands at the time of the Japanese invasion won him the Congressional Medal of Honour and have been described in the book *They Were Expendable*. Although now they had had little fighting against E boats, and no other enemy ships ever penetrated into the Western Task Force Area, our Coastal Forces and the U.S. squadrons did not want for adventure. The business of maintaining themselves in that mine-infested anchorage in all weathers—including one of the worst summer gales in living memory—was full of variety and interest.

When the S.G.B. flotilla had originally been attached to Admiral Kirk's Western Task Force, Lt. Cdr. Baker realised that "the flotilla would be based on thin air for an indefinite period, and that maintenance, food, water and fuel would play at least as big a part in its life as enemy action." His estimate had indeed been right, as will be seen in the extracts from his report which follow.

The convoy which the S.G.Bs. had been escorting on D day arrived safely in the transport area, and the patrol that night was uneventful. It was in the late afternoon of the next day —the 7th—that an emergency call arrived ordering them and Fanner's flotilla to go to the assistance of a hospital ship which had been mined. "The weather had moderated and the sun was shining," writes Baker, "as off we went 'hell bent for election'—four S.G.Bs. and seven M.T.Bs.—a fine sight. . . . Not one, but three, hospital ships were sighted well away to the westward of their reported position—no doubt the reason for their being mined. Two of them, the *Dinard* and *St. Julien*, were damaged and down by the bow, but in no immediate danger of sinking. The 63rd M.T.B. Flotilla was detached to escort the undamaged one back to the swept channel and the S.G.Bs. stood by the others until tugs could be obtained . . .

"Another night of air-raids, bombs and mines. *Grey Seal* sighted our first glider bomb. The A.A. barrage from the anchorage was intense, but how effective is hard to say. . . . As a sight it was quite beautiful, a lovely clear sky lit up by blazing barrage balloons, falling planes, and everywhere criss-cross red with brilliant tracer.

"On returning from patrol on the morning of the 9th, ships were able to fuel from small American 'Y' tankers. This was a great improvement on the fuelling trawlers, as these tankers were modern ships with proper pumping arrangements. By this time all ships were getting short of provisions, so a search was made for the depot and provisions ships said to be provided for supplying craft based on the far shore. The first call was made on H.M.S. *Capetown*,[1] but this did not prove a success as she was acting as shuttle control ship and had her work cut out to compete with smaller craft and her American staff. We learned from her that the *Eleazer Wheelock*—a Liberty ship—anchored inshore would provide all our wants. We found her busily unloading motor transport and were told to try the *Bernard Carter*. This was a great success, and one week's supply of food and a certain amount of American comforts were obtained. Such things as fresh meat, bread and vegetables were not catered for, but the tinned food was magnificent and included such things as pineapple, peaches and real sausage."

Only on one night—10th/11th June—did the S.G.Bs. have the opportunity to engage enemy ships. For a few brief minutes *Grey Wolf* (Lt. C. Martin, R.N.V.R.) and *Grey Goose* (my old ship, now commanded by Lt. P. N. Hood, R.N.V.R.) fought two E boats and claimed hits on at least one of them. On the night before, *Grey Fox* had fired three rounds of high explosive at a Junkers 88 and immediately afterwards a plane had been seen to crash not far away, but no claim was made because so many other ships had been firing. In spite of these episodes, the accent remained upon the simpler problems of life.

"Between the 12th and 16th," continues Baker, "nothing out of the ordinary occurred to break the monotomy of patrols, bombing, mines and searches for food, except the flooding of *Grey Wolf's* W/T office and galley with oil fuel by an over-enthusiastic tanker, and a perfect illumination programme by enemy aircraft on the night of 14th/15th. Not only did they use chandelier flares but also ground markers which burnt for hours. . . . These ground markers

---

[1] The British cruiser.

were found to be flares burning inside a sort of biscuit-box affair floating on the water. Thereafter P.T. boats were specially detailed to sink them, and did a very good job the next two nights, getting them out within five minutes by firing at the boxes with tommy-guns from a range of 6 feet."

A routine had been organised for the S.G.Bs. to return to the U.K. for forty-eight hours one at a time in rotation.

" Everyone was settling down to our odd existence," Baker goes on, " and mails and fresh food were coming over from Portland regularly by the ships returning from their stand off. The first torpedo-bomber attack developed at dusk on the 18th. *Grey Wolf* and *Grey Goose* had reported to *Frankford*[1] that night for orders and were just leaving after coffee and doughnuts when her after 5-inch battery opened fire. It was a beautiful sight, but *Grey Goose*, who was on the engaged side, didn't appreciate it. She was lucky to get away with a few broken electric-light bulbs and one cup of cocoa ' lost overboard by accident.' The owner seemed slightly aggrieved when he found himself holding nothing more than the handle. . . .

" Up to date we had had no serious breakdowns apart from a few minor machinery defects. Now the weather decided to take a hand and really test us out. The sun had risen in an angry sky, and by ten o'clock on the 19th the wind was freshening from the N.N.E.—the worst possible direction—and the barometer was dropping fast. The day was spent secured alongside one of the ships of the Gooseberry[2] inside the Mulberry. This provided adequate shelter except at high water—it was just on spring tides. At high water, however, the waves were breaking right over the merchantman's hold and playing merry hell with our wires and fenders, but what was worse, our main inlets had an irresistible attraction for the junk now floating everywhere, and were continually choking."

Baker describes how by the evening it was blowing a gale, but in spite of that two of the S.G.Bs. went out on patrol. *Grey Wolf* was left behind immobilised by a choked inlet, which she was trying to clear in spite of the risk of flooding her engine-room, and *Grey Shark* was standing by her in case she required assistance.

" Nobody slept that night," he goes on. " The seas were short and steep, quite the worst any of us had ever met in the Channel. *Grey Goose* reported her bilge pump seized up—she was known to be holed forward where an L.C.T. had savaged her in a last expiring effort before it sank—we were all getting short of fuel as we struggled to keep station, and nasty visions of *Grey Wolf* with the water mounting steadily in her engine-room kept flashing through my mind. At dawn on the 20th we fought our way back into the Mulberry to see how the others had fared. Fuelling was still out of the question as it was blowing harder than ever, with a very nasty breaking sea. *Grey Wolf* had sustained hull damage aft while immobilised, but had partly cleared her main inlet. *Grey Goose*, with a patched extractor and a shaky bilge pump, was in little better shape. I decided to sail *Grey Shark* for England (she was due to go, anyway), and follow with the rest of the flotilla if the weather did not improve by 1600. The scene inside the Mulberry was one of unutterable chaos ; literally hundreds of landing craft from L.C.V. to L.S.T. were ashore piled one upon another. The Gooseberry was breaking up, and what little sea room remained was packed with wreckage; " Dukws "[3] and more and more landing craft, coasters and barges dragging steadily towards the beach. The weather showed no signs of moderating. It was time to quit. Could *Grey Goose* and *Grey Wolf* make it? *Grey Goose* reported she would be ready at 1950, *Grey Wolf* said ' No.' I hated

[1] A U.S. destroyer.

[2] The name used for the merchant ships which had been sunk to form the first shelter on the sites of the two artificial ports or Mulberries.

[3] Amphibious lorries.

leaving her, but it was better to lose one ship than three. I requested permission to proceed from *Frankford*—approved if we thought we could manage.

"*Grey Seal* and *Grey Goose* joined up astern of a homebound convoy at 2026 and made good 7 knots, arriving back at Portland at 0940 on 21st June, *Grey Goose* fighting her leaks with a bucket chain throughout the night. To our infinite relief *Grey Wolf* arrived in at 2227 the same night. She had tried to shift berth the night before to reduce pounding, but had lost suction after a particularly vicious roll and drifted on top of a collection of barges, making the damage to her stern worse. She got under way again and anchored under the lee of an L.S.T. The main inlet choked twice more during the night and she finally got under way for England at 1245. A very fine effort by the Chief Engine-room Artificer and engine-room staff, who worked for thirty-six hours non-stop, often in the dark and always soaking wet.

" So ended our first spell off the Normandy coast."

THE P.T. BOATS IN ACTION

When Cherbourg fell the American P.T. boats were left with little to do at a time when the continuous hard running on the eastern flank was steadily reducing the number of available British M.T.Bs. Lt. Cdr. Bulkeley was now commanding a destroyer and the P.T. squadrons were under Lt. Allen H. Harris, U.S.N.R. Harris and his officers and men leapt at the opportunity of action against German ships, which up till now they had almost entirely missed, and a number of P.T. boats were immediately attached to the forces operating on the eastern flank off Cap d'Antifer. Not all the P.Ts. were employed here, for as the American armies pushed westward into Brittany the Coastal Forces in the Plymouth command could be operated farther and farther west, even round the corner of Ushant and down the Atlantic coast. The Channel Islands, which had hitherto been occupying the attention of these Plymouth boats, now came within the sphere of the American Naval Commander at Cherbourg, Admiral John Wilkes, and when the British boats moved west the P.Ts. took their place.

This plan was developed early in August, and I was sent to Cherbourg as Liaison Officer to " indoctrinate " the P.T. boats (to use the American phrase) and to help to establish a head-quarters ' plot.' My place at F.O.B.A.As. headquarters at Courseulles was taken by Bradford when his flotilla was withdrawn to refit and re-form after its arduous service in the very fore-front of the battle.

No staff officer ever had a more satisfying brief than that which Captain Clarke—Admiral Wilkes' Chief of Staff—gave me soon after my arrival at Cherbourg. I was to work out the details for the operations in the Channel Islands, I was to brief the Commanding Officers of the ships employed, and then, said Captain Clarke, I was to " go out and do it." In the weeks which followed we operated almost nightly amongst the islands, trying to prevent the shipping from moving between one and another and to prevent contact between the islands and the German garrisons which were still holding out at St. Malo and the Isle de Cezembre. Just as the earliest M.T.B. operations in that area had involved co-operation between Coastal Forces and destroyers, so once again destroyers and destroyer escorts made up a part of our nightly force with the P.T. boats, and occasionally also with some of the M.T.Bs. from Dartmouth.

On one particular night, for example, our mixed force met before dusk about 15 miles west of Jersey. The weather was calm and the Senior Officers of each unit went on board one of the destroyers to attend a briefing conference. This destroyer was H.M.S. *Saumarez* (Captain P. Cazalet, R.N.), and at the conference were Lt. Bill Godfrey, U.S.N., the Senior Officer of the P.T. boat unit, Lt. John Collins, R.C.N.V.R., Senior Officer of a unit of Canadian " D " Class M.T.Bs., and Capitaine de Corvette Ièhle, Senior Officer of the Free

French 70-foot M.T.B. flotilla. We spent most of the night in action, for an enemy convoy appeared soon after the conference had broken up, and as the first light of dawn began to show in the east those of the party who had been involved in the fighting mustered once more on board the destroyer to report to Captain (D). The co-operation had been excellent.

The P.T. boats had many such battles until the enemy hardly dared to move his ships, and St. Malo and Cezembre had fallen. Our routine was to meet in Cherbourg at four in the afternoon with the plans for the night; then set off at five in the P.T. boats for a rendezvous with the destroyers amongst the islands. At daybreak we returned to Cherbourg and, after a belated breakfast, planned the operations for the next night. The signals had to be made out, and telephone calls put through to Portsmouth and Plymouth, then briefing, in the Green Barracks next to the old and half-destroyed E boat shelter, and then away once more into the islands for our nightly vigil.

There came a time when the enemy in the Channel Islands was held to be no longer dangerous. The destruction and loss of life attending an assault would not have been commensurate with the advantages to be gained by liberating this territory. In short, the Channel Islands were no longer of military importance.

I returned from Cherbourg to Portsmouth just in time for the most dramatic and the most successful period which the Coastal Forces ever had in the Narrow Seas—the period of one week between 23rd and 30th August, 1944, when the Germans attempted to evacuate and also to reinforce Le Havre. The actions during this tremendous week were mainly fought in the area between Cap d'Antifer and Fécamp, the area which was under the control of the Commander-in-Chief, Portsmouth, and it is necessary to go back a few weeks and consider how the battle had been developing on this eastern flank of ' the spout,' where the fighting had grown steadily fiercer since D day.

Many of the flotillas whose adventures we have already followed operated at some time or another in this area, but there was one, led by Lt. J. D. Dixon, D.S.C., R.N.V.R., which, after being constantly in action during the first weeks off the Cherbourg peninsula, was in the forefront again off Cap d'Antifer. Dixon had been wounded in a spirited fight off Cherbourg about three weeks before D day, but in spite of that he was back again to lead his seventy-one-foot-six boats to sea when the invasion began, although he still walked with a pronounced limp and the medical authorities refused to accept responsibility for him. It was evident that it would take more than that to keep Dudley Dixon out of the fighting.

His divisional leader, Lt. J. Collins, R.N.V.R., who was always called " Jumper " Collins, led a unit into action three times in the first week of July against E boats on the eastern flank. In each case his unit of two boats (the second commanded by Lt. C. G. Glennie, R.N.V.R.) was outnumbered, but in each case the enemy retired. At four o'clock on 2nd July, the two of them tackled six E boats; soon after midnight on 4th July they tackled two groups of E boats with at least four boats in each; and soon after one o'clock on the morning of 8th July they took on four more, 19 miles west of Cap d'Antifer. In the very fierce battle which ensued, Collins was killed on his bridge.

All through July the battles went on, and they were not without casualties. In the early hours of the 27th, for instance, the Senior Officer of the 1st M.T.B. Flotilla,[1] Lt. T. J. Mathias, R.N.V.R., led a unit of three seventy-one-foot-six boats to attack what he believed to be a party of four E boats. His plan was to cut across the enemy's rear in order to get between him and his harbour, but as he passed astern of the fourth E boat, he saw a fifth heading straight for him, and behind it a sixth. There was nothing to be done. Collision was inevitable, and the

[1] This was Hichens' old flotilla (renamed), and consisted mainly of boats which had not been equipped with torpedoes but were still entirely gunboats.

E boat—*S*.182—ploughed into the M.T.B., which immediately blew up. The second M.T.B. was following in such close station astern that she was unable to avoid the wreckage of the first, and she too was so badly damaged that she had to be sunk. *S*.182 also sank and some of the survivors were taken prisoner, and one other E boat was heavily damaged by gunfire. Mathias himself was rescued, badly wounded, but ten of his crew were missing. A week after this action one survivor from *S*.182 apparently drifted ashore in German-held territory. He told a strange tale—that when their boat sank five of the crew, including the Captain, had climbed on board another boat, only to find that it was British, so they jumped overboard again and got into a raft.[1] During the week that followed, the raft drifted in the Channel and all but the one survivor died.

The morale of the E boats, who knew that they would be tracked wherever they went almost from the time that they emerged from their harbours, remained at a very low ebb. Any determined attempt to reach the assault anchorage, or even to get on to the main convoy routes of " the spout," was by this time quite unknown. They scored only one success against our supply shipping. This was a skilful attack on a convoy off Beachy Head at the end of July, led by a new-comer to the Channel, Kapitänleutnant Matzen. Otherwise the E boats had little stomach for battle, though in all justice it must be conceded that tactically their position was almost hopeless. Even the dash of such commanding officers as Baron Nikko von Stempel and Hugo Wentler, whose exploits were legendary in E boat circles, could not overcome the tactical disadvantage in which they found themselves during July, 1944.

In early August the U.S.P.T. boats began to operate with our M.T.Bs. on the eastern flank. In addition, it had been decided to call in the support of destroyers to work in close conjunction with the M.T.Bs. and P.T. boats in order to soften up the opposition.

THE LAST WEEK OFF CAP D'ANTIFER

The scene was now set for the last series of naval operations which the Germans attempted before the fall of Le Havre. On 23rd August the military situation indicated that, if the enemy were to rescue any of the shipping which remained there, he would have to start getting them away very soon. The operations of our patrols were planned accordingly, and disposed off Cap d'Antifer and Fécamp in much greater strength than usual.

Let us pause for a moment to see how these operations were prepared, for it was on this preliminary planning that much of the subsequent success depended. Each morning the details of the previous night's activities were passed, by those who had taken part, to the operating staff of the Captain, Coastal Forces (Channel), in the tunnel at Portsmouth Combined Headquarters, in time for the lessons which had been learnt to be incorporated in the plan for that night. The plan itself, drawn out in coloured wax pencil on a small Perspex-covered chart, was approved and if necessary adjusted by C.C.F. (C.) (Captain MacLaughlin) and the Chief of Staff to the Commander-in-Chief (Commodore Bellars), and then converted into the form of a signal addressed to all the ships and authorities who might be concerned. In the afternoon the small Perspex-covered chart was taken down to H.M.S. *Dolphin*, the Submarine Base, now temporarily the Coastal Force Base, where a large number of officers were assembled for the briefing. These included the Senior Officers of the M.T.B. flotillas, the Commanding Officers not only of the M.T.Bs. but also of the frigates and destroyers, and the Navigating Officers. The room was not very large and it was always crowded—crowded with men who knew their job. It was the Briefing Officer's task to explain to them in every detail the plan which he had himself prepared that morning, to tell them the object of the operation,

---

[1] No British boat records any such occurrence.

to give them all available intelligence and to clear up any ambiguities which might have arisen from the written signals.

As Staff Officer (Operations) to C.C.F., it was Lt. Dreyer who usually carried out this briefing. When I was at Portsmouth he and I took it in turns, but while I had been in France he had done it almost without a break day after day, taking up his station on the plot in the tunnel later each night. It was hard work and a heavy responsibility, but none realised better than the officers who assembled daily in that little room at *Dolphin*, to carry out the operations he had planned, how much of their success depended on the work of Christopher Dreyer. It was during this last and most active week of all that his work showed its most spectacular results, although the planning which led to the successful defence of the invasion convoys, and in which Dreyer played so important a part, had no doubt a greater influence on the war.

Also at these conferences were the Coastal Forces officers who went to sea every night with the frigates. The names of Philip Lee, Guy Hudson and Guy Fison will not be forgotten in the records of those last momentous days of fighting in the Channel.

At the end of the briefing conference the plan of attack, once the enemy had been found, the method of deployment and the special signals that would be used, these and many other details would be discussed. The key word was " understanding "—a complete understanding of what each would be likely to do in every possible eventuality. Dreyer had a phrase to describe the men who assembled in the briefing-room at *Dolphin* when he used to say that so and so " knew precisely what he was about."

On the afternoon of 23rd August the room was more crowded than usual, for the patrols had been almost doubled, and after the conference the officers went back to their ships in high hopes of a lively night. They were not disappointed, for an evacuation convoy did appear and the partnership of Kirkby and Arnold Forster, which had begun four days before with the sinking of an R boat and the capture of eighteen of its crew, was now continued. Lt. G. J. Kirkby, R.N., in command of the " Hunt " Class destroyer H.M.S. *Melbreak*, engaged the enemy for more than half an hour in spite of the continuous illumination and shelling from the batteries ashore. During that time he sank one coaster and damaged a trawler. Meanwhile the M.T.Bs. had managed to get inshore of the enemy and torpedoed another coaster. Later on that night, however, the Germans sailed a supply convoy from Fécamp towards Le Havre, and although it was attacked it got through. On the next night, therefore, our forces were given, as their main object, the prevention of reinforcements from reaching Le Havre, and they were disposed primarily against any such west-bound shipping, the destruction of the east-bound evacuation convoys becoming a secondary object.

Once again it was a busy night, for the inevitable E boats came out to create their diversion and the first four of them were chased and engaged with good effect at about eleven o'clock by three P.T. boats under Lt. S. E. Saltsman, U.S.N.R., in spite of the attentions of the shore batteries. At 11.15 the first convoy appeared south of Cap d'Antifer. It was coming north from Le Havre and four M.T.Bs., under the command of Lt. Shaw, went in to intercept. There were eight ships in the convoy which, according to the report, " put up sharp and prolonged resistance," but eventually Shaw managed to get in and fire torpedoes.

" One trawler blew up," he writes, " and we withdrew having suffered two minor casualties and no damage. This was particularly lucky, as the enemy, who presumably knew he was going to have to fight his way all along the coast, had been firing a tempestuous barrage to seaward for half an hour before we attacked." E boats appeared on the scene again, and once more P.T. boats engaged them, damaging one. The frigate H.M.S. *Retalick* (Lt. J. S. Brownrigg, R.N.) and the destroyer H.M.S. *Talybont* (Lt. J. Holdsworth, R.N.) also tackled these E boats and set two of them on fire.

Meanwhile the convoy had split, and a unit of M.T.Bs. under Lt. L. E. Yock, R.A.N.V.R., was ordered to attack two coasters which were close under the cliffs of Cap d'Antifer, but the shore batteries became too fierce and accurate. As the unit disengaged, however, it found two R boats, and set one of these on fire and silenced the other, before withdrawing out of range of the coast guns.

Arnold Forster was out that night too. He was embarked in a boat commanded by Lt. P. G. A. Irvine, R.N.V.R., and his other two commanding officers were Lt. P. J. Liddell, R.N.V.R., and Lt. P. R. Everett, R.N.V.R. He had watched the P.T. boats in the first battle with the E boats and had seen the shore batteries opening fire. " As soon as we saw the flash," he writes, " we started up as usual and got ready to move, but they weren't on to us this time and we cut again.

" Much later we were sent to investigate a ' probable E boat ' which *Retalick* and *Talybont* had hit and stopped. So we all got ready to board. One of the most dangerous moments in Coastal Forces life is when the members of the boarding party come on deck, and start loading themselves up with horrid little lethal weapons of various kinds. Usually their eyes are not yet adapted to the dark and they start tripping over things.

" We saw the target burning brightly when we were about 5 miles from it and when we were about a mile away it blew up quite nicely, so we unloaded some of the boarding party's really dangerous implements and the bridge at once became a considerably safer place for its occupants. At a thousand yards we illuminated and found nothing but an enormous cloud of smoke and a smell of Diesel oil. Soon after we were ordered to go and attack an east-bound convoy, and we set off to intercept it. We still had about 2 miles to go when a signal came through that there was also a west-bound convoy approaching us on our port beam. It looked as if we were going to get fairly well mixed up with them all, when the shore batteries suddenly illuminated *Talybont* away to seaward of us, and both convoys opened fire on her. Before long they were both firing at us as well, while we could see nothing at all except the gun flashes. We came out and worked round one convoy before going in for another attempt on the second, but this time they saw us at about a mile and kept up a fairly accurate fire for about ten minutes, which left us feeling rather exhausted but with only superficial damage. This seemed to be a good moment for a cup of tea. But we didn't get a chance to enjoy it before it was our turn to go and chase after the west-bound again.

" At seven minutes past five on the morning of the 25th we finally turned in to attack from a position about 10 miles north of Fécamp. The weather, according to the report I wrote at the time, was fine and clear, and I remember noticing that the horizon to the northeast was already showing signs of what turned out to be rather a decorative sunrise. The frigate's signal ' Despatch is necessary owing to increasing light ' deserved a ruder answer than it got.

" We carried on at 10 knots, altering course occasionally so as to close the enemy on a steady bearing. At 0529 the range was down to 18 cables[1] bearing 138 degrees, but we still couldn't pick them out against the land. They were in line with the hill close east of Fécamp and hard to see against that background.

" I looked astern to see how our boats were standing out against the light horizon to seaward, before telling them over the radio to get into quarter-line for the torpedo attack. The camouflage seemed pretty good, in spite of the background, and, as I watched, the boats began to pull out into quarter-line on their own. This was the result of a deep-rooted and, I hope, unjustified suspicion on the part of the Commanding Officers that I was sure to forget to make the signal.

[1] One and four-fifths miles.

" With the unit in starboard quarter-line we went on in at 10 knots for another two minutes before Peter Liddell, who was Fleet Number Two, said over the radio in a resigned tone of voice that he could now see the enemy pretty well on the whole, he didn't know whether anyone else could, or indeed whether we were at all interested, but if we were, the enemy was bearing Red thirty. This, I may say, was quite a normal occurrence in the 13th Flotilla. Peter invariably saw the enemy first, whereupon everyone else found to their intense surprise that the whole ocean was covered in hostile shipping and wondered why on earth nobody had noticed them before. Anyway, on this occasion there were seven or more Type III Tank Landing Craft with pointed bows and built-up gun platforms for their 88's.[1] They seemed to be in two ragged columns, and from where we were they were bunched up in three groups, so we closed for another three minutes before making individual attacks on each group. All boats fired between 0534 and 0538, turned off to port and formed up in line ahead. In view of this same convoy's good shooting when we had approached it earlier the same night, we were agreeably surprised to find them so fast asleep. The scene was so peaceful, in fact, that I was just beginning to think that we had missed the lot when Percy Everett's target blew up and disappeared in a most impressive cloud of smoke and red sparks, which tended to confirm our suspicion that the convoy was trying to take ammunition down to Le Havre. There were no more hits, which was disappointing, and by the time the bits and pieces of Percy's target had settled down, our unit was in line ahead again. Peter Irvine and his coxswain and I decided that if the enemy hadn't noticed us by now, he never would, and we might as well start smoking again. We returned to the northward at 10 knots for a couple of miles before increasing speed and setting off for home."

La Combattante Again

On the following night the battle was continued if anything more fiercely than before, and it is only by enumerating each and every action that a true picture can be given of the fullness of those nights. Once again the round began with diversionary E boats which were chased by three M.T.Bs. under Lt. Dixon. As usual, they retired at high speed and finally joined a convoy which was forming up outside Fécamp. With the frigate H.M.S. *Thornborough* (Lt. Cdr. C. G. H. Brown, R.N.) in support, the M.T.Bs. moved south to attack this convoy. Dixon found one large and two small coasters with the E boats in company about 400 yards off shore and heading westward towards Le Havre. Under the bright glare of starshells and constant fire from the shore batteries, he engaged the enemy for ten minutes, setting one coaster on fire and damaging an E boat. Under cover of this diversion the Fighting French destroyer *La Combattante*[2] was able to creep in on the convoy undetected. At 3,000 yards Capitaine de Corvette A. Patou, D.S.C., F.F.N., gave the order to open fire. The time was half-past two in the morning of 26th August. Two coasters were set on fire at once, while a third blew up a quarter of an hour later. Patou kept up his attacks for three-quarters of an hour, at the end of which he had sunk two more ships and an E/R boat, and yet another had beached itself off Iport. All that remained afloat was one T.L.C. and one large R boat of the new type with a funnel. These two turned back towards Fécamp, but Lt. Shaw, with

---

[1] Although called by us Type III Tank Landing Craft, because the landing craft for Hitler's proposed invasion of 1940 were subsequently armed and used for these patrols, more recently they had been built especially for patrol work and armed with two—or in some cases three—88-mm. guns. The Type II T.L.C. was not so heavily armed, but could carry a large number of mines.

[2] It will be remembered that it was *La Combattante's* gunnery which sank two E boats in the spring before D day.

a unit of three boats, moved in to intercept and cut off their retreat. He fired six torpedoes and sank them both—the relief convoy had been wiped out.

Meanwhile a party of R boats with a T.L.C. and a trawler had been attacked on their way from Dieppe to Fécamp, first by Lt. Strang and later by three P.T. boats under Lt. W. (" Rosie ") Ryan, U.S.N.R. Though many gun hits were scored no torpedo hits were observed, and in due course the enemy reached Fécamp. So ended the third round of the contest, during which there was hardly a moment of the night without fierce fighting along this short stretch of the enemy's coastal route.

Back at Portsmouth Combined Headquarters, on the morning of 26th August, some anxiety was felt when plans were being made for the fourth round. The enemy must by now be well aware of our initial dispositions, which could only be varied very slightly each night, and it seemed that some sharp reaction might now be expected. At the briefing at H.M.S. *Dolphin*, the patrols were warned to expect torpedo-bomber attacks or extensive minelaying by aircraft or surface ships. But, in the event, there was no new reaction. The enemy took his beating and relied only on his shore batteries and the efforts of his escorts.

Of a group of eight ships attacked that night off St. Valery, west bound, two T.L.Cs. were sunk by two M.T.Bs. when Liddell scored yet another success by leading Everett in to an unobserved attack, and the destroyer H.M.S. *Middleton* (Lt. I. N. D. Cox, D.S.C., R.N.) attacked and beat up the remaining six, one of which appeared to be driven ashore. Then Lt. Sam Saltsman led in three U.S. P.T. boats to score another torpedo hit. And finally Lt. P. Aspinall, R.N.V.R., with two boats of the 14th Flotilla (the second commanded by Sub-Lt. I. Brett, R.N.V.R.), fired four torpedoes and scored two more hits which produced very large explosions. It was the last attempt which the enemy made to reinforce his beleaguered garrison by sea.

On the following night the final remnant of German shipping sailed from Le Havre to the north-eastward, after filling the harbour with mines as they had done at Cherbourg. It was attacked by Dixon with three M.T.Bs. and Patou with *La Combattante*. The M.T.Bs. torpedoed two coasters, which are believed to have sunk, and *La Combattante* set another on fire and damaged a fourth. The surviving ships dodged into Fécamp, and on the following night our patrols waited outside for them in vain. On the night after, however, the enemy moved on, starting before dusk, for they evidently preferred to risk the chance of air attack rather than face up to our destroyers and M.T.Bs. During that week we had been running our Coastal Forces at high pressure, and on this night there were a number of breakdowns, so that only the frigate *Retalick* and the destroyer *Cattistock* (Lt. R. G. D. Keddie, D.S.C., R.N.) arrived on the scene to begin the battle. Both ships attacked, and almost immediately *Cattistock* was hit by a shell on the bridge, which wrecked her gunnery control equipment and killed her Captain. *Retalick* continued to chase and later, having repaired their defects, a mixed unit of M.T.Bs. under Lt. Cdr. Stewart Marshall raced up to attack before the convoy reached Dieppe, but they were too late and the enemy ships slipped into the harbour.

They had been able to escape through an unlucky series of breakdowns and an unlucky hit on the *Cattistock's* bridge. " It is with deep regret," writes the Commander-in-Chief, Portsmouth, in his report to the Admiralty, " that the loss of Lt. Keddie is reported. He was an inspiring and gallant officer who showed great promise."

On reaching Dieppe the enemy ships had passed out of the Portsmouth Command area. The next leg of their journey was through an area in which the R.A.F. made a concentrated attack, and then they had to run the gauntlet of the Dover Strait where once more there were M.T.Bs. to harass them. The Dover boats had had little action except occasionally against E boats operating from Boulogne. Now came their opportunity as the enemy was hounded up the Channel. On the night of 1st September, two M.T.B. attacks were launched. The first, under the command of Lt. Basil Ward, D.S.C. and bar, R.N., sank one ship and the second, under the command of Lt. Cdr. E. H. Larive, D.S.C., R.Neth.N., sank two.

Thus it was that, as the Allied armies ashore drove the Germans out of France, so the Allied Navies drove the German shipping out of the Channel and up through the Narrows to the coast of Belgium and Holland. The Coastal Forces war in the English Channel had been brought to a victorious conclusion.

Let us take stock of the achievements. In the battles off Cap d'Antifer during that final week four coasters, nine T.L.Cs., two trawlers, one E boat and two R boats are believed to have been sunk, and one coaster, one T.L.C. and one R boat driven ashore. For this destruction, which was shared between frigates, destroyers and M.T.Bs., *not one British vessel had been lost.*

But the main object of the Navy in the invasion had been defence, so that the sinking of enemy ships in convoy was only, as it were, a sideline. That being the case, it is interesting to compare the figures of ships sunk by M.T.Bs. with those of ships sunk by E boats. These figures cover the area of the Portsmouth Command and the Assault Area—an area enclosed, roughly speaking, by lines from Worthing to Fécamp and from Portland to Cap de la Hague— and they cover the period from D day until the end of August, after which, as we have seen, no enemy ships remained in the area.

By M.T.Bs.
Sunk : 7 coasters, 1 M Class minesweeper, 1 corvette, 9 T.L.Cs., 3 trawlers, 4 E boats, 8 R boats, 1 tug. *Total* 34.
Driven Ashore : 1 T.L.C., 1 R boat.
Possibly Sunk : 1 coaster, 1 M Class minesweeper, 1 trawler, 6 R boats.
By E Boats
Sunk : 1 M/T ship, 2 coasters, 1 destroyer, 2 L.S.T., 1 L.C.T., 1 L.C.I., and 3 M.T.Bs. *Total* 11.
Damaged : 1 battleship, 4 merchant vessels, 1 L.C.T., 2 frigates.

Altogether during that period we lost seven M.T.Bs. and three M.G.Bs. Three of the M.T.Bs. were lost in action with E boats, as we have seen, and of the remainder the majority were sunk by mines.

Early in September, as all available M.T.Bs. were making their way from Portsmouth towards the East Coast bases to continue the struggle in the North Sea, the following signal was received from the Admiralty:

" Their Lordships are particularly impressed with the recent fine work carried out by Coastal Force craft off the coasts of France and the Low Countries, and congratulate not only the crews themselves but also those concerned with the direction and administration of the craft. Their efforts have contributed largely to the success of operations in France."

The mention of the coasts of the Low Countries is important. The boats working near the Seine Bay were in the centre of the fighting, but those which threatened the German sea routes leading from the Fatherland towards the invasion fronts also made an important contribution.

While almost all eyes had been turned towards Normandy, there were still flotillas on the East Coast which had been carrying on the more normal types of M.T.B. fighting in the old familiar waters off Holland.

CHAPTER XVII

TORMENTING THE PATROLS

WHILE the invasion of Normandy was progressing in the Channel, targets for our M.T.Bs. were comparatively few off the coasts of Holland and Belgium. After the bombing raid on Le Havre, it is not surprising that the Germans were unwilling to commit any more of their warships to the struggle in the Channel. Even the E boats were having a difficult time and, though it was necessary to reinforce them, they had at least got shelters in which to hide whenever they were in harbour. To send more destroyers and "M" Class minesweepers would just be throwing them away. What was more surprising, however, after the heavy air attacks on their land communications, was that the Germans did not increase their coastal convoy traffic, particularly as they would surely have guessed, and rightly, that many of our East Coast flotillas had been transferred to the Channel. That they did not increase this traffic must, to a large extent, be attributed to the threat which was maintained by the few remaining M.T.B. flotillas still operating from the three East Coast bases—*Midge, Mantis* and *Beehive*. This threat was maintained by continuous and highly successful attacks on such shipping as could be found in those waters—principally patrols of trawlers, gun-coasters and "M" Class minesweepers guarding the convoy route against M.T.Bs. and the coast against further Allied landings.

These attacks were brought to a very decisive pitch of perfection by a handful of M.T.B. Commanders, such as Wright, MacDonald and Gemmel, who, like their colleagues in the Channel, "knew precisely what they were about." Lt. Cdr. Gemmel, for example, had brought his flotilla back to the East Coast after its adventures in Norway. On the night of the 9th June, off Egmond, he met a force of four trawlers, of which he torpedoed three; a little later three more trawlers appeared on the scene and one of these was also torpedoed. About a month later Lt. R. G. Eburah, R.N.V.R., led an attack off Scheveningen in which two trawlers and a guncoaster were torpedoed; and so it went on.

Lt. Cdr. D. G. H. Wright, D.S.C., R.N.V.R., who had commanded flotillas of both seventy-foot and seventy-one-foot-six M.T.Bs., took over the "D" boats of the 58th Flotilla from Gemmel, and towards the end of August, under Wright's leadership, they repeated their June success in a brilliant action off the Hook of Schouwen to the north of Walcheren. Five "D" boats stalked four enemy patrol ships—a trawler, a guncoaster, an "M" Class minesweeper and a T.L.C. Each M.T.B. took a different target except that two aimed at the "M" Class, which was the largest. When Wright gave the executive signal to fire torpedoes, his force was apparently still unseen. All the boats fired, and every one reports that his target was hit. Two torpedoes hit the trawler, one hit the guncoaster, which evidently did not sink, as it continued to fire its guns for some time. Two torpedoes hit the "M" Class sweeper, which was seen to sink, and one hit the T.L.C. bringing up the rear.

"German patrol boats," announced Berlin, "last night repelled an attack by British Light Coastal craft off the Schelde Estuary. In a bitter engagement our vessels succeeded in sinking an enemy coastal craft. Heavy damage and fires were caused on several other enemy ships. One of our vessels was lost, but the Commander and the greater part of the crew were saved." It seems hardly necessary to add that the M.T.Bs. returned safely to harbour with one boat slightly damaged and no casualties whatsoever.

Another important leader at this time was Lt. G. J. MacDonald, D.S.O., D.S.C., R.N.Z.N.V.R., who as Senior Officer of the 21st M.T.B. Flotilla had carried on the traditions laid down by Dickens on the East Coast. This New Zealander led his flotilla into action successfully time after time, and earned for them and for himself a great reputation in Coastal Forces. Since that night in March 1942 when I had first met him, wet and bedraggled, in the moonlight on board his burning M.T.B. in the Dover Strait, the night on which he won his first D.S.C., he had earned two bars to it and a D.S.O. His was a record of exceptional skill and infinite spirit.

ANOTHER WINTER

These battles in the typical pattern went on after the enemy had been driven north-eastward through the Straits. But in addition a new defence problem had arisen.

Arnhem is a name which will not be forgotten. The airborne landing there did not succeed, but, as in many failures, endurance and courage were there displayed upon a scale which will always be remembered in history. Arnhem, however, was something more; it was the start of a new phase in the war. Had Arnhem succeeded, the collapse of organised resistance in Germany might have followed before the winter. As it turned out, we were faced at once with an extension of the war at least until the following spring and possibly longer still. That meant that there would be an army to supply for many months along sea routes that would have to be defended, not against the improvised attacks of an enemy who was still reeling and falling back after his defeat in France, but against the well-prepared and carefully organised attacks of a desperate opponent who had won for himself a much-needed breathing space.

The capture, intact, of the port of Antwerp with its tremendous harbour facilities was the key to the supply situation, and it was the defence of a new lane leading into the River Scheldt which became the task of the Navy during the winter of 1944/45.

Before this route could be opened to our ships, the enemy had to be cleared first from the south bank of the estuary and then from the north bank, formed by the island of Walcheren, where once again Coastal Forces were used as the navigational leaders of our assault. Until this had been achieved, however, Ostend was the most northerly port held by the Allies, and it was to Ostend that Cdr. Brind took the Coastal Forces Mobile Unit (by road via Brussels) as soon as the port fell, for its work in the Mulberry at Arromanches had finished with the evacuation of Le Havre.

Thus the well-appointed E boat base at Ostend became a Coastal Forces base, from which the inshore M.T.B. patrols could be manned, first to protect the channel to Ostend itself and later to protect the channel to Antwerp—the channel in which the minesweeping M.Ls. played so vital a part.

The majority of these patrols, however, were still manned by boats working from the East Anglian coast. It was against these lines that a new E boat campaign was launched by the enemy with flotillas which had been reconstituted since the severe handling they suffered during the summer.

It was during the early stages of this campaign that perhaps the most decisive battle against E boats of the whole war came to be fought.

One night in September, the frigate H.M.S. *Stayner* (now under the command of Lt. A. V. Turner, D.S.C., R.N.V.R.) was patrolling north of Ostend in company with a single unit of two " D " boats from Lt. Cdr. Wilkie's flotilla. The Senior Officer of this Unit was Lt. J. F. Humphreys, R.N.V.R., in M.T.B. 724, who had with him M.T.B. 728, under the command of Lt. F. N. Thomson, R.N.V.R.

Besides their normal mining and torpedo sorties, the E boats were occasionally used at this time for running the blockade to Dunkirk, where the German garrison was now besieged on the landward side. When these runs were made other E boats often used diversionary tactics, as they had attempted to do off Cap d'Antifer and elsewhere. It is probable that the unit of three boats of the 10th E boat Flotilla under the command of Kapitänleutnant Karl Müller, which met our force soon after eleven o'clock on the night of 18th September, was engaged on some such diversionary duties. As they steered south-west in arrowhead formation, Müller sighted the wakes of two boats on his port bow and began to turn away. The E boat on the port wing of the arrowhead, however, did not turn quickly enough, and the two M.T.Bs. engaged it to such good effect that in a matter of seconds it was burning brightly and soon after it lay stopped, to be despatched in due course by the *Stayner* herself. Humphreys passed it by and led on to engage the other two, and it was at this juncture, according to Müller, that the two E boats came into collision. He claims that his E boat stopped as a result of this collision, but it is equally certain that it was heavily hit by the two M.T.Bs. The third E boat was recalled to the assistance of his damaged leader, but instead of him the M.T.Bs. arrived on the scene to find Müller and his crew abandoning ship. A few minutes later the remains of the E boat blew up and sank.

Two out of three had been disposed of, now for the last one. Returning towards its damaged companions, it was met by the M.T.Bs. and made off again at 40 knots, but, in the few seconds of the brief engagement, the gunnery of the British boats was as effective as before. Although the enemy outdistanced the pursuit, the death blow had been struck. In the E boat one engine had been hit, and so had the cooling system of another; after running a mile or so the engine seized up and the enemy was reduced to a crawl. Soon the M.T.Bs. came up, but so dark was the night that they did not see the crippled E boat until they were on top of it. Humphreys first sighted it 6 feet from his starboard side. He had missed ramming it inadvertently by inches. Over the R/T he told Thomson in the boat behind, who altered course just in time so that the E boat passed down his port side. As he did so his gunners opened fire and the enemy vessel burst into flames and blazed like a torch. So far the operation had gone without a hitch, but it is only fair to record the bad with the good, and now came a piece of unavoidable bad luck. It will be observed that the M.T.Bs. had passed one on either side of the E boat. But Humphreys could not know this. Return fire from the E boat had started a small fire in Thomson's boat and Thomson reported it to Humphreys, and then his R/T went out of action. Hearing this report and seeing the blazing boat astern, Humphreys very naturally connected the two. What, then, was the boat speeding away on a divergent course on the starboard beam? It must be the E boat; and so it was that 724 opened fire on 728; 728, thinking that here must be another enemy, returned the fire. The firing only lasted a few seconds, but we have already seen how accurate was the gunnery of these two boats and regrettably enough some hits were scored. The two lost contact with each other, and Humphreys went back to lay a smoke-screen round what he believed to be the burning wreck of Thomson's boat. It was only when he closed in to pick up the survivors that he was amazed to discover they were German.

Thus two M.T.Bs., at a cost of three killed and one wounded, had, with the support of *Stayner*, wiped out a whole unit of three E boats. Over sixty prisoners were taken, amongst them Müller himself—a veteran in the E boat service, who was known to his friends as " Charlie " Müller. He claimed to have fought in no less than 164 actions, and had been awarded the Ritterkreuz.

This debacle, however, did not prevent the E boats continuing their attacks on the Antwerp channel, under von Mirbach and his colleagues. Indeed, they even renewed their sorties against the East Coast convoy route, so that our Coastal Forces were fully occupied throughout the winter with their usual patrols—patrols which as usual meant long and tedious nights at sea with only occasional contact with the enemy. Flotillas under the command of such leaders as Lt. Cdr. S. D. Marshall, R.N.V.R., Lt. Cdr. P. Wilkinson, R.N.V.R., Lt. P. Magnus, D.S.C., R.N.V.R., Lt. Cdr. J. R. H. Kirkpatrick, D.S.C., R.C.N.V.R., Lt. Cdr. A. R. H. Nye, D.S.C., R.N.V.R., and several others, as well as Dixon, Wright, Shaw, Mac-Donald and Wilkie, were active in defending our supply lanes against E boats, human torpedoes, explosive motor boats and the new midget submarines in what was clearly the last offensive effort of the German Navy before the final collapse of the Third Reich.

THE ATTACK PRESSED HOME

This book would not be complete without the detailed record of one further battle, a battle as full of the colour and essence of M.T.B. warfare as any which was ever fought in the Narrow Seas.

If the occasions which call for fortitude and courage in an M.T.B. action are related in any way to victory or defeat, it is often enough in an inverse ratio, for it is in adversity that those qualities in the human spirit shine most brightly. In the autumn of 1944, however, a battle was fought in which great boldness well earned the success it deserved, although not without cost, both in men and boats, and fortitude and courage were called for in full measure. Most of the action took place during one fiery hour between half-past midnight and 1.30 a.m. on the morning of 1st October, when five of our M.T.Bs. made their attack on an escorted convoy coming towards Ijmuiden from the south; in short, an evacuation convoy from Rotterdam or the Hook.

These five M.T.Bs. were from the 11th Flotilla, and they were organised in two divisions:

> M.T.B. 351 (Lt. N. C. Morrow, R.N.V.R.).
> M.T.B. 360 (Lt. D. A. Hall, R.N.V.R.).
> M.T.B. 349 (Sub-Lt. K. E. Harris, R.N.V.R.).
>
> M.T.B. 347 (Lt. A. D. Foster, R.N.V.R.[1]).
> M.T.B. 350 (Sub-Lt. H. G. Franklin, D.S.C., R.N.V.R.).

The Senior Officer of the force, who was embarked in M.T.B. 351 was Lt. F. W. Bourne, D.S.C., R.N.V.R.

The boats arrived on their hunting-ground at a quarter to nine in the evening, close to the harbour of Ijmuiden, and sighted a dark object which proved to be the masts and funnel of the liner *Strasbourg*, sunk by Bradford in the previous March. It was not until nearly mid-

---

[1] Not to be confused with Lt. M. Arnold Forster, D.S.O., D.S.C., R.N.V.R.

night, however, that they sighted a suitable quarry about 4 miles to the south of them, for the moon was nearly full although it was hidden in cloud. For three-quarters of an hour they manœuvred to attack what turned out to be a convoy and its escorts, amounting in all to at least fifteen ships. Intermittent rain squalls and low clouds had greatly reduced visibility by the time that the three boats of the first division closed in to fire their torpedoes. Bourne's report, of which extracts follow, is direct and simple in its statement of fact, but none the less it conveys the extraordinary tension and excitement of the approach:

" As the first division was closing the enemy, a T.L.C. was sighted slightly on the starboard bow at a range of 400–500 yards. . . . The first division altered course to starboard under the stern of the T.L.C. at a range of approximately 100 yards and then back again to south 70 east. At the same time, visible to starboard at a range of four or five cables was a trawler. Due to the very low visibility, the first division had broken through the convoy's screen without being observed. The main target, at 0035½, fired starshell and illuminated the first division. Rockets[1] were then fired by the first division over the main target, which was seen to be a three-island merchant vessel of 2,000 to 3,000 tons, followed by a flush-deck single-funnel motor vessel, also of 2,000 to 3,000 tons. The order to stand by was given by ' loud hailer,' and at 0036 M.T.B. 349 fired her torpedoes, taking line of sight at 800 yards on the bridge of the leading target; torpedoes were seen to run true between two lanes of tracer from the merchant vessel . . . "

M.T.B. 360 fired her torpedoes a second or so later, and a few moments after firing there was an explosion which threw up a great column of water. One at least of Lt. Hall's torpedoes had exploded, but a long way short of the target, and at the critical moment the resulting column of water obscured the target from M.T.B. 351 so that Lt. Morrow was unable to take aim. " As the unit was under heavy fire from light automatic weapons and 3–4-inch shells," Bourne goes on, " the first division was ordered to disengage to starboard, the unit altering to the westward. While so doing, at 0038, a heavy explosion occurred and a large cloud of black smoke was seen in the direction of the leading merchant vessel. Simultaneously M.T.B. 351 had a defect on her centre engine, causing the engine to seize up, and the disengaging speed was reduced to 14 knots under heavy cross fire from the screening trawler and the T.L.C. M.T.B. 351 replied with her Oerlikons on the nearest trawler, which had altered out of the convoy and turned to chase and succeeded in causing damage, starting a fire on the stern and scoring hits on the bridge, M.T.B. 349 being unable to fire her guns as the target was covered by M.T.B. 351.

" Meanwhile M.T.B. 360 in disengaging to starboard under cover of her own smoke-screen, was repeatedly hit by heavy-calibre shells, starting a fire under the bridge and in the W/T cabin. Her steering-gear became jammed and she veered off to port, opening fire with her Oerlikons and inflicting damage on a trawler. She then altered to the north, keeping station on the convoy. This manœuvre had the effect of stopping the fire on her from the enemy, as they possibly thought she was part of the escort. All main engines had been hit and badly damaged, and in making another attempt to clear the convoy she received several more hits, as the enemy resumed fire. This finally stopped her, and, sinking and burning furiously, she was abandoned by her crew."

From Bourne's report it is only possible to guess at the horror of the ordeal through which Hall and his crew had passed. He himself was wounded, his coxswain was so badly wounded that he died later; his First Lieutenant and four ratings were missing, believed killed; two other ratings were missing and two were seriously wounded.

The two M.T.Bs. of the second division were 1,000 yards from the main target at 0039,

---

[1] Illuminating rockets carrying parachute flares beyond the target to silhouette it.

and Lt. Foster in 347 was preparing to give the order to fire torpedoes when his boat was hit. "A 3- or 4-inch shell tore a large hole in the starboard torpedo-tube, cracking the air bottle of the torpedo; it also blew the after Oerlikon gunner over the side and wounded two other gun's crew ratings. Smaller calibre shells hit the port torpedo-tube, bridge, mast and Oerlikon ready-use locker, setting a pan on fire. At 0040½ opened fire on trawler to starboard with after Oerlikon, many hits seen on the bridge and superstructure. Range of motor vessel 800 yards. Passed order to fire torpedoes to M.T.B. 350, who did not receive the order. Both tubes in 347 failed to fire. The seaman torpedoman on the port tube reported the breach block was damaged and unable to be fired; the starboard tube was obviously useless."

At 0041 Foster disengaged to starboard and lost sight of 350. Sub-Lt. Franklin decided to stand on and attack alone.

"At 0040½ the target was illuminated and at 0041 M.T.B. 350 fired both torpedoes at a large flush-deck supply ship, estimated tonnage 2,500, range 500 yards, track angle 75°, enemy's estimated speed 10 knots. Shortly after firing, two large explosions were observed on the target, one amidships and one on the port quarter, but it is regretted no results of these hits were observed, as by this time heavy tracer was blinding the Commanding Officer, who disengaged to starboard down between the lane of enemy ships on a reciprocal course to the enemy, passing a small trawler at 25 yards range. This was severely mauled by the gunners, and two fires were seen to start, one on the bridge and the other on the quarter. This trawler was followed by a tug and then a large enemy destroyer, possibly a 'Narvik.' This was the end of the convoy, and observing a burning M.T.B. away to the northward, M.T.B. 350 turned to starboard to close her and render assistance, noticing also that there were two enemy trawlers close to the blazing wreck, one of them firing 4-inch shells at it. At approximately 0048 M.T.B. 350 illuminated the burning boat and the trawlers, and at 0048½ stopped about 200 yards from it, seeing then that it was M.T.B. 360. At 0049 M.T.B. 350 started to pick up survivors from M.T.B. 360, and by 0100 had rescued five ratings."

The Last Adventure of M.T.B. 347

Franklin's determination in pressing home his attack to 500 yards in the face of such fierce opposition was beyond all praise. No less remarkable was Foster's continued approach after his boat had been hit, in the hope that the second torpedo might still be able to be fired. Foster's boat was by now in a bad way. "During this mêlée," the report goes on, "M.T.B. 347, while still disengaging to starboard at 0041, had extinguished the fire in the ready-use locker. At 0041½ M.T.B. 347 was hit in the engine-room. One 3- or 4-inch shell exploded on the after end of the centre engine, blowing down the engine-room tiller-flat bulkhead, lifting the deck off the tiller flat, making a large hole in the bottom of the boat below the centre engine, damaging the auxiliary engine, and assisting the centre engine Dumbflows through the port side of the boat. A few seconds later another large shell hit the starboard engine, and smaller shells struck the port engine outboard exhaust manifold and damaged the electrics. The steering-gear was put out of action, and the C.S.A. gear[1] and other upper deck fittings were removed. The Motor Mechanic, with a shell splinter in his shoulder, was the only casualty from these hits. The Motor Mechanic ordered the engine-room, which was full of exhaust fumes, to be cleared. Bunk cushions were brought aft and attempts were made to plug the hole in the bottom of the boat by the engine-room crew, while holding their breath, as the smoke helmet had been shot away. At 0042 two explosions and columns of water, followed by a cloud of smoke, were seen on the motor vessel, which was now about a cable to port.

---

[1] Smoke-making apparatus.

M.T.B. 347 proceeded at about 4 knots on the inboard bank of cylinders of the port engine, and on hand steering, course south-east. At 0045 crossed the bow of a trawler which was burning fiercely aft. Oerlikon fire was opened on this ship at 100 yards' range and many hits were seen on her bridge, which was left burning. Her return fire hit M.T.B. 347 forward, causing her to make water in the forward heads. This leak was stopped with mattresses. At 0046 the helm was put hard a-starboard to bring the boat on a reciprocal of the enemy's course.

" Unfortunately the rudders jammed in this position. The boat circled slowly, completely out of control, and struck the next enemy in the line a glancing blow amidships with her port bow. This ship was a minesweeper with sweep out aft and flying a balloon. She was firing on both quarters and did not appear to see M.T.B. 347. As the Oerlikons were being reloaded by the one remaining gunner, and in view of the extreme proximity, the Commanding Officer decided not to attract her attention by firing with ·303. While circling away the steering-gear was freed and the boat was brought to the reciprocal of the enemy's course. As she drew clear of the minesweeper, she was hit on her starboard bow by a large shell, presumably fired by one of the inshore escorts. This escort opened inaccurate fire on M.T.B. 347, but a small fire was started in the wheelhouse. This was extinguished at once. About this time three trawlers were seen to port, range about 1,000 yards. Two minutes later the next enemy in line, a small tug, was abeam range 75 yards. She was engaged and heavily hit on the bridge by the Commanding Officer, who had manned the after Oerlikon. Fire was then switched to another dark shape, which was now abeam, range 250 yards. The remaining rounds in the pans, about ten in all, were fired, but no hits were seen. This target was then silhouetted and seen to be a large destroyer. Fortunately she did not open fire.[1] By the time M.T.B. 347's guns were reloaded, she was no longer visible and no other ships could be seen.

" During these actions a fire in the engine-room had been reported and the methyl-bromide extinguishers had been released with success. The time was now about 0055 and a burning wreck was seen to the west. A south-westerly course was steered to clear this, as its identity was not known. The R/T receiver was still working and the Senior Officer could be heard calling M.T.B. 347 up. The aerials were re-rigged and attempts were made to answer, without success. At 0110 the port engine stopped, and the engine-room crew tried hard to restart it again while holding their breath. Water was now over the starters and their efforts were in vain."

Foster realised that his only hope of getting the boat back now was by a tow, and the chances of that seemed rather remote. He could see three boats lying off the burning wreck about a mile to the northward, and since he thought they were friendly he tried to attract their attention by firing several pyrotechnics. Meanwhile he prepared to sink his boat should they prove hostile. But she was sinking, anyway, of her own accord.

" At 0120 the boat began to settle by the stern, and after ordering the wounded to be put on the raft and confidential books to be sunk, the order was given to abandon. At 0130 M.T.B. 347 sank by the stern and disappeared."

The three boats by the wreck of 360 had, indeed, been M.T.Bs. While Harris in 349 took his boat alongside the bows of the burning hulk to rescue Hall, the Commanding Officer, and the Coxswain, who, because of their wounds, had been unable to abandon ship; Bourne and Franklin had been covering him. On seeing Foster's distress signals, Bourne set off at once to his assistance. On the way he sighted three trawlers and an E/R boat, but he managed

---

[1] From the disposition of the enemy convoy it seems likely that this destroyer was being towed away from Rotterdam, where, no doubt, she had been refitting, which would account for the minesweeper sweeping ahead of her and the tug, and would also account for the fact that she did not reply to 347's fire.

to avoid them, and eventually found the raft, from which all but one of 347's gallant crew were rescued—all but the gunner who had been blown overboard at the beginning of the action.

The three remaining boats, little damaged, returned to Felixstowe with their survivors. They had lost two of their number, and nine men killed or missing. They had torpedoed two merchantmen and damaged at least two trawlers and a tug. Who shall say that they were not the victors? By their spirit in this battle alone the names of Alec Foster and Henry Franklin will long be remembered in the annals of the Coastal Forces.

The End in Sight

Foster was involved in a close-range battle once again, on the night of 6th April, 1945, this time against E boats. Just before the collapse of Germany the E boats in the North Sea put forth an intensified effort. Although it availed them little, it led to a series of unusually fierce actions in which the enemy was ready to stand up and fight back whenever he met our Coastal Forces.

The night of 6th April was very dark, and in intercepting a group of five E boats, the leader of a unit of three M.T.Bs. (under the command of Lt. J. May, R.N.V.R.) came into collision with one of the enemy. The M.T.B. was rolled right over with the loss of all but three of her crew. Foster rammed another E boat and, after breaking free, he hit it six times with his 6-pdr. at 25 yards' range. Then unfortunately he ran over the upturned wreck of May's M.T.B., and his boat was so badly damaged that she could only proceed stern first. One E boat lay disabled and firing red flares about 200 yards away, and Foster engaged it until it was evident that it could not escape. It is now known that both the rammed E boats sank and that a third one was lost that night as a result of a separate action.

On the following night, in spite of a strong wind which made gunnery difficult, Lt. Dixon, in a very brilliant action, sank two E boats by gunfire, while his own force suffered no damage whatever. The Germans claimed that the first of their boats was stopped by the gun-fire and that the second ran into it from astern. However that may be, the efforts of Dixon's unit cost the enemy two E boats, and won him his third D.S.C.

Only once more did the E boats venture out, and once again they were engaged at 20 yards' range. Then they had shot their bolt. During this closing period of the European War a very effective co-operation between the defensive patrols and reconnaissance aircraft was brought into play. So effective was it, in fact, that, as in the Seine Bay during the previous summer, the spirit of the E boats was suddenly broken. For more than three weeks before VE day all E boat operations ceased. On the sea, as on the land, the Germans were beaten.

In the struggle against the enemy's special weapons, the explosive motor-boats had scored no greater success in Holland than they did in Normandy. The midget U boat, however, was more dangerous, and it was against this that the Coastal Forces, and particularly the M.Ls., did such excellent work. Out of a total of 81 captured, sunk or probably sunk, Coastal Forces accounted for 23—a larger share than any other arm.

Both the Norwegian flotilla and the Fighting French flotilla—off the coast of Norway and in the Bay of Biscay respectively—were fighting until very shortly before VE day, and the last two Coastal Forces battles of the European War were fought by boats of Lt. Ièhle's 23rd Flotilla off the west coast of France. On the night of 2nd/3rd May they shot up a trawler, and two nights later, off La Pallice, they fired torpedoes at four trawlers without result. So ended the fighting in the Narrow Seas.

One last scene remained to be enacted a few days after the unconditional surrender of Germany, when two E boats flying the white flag sailed from Rotterdam for Felixstowe.

They came, not, as was popularly supposed at the time, to surrender—for the German armed forces had already surrendered—but in order to bring the German Admiral Bräuning, carrying the charts of the enemy's minefields, to confer with the Commander-in-Chief, Nore. He brought two E boats in case one should be mined or break down. They were met at the South Falls buoy off the Thames estuary by ten M.T.Bs. of various types, which were to escort them for the 50 miles to Felixstowe. On board these ten M.T.Bs. were most of the Senior Officers of the flotillas based on the east coast—amongst them Wright, Marshall, Clayton, MacDonald, Magnus, Dixon, Price, names which have figured already in this book. The Senior Officer present was Lt. Cdr. J. H. Hodder, D.S.C., R.N.V.R. Thus it came about that, on 13th May, 1945, I found myself in John Hodder's " D " boat for my last experience of Coastal Forces, well remembering my first experience of them, in his " C " boat, more than three years before.

As we lay waiting at South Falls at about 2 p.m. on that sunny Sunday afternoon, two specks were sighted on the horizon, and soon they were recognised as the expected E boats. Five minutes later they had been ordered to stop and we were manœuvring to come alongside the sleek, low hull of the leader, with a black panther painted on its side. With two signalmen, Wright, Pryor [1] and I jumped on board, and then the M.T.Bs. formed up on either side and the formation set off for Felixstowe. On the E boat's bridge was the German Admiral, full of salutes, a dry little man in a grey leather coat. Korvettenkapitän " Bobby " Fimmen—the Senior Officer of the 4th E boat Flotilla since the death of Lützow,[2] was also on board, and so, too, was Korvettenkapitän Rebensburg, who, as Staff Officer (Operations) to the E boat chief, Kapitän zur See Petersen, had been my opposite number during the previous summer. It was against him that Dreyer and I, while on the staff of C.C.F. (Channel), had planned and counter-planned.

On the passage from South Falls to Felixstowe the formation made 20 knots—the best cruising speed for " D " boats—although the German boats had been making 32 knots from Rotterdam to South Falls. The wind was freshening as we turned in towards the Orwell estuary, and we watched Hodder in the boat ahead putting on his oilskin as the spray burst over the bridge, whilst we in the E boat sat up on the canopy at the back of the dustbin and remained perfectly dry. There was no doubt about which was the drier type at 20 knots. By the same token, however, it was noticeable that the E boat rolled much more than the M.T.B., and was therefore a much less steady platform for gunnery.

With some difficulty we persuaded the Germans to fall their crews in on deck as they entered harbour, where a great crowd of spectators was assembled on all the piers and jetties. The E boats berthed alongside Hodder's boat, a manœuvre which, with their large screws and considerable astern power, was carried out at a most spectacular speed in the small basin. The armed guards filed on board and for the first time an E boat was available for the study of the Admiralty experts.

"THE TRUE GLORY"

Here, to conclude the story, are some relevant statistics of the world war of 1939–1945. At the beginning of it we had 28 Coastal Force craft, of which 12 were at Malta, 6 at Hong Kong and the remaining 10 in England. By the end of the European War 1,560 had been built. By 1944 there were about eighty times as many officers and ratings in Coastal Forces as there had been in 1939. Those men in those boats were involved in 780 separate naval actions —464 of them in Home Waters round the British Isles. There has only been space to describe

[1] Lt.-Cdr. M. A. Pryor, R.N.V.R.
[2] See page 171.

a small proportion of them in this book. [Of the 316 actions which took place in other theatres of the war, perhaps a book (or more than one) will be written by those who fought in them. I hope so.]

In those 464 battles in Home Waters, 269 enemy vessels were sunk or probably sunk for the loss, through enemy action, of 76 Coastal Force craft. Such are the figures which measure the achievement of the Coastal Forces in the Narrow Seas round Britain. They are figures which should have established the usefulness of this branch of the Navy sufficiently at least to make sure that its tradition is not cast aside in time of peace, as the tradition of the C.M.Bs. was cast aside between the two wars. It has come a long way since the early days of the " Costly Farces," and the lessons it has learnt must not need to be learnt all over again.

If we believe that the future of mankind depends upon a lasting peace, if we are determined that war with its attendant horrors and the frightful destructive potentialities of atomic power, shall never come again to plague the world, then it is essential that we and those other peoples who believe in like principles should be strong enough to defend them—strong enough to deter the would-be aggressor from his purpose. That means that we must retain a strong Navy, and in a strong Navy there must be a place for the Coastal Forces. We shall have need of them so long as armed force continues to play a part in the affairs of men.

That is the end of this history of five years of bitter fighting in the Channel and the North Sea, during which our Light Coastal Forces patrolled the no-man's-land between the two front lines from the darkest days, when Hitler's invasion seemed upon us, until the time when the German Navy was finally beaten. They carried on the great sea tradition of our country until the job was done—until it was thoroughly finished. Theirs was the spirit of Drake when, in 1587, after sailing into the harbour of Cadiz and there destroying the assembling ships of the Spanish Armada, he wrote, in a letter to Sir Francis Walsingham, a sentence which is as apt today as it was nearly 360 years ago:

> " *There must be a beginning of any great matter, but the continuing unto the end, until it be thoroughly finished, yields the true glory.*"

Index